THE OXFORD BOOK OF AUSTRALIAN ESSAYS

Edited by Imre Salusinszky

Melbourne

OXFORD UNIVERSITY PRESS

Oxford Auckland New York

OXFORD UNIVERSITY PRESS AUSTRALIA
Oxford New York
Athens Auckland Bangkok Bombay
Calcutta Cape Town Dar es Salaam Delhi
Florence Hong Kong Istanbul Karachi
Kuala Lumpur Madras Madrid Melbourne
Mexico City Nairobi Paris Port Moresby
Singapore Taipei Tokyo Toronto
and associated companies in
Berlin Ibadan

First published 1997

National Library of Australia
Cataloguing-in-publication data:

The Oxford book of Australian essays.

ISBN 0 19 553739 4.

I. Salusinszky, Imre, 1955– . II. Title: Book of Australian essays.

A824.008

Edited by Cathryn Game
Text and cover designed by Anitra Blackford
Cover illustration by Ned Culic
Typeset by Anitra Blackford
Printed through South Wind, Singapore
Published by Oxford University Press
253 Normanby Road, South Melbourne, Australia

CONTENTS

PREFACE

Many friends and colleagues have helped me with their suggestions for this anthology. I would particularly like to thank the following: Jane Adamson, Robert Adamson, Don Anderson, Jill Barnard, Chris Bradley, Penelope Buckley, Pat Buckridge, David Carter, Michael Christie, Hugh Craig, Tim Dolin, Hume Dow, Tim Duncan, Juno Gemes, Kerryn Goldsworthy, John Gullock, Cliff Hanna, Laurie Hergenhan, Michael Heyward, Frank Higgins, Ivor Indyk, Nick Jose, Brian Kennedy, Noel King, Harold Love, Colin Lyons, Brian Matthews, David Matthews, Andrew Metcalf, Stephen Mills, Adrian Mitchell, Helen O'Neil, Bill Perrett, Jeff Richardson, Mitchell Rolls, Peter Steele, R. J. Stove, Christina Thompson, David Tribe, Chris Wallace-Crabbe, Robert Wilson.

Two people who have advised and guided me throughout this project are my wife, Karen Barrett, and my publisher, Peter Rose.

It is also a pleasure to acknowledge my frequent recourse to *The Oxford Companion to Australian Literature* (2nd edn, 1994, ed. Wilde, Hooton, and Andrews), especially in compiling the Notes on Contributors.

I have used an ellipsis in square brackets [...] to indicate cuts made to the original text.

ILS

INTRODUCTION

Although the Australian essay might not have attained to the seriousness of its British, or the urbanity of its American, counterpart, for sheer democratic variety you cannot beat it. Here I have tried to select pieces that reflect, or reflect upon, the Australian experience, taking that in its broadest sense — so that the result will be a book of Australian essays, not essays by people with Australian passports. But even within this self-imposed limitation, the variety of themes, styles, and stances is remarkable; and indeed, the relationship *between* the pieces seems to tell us more about an 'Australian identity' than the content of any of the individual essays themselves: there is something elusively but decidedly Australian about the way that Lennie Lower and Germaine Greer, Brent Crosswell and David Malouf, can sit so easily and comfortably and *necessarily* next to each other.

If the Australian essay today, taken as a whole, conveys this sense of cornucopia, it is a sense that it has only acquired in the last half century. Writing in 1930, H. M. Green declared that 'in essays Australian literature is even weaker than in drama', and from where he stood, he was probably right, because the Australian essay is a latecomer in a culture that is itself a latecomer. The familiar essay — inconclusive, personal, humorous, conversational — had few outlets in Australia in the first half of the nineteenth century. Men were not writing essays in any numbers until at least the middle of the century, and women not for another four or five decades after that. And although Marcus Clarke could declare by the 1870s that there was no better place than Australia to be a freelance journalist, even the great blossoming of magazines and journals during that period did not seem to provide a fertile enough ground for the essay to flourish. Most of what you will read in the promisingly dignified-looking *Melbourne Review* or *Victorian Review* in the 1870s or '80s is either relentlessly practical — tariffs, temperance, smut (in wheat) — or else bypasses the middle ground of the essay entirely and enters the metaphysical terrain of the homily. Meanwhile, in Sydney, in the less dignified *Southern Cross* or early *Bulletin*, you will find reviews, notices, articles, stories, poems, some literary criticism, endless political diatribe (of a level of personal viciousness alas unknown today), and the race results 'by electric wire from Melbourne'. You will, however, find precious few essays, though some of those you do find *will* be precious, since they will be written despite, or against, the grain.

H. M. Green believed that the enemies of the essay in Australia up to the 1930s had been lack of leisure and lack of a market. (Its enemies today are academic prose — and lack of a market.) It is true that the rhythms of a pioneer culture are driven by action, not thought, and that the literary forms thrown up by a pioneer culture tend to be driven by story, not idea: hence the precocious strength of the novel and the short story, the travelogue and the diary, in colonial Australia. Fledgling communities huddled together in a hostile environment specialise in cautionary tales about the anticipation of danger and, more rarely, heroic tales about the overcoming of danger; they do not specialise in the free play of the intellect. While the essay may employ narrative, or indeed description or argument, among its strategies, merely telling a story can never be its aim — which is, usually quite explicitly, to convey a new understanding.

Green is right too to think of the essay as a creature of leisure. Thus it is when institutions of leisure, including those great fat high-leisure palaces the universities, begin to come 'up to speed' (if that is an appropriate phrase here) in the twentieth century that, in terms of numbers, the essay in Australia begins to take off. The three previous collections of Australian essays — Mackaness and Holmes (1933), Cowling and Maurice (1936), and even Rodd (1968) — all confirm Green's sense of a slimness of pickings. They all have a slight 'for schools' feel about them; they all delve into adjacent genres like the sketch, the memoir, the travelogue, the potted bio, even the short story; and they all rely heavily on selections from Walter Murdoch.

Institutions that encourage the play of ideas that Green calls leisure, whether more or less formal, tend to be metropolitan. The Australian essay is of the city, even when, as so often, it gazes out at the bush. (In a limited sense the Australian essay *is* the city's take on the bush.) Another way of saying this is to make the rather banal point that the essay depends on civilisation. But it is less banal to say, as Vance Palmer implies, in the essay reprinted here, that civilisation might depend on the essay.

Sir Walter Murdoch and Clive James are probably our two most technically skilled, as well as our funniest, essayists, and still the only major Australian writers to have specialised in the genre. Murdoch is hardly read now — probably best known for his years as Chancellor of the University of Western Australia, for giving his name to another university, and for his famous grand-nephew — but in his day, the 1930s and '40s, he was immensely popular, and his collections were huge best-sellers. Murdoch's work always carries a strong whiff of the Edwardian British world into which he was born and educated, perhaps too much so for contemporary readers.

Murdoch believed that 'the essay is to prose what the lyric is to poetry; it is intensely personal'. Certainly the essayist is closer to the lyric poet than to the writer of fiction, because deep in the essay there is the convention that the essayist is overheard thinking aloud, rather than heard directly. Instead of telling us what she thinks we ought to know, the essayist lets us listen in as she finds out what it is she knows. Hence the editorial is never an essay; nor is the republican (or monarchist) harangue, that major environmental hazard of our time. Vincent Buckley, in his 1964 essay on 'The Search for a National Identity', argued that our finest poets sought personal identity, not national identity, and that if they contributed anything to the latter it was as 'by-product'. The same is true of our best essayists: they tend to look at the 'big picture' from the corner of the eye, or through the lens of a lived detail, if at all.

Like Vance Palmer, Murdoch (writing in 'The Essay') believed there was some essential connection between the essay and civilisation:

> If the essay should come to displace the novel in popular favour, it would be a clear sign of an advance in civilisation. When we are prepared to sit down and listen to an easy, informal talk by a wise, humorous, kindly observer of life, without demanding that he shall tell us a story, we show that we are growing up.

One sense in which he is right about the essay as a grown-up taste is that, more than any other genre, it is haunted by irony: you write an epic poem about Gary Ablett; you write an essay about Vinny Catoggio. (The essay's ironic temper is another quality that distances it from high-toned political exhortation, or 'the vision thing'.) In *The Stockyard and the Croquet Lawn*, G. A. Wilkes has argued that the sceptical and ironic undercurrents in colonial Australian literature have been obscured by the dominance of the nationalist account, and the history of the essay supports this argument. For example, it is no accident that in his essays, more than in his poems or stories, it is impossible to take Lawson's attitude to the bush as anything but grimly ironic. In fact, Lawson's essays figure the bush as a nightmare landscape of thwarted human ambitions and desires, like Dame Mary Gilmore's no less powerful vision of human creative potential in the bush becoming stunted like a bent twig.

In the general flowering of the Australian essay that has occurred over the last fifty years, the story is not always predictable. The late 1950s and early 1960s, which we think of, or have been taught to think of, as a 'grey' period in Australian cultural life, are in fact the heyday of the essay. It was a great time for journals like *Meanjin*, *Quadrant*, *Overland*, *Australian Letters*, and (just) the *Bulletin*; and of course at this stage the humanities everywhere had not yet retreated from public speech into a sterile and introverted jargon. But there is also something about the urgency of the issues confronting Australian life in the late 1950s that concentrates the minds of trained intellectuals and keeps them addressing broad human concerns in the language of ordinary women and men. The very sense of threat to free public life keeps a vigorous public sphere of discussion alive. It was, as Geoffrey Dutton called it, a vital decade, and no period before or since has given us public essayists of the strength of James McAuley, Manning Clark, Vincent Buckley, Arthur Phillips, Alister Kershaw, and Frank Knöpfelmacher.

And by contrast, what of the much-vaunted 1970s, the decade that — and shouldn't this be the other way around? — began in wine and ended in rage? Well, while there are some good things there, overall the period is not strong in the essay. In contrast to its riotous cousin satire, irony prefers to take a sober and realistic accounting of life's little disappointments. But read some of the children of Gough in full flight now, and you find that they have given drunken raving a bad name.

The history of the Australian essay teaches us much, but proves nothing, except perhaps the truth of the saying that what goes around comes around. When we read Samuel Rinder's essay spiritedly defending the rights of 'foreigners' to be considered as Australian as currency lads, and to be given an equal political voice, with just a few terms altered we could be reading a contemporary meditation on race, identity, and culture — for example, Graham Little's essay, written a century later. I would like to think that this means we are embarked on what educationists call a 'spiral curriculum': always circling around the same themes, but with a gathering sense of their significance. But sometimes it feels as if the old line about marriage — you always argue about the same things: it's just that you swap sides every few years — could apply as accurately to cultural dialogue.

Recent talk of a renaissance in the essay might be premature. While there are certainly more outlets for the essay now, many of them seem almost as chary of the poor middlebrow reader and his or her attitudes and interests as the hardcore academic journals. And while the main (though not exclusive) driving force for the essay will tend to be intellectuals, especially university intellectuals, there are numerous disincentives for Australian academics interested in the public essay. If you want to make money, don't write essays: write reviews or journalism; if, as is more likely, you want advancement, again don't write essays: write academic articles. Genuinely informal writing requires as much skill and application as formal prose; to adapt a remark of Northrop Frye, the skill required for the essay is a special skill, like playing the piano, not the expression of a general attitude to life, like singing in the shower. Far from encouraging the Australian intelligentsia to develop this skill, a great deal seems set up to encourage it to do what it does best anyway, i.e. disappear up its own discursive formation.

In the preface to one of his own books of essays, Les Murray remarks that they are part of an experiment to discover 'whether it is possible any longer to be an individual in Australia'. In this anthology I have looked for essays that participate in that same experiment. Glancing back now across the sixty-one chosen from among the several thousand looked at, I see that I have also favoured essays in which the essayist tells us something that she or he has learned, not from books but from experience. Perhaps the rhythm of action, including the rhythm of the failure or collapse of action, has left its mark on the Australian essay after all.

'SIMON STUKELEY'

from *The Hermit in Van Diemen's Land*

Among the several institutions established in this beautiful and rapidly advancing Colony, which at once bespeak a sound knowledge of the best principles of Government, and a paternal interest for the prosperity of the inhabitants, none has pleased me so much, nor has so exalted its rulers in my estimation, as the schools for the care and education of orphan children. Were I inclined to moralize, how many deductions would present themselves, from even a partial consideration of this important subject; but the benefits arising to the community, from the instruction of youth, from checking the evil propensities of our nature, and substituting in their places, the seeds of virtue and of true christianity, have been well known from the earliest ages. They have been thought worthy the special injunction of Holy Writ; they have found a place in the breasts of the wise and good of all countries, but in no spot, perhaps, throughout the world, are they more deservedly called into action, than in a Colony, which serves as a cloacina to the Mother Country, and many of whose inhabitants are, consequently, the very last persons to whom the charge of youth ought to be entrusted. But all such institutions, good in themselves, become more or less useful, according to the management which obtains with respect to them, and according to the character of the individuals who are selected for this interesting trust; and here again, in Van Diemen's Land, there is, I apprehend, or rather alas! there has been, abundant cause to admire and approve the choice which has been made. I use the past tense, not with any view of disparaging those who still perform the duties relating to such establishments, but as referring to a sad event of recent occurrence, which gave rise to a scene of deep interest, and of which I have been an intimate spectator.

Accident, some little time ago, brought me acquainted with a very worthy couple, with whose story were connected many affecting incidents. The Gentleman, bred and educated in the bosom of Mother Church, anxious to disseminate the doctrines upon its truths and precepts, had accepted a situation at a pestilential settlement on the coast of Africa, regardless of all personal considerations, and mindful only of the warfare, wherein he was enlisted. His wife, a delicate and accomplished lady, accompanied him, sharing all his fatigues and difficulties, and exposed to the influence of perhaps the most unhealthy climate in the world. The rest is soon told — shattered in constitution, and suffering in health, the Gentleman's appointment, and his career of usefulness, were changed for this distant Island, the salubrity of the air here, being probably considered the best mode of repairing the effects of their former residence. But scarcely were they inducted in the joint charge of the School for Female Orphans, ere a slow, but insidious disease began to shew itself, creating bodily pain of the most excruciating nature; baffling the utmost efforts of human skill, and at length terminating in a release from all mortal cares and anxieties. It was the funeral of this patient, this excellent person, which occasioned the reflections giving rise to my present remarks; and although the subject is somewhat different to that which I now and then bring before my readers, methinks that the object I have in view by my essays, is quite as likely to be attained by holding up departed virtue and innocence to imitation, as by exposing living follies as a warning or beacon to others how they may avoid them.

After the solemn minute bell had been some time tolling, the mournful procession left the late abode of peace and sincere conjugal affection, where the deceased had breathed her last, and entering the body of the Church, the last sad rites were administered in a slow impressive manner, well befitting the occasion.

The greatest sufferer by far, exhibited on his countenance, that calm resignation which can only arise from a mind well at peace with itself, and when those beautiful words 'I am the resurrection', &c. were uttered by the officiating Clergyman, an expression of hope and consolation usurped for a moment the place of the solemn melancholy which sat upon his brow, and he seemed to feel 'we shall yet be united'. When the sorrowing group turned their steps towards that 'bourne whence no traveller returns', and where the remains of all that was lately good, amiable, and accomplished, were about to be removed for ever from mortal sight, the scene became interesting and affecting in the extreme. A number of little Orphan Boys, about sixty or more, varying in ages from perhaps two or three to twelve or fourteen years old, formed the van of the procession, all dressed alike in a dark cloth suit, straw hats with crape bands; next to them came about fifty Orphan Girls, walking like the others, two and two, and habited in neat stuff frocks, white aprons, and straw bonnets with crape. The pall was borne by Clergymen, and at the head of the body of real, sincere mourners who followed, was the Lieutenant Governor himself, clad in his military undress, with the usual crape symbols, thus shewing the high sense he entertained of the merits of the deceased, by assisting the unfortunate husband through this, his hour of severe affliction; the rest of the party was composed of a long train, comprehending the foremost in rank, talent, and influence of the Colony. It was, indeed, a funeral of the heart, not the idle pageantry which too often attends such scenes, but the mourning of the spirit which we are led to believe is ever acceptable; and, if human sympathy and condolence be capable of mitigating sorrow, surely that of him who had thus been separated from all that was dear to him, must ere now have been somewhat diminished. Among the parts of the service not the least interesting, the full solemn notes of the organ yielding their touching melody as the instrument was played with exquisite taste and feeling, in accompanying an anthem adapted for the occasion, which was sung by the children, particularly impressed me; and I could not help feeling how much had been done in the short space of five and twenty years, towards adapting a wild and savage waste into a fit abode for an Englishman. The Arts and Sciences have indeed gone hand-in-hand here with religion, and have created a striking example of what may be accomplished, where zeal, energy, and talent direct the helm. [...]

1829

SIR JAMES MARTIN

Sun-Set

Having in my last sketch given an account of sun-rise, as seen from South Head, it may not be inappropriate here to describe the appearance of sun-set as I once saw it, from the same position.

Having been out one remarkably fine day, visiting the Lighthouse and its vicinity, as the sun was declining towards the western horizon, the heavens presented such a beautiful appearance, that I determined to wait and contemplate the approach of an Australian sun-set. The sky was slightly covered with a mixture of dark and fleecy clouds, which, contrasted with the deep blue of the atmosphere, afforded a very picturesque appearance. Italy, I felt convinced, with all her charms, her orange groves, her balmy breezes, and her splendid skies, might well be proud of such an evening.

When the sun had almost sank below a light strata of clouds that skirted the horizon, the sight that it presented was exceedingly beautiful. The various picturesque tints which its rays gave to the vapoury screens, which seemed to envelope it, had a delightful effect. Far inland could I discern the blue mountains rising high above the surrounding lands, and appearing at different places like a sea in the distance. Here and there a conical hill reared aloft into the atmosphere, looked like a dense azure cloud resting upon the mountains. Intervening between this and the spot where I was standing lay the splendid harbour of Port Jackson, bearing on its tranquil bosom ships and boats of every description. The masts and rigging of the vessels appeared like a splendid forest amidst the waters, and the monotonous noise of oars conveyed along the surface of the deep, sounded musically upon the ear. A portion of Sydney, in the form of an amphitheatre, was visible over an intervening headland, at the extremity of which was built the picturesque and frowning battery of Fort Macquarie. In short, everything that I gazed upon was eminently calculated to enliven the scene, and envelope it in a mantle of magic splendour. No spot could present a much neater view than that which I then beheld, slightly dimmed as it was by the approaching shades of night.

The sun at length was beginning to disappear below a cloud and twilight was rapidly approaching. A bright golden tint overspread the whole face of nature — the sky — the land — the water — the shipping and the buildings — all partook of the brilliant rays of the departing luminary. The portion of the harbour intervening in a direct line between me and the sun looked like a sea of molten gold; and wherever a boat passed across it, my fancy pictured to me some joyful ferryman, urging his light skiff gaily along in the regions of the blest. Happy land, ejaculated I, how little do your thoughtless inhabitants appreciate the beauties which nature has liberally bestowed upon you. Alas! that England should make you the repository to which all her excess of crime and depravity is sent — to which the refuse of her people — the outcasts of society — are transported!

In a few minutes the sun was entirely hidden from my sight, but still its influence had not departed. By degrees the vivid tints which its rays had shortly before given to everything around became less brilliant — the golden colour changed to a yellow — the yellow to a red — the red to a blue — the blue to a dun — until finally twilight had begun to reign. The various and rapidly changing tints becoming gradually more beautiful until they were all gone, had an enchanting influence upon the senses.

When the objects before me were almost enveloped in the shades of darkness, I was still lingering on the spot whence I had beheld the setting of the sun. My eyes were still turned longingly towards the west, and although night began to settle upon the mountains, I yet gazed as though the golden scene were still before me. The charm which bound me to the place was not broken until night had advanced, and the silver moon, brilliant and beautiful, had arisen to assume her sway. The pale orb and the twinkling stars aroused me from the slight and transient lethargy into which I had fallen, and warned me that it was time to retire.

Were it possible, I would gladly spend every day of my existence in witnessing a sight so glorious as the one which I had just beheld. Continual enjoyment instead of cloying would but augment my desire.

To those who have never witnessed an 'Australian sun-set' in spring, the foregoing account may appear highly coloured and greatly exaggerated; but, instead of exceeding it, in my opinion, falls short of the truth. However, let those who have an opportunity judge for themselves.

1838

SAMUEL RINDER

The 'Foreigner' in Australia

I am indebted for the above title to Mr Meudell, who, in his article on 'Australia for the Australians', politely designates as foreigners the whole body of colonists who have had the misfortune to be born in other countries, and who, in that young gentleman's opinion, are only nuisances and obstacles to progress that should be got rid of as early as possible. As an old colonist myself, I object to such summary treatment, although Mr Meudell can certainly quote examples in his favour as old, not merely as the Greeks, but dating back to the days of the Aryan house-father —

> 'When Leonidas arrived at the scene of his desperate defence of Thermopylæ, he was accompanied,' says Herodotus, 'by the three hundred men which the law assigned him, whom he had himself chosen from among the citizens, and who were all of them fathers with sons living! According to modern notions, a forlorn hope would naturally be composed of men who had not given hostages to fortune. Such, however, was not the light in which the matter presented itself to the Greek mind. The human plant had flowered, and the continuance of the house was secure. It was, therefore, of comparatively little moment what befel the man whose duty to his ancestors had been fulfilled.'

Thus, 'Young Australia', at the very moment of declaring its revolt against old-world notions, and exulting in the vast superiority of the new race, which is to push the old one from its seat, does but repeat one of the most ancient of them all — as old, indeed, as the Archaic world, in which the continuance of the house and the worship of the ancestor were the primal duties. Unlike his mythic forefathers, however, the young Australian, if we are to accept Mr Meudell's description of him, is not at all inclined to the practice of burying his departed parent beneath the hearthstone and worshipping his spirit.

> 'In this hearth,' says Dr Hearn, 'where in his lifetime he had himself so often sacrificed, the departed house-father received, at the hands of his successor, his share of every meal, and heard from his lips in his own honour those familiar words of praise and prayer that were the heirlooms of his race.'

The 'departed house-father' of the young Australian is not likely, it seems, to have any such experience. Already, even before he has passed into the spirit land, his eager sons are anxious, we are told, to step into his shoes, and he may say, with the dying king:

> *'I stay too long for thee — I weary thee;*
> *Dost thou so hunger for my empty chair*
> *That thou wilt needs invest thee with mine honours*
> *Before thy hour be ripe?'*

We old Australians, to quote Mr Meudell, are 'foreigners' — trespassers on the land that we have given to our sons. Our intellects are 'stunted as the feet of a Chinese dame', and, says our cruel critic, 'despite their time-honoured boast of absolute freedom, many of our fathers actually did not know what freedom was till they came hither!' How the young cockrel crows! And how we crowed, too, when the down was on our lips, and we felt that our certain mission was to set the whole world straight. In those days 'Young England' was as fierce and as self-confident as Young Australia is in these, and possibly felt as much contempt for the old fogies who had made England arbitress of Europe, and first in arts and arms. But, conceited as we certainly were, I do not believe that the boldest of us would have ventured to attack the old folks as savagely as Mr Meudell does. We unfortunate elders have exchanged, we are told, 'the frigidity and comparative destitution of the silver-coasted isles, with their time-honoured associations and domestic exigencies (whatever they may be), for the bright skies, genial climate, and comparative affluence of this Australia Felix.' Poor souls — Englishmen, Irishmen, Scotchmen — driven from our miserable, poverty-stricken homes, where we were, it seems, 'accustomed to want as regards food, and filth as regards houses and clothing,' to the great Southern elysium, where our sons can teach us — to suck eggs!

> 'Every age,' says our young Solomon, 'reveals the fallacy of what was previously held to be indubitable truth, and, therefore, the Australians have an advantage over men educated in an old age and in an old world. The rising generation has been nurtured under a new and dry light, mental and moral, while the old decaying one was forced in a hot-house of falsity.'

The metaphors are somewhat confusing, but no doubt the difficulty of understanding our mentor's meaning is due, not to his lack of power to express it, but to our obtuseness; though how the old decaying generation has contrived to produce out of its rottenness such brilliant successors, is a puzzle that one may well be content to give up. The usual fruits of decay are mushrooms, or more frequently, poisonous fungi. In which of these somewhat low organisms shall we class our coming rulers?

As a striking proof of the advanced condition of Young Australia, and of the high state of culture to which it has been brought under the 'new and dry light', we are offered a comparison of the number of brides and bridegrooms who sign their names with a mark in Victoria and in any other colony, or in Great Britain, Ireland, or France. This, we are told, is the very best proof that the standard of State school education is higher here than in England, and that 'education is more widely diffused among the lower classes'. For this happy state of things we are, of course, indebted to the scholars — not to the teachers, who are chiefly 'foreigners', nor to those who established and have administered our educational system, and who certainly belong to the decaying generation. If the statement be correct, it is a good proof of the precocity of our youngsters, for the system is hardly old enough to allow the State-educated brides and bridegrooms to outnumber those who have had no such advantages.

And now, after all this bragging, let us see what Victoria owes to her colonists, and what to her sons and daughters. In the very same number of the *Review* in which Mr Meudell's article appears we have an admirable sketch of the life of one of the 'foreigners' to whom she is chiefly indebted for her University, her Public Library, her Royal Society, her National Gallery, and her National and Technological Museums. This noble scion of a 'decayed generation' is, alas! one of those whose death the Australian champion seems to think is rather matter of rejoicing than of sorrow; or if there be some slight regret, it is mitigated, we are told, by the belief that the places of the lost ones will be easily filled. It may be so, but the signs are not yet. Surely this young Victorian forgets that to the unwearying energy, the strong self-reliance, the clear heads and stout arms of her early settlers, his country owes the very wealth and culture of which he boasts, and to the growth of which he and his fellows have as yet contributed so little! Step by step the wild lands have been reclaimed; stone by stone the noble cities built; mile by mile the far-reaching lines of rail and wire have been stretched; foot by foot the buried treasures sought and found; one by one the schools of art and learning erected and endowed. By whom? Not by the 'young Australian', surely! Did that freedom, which he boasts as his, spring self-begotten from the earth? Was that noble educational system which he praises born of the soil? Have the grand gifts which the fast-vanishing generation of 'foreigners' will bequeath to their sons dropped from the clear Australian skies? The gifts of art and science, of learning and culture, of commerce and manufactures, of ripening harvests and glittering ores; the shady groves of Academe; the gathered treasures of literature, and of the sister arts; the temples of religion and of justice; the palaces of commerce, and the huge piles that quiver to the throbbing pulses of the tireless giant whose hot breath and iron sinews obey the master's slightest touch; the parks and gardens; and the thousand homes of comfort and of health; — are all these nothing in the eyes of those of our race who are so soon to fill our vacant places? Do our sons owe us no better guerdon than this sneer at our now rapidly diminishing numbers — at our early and bitter struggles? Not so is kept the memory of the fathers of the Great Republic, to be able to claim whose ancestry is to be —

'The heir of all the ages, in the foremost files of time.'

And what, may we ask before we go, are these sons of ours doing to carry on the work so well begun? Some of them, we know — many, we hope — are working hard to better our endeavours — to build up to greater height and nobler proportions the edifice of which we have but laid the foundations. But how many are rather drags on the work, hindrances to the progress of the land they profess to love so well. Mr Meudell longs for the day when native Victorians alone shall sit in her legislative chambers and make her laws. Has that experiment been, so far, a great success? Have our native-born legislators done much to raise the character of our parliaments, or shown themselves more capable than the intruding 'foreigner' of 'comprehending the grand truths of political economy'? Have they, indeed, given the slightest ground for Mr Meudell's declaration that 'Australia will never be properly governed till she is ruled by native-born Australians'? The temptation to individualize is strong, but I forbear. That the coming race is capable of great things, we willingly and gladly acknowledge. That many of our sons are full of promise, and that some are already in the full vigour of great performances, are matters of quiet joy to the old fellows, who see in these their youth renewed. But, on the other hand, there is a very great number in whom not only is there little promise of good, but very much of evil; and, as yet, with a few exceptions, the capacity to rule has not been greatly developed in Young Australia, while the capacity to obey, which must precede the other, is sadly wanting. But that these qualities will come in good time we hope and believe; and that with them will also come more generally that power of steady application, persistent industry, and grave earnestness, which have raised the 'foreign' empire of Britain to such a high position among kindred states. That in many of the young sons and daughters of the South these great qualities are at present either dormant or absent is unfortunately too true, and it would almost seem that our Italian skies and genial climate are helping to develop a race having the characteristics rather of lands fanned by the soft airs of summer seas than of those rugged shores on which the fierce tempests of the North beat ruthlessly; of Sicily and Florence rather than of sturdy Kent or Stony Caithness; of the banks of Tiber or Arno rather than of Shannon, Thames, or Clyde. The love of out-door games and athletic exercises is a redeeming trait; but the very proficiency in these sports, of which we hear so much, and the eager interest shown in the peaceful victories that are blazoned in columns side by side with stirring incidents, that make the great world pause, furnish but another instance of the passion for pleasurable excitement that must be gratified at the cost of nobler aims. Cricket, football, racing, rowing, are excellent and English. They are grand games, and the love of them should be fostered; but here they bid fair to become the serious business of the day instead of its rest and relaxation. They cannot be called 'muscular Christianity', for I suspect that few of the gymnasts care much about their fathers' faith, however anxious they may be to step into their shoes. The grand old motto, 'Fear God and honour the king', has little force for them, and obedience to the 'first command with promise given' is hardly common enough to ensure for the young Australian the fulfilment of the promise 'that thy days may be long in the land which the Lord thy God giveth thee'. Happily, this description does not apply to all, but the world is apt to judge of the bulk by the sample, and the sample of Young Victoria who pose in public are not prepossessing. We know well that a numerous body of young men are working with their might, and striving with all their strength, to fit themselves for the battle, and it may be that the bad specimens who occasionally come to the top are but the scum thrown up by the bubbling waters beneath, which are purified in the process. Most of the world's work is done by men whose names are hardly known outside the little circle in which they move, and, doubtless, there are many of this stamp among the younger generation, as well as a chosen few who are born to be leaders of men.

Thus, then, we may hope that as the new race comes in greater numbers to the front, the old blood will show itself, flowing, perhaps, a little more rapidly under the Southern sun, but still beating with the same steady pulse that has given coolness and courage in so many hard-fought fields, both of peace and war. Mr Meudell says rightly that our time is short, but he need not wish, therefore, to make it shorter. The dearest wish of our hearts must be to see our sons take our places, and fill them better than we have done; to see carried to its full fruition the hope that has buoyed us up through many a weary struggle; to watch the gradual clearing of the clouds that somewhat shadowed the early morning of the new land we love so well; and to welcome with pride and joy the growing glories and increasing strength of the young giant by whose cradle some of us have stood — the latest born of nations, the stalwart son of the great mother whose children inherit the earth, and who rests —

'Broad-based upon the people's will,
And compassed by the inviolate seas.'

1882

D. H. DENIEHY

On Certain Aesthetic Disabilities of Native Australians

Looking over the second edition of Mr Frank Fowler's 'Southern Lights and Shadows', which has just reached Australia, the following passage struck us as amusing in its way: 'I first noticed that a large and an æsthetically valuable part of English literature was necessarily a blank to the native Australian. I mean all that portion which relates to winter, its charms and peculiarities — the yule log, old Christmas, the mistletoe and the holly: the fooprints, let us say, of the muse in the snow. To read Tennyson's "Death of the Old Year" to a young Australian, would be like reading Hafiz to a Laplander.' As is often the case with writers who find it easier to supplement a statement of fact with an image — which always has a knowing air about it, besides being pretty, — than to support its pretensions to *vraisemblance* by reasons, the simile perhaps proves more than was intended. Why should not a Laplander relish Hafiz as well as Horace, provided he could have it in good Norse as Mr Frank Fowler gets it in Sir William Jones's English. The poet of Shiraz, with as little of positive Sufism about him as Beranger, sang of women and wine; and of these things a Laplander has quite as lively conceptions as a Cockney. Lord Dufferin found the Lapp women pretty, and the men, the bishop included, the jolliest dogs in all creation. But if as a necessary condition for understanding poetry, one must live or have lived in the climate, and among the circumstances under which it was produced, where are Mr Fowler's own qualifications for appreciating Hafiz? How to Moore's admiring 'Dubliners' is all that is sung about the 'Feast of Roses' and the other graceful revelries of the vale of Kashmere in 'Lalla Rookh', to be other than 'necessarily a blank'. But a more puzzling question still; how did the late Mr Thomas Moore — himself, of whose numerous services to society, travelling in the East certainly formed no part, manage to create the poetry itself? Travellers, we are told, admit the 'costume and feeling' of the poem to be correct. And yet, Tom managed it all, with his 'study of imagination' and the books of Lord Moira's library hard by Sloperton. And again, how does that large section of English readers unacquainted with the manners and customs and what Dr Woolley would perhaps term 'the law' of piratical ethics in the Greek archipelago —

> — *'The land where the cypress and myrtle*
> *Are emblems of deeds that are done in their clime.'*

get along with Lord Byron's very popular poetry?

Mr Frank Fowler's statement on this point about us native Australians, is just as true as most statements of fact in a book, otherwise really sparkling and picturesque. The gamins of Sydney, who are nocturnally interrupted in their *sommeil de Bohéme* in brick-kilns and removed by the police 'for protection', and the lads of better class who are everlastingly cricketing in the public grounds of the metropolis, have small ideas of these things. But this is not because they have not eaten a Christmas dinner, with the frost upon the pane, or taken a part in the osculatory amenities beneath the mistletoe, or have not known that other 'footstep in the snow', which Mr Fowler has forgotten to mention, the entrance of harmony to rule 'the anarchy of dreaming sleep', in the shape of the midnight music of 'the waits'. It is, simply, because they know nothing at all about literature, and have never had their imaginations trained to realise things beyond the reach of their daily experiences. Their power of appreciation, as compared with that of their cultured countrymen, is just as one should compare an untravelled English youth's notions of the bright, sunny, highly coloured qualities of out-of-door Italian life and Italian scenery, as gathered from such writers as Walter Savage Landor, and Robert Browning, with the loose notions about 'furrin parts' of the big-caped cab-driver, who slaps his hands in the chills of an early December morning, on Tower-hill. The wintry tone, and the high relief into which in-door comfort is thrown by it, which eminently belong to Mr Dickens's Christmas Tales, were quite as well understood here, as books which do not repeat experiences common to *any* local society can be, and in which category a large portion of books in every literature stands. That we enjoy as keenly as one who cherishes images of the snow on the holly-bough, and the rumbling of the December wind in the chimney, and the happy Christmas faces that throng the dearest and sweetest of his memories we do not say. Nor is it necessary we should. We are not informed as we might have been with truth, that we do not as fully *enjoy* things of this kind as people in England. We are told 'they are of necessity a blank' to us.

Mr Fowler, whose knowledge of Australia is, we believe, confined to what he experienced in Sydney, and on a trip once taken up the Hunter, seems to have forgotten there are portions of the territory, where the natives have a taste of the qualities of frost and snow as fully as the inhabitants of the British Isles. To add to *their* climatic experiences, some realisation of that equipage of genial and affecting images which environ an English Christmas, is by no means one of the hardest 'tricks of strong Imagination'.

1859

'PETER 'POSSUM'

The Compliments of the Season

What an impotent, impudent sham — what a dreary humbug — an Australian Christmas is! Mercury at eversomuch, pink bonnets and white jackets; red dust macadamising your throat, and tickling your nostrils like cayenne, when the wind blows; black leaves hanging grim and silent as undertaker's mutes in the scorching sunlight, when the breeze is dead; myriads of locusts rattling away like shipwrights' hammers on an iron steamer; indoor festivals at which the guests, in spite of open windows and illegitimate shirt sleeves, look brown and oleaginous as the uneatable roast beef; outdoor gatherings — *picnics*, forsooth — for the consumption of cold fowl, champagne, and strawberry ice. *That* Christmas! Bosh!

Oh, for a good old English Christmas Week, in rural places and pre-railway times! The 'up' coaches feathered with game and turkeys; the 'down' coaches bright as sunlit greenhouses with a broad smile of uncaged schoolboys, puffing out their cheeks like mischievous cherubs as they salute every one they pass with a hailstorm from their pea-shooters; the mellowed anticipatory mirth of Christmas Eve — to Christmas night what silver is to gold; the jubilant bells breaking out at midnight — sweet yet startling, like angel-voices long ago in Palestine — to herald Christmas in; the peep out on Christmas morning, through the arabesques of the frosted pane, upon the pure, peaceful hush of snow for many a mile: on cottage-roofs, ruffed round with icicles; in cottage-gardens, printed with the fanlike footmarks of the hunger-tamed, brown birds — black from their contrast with its spotless white; wrapping the old church-tower in its thousandth winter-robe, powdering its polished ivy-leaves, shrouding the swelling graves; gathered in deep drifts in ditches; burying the bending hedges; turning the sliced haystacks into monster twelfth-cakes; stretching far as the eye can reach over the now unfamiliar-looking fields.

The 'merry, merry bells of Yule' peal through the little village over its circling meadows, and from the hamlet homes, and the outlying farms, men, women, and children troop merrily to church: grayheaded patriarchs, grandames in scarlet cloaks; stout yeomen in top boots, matrons with broad, sunny faces that typify their hearts; rustic belles, with cheeks redder than their ribbons; rustic beaux, sheepish, large-fisted, and sleek-haired; less pretentious ploughmen in Jim Crows, green smocks, and leather leggings; bullet-headed little boys, roguish and loud; curly-pated little girls, demure and silent.

And then the hearty greetings from young and old and rich and poor (once a year, at all events, brotherly and gay) as one walks briskly up the churchyard path; the happy family-clusters in the crowded pews — scattered at other times, but households once again in this uniting season; the freshness of the service on this the birthday of its Founder; the pleasant sameness of the old vicar's old Christmas sermon — to his old parishioners, a thirty-years familiar friend; the joyous Christmas dinner, with its mountainous supply of *utile* and *dulce*, and their most business-like consumption (languid, beggarly picnics, indeed!); the country dances, forfeits, hunt-the-slipper; the kisses snatched from coy and yet not unwilling maidens beneath the mistletoe (which too soon, alas! hangs berryless); the roasted chestnuts, punch, and ghost-stories before the blazing fire; the closing frolic, crowning supper, and valedictory hot elderberry wine — that's what *I* call Christmas!

'A Merry Christmas and a Happy New Year!' — how the old greeting awakens memories of similar good wishes, from other lips, in other lands: from those lips, in the dear old familiar places, perchance, never to be heard again! *Heimweh* casts a sad shade on Christmas festivities in this part of the world. Their warmth to many a one is thermometrical alone. Watching family-gatherings — like Charles Lamb's friend at Mackerey End, the only one who had no cousin there — the stranger feels more than ever strange. *His* Christmas Tide is hardly 'merry.'

And what of his New Year? as, on the last night of the old, he sits listening in his solitude to the ticking of the clock — solemn at such a time as the audible beating of a dying heart — in throngs

The Beloved, the True-hearted,
Come to visit him once more;

those from whom he is severed by the ocean, and those between whom and him there spreads that wider, sailless sea. Phantoms of vanished joys arise; old sorrows, too, long cherished sacredly in the soul's secret places; and bitterly he feels that now there is none to share with him his pleasure or his pain. 'A Happy New Year' — however goodnaturedly uttered — seems but a mockery to a lonely heart.

But enough of this. Christmas, after all, everywhere teaches the same lesson of the charity that thinks no ill, of world-wide love. One Janus-glance backwards may be allowed in January; but the god had a second face, and, like it, we, too, ought to look bravely on the future.

As the household, forgetting the day's troubles and forgiving all its little wrongs, meet in the evening in a cheerful circle round the hearth of Home — Demophoon-like, deriving purity and strength from its golden blaze, — so should the whole Christian family close the year with a like sanctifying, animating glee — cleansed from the soils of the old year at its concluding festival — casting off old spites, and pettinesses, and impurities as a rescued beggar sloughs his squalid rags — we should step hopefully over the threshold of the new, and uncomplaining enter on its toils.

1858

FREDERICK SINNETT

from *The Fiction Fields of Australia*

Man can no more do without works of fiction than he can do without clothing, and, indeed, not so well; for, where climate is propitious, and manners simple, people often manage to loiter down the road of life without any of the 'lendings' that Lear cast away from him; yet, nevertheless, with nothing between the blue heaven and their polished skins, they will gather in a circle round some dusky orator or vocalist, as his imagination bodies forth the forms of things unknown, to the entertainment and elevation of his hearers. To amend our first proposition, then, works of fiction being more necessary, and universally disseminated, than clothing, they still resemble clothing in this, that they take different shapes and fashions in different ages. In the days of Chaucer —

> *First warbler, whose sweet breath*
> *Preluded those melodious bursts that fill*
> *The spacious times of great Elizabeth*
> *With sounds that echo still —*

didactic and descriptive poetry was almost the only recognized vehicle of fiction. Then came the bursts that Chaucer preluded; and in Shakspere's days the dramatic form prevailed over all others. For some time afterwards every kind of feeling and thought found its expression in miscellaneous verse; and (though he was, of course, not the first novelist) Fielding, probably, set the fashion of that literary garment of the imagination, which has since been almost exclusively worn — the novel.

In the shape of novels, then, civilised man, at the present day, receives the greater part of the fictitious clothing necessary to cover the nakedness of his mind; and our present inquiry is into the feasibility of obtaining the material for this sort of manufacture from Australian soil. We are not, of course, questioning the practicability of writing novels in Australia. Thackeray might have begun 'The Newcomes' in Kensington, and finished the book in Melbourne, as well as on the Continent. Our inquiry is into the feasibility of writing Australian novels; or, to use other words, into the suitability of Australian life and scenery for the novel writers' purpose; and, secondly, into the right manner of their treatment.

A reference to the second topic almost forestalls the necessity of our stating the distinct conviction by which we are possessed, that genuine Australian novels are possible; and, as a corollary from their being possible, it follows, with apparent obviousness, that they are desirable, inasmuch as it is desirable that the production of things necessary or comfortable to humanity should be multiplied and increased.

First, however, we must deal with the possibility; for, it has been our lot to fall in with men, by no means altogether given over to stupidity, who deem, what Signor Raffaello calls, 'this bullock-drivers' country' to present a field, not by any process whatsoever to be tilled and cultivated so as to produce novels, for some ages to come. The real reason, we take it, why our incredulous acquaintances arrived at the opinion they expressed, is, that such cultivation has not yet prospered to any remarkable extent; and that it is always difficult to believe in the possibility of anything of which there is no existing example and type. But, as this particular reason for disbelief is one which, while it has much actual weight over men's minds, is not often openly advanced, some more specific and respectable arguments were required, and, accordingly, were soon forthcoming.

In the first place, then, it is alleged against Australia that it is a new country, and, as Pitt said, when charged with juvenility, 'this is an accusation which I can neither palliate nor deny.' Unless we go into the Aboriginal market for 'associations', there is not a single local one, of a century old, to be obtained in Australia; and, setting apart Mr Fawkner's pre-Adamite recollections of Colonel Collins, there is not an association in Victoria mellowed by so much as a poor score of years. It must be granted, then, that we are quite debarred from all the interest to be extracted from any kind of archeological accessories. No storied windows, richly dight, cast a dim, religious light over any Australian premises. There are no ruins for that rare old plant, the ivy green, to creep over and make his dainty meal of. No Australian author can hope to extricate his hero or heroine, however pressing the emergency may be, by means of a spring panel and a subterranean passage, or such like relics of feudal barons, and refuges of modern novelists, and the offspring of their imagination. There may be plenty of dilapidated buildings, but not one, the dilapidation of which is sufficiently venerable by age, to tempt the wandering footsteps of the most arrant *parvenu* of a ghost that ever walked by night. It must be admitted that Mrs Radcliffe's genius would be quite thrown away here; and we must reconcile ourselves to the conviction that the foundations of a second 'Castle of Otranto' can hardly be laid in Australia during our time. Though the corporation may leave Collins-street quite dark enough for the purpose, it is much too dirty to permit any novelist (having a due regard for her sex) to ask the White Lady of Avenel, or a single one of her female connections, to pass that way.

Even if we survive these losses, the sins of youth continue to beset us. No one old enough for a hero can say,

'I remember, I remember the house where I was born,'

apropos of a Victorian dwelling. The antiquity of the United States quite puts us to shame; and it is darkly hinted that there is not so much as a 'house with seven gables' between Portland and Cape Howe.

Mr Horne, in his papers on dramatic art, observed very truly, that one does not go to the theatre (or the novel) for a fac simile of nature. If you want that you can see nature itself in the street or next door. You go to get larger and more comprehensive views of nature than your own genius enables you to take for yourself, through the medium of art. In the volume of Shakspere's plays, for example, is compacted more of nature than one man in a million perceives in a life's intercourse with the world. Shakspere, like all the kings of fiction, was a great condenser. We are not detained by him, except occasionally, and for subsidiary artistic purposes, with mere gossip about the momentary affairs of the men and women brought upon the scene. A verbatim report of a common evening's conversation would fill a book, and the greater part of what would be reported would be quite uninteresting, uninstructive, and unconducive to the purposes of art. The author of genius leaves no apparent gaps in the discourse; and brings about in the reader's mind a half-illusion that he is listening to a complete and unstrained dialogue; whereas, in fact, the speeches are so concise, and in such sequence, that we only have the essence of any possible conversation. Conversation is one of the essential processes of the writer of fiction, whatever form he may adopt — otherwise the description of years of life would take years to read.

Now, in the old world, we are accustomed to this kind of conversation; to conversations not reported verbatim, but artistically. From Shakspere downwards hundreds of authors have performed this service with admirable general fidelity; and have, at the same time, with artistic skill, concealed the evidences of their own labor as effectually as the sculptor does, in whose smooth and finished marble no mark of the chisel is to be discerned. This much, which is entirely due to the manner of the narrative, we have suffered ourselves to believe an attribute of the matter; and, because daily life, which is not much more prosaic on one part of the earth's surface than on another, has been, in the old world, so often and so admirably converted to the purposes of art, we fancy it to be peculiarly adapted to those purposes. Here we have not been accustomed to see nature through the medium of art, but directly; and though, to the eye of genius, 'the earth and every common sight' possesses a 'glory and a freshness,' and needs needs no abridgement or coloring, yet to possess such powers of perception is the privilege only of one among thousands. The great mass of mankind can only hope to catch glimpses of the glory of 'every common sight,' when genius holds it up for them in the right light. This genius has not yet done for Australian nature. Most of us have had more than enough of positive Australian dialogue, but we have never read an Australian dialogue artistically reported. We have heard squatter, and bullock-driver, and digger, talk, and we think it would be very uninteresting, no doubt; and a verbatim report of the conversation of Brown, Jones, and Robinson, in the old world, would be equally uninteresting, but we know by experience that genius can report it so as to be interesting — yet to leave it the conversation of Brown, Jones, and Robinson still. The first genius that performs similar service in Australia will dissipate our incredulity, as to this matter, for ever.

[...]

With respect to feelings and passions, then, which of them is there excluded from Australian soil? Certainly not that master passion which is the fiction writers' most constant theme.

All thoughts, all passions, all delights,
That ever move this mortal frame,
Are but the ministers of love,
And feed his sacred flame.

'Love rules the court, the camp, the grove,' and Australians as effectually as dwellers in old countries; and all the joys and sorrows of that emotion — which wise people, aged sixty and upwards, and other non-combatants in Cupid's warfare, laugh at and long for — are present for the novelist to deal with, as he tells, in some new form, the oft-told tale of which mankind never tires. Nay, the very fact that numberless lovers are here separated from their loves, should suggest a thousand various stories and situations, peculiar, in their details, to the soil, and yet dealing with a cosmopolitan and universal interest.

Is the opposite feeling of hate banished from Australia? We could contentedly give up the possibility of Australian novels for the assurance that we resided in such a utopia. Alas! that such a perfect reality cannot be obtained by the sacrifice of so much novelists' capital.

[...]

One word as to scenery. Many worthy people thought railways would put an end to romance in England. The new police act, it was conceived by others, would be equally destructive to the raw material of novels. The romance of robbery, some imagined, ended when robbers ceased to wear gold-laced coats and jack boots, and to do their business on horseback. The genius of fiction, however, can accommodate herself to greater changes than these, and remains just as fresh and as blooming under circumstances that make people, unacquainted with the invulnerable hardiness of her constitution, predict her immediate decline and death. For our part we hold that there is comparatively little in the circumstance, and almost all in the genius that handles it; but those who believe in mounted robbers, and mourn over the introduction of railways, should feel that in Australia the novelists' golden age is revived. When Waverley travelled up from London, to visit his northern cousins, the Osbaldistones, he went on horseback, and took a fortnight over the journey — that is the way we manage here to this very day. There was a great deal of 'sticking-up' then, and there; and there is here, and now. Sir William of Deloraine had to swim the stream that it would have spoiled a magnificent description for him to have crossed by a cast-iron bridge, as he would do in the reign of Victoria; but in the colony which bears her name, the Central Road-Board cannot be accused of having destroyed the romance of the water-courses. How, in the name of gas-pipes and rural police, is a traveller to be lost and benighted in England now-a-days. Here he can be placed in that unpleasant but interesting predicament, without violating, in the least, the laws of perfect probability. Look at the railway map of England, and see where

Now spurs the lated traveller apace
To gain the timely inn.

He has no control over the iron-horse that whirls him along, and when he gets to the terminus he gains the timely inn in a Hansom cab. Here the description applies with precise accuracy. In short, the natural and external circumstances of Australia partake much more of what we used to call romance than those of England, but we refuse to claim any advantage on this score, and content ourselves with reasserting that those who know how to deal with it can extract almost as much out of one set of circumstances as out of another, wherever the human heart throbs and human society exists.

We explain the absence of any really first-class Australian novels simply by a reference to the mathematical doctrine of probabilities. It is only once in many years that there steps forth from among the many millions of the British people a novelist able to break up new ground, and describe phases and conditions of life undescribed before. [...]

Well, then, we argue, if only now and then out of the population of all England there arises a novelist capable of breaking up fresh ground, it is not to be wondered at that no such man has yet arisen here. Geniuses are like tortoiseshell tom-cats — not impossible, only rare. Every ten years one is born unto great Britain, but probably none exists in Australia, and a reason precisely analagous to this makes it improbable that we have at present among us any one capable of doing justice to Australian materials of fiction. There are not cats enough in Australia to entitle us to a tortoiseshell tom yet, according to the doctrine of averages.

We have to confess that we labor under the same disadvantages as afflict the hacks and copyists, and we cannot, therefore, point out how the great untouched Australian quarry is to be rightly worked. Only as we roam about the motley streets, or ride through the silent bush, we have just sense enough to feel that, when the capable eye comes to look upon them, all these rude amorphous materials may be arranged in form of the highest and most artistic beauty. The recorders are tuneless only because there is no one who knows how to play upon them; in the right hands they will 'discourse most eloquent music'.

[...]

1856

HENRY KENDALL

A Colonial Literary Club

In the year of grace one thousand eight hundred and — , on a spot not a hundred miles from Collins-street, East Melbourne, there existed a literary club. Putting aside the strong probability that it is flourishing at the present moment, I will proceed to sketch it as it was at the date first mentioned, and to introduce in a casual way a few of its more remarkable members.

There are clubs and *clubs*. The one forming my subject most decidedly belongs to the latter division — that is to say, without reference to its members, the club does. In order to give the interested reader some idea of its character., I can do no better than describe how I first became acquainted with it, and what my impressions amounted to on the occasion. To begin then, at the beginning. Circumstances — to wit, bailiffs, dear reader — having compelled me to leave Sydney for a short time, I took ship to Melbourne, where I landed on an ominous first of April, decidedly ominous to a man starting life in a strange city, with a stock-in-trade consisting of two or three letters of introduction, and a sum in money not exceeding 4s. However, I made the best of it, and finding friends in Bohemia, I was baptized, and became one of the glorious brotherhood who live on their wits. In this society I fell in with Perks, and in Perks's society I tumbled across the Colonial Literary Club.

The last-named affair came about one afternoon in this wise. Perks and I were smoking, and Perks, poor fellow, was well — yes a trifle 'on'. Not much, but just enough to set him up on stilts, and to impart to his voice and manner the dignified and distinct characteristics of a patron. 'Smith,' he save gravely, 'I must make you an honorary member of the Golgotha. The fact that you are known to be addicted to scribbling will settle the matter of qualification, and as to the seconder, "I" will see to him. Let us imbibe another beer, and start at once.' My reply to the foregoing was eminently characteristic! That I was a scribbler I was too vain to deny, the invitation to beer I was too modest to refuse; but it must be confessed here there was some uneasiness in my mind with regard to the Golgotha. What Perks meant by the sinister noun I really could not guess, but I had an alarming presentiment that the little fellow was about to force me into a society of ghouls. However, the mystery was soon cleared; and if I did not go to bed the following night exactly bewildered by fireworks of intellect, I certainly retired with an immeasurable sense of relief. 'The Golgotha, my boy,' quoth Perks as we sauntered past the office of the local Daily Thunderer, 'is a den that we fellows have dignified with the name of club. There the geni who presided over the nicotine, strong drink, aesthetics, and the cloacae, respectively, are worshipped by some ten score of enthusiastic disciples. There, in fact,' concluded my friend, dropping from his stilts, 'you will meet with good men, capital talk, fair liquor, and infernally evil smells. But here we are.'

At this point Perks popped into a dingy passage leading towards what appeared to be a bill-sticker's back skillion. About half way up this corridor there loomed through the darkness a narrow, suspicious-looking flight of stairs. At the foot of this my little friend paused, and instructed me to follow him, warning me at the same time to be careful of the steps. Careful I certainly was, but a more villainous ladder I never ascended. However, we scrambled to the top, and lo! the full glories of the Golgotha burst upon me. Facing the landing, an old door opened into an aromatic room, which, I was informed, did duty as 'the reading, talking, and smoking-den'. The most remarkable items of its furniture were the spittoons — useful utensils in their way, no doubt, but distressingly plentiful and palpable at the Golgotha. Passing through a suggestive lavatory, we entered the library, where I found a stock-in-trade, consisting of a couple of desks, four or five chairs, a table, two shelves bristling with ancient magazines and effete blue-books, certain other sundries of a doubtful character, and a melancholy waiter. An apartment, called by courtesy the dining-room, and devoted principally to a brace of dissipated newspaper reporters, was the only other feature that arrested a somewhat disappointed stranger's attention; but from the club rooms I turned with not a little curiosity to survey the club members.

There were about twenty of these gentlemen present, some swallowing, some smoking, some discussing local politics, some doing nothing at all. One elderly member of the company — a biped with a fiery nose and a puffy voice — was holding forth on horseflesh, and I immediately suspected him to be what he was, i.e., a sporting editor. The arrival of Perks with a full-fledged honorary did not attract much attention, but the coat worn by said honorary did. 'D __ d good coat that of yours, Smith,' said one, after the formalities of introduction had been gone through, 'd __ d good coat, whose cut is it, eh?' 'May I inquire as to the figure?' was the modest request of another. 'Looks like one of Milton's make,' observed a third; 'I could almost swear to Milton.' To these criticisms and questions I replied in the best way I could, mentioning amongst other things that my respected and long suffering creditor, Mr Millett, was the tailor, and that the figure amounted to a certain sum which I had no hopes of being able to pay. Mr Millett's whereabouts was then eagerly inquired for, but my answer ruined that gentleman's momentary intercolonial reputation. His name was, figuratively, pitchforked out of doors — Sydney tailors (like all else appertaining to Sydney) being in the eyes of the Melbournites abominations. I may mention that I, even I, accomplished Bohemian as they afterwards admitted me to be, suffered not a little in their estimation through the fact that I hailed from the metropolis of New South Wales. I do not know what saved me, possibly it was the assurance that I had proved myself to be too good for Sleepy Hollow by not paying my way there.

There were some queer fellows at that Golgotha. On the occasion of my first visit, I was presented with a copy of the bylaws and regulations of the club — a document which informed me that all candidates for membership were strictly subjected to its first rule but I was never able to perceive the harmony between this information and surrounding facts. The rule referred to provided for the election of men accredited in literature, science or art, and for their election only; but presuming I understand what is generally meant by literature, science, and art, I am ready to assert that there were not more than twenty accredited professors of these in the club. In fact some of the members had never ventured in composition beyond a letter, in science beyond a stale truism, or in art beyond a schoolboy's attempt on a slate. One leading spirit of the institution was a doctor's son whose qualification was that he knew a gentleman who had a brother, who during the Rev. Charles Kingsley's schooldays had acted as a 'fag' to that genius. Another eminent member had been elected on account of his literary tastes, which latter must have been a source of considerable profit to the local Bell's Life. A third gentleman, who, by-the-way, appeared to be the self-elected champion of the dignity of the institution, maintained his position by the means of his reputation as a fair police-office reporter. This member — little Birch they used to call him — was probably the smallest as well as the most amusing cad in the company. I have no doubt that, according to his creed, the Golgotha was the grandest club in creation, its members the grandest wits alive, and he the noblest Roman of them all. Notwithstanding the accredited literary abilities of Birch, his syntax, or rather the examples of it, which came under my notice from time to time were as wide apart from orthodox notions of English grammar as that of your ordinary Berkshire boar. It is probable, however, that, like Herr Wagner, the composer of 'music for the future', little Birch and his lucubrations were too perfect to be considered by his contemporaries anything but palpable nonsense.

There were other men there of the Birch type, but I prefer to leave them alone for the present, and to glance at a few of those who had a 'strain of the thoroughbred' in them, and first of all — Perks. A casual observer of this young writer would very likely set him down as being merely a brilliant mime with a considerable stock of vanity, and a clever way of persuading everybody that he knew everything. Perks was not a genius, but he was something more than a brilliant mime. There was stuff in the man — good stuff too, only he himself did not appear to value it. Nothing seemed to satisfy him better than the borrowed and theatrical garb under which he contrived, too successfully sometimes, to hide his inherent gifts; in short, to affect the cynicism of a Coldstream, to carry that affectation into ordinary conversation, to make it the staple of his literary work, to look, talk, and write like a 'blase' libertine, constituted the chiefest delight of my juvenile friend — my budding philosopher. Occasionally, however, in rare and happy moments, he would fling his cant aside, and speak or write out his own thought like a man, and it is to those brief spaces of time that we are indebted for all that is worthy of association with his name. Should any of my readers be curious to know more of this gentleman immortalised hereunder the nom-de-plume of Perks, they can hunt up the files of a great Melbourne weekly and glance over its gossip, with a perfect faith that they will find his portrait painted there in glowing colours by himself.

[...]

I approach the next name with a sorrow that many, many years will not subdue, a name that is associated with so much that was loved in the days that were, so much that is missed in the days that are. A noble memory sanctified by the awful baptism of death, hallowed by the tenderests lights of an abiding friendship. Few of those who knew Adam Lindsay Gordon, that royal spirit so gifted, so human, and so unfortunate, will wonder that the head which now lingers by his grave is uncovered. Few who were acquainted with the fine, fearless, kingly nature which was hidden behind an unassuming, even shy exterior, will marvel at the loyalty which proffers this tender blossom of its regard for the dead. Gordon, like many others of the supreme brotherhood, shrank from all conversation on the subject of his own attainments or literary work. His was, in the extreme sense, a self-withdrawn life. Nobody, looking at him for the first time, without previous knowledge of his gifts, would dream that the man was a genius; while few, if any, after a successful penetration of his reserve, would dare to deny his title to that august name. Cut off as he was in the zenith of his splendid powers, snatched away on the threshold of fame, fortune, and happiness, destroyed by the same hand that gave us the too insufficient evidences left of his superb faculties, how mournfully pertinent are these lines, the last from his pen:

Child! Can I tell where the garlands go?
Can I say where the lost leaves veer,
On the brown burnt banks where the wild winds blow
When they drift thro into the dead wood drear?
Girl! when the garlands of next year glow,
You may gather again my dear
But! go where the last year's lost leaves go
At the falling of the year.

At the 'falling of the year' he went, and we who admired and loved him so much can only come with poor white flowers like this, and strew them with faltering hands upon his grave.

1871

'THE VAGABOND'

A Brutal Football Match

In Victoria like every athletic sport, football is followed by all — larrikins, mechanics, clerks, and (self-esteemed) young aristocrats. It seems, amongst a certain class, to be even more popular than cricket. The favourite amusements of a people are signs of the times well worth studying. When I go to a new country, I make it a rule to read the newspapers (if I am master of the language), and to attend the churches and places of public amusement. I have learnt much from the press here; the churches have told me no new thing; and the amusements have principally bored me. But football, as it is carried out here, is a new study, and it has given me some curious ideas as to the civilization and humanity of the coming Victorian race.

I am not going to indulge in a tirade against athletic sports, although I have a suspicion that the tendency of the age here, as in England, is to the excessive cultivation of the bodily powers to the neglect of the mental. It is, no doubt, a good thing to be able to jump a five-barred gate, to run a mile in five minutes, and throw fifty-sixes over your head until further notice. But all virtue does not consist in training, and the country will not be saved by such gifts. *Mens sana in corpore sano* I believe to be generally true, but the principle may be carried to excess, and a healthy mind certainly does not exist where cruel and brutal sports are indulged in. Football, as now carried on here, is not only often rough and brutal between the combatants, but seems to me to have a decided moral lowering and brutalizing effect upon the spectators. The records of the past season show that several promising young men have been crippled for life in this 'manly sport'; others have received serious temporary injuries, and laid the foundations of future ill-health, the luckiest getting off with scars which they will bear with them to their graves. Now, is the general good derived from the encouragement of physical endurance in the players, and the amusement given to the spectators, worth all this? I think not, and hold that the evil does not stop here, but that society is demoralized by such public exhibitions as the 'last match of the season' between the Melbourne and Carlton Football Clubs, which I witnessed. I arrived early at the spacious piece of ground which has been given to our Catholic friends for religious purposes, and has been let by them for the highly religious performances of Blondin, football matches, &c. [...]

The six or seven thousand spectators comprised representatives of nearly all classes. It was a truly democratic crowd. Ex-Cabinet Ministers and their families, members of Parliament, professional and tradesmen, free selectors and squatters, clerks, shopmen, bagmen, mechanics, larrikins, betting men, publicans, barmaids (very strongly represented), working-girls, and the half world, all were there. From the want of reserved seats, or any special accommodation for ladies, the mixture all round the ground was as heterogeneous as well might be. I mingled with the throng everywhere, and had a good chance of arriving at the popular verdict respecting football, as at present played. The Carlton Club were playing on their own ground, and the feeling of the majority was in their favour, and from the commencement was so expressed rather offensively towards the Melbourne Club, which is considered, I believe, to be a little more high-toned, and consequently antagonistic to democratic Carlton. At the commencement I got a position at the rails between a seedy but highly respectable-looking old gentleman, a commercial traveller, and several hardy sons of toil [. . .]

If an intelligent foreigner had been present, watching these young men clad in parti-coloured garments, running after an inflated piece of leather, kicking it and wrestling for it, receiving and giving hard blows and falls, he must have thought it the amusement of madmen. The spectators, who howled, and shrieked, and applauded, he would have thought equally mad. It is true that, as a spectacle of bodily activity and endurance, the show was a fine one, but the cruelty and brutality intermixed with it, and which the crowd loudly applauded, and appeared to consider the principal attraction, was anything but a promising evidence of a high civilization. I was told by several that it would be a pretty rough game, and they gloated in the fact. As the play went on, and men got heavy falls, and rose limping or bleeding, the applause was immense. 'Well played, sir,' always greeted a successful throw. 'That's the way to smash 'em,' said one of my neighbours. 'Pitch him over!' and such cries were frequent, and the whole interest and applause seem centred in such work. It was no fair conflict either; a man running after another who has the ball, seizing him by the neck, and throwing him down, does not, to my mind, do a particularly manly thing. It inculcates bad blood, as the victim is sure to spot his oppressor, and be down on him when occasion offers. Early in the game it was apparent that a bad feeling existed between the players. There was a dispute as to the first goal kicked by the Melbourne club: Was it a 'free kick' or not? The umpire's decision was loudly canvassed, and angry players congregated in the middle of the ground. 'There's going to be a scrap,' said a Carltonite, delightedly, and called out to one of the players, 'Go into the __, Jim.' Indeed, it seemed to me as if hostilities had already commenced. There was a squaring of shoulders, and the central mass heaved and surged for a minute, and then the would-be combatants were separated. Shortly after this, the umpire took up his stick, and walked off the ground, and the game was suddenly stopped. I asked this gentleman what was the matter, and he said the Carlton players used such blackguard language to him that he would not stand it; and in this, I think, he was right. One friend said, however, that he was wrong. 'The umpire always has a hard time of it,' said he; 'the only thing he can do is to wear several brass rings, if he hasn't got gold ones, and let the first man who disputes his decision have it straight.' This idea was received with great favour by the crowd, and is an instance of the good feeling generally engendered by this 'manly sport'.

After a fresh umpire was procured, the game became as rough as it well could be, without absolute fighting. Luckily the Rugby game, in which a man who holds the ball can be kicked until he releases it, is not played here. Still 'hacking' was sometimes indulged in under cover of play, and I was not at all surprised to hear that a man had his eye kicked out at this very ground a short time back. The 'scrimmages' were frequent, and altogether the violence used was often totally unnecessary and gratuitous. I watched several individual players. One man would throw or push another down after he had kicked the ball, and without, as far as the play was concerned, any excuse or provocation. The aggrieved one would 'spot' his antagonist and repay in like manner. This system of aggression was altogether, to my mind, cowardly and uncalled for, and yet was loudly applauded by the spectators. Towards the end of the game one man fainted; several must be lame for weeks, and every man must have been bleeding or scarred. The gentleman who played in spectacles was plucky, but I would advise him to relinquish the game before he receives further injuries. The victory of the Melbourne Club proved unpopular with the larrikins, who commenced stoning the players outside the gates. One offender, however, received a good thrashing for his pains. I consider that football, as played at this match, is a disgrace to our civilization.

1876

MARCUS CLARKE

Adam Lindsay Gordon

The poems of Gordon have an interest beyond the mere personal one which his friends attach to his name. Written, as they were, at odd times and leisure moments of a stirring and adventurous life, it is not to be wondered at if they are unequal or unfinished. The astonishment of those who knew the man, and can gauge the capacity of this city to foster poetic instinct, is, that such work was ever produced here at all. Intensely nervous, and feeling much of that shame at the exercise of the higher intelligence which besets those who are known to be renowned in field sports, Gordon produced his poems shyly, scribbled them on scraps of paper, and sent them anonymously to magazines. It was not until he discovered one morning that everybody knew a couplet or two of 'How we Beat the Favourite' that he consented to forego his anonymity and appear in the unsuspected character of a versemaker. The success of his republished 'collected' poems gave him courage, and the unreserved praise which greeted 'Bush Ballads' should have urged him to forget or to conquer those evil promptings which, unhappily, brought about his untimely death.

Adam Lindsay Gordon was the son of an officer in the English army, and was educated at Woolwich, in order that he might follow the profession of his family. At the time when he was a cadet there was no sign of either of the two great wars which were about to call forth the strength of English arms, and, like many other men of his day, he quitted his prospects of service and emigrated. He went to South Australia and started as a sheep farmer. His efforts were attended with failure. He lost his capital, and owning nothing but a love for horsemanship and a head full of Browning and Shelley, plunged into the varied life which gold-mining, 'overlanding', and cattle-driving affords. From this experience he emerged to light in Melbourne as the best amateur steeplechase rider in the colonies. The victory he won for Major Baker in 1868, when he rode Babbler for the Cup Steeplechase, made him popular, and the almost simultaneous publication of his last volume of poems gave him welcome entrance to the houses of all who had pretensions to literary taste. The reputation of the book spread to England, and Major Whyte Melville did not disdain to place the lines of the dashing Australian author at the head of his own dashing descriptions of sporting scenery. Unhappily, the melancholy which Gordon's friends had with pain observed increased daily, and in the full flood of his success, with congratulations pouring upon him from every side, he was found dead in the heather near his home with a bullet from his own rifle in his brain.

I do not purpose to criticize the volumes which these few lines of preface introduce to the reader. The influence of Browning and of Swinburne upon the writer's taste is plain. There is plainly visible also, however, a keen sense for natural beauty and a manly admiration for healthy living. If in 'Ashtaroth' and 'Bellona' we recognize the swing of a familiar metre, in such poems as the 'Sick Stockrider' we perceive the genuine poetic instinct united to a very clear perception of the loveliness of duty and of labour.

'Twas merry in the glowing morn, among the gleaming grass,
To wander as we've wander'd many a mile,
And blow the cool tobacco cloud, and watch the white wreaths pass,
Sitting loosely in the saddle all the while;
'Twas merry 'mid the blackwoods when we spied the station roofs,
To wheel the wild scrub cattle at the yard,
With a running fire of stockwhips and a fiery run of hoofs,
Oh! the hardest day was never then too hard!

Aye! we had a glorious gallop after 'Starlight' and his gang,
When they bolted from Sylvester's on the flat;
How the sun-dried reed-beds crackled, how the flint-strewn ranges rang
To the strokes of 'Mountaineer' and 'Acrobat;'
Hard behind them in the timber, harder still across the heath,
Close behind them through the tea-tree scrub we dash'd;
And the golden-tinted fern leaves, how they rustled underneath!
And the honeysuckle osiers, how they crash'd!

This is genuine. There is no 'poetic evolution from the depths of internal consciousness' here. The writer has ridden his ride as well as written it.

The student of these unpretending volumes will be repaid for his labour. He will find in them something very like the beginnings of a national school of Australian poetry. In historic Europe, where every rood of ground is hallowed in legend and in song, the least imaginative can find food for sad and sweet reflection. When strolling at noon down an English country lane, lounging at sunset by some ruined chapel on the margin of an Irish lake, or watching the mists of morning unveil Ben Lomond, we feel all the charm which springs from association with the past. Soothed, saddened, and cheered by turns, we partake of the varied moods which belong not so much to ourselves as to the dead men who, in old days, sung, suffered, or conquered in the scenes which we survey. But this our native or adopted land has no past, no story. No poet speaks to us. Do we need a poet to interpret Nature's teachings, we must look into our own hearts, if perchance we may find a poet there.

What is the dominant note of Australian scenery? That which is the dominant note of Edgar Allan Poe's poetry — Weird Melancholy. A poem like 'L'Allegro' could never be written by an Australian. It is too airy, too sweet, too freshly happy. The Australian mountain forests are funereal, secret, stern. Their solitude is desolation. They seem to stifle, in their black gorges, a story of sullen despair. No tender sentiment is nourished in their shade. In other lands the dying year is mourned, the falling leaves drop lightly on his bier. In the Australian forests no leaves fall. The savage winds shout among the rock clefts. From the melancholy gums strips of white bark hang and rustle. The very animal life of these frowning hills is either grotesque or ghostly. Great grey kangaroos hop noiselessly over the coarse grass. Flights of white cockatoos stream out, shrieking like evil souls. The sun suddenly sinks, and the mopokes burst out into horrible peals of semi-human laughter. The natives aver that, when night comes, from out the bottomless depth of some lagoon the Bunyip rises, and, in form like monstrous sea-calf, drags his loathsome length from out the ooze. From a corner of the silent forest rises a dismal chant, and around a fire dance natives painted like skeletons. All is fear-inspiring and gloomy. No bright fancies are linked with the memories of the mountains. Hopeless explorers have named them out of their sufferings — Mount Misery, Mount Dreadful, Mount Despair. As when among sylvan scenes in places

Made green with the running of rivers,
And gracious with temperate air,

the soul is soothed and satisfied, so, placed before the frightful grandeur of these barren hills, it drinks in their sentiment of defiant ferocity, and is steeped in bitterness.

Australia has rightly been named the Land of the Dawning. Wrapped in the mist of early morning, her history looms vague and gigantic. The lonely horseman riding between the moonlight and the day sees vast shadows creeping across the shelterless and silent plains, hears strange noises in the primeval forest where flourishes a vegetation long dead in other lands, and feels, despite his fortune, that the trim utilitarian civilisation which bred him shrinks into insignificance beside the contemptuous grandeur of forest and ranges coeval with an age in which European scientists have cradled his own race.

There is a poem in every form of tree or flower, but the poetry which lives in the trees and flowers of Australia differs from those of other countries. Europe is the home of knightly song, of bright deeds and clear morning thought. Asia sinks beneath the weighty recollections of her past magnificence, as the Suttee sinks, jewel-burdened, upon the corpse of dread grandeur, destructive even in its death. America swiftly hurries on her way, rapid, glittering, insatiable even as one of her own giant waterfalls. From the jungles of Africa, and the creeper-tangle groves of the Islands of the South, arise, from the glowing hearts of a thousand flowers, heavy and intoxicating odours — the Upas-poison which dwells in barbaric sensuality. In Australia alone is to be found the Grotesque, the Weird, the strange scribblings of Nature learning how to write. Some see no beauty in our trees without shade, our flowers without perfume, our birds who cannot fly, and our beasts who have not yet learned to walk on all fours. But the dweller in the wilderness acknowledges the subtle charm of his fantastic land of monstrosities. He becomes familiar with the beauty of loneliness. Whispered to by the myriad tongues of the wilderness, he learns the language of the barren and the uncouth, and can read the hieroglyphs of haggard gum-trees, blown into odd shapes, distorted with fierce hot winds, or cramped with cold nights, when the Southern Cross freezes in a cloudless sky of icy blue. The phantasmagoria of that wild dream-land termed the Bush interprets itself, and the Poet of our desolation begins to comprehend why free Esau loved his heritage of desert sand better than all the bountiful richness of Egypt.

1876

LOUISA LAWSON

The Australian Bush-Woman

The Government statistician estimated that at the end of 1887 there were in the colony of New South Wales about 471,000 women and girls, so that I suppose there were at that time, in various stages of growth, about 471,000 different kinds of woman. This is rather too large an assortment to be separately described in the *Woman's Journal*, unless you will place me on the staff as a life contributor. This suggestion can be considered at leisure. Meanwhile, for hasty purposes, my colonial sisters may be roughly sorted into three heaps — city women, country women, and bush-women, and it is of the last I will write, for it is of their grim, lonely, patient lives I know, their honest, hard-worked, silent, almost masculine lives. My experience lies chiefly among the women of New South Wales, but I think in the main, and as far as generalizations can describe a large number of units, my description will apply to the bush-women of all Australia.

The city women in Australia are for the most part like all other English-speaking women. Their civilization is pretty nearly up to date, and the tragi-comedy of their lives is of a type common to all the cities of the world. The country women have also no features which are unique. As everywhere, they drag behind the town in fashions, they imitate the town in a leisurely, bucolic way; they are a little healthier, a little less clever, and a little less artificial. But the bush-women are a race apart. No 'foreigner' can seem so strange to them as a city woman does. A bush-woman in town is as lonely, as helpless, as homesick, as an Esquimaux landed at Honolulu. What does she know of domestic comforts? She desires none. There is nothing for her to do. She cannot keep house: she who comes perhaps from rounding up lost cattle or ring-barking trees. She is independent, taciturn, and the regularities and measured methods of town life appal her. If the cattle were lost, she would be all day long in the saddle, working as well as any of the men, and she would do what little had to be done in the house on her return — whenever that might chance to be. It would not anyhow be much more than the making of a 'damper' in a tin dish and putting it in the ashes. She is not one to be easily moulded to the hours and times of city customs. For by bush-women I mean not the wives of settlers in accessible country, near a railroad or town, but the wives of boundary-riders, shepherds, 'cockatoo' settlers in the far 'back country;' women who share almost on equal terms with men the rough life and the isolation which belong to civilization's utmost fringe.

Progress begins at the seaports, and it [is] a long while before the ripples reach the bush-woman. It is less than five years since I saw one start out to tend sheep, taking among her few necessaries a flint and steel. Half a century of advance lies between her and her daughters, educated at the public schools; but the bush-woman herself, Australian-born, and the daughter or granddaughter of a pioneer, retains her characteristics in spite of the march of the times.

The bush-woman is thin, wiry, flat-chested and sunburned. She could be nothing else, living as she does. She lives on meat; sometimes she does not even eat bread with it. She rarely sees vegetables, and no costly bouquet of orchids could so surprise and delight a city dame as a cabbage would gratify and amaze a bush-woman. She is healthy and full of vigour, but it is a leathery, withered, sun-dried health. You would call her a poor starveling in appearance, if you contrasted her with one of the fair, fresh-looking, plump city women whom two miles' walking would utterly exhaust. If the energy of the bush-women could only be put to some profitable use, they might be millionaires; but they live in perpetual feud with the sun. They try to keep bees, but the heat starves them out. If they have cattle, the drought or the pleuro kills them. When they do get a wet season, the flood rots all they have in the ground. Two-thirds of their labour is wasted. They are lank, yet wiry, sun-cured while alive, but able to do, and almost always doing, the work of a strong man. In the city, a wet day is accursed; it makes people melancholy; every one abhors dulness and damp; but the bush-woman's ideal home is a place where it *is* dark and wet, some damp, lush, grassy hollow. Let her be ever so miserable, ever so ill-fed and hard-worked, her life becomes full of bliss when she hears the rain pattering on the roof. There is no sorrow that a good shower will not wash away.

Though she is not egotistical, she has no patience with the ways of city folk. She is disgusted at their fastidiousness. They want soft, comfortable beds; but she can sleep anyhow. Often, in the self-abnegation which is natural to her, the supreme recognition of the claims of hospitality, which is only with her a habit and ingrained custom, she relinquishes her bed to a stranger and sleeps on the floor. As to food, the heel of a 'damper' and the fag-end of a piece of beef will do for her. She is utterly self-neglectful. The white plump women of the city seem soft to her. They cannot walk a mile without fatigue, while she will tramp five miles with a heavy child on her hip, do a day's washing, and tramp back again at night. She works harder than a man. You may see her with her sons putting up a fence, or with the shearers, whistling and working as well as any. She has a fine, hard patient character; she is not emotional, nor very susceptive, but she has no conception of the little jealousies, the spite and petty meanness of city women. Her generosity to any sort of stranger is natural, for society of any kind is at a premium. The monotony of the ever-green (or rather ever-brown) Australian bush, and its years of unbroken drought, tend to make time seem as if it had no changes and no periods. To hear of a life she does not know, to get news and speech of outside things from even the most worthless stranger, is payment enough for all the shelter, food, and assistance that she offers. It is such an incursion of novelty into her dreary domain of changeless months, that it is a pleasure and a relief no town-bred woman can understand.

Of her own life she never speaks. To her oldest friends she does not talk of her hardships, though her life may be nothing but a record of ill-usage. She may be an isolated woman prey, alone in the wilds with a brutal husband, yet she does not complain; she suffers silently. She thinks her lot peculiar to herself. Resource she has none, nor escape, nor redress. She is tough and patient, and works till she dies without murmuring. Reform can never come through her, for should one speak to her of anything touching her own life or fate nearly, she would look at her askance, and shrink from her. People who think must be 'cranks,' for he who lives in the bush and thinks, goes mad. She may have ideas, but she never exchanges them. She is a slave, bound hand and foot to her daily life. If an educated man — and there are such, with strange histories behind them — goes into the bush and becomes shepherd, hut-keeper, or the like solitary exile, his mind recoils on him. In the solitude he becomes at the least a 'crank,' and there is no more respect for him. So with a bush-woman; she does not speak of what she has discovered or thought out, she does not go beyond her daily life, because they would say 'She hasn't got all her buttons,' she is a 'crank'. Nevertheless she is not mindless; she loves poetry and pictures, and what newspapers come in her way she reads carefully. She often knows more of letters than her sisters of the city, for what she reads she reads earnestly and remembers. She cuts out the articles which she values and preserves them. You would not suspect they lay among her treasures, for she says nothing. Her thoughts and actions are all alike uncommunicated and self-contained.

She has no pleasure nor comforts. When she is sick, she leaves it to nature, or treats it with one of the three remedies she recognizes as a complete and sufficient pharmacopoeia — salts and senna, castor oil and Holloway's pills. She would laugh at a medicine-chest; she could not be bothered with it. Many of these women even endure a confinement almost without aid. Some will mount a horse and ride for the nurse themselves. In one case the husband, with the customary indifferent, indolent, non-interfering habit, left his wife to ride alone to the midwife. She became ill on the way, and was never seen alive again. The native dogs watched her agonies and ended them.

There is one thing the bush-woman hates — it is discipline. The word sounds to her like 'jail.' System, regularity, method, her life has nothing to do with. The domestic affairs of town women, which are ordered with the precision of an almanac, are an abhorred mystery to her. You could not put her to worse torture than by setting her to dust the drawing-room every morning at a fixed hour. Her home among the eucalyptus bush or on the 'ironbark' ridge is guiltless of drapes and mantel boards and ornaments; her domestic duties are merely the simplest of cooking; her life is out-of-doors in the broiling sun and the dry wind. She can handle a stock-whip better than a duster, she can swear mildly when the cattle are very refractory and the dogs utterly unmanageable, and she would far rather break in a horse than flutter around pictures with a feather broom.

There is also one thing in which she becomes particularly expert, the weather signs. The one hope of her life is for rain. She is always on the watch to wrest from nature the earliest news, and she can tell you whether the showers will come or the drought continue. She hates the cry of the 'hard times bird' who shrieks in the dry, dewless nights and parching days of drought seasons; she watches the colour of the sky, the clouds, the sun as he rises and sets; she hearkens to the frogs, and can tell them from the colour which the atmosphere gives to distant objects whether the drought will break and the cattle live.

The bush-woman's husband, if he be also Australian born, is like herself, spare and wiry. He is inured to wind and weather, cold and heat, and what is better, he can *fast* well. He is not, as a rule, dissipated, nor is he brutal to her. He has a tendency to leave her to manage the business, and he is rather indolent and neglectful. He will sit with others talking, while she, a thin rag of a woman, drags two big buckets of water from the creek, for instance, and if he stands by while she chops the wood, he sees no unfitness in the arrangement. They are a comparatively cold and impassive pair, inured to weather and hardships and rough living. They are never jealous of one another, and rarely unfaithful, so that the bush-woman, if married to an Australian, has generally a smooth life enough. She is fortunate in such a marriage, for the native is innately mild and not ill-natured, even in a life which seems to intensify in other men all the brutality they possess. To generalize roughly, one must say that the bush-woman's life is, however, on the average, a sad one. The Englishmen, Germans, Scandinavians, and, indeed, all the men of whatever nationality who took to bush life, were generally of rough, coarse character, or, if they were not of such nature originally, the solitude and the strange, primitive life must have made them so. In those remote and isolated spots, man is king and force is ruler. There is no law, no public opinion to interfere. The wife is at the man's mercy. She must bear what ills he chooses to put upon her, and her helplessness in his hands only seems to educe the beast in him. There is a vast deal of the vilest treatment. Some are worked to death and some are bullied to death; but the women are so scattered and so reticent that the world hears nothing of it all. In town, the fear of the law operates insensibly; we know that a woman can, if she needs, reach a police-station in five minutes, and charge her husband with an assault; but out in that loneliness of mountain and plain, where is the redress, where the protection? She cannot ride a hundred miles in search of a magistrate; she cannot leave the hut and the sheep and the cattle to look after themselves in her absence; the law is not accessible, even if she would use it; if she writes a letter, it may lie a fortnight before the chance comes of sending it on. Besides, she is not the kind of woman to run to the law. She keeps her sorrows to herself, and endures everything. I have known a woman to be up in a tree for three days, while her husband was hunting for her to 'hammer' her. It is horrible to think such things are possible, yet worse things happen daily. Time and our efforts may help to mend the world.

A bright and promising story follows the saddest part of this narrative of the bush-woman's life. The best qualities of her live in her girls, and they will make their mark on a fairer page of Australian history. I have heard it urged against them that they are very shy. It is a true bill. They are as shy as the kangaroos and emus, their wild fellow-lodgers in the bush. You may catch sight of two girls astride a horse. They see you and are gone in a flash. They have no curiosity about strangers. I remember a man telling me that he had often caught a brief glimpse of a girl about a certain district, and that some day he meant to get a horse and run her down. In the old days the children used to get a little schooling in the evenings from some shepherd who could boast of education; but now wherever a dozen children can be got together, there is a school. Many of them walk or ride very long distances, but they get there; for the bush-woman is anxious for her children to get on, and is proud of their successes. Anything is good enough for her, she thinks, and if any comfort or advantage comes with growing civilization, it falls to the children's share. The girls are of very quick intelligence; they learn everything rapidly, and surpass the boys. Where they have a chance they make clever women, and a great number become schoolteachers, but in those who get no schooling this astuteness turns to slyness and cunning. Take them all round, they are fine girls, always ready in an emergency, and capable of anything. Tough, healthy, and alert, they can cook or sew, do fancy-work or farm-work, dance, ride, tend cattle, keep a garden, break in a colt. They are the stuff that a fine race is made of — these daughters of bush-women. The men are more idle, and besides they have always the drink washing away their prospects; therefore we look to the girls for the future.

So as the bush-women, one by one, end their sad, lonely, hard-worked lives, these girls, quick, capable and active, will be ready to step into their places, and the iron strength of character, the patience, endurance and self-repression which the bush-women practised and developed, passing to a generation more enlightened and progressive, will give us a race of splendid women, fit to obtain what their mothers never dreamed of — women's rights.

1889

PHILIP MENNELL

New Chums

The term 'new chum' is one of so wide and indefinite an application that, were I not to narrow its significance after a somewhat arbitrary fashion, I should find myself, in endeavouring to portray a few of the chief characteristics of the species, inditing a book instead of a sketch. How long the poor immigrant caterpillar must remain in the dark chrysalis of new chumship before he can be supposed to have expanded into the full-blown Colonial butterfly is a question upon which a great variety of opinions prevails, even amongst 'old hands' (I use the term, not opprobriously, but in a perfectly parliamentary and Pickwickian sense, to denote old Colonial residents). Some limit the period to five years, the duration of an ordinary trade apprenticeship; some think seven years 'the cheese'; whilst others, again, whom we charitably credit with an awful experience of new chum ignorance and stupidity, would, like Laban, of Biblical celebrity, protract the date of emancipation 'yet other seven'. Leaving these highly respectable parties to their opinions, I will briefly explain what, for the purposes of the present sketch, I mean by the term. In the first place, I restrict its application to the new arrival, who, having landed with no capital beyond a few pounds, has hitherto failed in obtaining remunerative employment. I do not intend to refer to the new chum of the labouring class, who, if he be energetic and pushing, will very soon find himself outside the category of the unemployed. In short, I confine myself to such new chums as have not been inured to manual toil — members of the middle and upper middle-class at home, bred up to professions, mercantile clerkships, or — more commonly still — to nothing at all. In a word, I treat of the newly-arrived unattached gentleman-immigrant, who, notwithstanding all the warnings of prudence and experience, is constantly being landed — and, I am sorry to say, stranded — upon Australian shores. It is his joys and sorrows, shifts and troubles, economies and imprudences that I sing. He is a much-tried individual, and his circumstances make him a meek and unobtrusive one. I therefore owe him an apology for dragging him out of his obscurity into the dazzling light of garish day. Let him rest assured that I should not have done so had I not hoped to point a moral as well as to adorn a tale. After the confinement, the constraint, and the dreary monotony of a long sea voyage, a reaction in this direction of indulgence — not to say over-indulgence — is very apt to set in on the part of immigrants on landing. This is generally so powerful in the case of the class of new chums to which I am referring as to overcome in a moment all those righteous and sober resolutions in which none are more prone to indulge, whilst under the influence of those remorseful self-introspections which are sure to obtrude upon the mental listlessness and inaction of a prolonged passage. The new chum of the fast order settles himself down at an expensive hotel, devotes his day to the billiard table, his nights to the *demi monde.* The crisis of his affairs is soon reached. Rung by rung he descends the ladder. His funds and his borrowing powers, if any, are soon alike exhausted. He 'pops' or sells his watch and chain; the same with the rest of his available jewellery. Article by article, his clothes follow till mine host, seeing how matters stand with him, and distrusting the security of his attenuated wardrobe, gives him a broad hint to quit. This hint, however, loath, he is compelled to take, and packs accordingly — not his luggage (that is *non est*) — but himself. Thrown penniless upon the world, he drops at once to a level with the ordinary pauper loafer, who, however, has this great advantage over him, that he thoroughly knows his ground, has had a large experience in the cadging art, and though, like our new chum, he cannot, or will not, dig, unlike the former, to beg is *not* ashamed.

The early colonial career of the new chum of the steady-going type, unless he be gifted with the rare prudence of accommodating himself to his new position, and settling down without delay to cheap quarters and strict economies, though less blameable, is scarcely less felicitous in its practical results than that of his faster *confrére.* He, too, though far too proper to go 'upon the burst', must have a few little indulgences after his long abstinence, must take up his quarters at a comfortable hotel, and enjoy a short spell before, as he elegantly and expressively phrases it, 'buckling to'. That word 'spell' is a very short word, a very easy word, a very innocent-sounding word, but, as used in Mr Steady-going's vocabulary, it is also a very comprehensive word, and, *par conséquence,* a very expensive word. It includes all manner of good living, good liquor — without excess, you understand — theatre-going, sight-seeing, *ad libitum,* hansoms unlimited, luncheons 'quite regardless', drives into the country, rides into the bush, a run over to Ballarat, visits to the ship, nobblers round, and a host of other things too numerous to mention. The result is that Mr Steady-going is almost as soon upon his beam-ends (that last remnant of my new chumship, the affectation of nautical phraseology, still clings to me, I see) as his more frolicsome brother, Mr Fast. He is, however, somewhat wiser in his generation. He clings to his watch, his etceteras, his portmanteau, his boxes, especially that big one which contains his dress suit, his white ties, his white kids, his patent pumps, his silk waistcoats, his shiny blue surtout, his twenty-five white linen shirts — all marked — to the last. As soon as he considers that the amount of his account is about coincident with the amount of his resources, he calls for his bill, peruses it, pays it, though it exhausts his finances to the last pound, with the *nonchalant* air of a traveller who is passing on to an adjacent and equally luxurious stage, looks out a cheap but respectable lodging, to which he transfers his goods by car, as per special bargain. His landlady, to whose inquiring eyes he presents a dazzling vista of well-cut clothes, white shirt front, gold watch chain, studs, sleeve-links, well brushed bell-topper, speckless boots, irreproachable 'Gamp', and, above all, substantial luggage, thinks, poor, silly woman, she has landed a prize, and does not dream of insulting him by presenting her account for a matter of some weeks. This gives him time, as he classically expresses it, to turn round. He presents his business introductions, if he has any; looks up every unfortunate individual upon whom he has, or imagines he has, any claim; puts the screw on Mr This, gives the tip to Mr That — all with a view to obtaining that employment which has now become a matter of absolute and immediate necessity to him. This sort of work employs his mornings. At one he dines — or, as, with a view to some distant suggestion of a late dinner, he will persist in calling it, lunches — at a sixpenny restaurant. Furtively he glides in, and cautiously; with many glances to right and left, he slips out. This satisfactorily accomplished, he repairs to his lodgings, has a rest, a wash, and a brush up, and turns out just in time to take his part in doing the Block* — a duty which he religiously discharges every afternoon. He feels, to be sure, that he is a sort of ghost at the feast, a kind of one too many, an interloper, almost an impostor; for are not his fine feathers tantamount to a false advertisement of a full exchequer? Still, he thinks it best 'on principle', and as a matter of business, 'to do the respectable', and very efficiently he does it. Mark his brisk air, his well-assumed expression of easy satisfaction, his light, jaunty step. See how naturally he 'coins his cheeks to smiles', which are simply the products of will, and have no origin in a heart which could find its only adequate expression in a language of sighs, and you will cease to wonder at that hackneyed Spartan boy who smiled whilst the fox beneath his cloak gnawed his vitals. By six the farce is over, and our friend retires to his threepenny coffee, with bread and butter *ad lib*, which in his case indicates at least sixpennyworth of butter, almost a whole loaf of bread, an hour and a-half's free sitting room, and the monopoly for that period of half-a-dozen newspapers. It is now time for him to be again upon the streets, or, perhaps, he turns into the library for a change. His stay there will, however, not be as long, as, with a mind ill at ease, he will in all probability find it impossible to settle down to steady reading, and to sit and think would be still more intolerable. He will therefore soon return to his old task of pacing Bourke and Collins Streets, varying the dull round with an occasional trip to the arcades, or the Hobson's Bay Railway Station. Not until his walk has degenerated, through sheer fatigue, into a toddle will he turn his steps homeward, and find repose — and he will be lucky if he always find it — in slumber. Such is a sample of his day. If he be thoroughly determined, and, putting aside false delicacy, press his claims, in season and out of season, he will in all probability gain a footing of some sort of another. If he fail, nothing can very long avert the catastrophe of his respectability, or prevent his sinking to the level of the more reckless gentleman whose descent to pauperism I have already depicted. 'Fallen,

fallen from his high estate.' Little by little his paraphernalia drops away. He is to be seen nightly hovering round the pawnshop, which it costs him I know not what pangs of agonising pride to enter. First go the small things, then he begins to deal in huge newspaper bundles, and you may know the end is near. His embarrassed air in demanding 'an advance', and the expression of mute misery with which he awaits the shopman's decision, are all against him. They tell of the rude presence of absolute necessity, and encourage that experienced functionary to drive a doubly-hard bargain with him. His clothes, he is told, are not of the 'colonial cut', and will be 'moth-eaten to pieces' before they are got rid of. Then, after a feint of not taking in his property upon any terms, the poor new chum is offered about a tithe of what he has asked on them. This he is fain to accept, but saves his pride by muttering something about 'not caring to carry them back home with him that night', and 'coming to-morrow and taking them out again, as he cannot afford to let them go at that price'. But, as he himself knows, and as the wily broker easily divines, there is very little likelihood that to-morrow — that 'rare and luxurious' to-morrow — will ever come. But the poor lie preserves his self-respect, or he thinks it does, which is about the same thing.

Driven from the haunts of respectability by the growing seediness of his attire, the new chum, such as I have described, in not a few instances makes a final rise of a few shillings, and starts on the tramp up-country. Here a proportion turn tutors or book-keepers (these are lucky), obtain work on stations, get into stores, or are otherwise absorbed into the ordinary life of the country. The remainder either have the fatted calf killed for them at home, blossom into 'sundowners', or worse still, degenerate into confirmed criminals. Of those who remain in town a small modicum obtain employment as waiters, grooms, boots, or even 'to be generally useful' about hotels, but they do not, as a rule, settle very well to their unaccustomed billets, and are, most of them, in communication with 'home', with a view to a speedy return to their old haunts. Their life may be described as a perpetual 'waiting for the mail'. Lucky will they be if their friends prove lenient and their expectations of a goodly remittance are realised. More often they get a stone instead of bread, a letter of recrimination and good advice instead of the letter of credit for which they so urgently plead. Nothing is more striking than the invincible repugnance manifested by the new chum, even when in direst need, to the receipt of public charity. He will do anything, dare anything, rather than accept it — go through any amount of private cadging, lie down in the cricket reserve, or pace the streets all night, as he is forced to do all day, rather than accept the 'hospitality' of the Immigrants' Home or Benevolent Asylum. Once he has been humiliated by the taint of public charity, his self-respect is destroyed, and there remains very little hope of his ever emerging from the slough of despond into which he has fallen. What becomes of him is best known to the criminal statistician and the philanthropist. I draw a veil over his latter end.

The new chum, whilst doing Melbourne, is, like the country cousin in London, an easily recognisable individual. The very cut of his coat collar betrays him. When his fortunes are on the decline his air of wild misery and undemonstrative desolation are truly pitiable. The one trust of his dreary life is when — it generally happens in the evening — he falls in with some of his old shipmates similarly situated to himself. Nearly every evening you see a knot of these unfortunates collected in front of the theatre or opera-house door, like a group of Peris gathered round the gate of a paradise which they cannot enter. It is the one glimpse of sociability which they get throughout the day, and they make the most of it. Very merry they grow over the burlesque delineation of their mutual miseries, of which, when together, they can only see the comic side. Then, if one of the number have had the luck to make 'a rise' during the day, he 'shouts' tobacco for the lot, or sometimes — *mirabile dictu* — 'nobblers round'. It is the old story of Nero and his fiddle over again. But if the whimsicalities which distinguish these chance-meetings prove even a temporary medicine for sick hearts, dashed hopes, tired limbs, and weary feet, who will cavil at this light-headed thoughtlessness? Sunday, from the absence of life and movement in the streets, is a dreary day for the new chum, if he keep to his Melbourne beat. If the day be fine, however, he will probably extend his walks to Sandridge or Williamstown, where he will find plenty of variety in inspecting the shipping. The sea air, is, however, too hunger-inspiring to be economical, and if his exchequer be too low to stand the drains of an increased appetite, he must be content to be unfashionable, and remain in town. Under these circumstances, or if the day be wet, he will, in all probability, if his clothes be sufficiently decent, sit under Canon Handfield, or the Rev. Charles Strong, always remembering to 'clear out' before the collection, that scourge of the penniless church-goer. I take it for granted that he is a Protestant, as I cannot see how, on a Sunday, the impecunious new chum can be anything else. Should he, however, be rash enough to think of attending High Mass or Vespers at a Roman Catholic Church, he will find himself confronted at the entrance by a couple of lynx-eyed money-takers, and the chink of the coin as the worshippers drop in will tell him only too plainly that in these boasted churches of the poor there is no place for him. If, therefore, he hanker after the 'sensuous worship' of Catholicism, he will have to be content with such harmonies as he can gather from the outside. On a week-day the penniless new chum would be ungrateful were he not something of a Roman Catholic, seeing what glorious shade and shelter the open churches of the creed afford to him from the glaring sun and pelting rain. On a Sunday, however, he must be a Protestant or nothing at all. If inclination, seediness of attire, impecuniosity, or all combined, make him the last, he will have to take refuge in the Fitzroy Gardens, where he will find free 'sittings', 'sermons in stones', and prayer, if he will, in the rustling of wind-shaken plants and trees. The new chum, however poor in pocket, is certain, after a few weeks upon the streets, to become rich in what Disraeli calls 'accumulated experience'. He knows every turn of every street in Melbourne; the whole architecture and outline of the city is at his finger ends, for he has inspected it in sunshine and in shower, by night and by day — nay, at all times of the night and day, and from every possible point of view. He is a sort of walking guide-book to its public parks and buildings, a kind of dictionary of 'things not generally known' to the mass of its inhabitants. He has thumbed every book in the Public Library, and has become a living encyclopaedia of literary odds and ends. He is something of a theologian, for he has attended in turn all the churches and chapels of Melbourne. He is something of a politician, too, pinning his faith to the Colonial party, which, for the nonce, is most prone to assert the Englishman's 'privilege of public meeting,' a right, the vindication of which by the current radicalism has secured him many things an evening's shelter in the Town Hall, and others equally well-warmed and lighted. He knows more law than many lawyers, the Supreme Court in term-time being one of his favourite refuges. He must needs be something of a philosopher, having traversed the extreme poles of its phases. Last, but not least, amongst his numerous qualifications, he knows better than anyone how to lay out threepence to the best advantage. All this knowledge makes him a very desirable, or, at any rate, a very amusing companion, and accounts for the fact, which would otherwise be inexplicable, of his seldom being without tobacco and, at least, one daily 'nobbler', the tobacco and the 'nobblers' being, in fact, the price paid for his society by his less gifted but more solvent associates.

I have now lightly depicted some of the habits and manners of one of the great 'social facts' of Australia. I have treated the subject from somewhat of a serio-comic standpoint; but I am not on that account unconscious of the shadow of tragedy which surrounds it. Pitiable as is the position of the unsuccessful new chum who has 'come out' of his own accord, that of the emigrant who owes his misfortunes to the cruelty or carelessness of unfeeling friends has still greater claims to sympathy. It seems to be no uncommon thing for persons at home, who wish to be relieved of the surplus incumbrances, in the shape of sons, nephews, etc., to ship them off to the colonies, with funds utterly insufficient to give them a fair start on landing, and without affording them any fair opportunity of gauging their prospects in emigrating prior to starting. In this way, not only are the victims themselves reduced to the shifts and makeshifts I have described, but the useless, and, I am sorry to say, criminal, population of the colonies is most wantonly and unnecessarily swelled. Parents and guardians, who dare not expose their *protégés* to destitution on the streets at home, think nothing of what is practically the same thing when a long voyage intervenes, and they are divided by thousands of miles from the miseries of which they are the cause, and the public obloquy which should be their meed. If the persons thus sent out are thoroughly able-bodied, they may, after a time, overlive their troubles, but their chance of doing so is small indeed when, as is often the case, they are physically delicate, or even mentally deficient. The victims of this kind of 'happy despatch' are not, unfortunately, confined to the sterner sex. A young girl at home commits a *faux pas*, and in order to avoid scandal, perhaps on the very eve of her confinement, when she most of all needs tender treatment, is put on board ship without any companion or attendant, except the ship doctor, who is not invariably the most skilful of his class. If she survive the sufferings of the voyage, and escape utter demoralisation on the passage, how can she hope, when landed in one of the great Australian ports, without friends, money, or character, to provide sustenance for herself and infant after an honest fashion? Ten to one she will be driven to find a living on the streets, and (*pace*, ye moralists) who is most to blame? The poor girl, or those who sent her out to certain destitution? It is not for me, the mere 'idle singer of an empty day,' to point the moral of the facts to which I have adverted; but should they be taken up and ventilated by others, I shall not have 'made a note' of them in vain.

*That is, taking part in the fashionable promenade in Collins Street — the Regent Street of Melbourne — in the afternoon, from about four to six.

1888

E. J. BANFIELD

The Gentle Art of Beachcombing

Before all things, it is essential that the beachcomber should have for the exercise of his art a strip of the tropics. The air must be balmy and the sea tepid, for he laves himself with judicious impartiality in either, as the mood of the moment persuades, and with little of the superfluity of clothes. He must be a fanciful Laodicean — neither hot nor cold.

The robes of civilisation being for the most part discarded, the sun will keep him from becoming uncomfortable from heat, while the sea must never be cold enough to give him a chill, no matter how long he elects to favor that commodious element. Ideal conditions being discoverable in the tropics alone, it follows that the majority of Australians who, with inexplicable perversity, elect to live within the temperate zone can have but vague perceptions of the high, yet virtuous, delights, the refinements and the vigorous impulses of the art.

There are, of course, those who defile the title of beachcomber with harsh and opprobrious significance, just as there are men who, making of the art a sordid calling or trade, cannot be expected to appreciate its niceties. The true beachcomber must be endowed with those qualities which gently constrain him from the recognition of the passing of time and of the least of the conventions. Nor must he confine his attention to things of the sea. He should be capable of a generous and catholic admiration for the beauties of Nature. He ought to be able to enjoy the lustre of an oyster-shell even when denied the more entrancing pearl. He should be able to distinguish one beach plant from another, though their ceremonious titles are unfamiliar. Craig, the gardener in *Adam Bede*, who gave Hetty Sorrel the hot-house flower which enhanced her prettiness at church, said, in apology for vocal deficiencies, 'A man that's got the names and natur' o' plants in 's head isna likely to keep a hollow place t' hold tunes in.'

There must be no hollow places in the head of the beachcomber if he is to extract all the sweetness and satisfaction out of his art. The sea will prattle to him as the boat slips along, yet in such quiet tone that the voice of the turtle — only a great and gulping sigh — will not be drowned. Casuarians will harp for him a humming accompaniment to the measured cadences of old ocean, and the tree of beautiful leaf, which lacks a familiar name, will waft pure and refreshing scent from flowers milk-white and gold. Nor will the beachcomber be indifferent to the joys which come, of the discovery of material blessings which have been laid out upon untrodden strands for his inspection.

Once this particular beachcomber waded, disrobed, in shallow, sunlit water, as limpid as the fictitious stream which King Solomon improvised at the foot of his throne when the Queen of Sheba attended his court. (You have not forgotten the purpose of the strategic stream? The gorgeous queen regarded it as a ceremonial device, and lifting her robes, displayed her shapely calves to the epicurean monarch, in accordance with his device.) The water resting on the verge of the dainty isle was just as delusively clear, but it was not deceitful. It revealed living coral, good to be avoided by the bare-footed, and many strange sea things — clams with patterned mantles grey, slate, blue, sage-green, brown and buff; anemones in various tints, some like spikes of lavender, irritant and repellent to the touch; some plate-shaped and cobalt blue, and clinging and caressing to the finger; some living vases with the opalescent tints of Venetian glass, which, abhorring the hand of man, retreat into the sand until only an inconspicuous fringe of neutral tint is visible; sea slugs, in almost endless form and variety of hue, were strewn among the loose rubbish of the reef, beneath which there lurked molluscs of several species. In the middle of a clump of brown seaweed, which had fallen apart like the hair on a woman's head, was a black streak signifying the gape of a shell-fish, which some folks erroneously term an oyster. The gape was about as long as the parting of a woman's hair and about thrice as wide.

As I crouched over to watch the functions of the animal within, my shadow intervened, and the cautious creature immediately retired, the valves closing with faultless apposition, so that no sign of its presence was visible. Changing my position, so that the pinna — to use the name judicious mortals have bestowed — should enjoy its place in the sun, the valves soon furtively opened. A slight movement on my part and they closed again, without revealing any hidden charms. After a few minutes a certain confidence was established between us, and the pinna emerged from its retirement, in so far as such creatures are permitted by Nature.

The mantle of this particular species of pinna is shown as a delicate fringe of lace in old gold and black. It waves or ripples along the upper edges of the confining valves, which are intensely black, with a pearly lustre. The pretty movements of the decorated mantle — one could imagine the skirts of a well-apparelled damsel — attracted admiration, and on peering into the shell I caught a glimpse of something precious. Tossed and twirled about just below the old gold fringe was a black pearl about the size of a pea. The prize was safe, so that I could, without risk of losing it, watch it in its eternal revolutions. It seemed as if the animal unceasingly attempted to rid itself of the incubus, the weight of which kept it about an inch below the aperture of the valves. Such a motion would naturally tend to the perfection of the prize. Whatsoever its lustre might be, it would certainly be a sphere of just and exact proportions. Besides, it was pearl in the making. As long as it remained within the pinna, and it could not voluntarily be rejected, its size would inevitably increase. It was the rolling stone to which time and the secretions of the animal would add weight, and, peradventure, beauty.

Was ever mortal, I pondered, privileged to watch over the growth of a pearl, and a black pearl? The activities of the mantle were slow, automatic and rhythmical as a pulse beats. Close scrutiny showed that the pearl was not absolutely free. It was enclosed in a transparent membrane, which, however, did not seem to interfere with its apparent revolutions. The envelope was the merest film. The pearl was retained in a particular position in the shell, its motions being perpendicular and revolutionary. Perhaps the rays of light which fell unequally on it through the water created the illusion of revolutions; but, if so, the magic of the light was very deceptive, for the whole of the functions of the parts of the animal revealed were watched with intense interest.

Was it possible for human nature to deny itself so easily gotten and pretty a prize? I confess that though I argued the possibility of the pearl increasing in size and loveliness, I also took into calculation the fact that pinnas are subject, like mortals, to ills, chances and mishaps. Left to be slowly tossed about the pearl would become greater; but size, though an important feature, is not the only desirable quality. And while it grew might not some other bare-footed beachcomber happen to discover it? Or might not one of the many ardent admirers of the pinna itself find entrance by drilling or by the violent crushing of the valves, and ignoring the treasure, destroy the organs and the substance by and from which it was being delicately elaborated?

Suppose, I argued with myself, I remove the gaping shell, I shall no longer be able to enjoy the rare, the unique pleasure of presiding over the gradual perfection of a pearl, an aesthetic advantage to which I alone had been made free. Could present possession of a little sphere of carbonate of lime, polished and sooty black, compensate for the continuance of the chaste joy of watching one of the most covert and intimate processes of Nature?

Balancing the immediate material gain with inevitable moral loss, I was almost persuaded to self-denial, when, with a sudden impulse begot of the consciousness of rightful acquisition, the pinna was forcibly yet carefully drawn out from the sand in which it was deeply embedded and in which it had been anchored by toughened byssus. Directly the valves were prised apart the pearl fell into my hand. It now adorns a ring of the most amiable of sisters.

Never before had I seen a pearl so loosely retained within the shell. Generally, in the case of the pinna, pearls are embedded in the muscles or other soft parts of the animal. Indeed, completely spherical pearls are seldom found elsewhere. Generally, too, the trivial pearls of the pinna are not primarily discernible, but have to be sought by passing the 'meat' through the fingers. On this occasion all previous experience was set at naught, so that it might seem that the prize had been presented to me by the animal as its perfect and most opulent work.

Pearls, black and white and brown — all, with rare exceptions, absolutely worthless — are not dealt out to the sanguine beachcomber every day and indiscriminately. Most of his wanderings are quite unsensational and unrewarded. Does not the freedom of untrodden isles, unsoiled beaches, undefiled seas content? Slippery-backed dugong may swirl away from his boat; he may see a kingfish shoot thirty feet up into the air and marvel at the stupendous impelling force; for him the alligator pike may dart out of the sea and skip along with the speed of a bird by merely flipping the placid surface with the tip of an agile tail. And when he returns to his humble dwelling and the limb of the turtle which the black boy has harpooned is hanging in the dusk, he will be sure to notice that the chill, quivering flesh is all aglow. Has someone, undetected, clotted it with phosphorous so luminous that print may be read by its light though the night be dark? No. Simply, phosphorous is one of the elements which are embodied in turtle, not in excess but in unaccustomed measure, making the flesh rich and nutritious. He will eat of the flesh and acknowledge it to be salubrious, and give thanks that it conveys to his system certain essences of the eternal sea which exhilarate. The turtle is a shy, shrinking, long-lived animal. Assimilate the white, phosphorus impregnated meat, and possibly you may become like unto him.

Do you now ask why I am a beachcomber?

1913

DAME MARY GILMORE

The Bent Twig

When from the incubation of years of experience and thought a book is written quickly and warm from the heart, it is possible that, like the chicken from the shell, it comes forth a little surprised at the haste with which at last it arrived at being, wondering somewhat at its own newness, and dazzled, perhaps, by the too brilliant light of the concrete and more public world! One says 'a book'. But, after all, that thing between covers is the self. Only in a mirror does a man see his back, and the 'self' sees itself only in a book. In everything else, in the acts and facts of daily life, it knows but the isolated word, the single action, and the individualized stress of personality. Books are not all alike, of course, even as to the self. Sometimes they mirror so small a part of the reality that, after one look, they are found to be so trifling that one does not look at them again. But once in a while the soul speaks, and not even the writer himself knows with what self-revelation. For at times one finds the depths come to the surface. The underworld of life awakes like a bird which a passing ray of light stirs in a dark forest. Then the loves of the heart are spoken, the shallows are broken through and submerged by that which comes flowing forth.

But often, when one long silent writes a book, the theorist, reading only what is written, says, 'This one did not write before because thought had not matured,' or 'because life had not touched him to emotion,' or 'because the hour had not struck.' But, like the clock in the tower, the hour of capacity strikes many times, and passes without our being in a position to take advantage of it. Thus, as the waters of Australia, capacity flows out unconserved to that ocean which knows no individual boundaries within its mighty limits. The storage-waters of art and science, of all things that better life, are scarcely drawn upon because the wells are not sunk, and the well-buckets are set dredging in mud for a bare existence. The pearls are lost that the pig may feed; the cream of life is too often set to do the work of the clay.

There was once a child who sang as soon as it learned that words meant feeling. It sang, like a bird, in the fury of the creative coming to expression, and, at the end of the outburst, sank never-wearied through excess of that spent force.

It sang because of an intensity of vitality which demanded expression; because of something that we call life stirring in its sleep, some spirit-harp answering wind and sun. It sang because life made it sing. And then the claims of life came and drowned the young, the singing years. Many times the clock of capacity struck; but the striking had to go unheeded.

And there was a sculptor who was a boundary rider. He cut sheep-shank bones into rings, and into saddles and bridles; saddles small enough to fit the little finger, with the tiny girth and every buckle and dee in its place. But he never cut marble. The marble was too far away. And who now on Mandamah ever remembers Shannon the Boundary rider?...There is, in a desk in Sydney, a little saddle which is perhaps all that is left of Shannon and a whole life's capacity. The hour was struck every time that man took out his knife and nicked a cut upon a bone; but circumstances shut the door of opportunity.

I knew a boy in Victoria. He could tell you when the first tiger-orchid came out, miles away from his home, and the kind of grass that showed its most likely place of growth. He discovered the first white boronia in his district, and knew the cry and call of every wandering bird. But he had no name for the flowers, and no classification for the birds. He had but dumb knowledge, depending on the pointing of a finger or the production of a plant, and but dumb thoughts, because none had come to give him language. He had facts without a name; his was genius without a wing. He held life's jewels in his hands, unpolished, denied their lustre.

The bush blossom called him, the insects led him. 'He knows very spider in the bush!' said the neighbours, interested in knowledge, if not in the things that made knowledge. To him a spider was creation; the created telling the power of the Creator. To those about him it was but a spider, a thing to be crushed under foot, matter in the wrong place. 'He is mad on the colour of them,' they said in their crude way. What was a spider but a grey thing, speckled black, or red or brown? But the red and the black, the grey and the brown, were a new world to this boy with his fine sensitive senses and his strong native feeling. Darwin loved not nature better than he. As with Agassiz, even the snake was not too deadly for his friendly searching eyes and hands.

A naturalist? ... At eighteen he was shearing. At twenty-three he was dead on the fields of France. In his death, the bush which is going, along with its myriad tribes and denizens, lost one who loved it; lost an interpreter, who said nothing to the world because none brought him the opportunity of learning the needed speech. He who would have made the wild plant a friend and fellow-housekeeper with man was like one who would learn French yet had no books, and no teacher. I grieve over that boy who never had a chance, for the rose is only scented where it blooms in the sun, and what is a mind but a rose of God?

There was another boy, near Tocumwal, on whom punishment fell constantly because of a white wall and a bit of charcoal. A burnt stick or a blue-bag drew out of him — as wind out of warm air, as light from the sun — something that longed for utterance. It was the Great God Himself, speaking out of a boy's mind in a lightning that would not be held. But the hand that should have balanced the palette held a plough; and the sight that should have measured form and steeped itself in colour measured milk in a cow-yard.

I once met a girl in Paraguay who, in mud from a river-bank, modelled lambs and cats and pigs (and Kewpies before there were Kewpies), choosing her colours as the clay allowed. The native Paraguayans marvelled, half afraid of the work so like yet so unlike the living, for she added an individuality of the bizarre to everything she did. '*Milagro!*' they cried, as they looked at the work, and *Miracle!* it was. But there was no one there to tell the child that she had in her hand a ladder which might reach from earth to heaven!

And there was a man who knew the track of the quail, and the haunt of the wild bee; who felt the heart-beat of a horse, and realized the ancestral fear of the dog....Poverty tied him, and only the dog and the horse read his message. The Bush, that should have made him, in its solitude ate him.

So, when I hear people talking of the benevolence of poverty as a helper to genius, and of how genius must 'out', I ask, 'Is genius independent of bread? Hath not genius appetite? Needs it not to eat?'

A cask can be emptied in either of two ways. One is by the slow process of drop by drop, which benefits no one; the other is by the free flow that quenches thirst, even the thirst of a world eager to drink and to be sustained. And genius that must 'out' so often has only the 'out' of that slow drop which is as useless to itself as to the world.

Even a plant must have time, a place and food, to grow. And what is thought but a plant of mind? Poverty! ...Poverty!...Poverty!...Ah! man the judge of another, you do not put your corn in poor ground if you want a full crop, nor turn the herd on stony ground if you want milk!...Poverty!...Poverty is like frost; it is a good experience for the warm and the well-fed, whether plant or man, but it kills the crop of the poor. The oven has baked many a woman's full song to hard crusts; the clearing has sent many a sculpture to splinters; the hand of the delicate touch has too often been calloused by the grindstone of life. The baked bread was eaten, and none knew of the song lost in its baking, the trees fell, and none heard the cry of the dream. 'Genius will out?' When I think of Genius and Poverty, I think of Hell without a bottom!

Minds are many. There are crows as well as nightingales. The cruelty is not in being a crow, but in silencing the nightingale. One may make brooms of roses instead of millet. Such a broom may sweep; it may even sweep best. But to use the rose as a broom destroys the rose; turns it from its true destiny; in the end it becomes merely broom. But no broom ever becomes a rose. There is no real exchange in these things. There is only the terrible loss of the subverted and the destroyed, and the cruelty of waste unhallowed by any compensating return of values.

1922

A. B. 'BANJO' PATERSON

The Amateur Gardener

The first step in amateur gardening is to sit down and consider what good you are going to get by it. If you are only a tenant by the month, as most people are, it is obviously not much use your planting a fruit orchard or an avenue of oak trees, which will take years to come to maturity. What you want is something that will grow quickly, and will stand transplanting for when you move it would be a sin to leave behind you all the plants on which you have spent so much labour and so much patent manure. We knew a man once who was a bookmaker by trade — and a leger bookmaker at that — but he had a passion for horses and flowers, and when he 'had a big win', as he occasionally did, it was his custom to have movable wooden stables built on skids put up in the yard, and to have tons of the best soil that money could buy carted into the garden of the premises which he was occupying. Then he would keep splendid horses in the stables, grow rare roses and show-bench chrysanthemums in the garden and the landlord passing by would see the garden in a blaze of colour, and would promise himself that he would raise the bookmaker's rent next quarter day. However, when the bookmaker 'took the knock', as he invariably did at least twice a year, it was his pleasing custom to move without giving any notice. He would hitch two carthorses to the stables, and haul them away at night. He would dig up not only the roses, trees, and chrysanthemums that he had planted, but would also cart away the soil he had brought in; in fact, he used to shift the garden bodily. He had one garden that he shifted to nearly every suburb in Sydney in turn, and he always argued that change of air was invaluable for chrysanthemums. Be this as it may, the proposition is self-evident that the would-be amateur gardener should grow flowers not for posterity, nor for his landlord, nor for his creditors, but for himself.

Being determined then to go in for gardening on commonsense principles, and having decided on the class of shrubs that you mean to grow, the next thing is to consider what sort of a chance you have of growing them. If your neighbour keeps game fowls it may be taken for granted that before long they will pay you a visit, and you will see the rooster scratching your pot plants out by the roots as if they were so much straw, just to make a nice place to lie down and fluff the dust over himself. Goats will also stray in from the street, and bite the young shoots off, selecting the most valuable plants with a discrimination that would do credit to a professional gardener, and whatever valuable plant a goat bites is doomed. It is therefore useless thinking of growing any delicate or squeamish plants. Most amateur gardeners maintain a lifelong struggle against the devices of Nature, and when the forces of man and the forces of Nature come into conflict Nature will win every time. Nature has decreed that certain plants shall be hardy, and therefore suitable to suburban amateur gardens, but the suburban amateur gardener persists in trying to grow quite other plants, and in despising those marked out by Nature for his use. It is to correct this tendency that this article is written.

The greatest standby to the amateur gardener should undoubtedly be the blue-flowered shrub known as plumbago. This homely but hardy plant will grow anywhere. It naturally prefers a good soil and a sufficient rainfall, but if need be it will worry along without either. Fowls cannot scratch it up, and even a goat turns away dismayed from its hard-featured branches. The flower is not strikingly beautiful nor ravishingly scented, but it flowers nine months out of the year, and though smothered with street dust and scorched by the summer sun you will find that faithful old plumbago plugging along undismayed. A plant like this should be encouraged and made much of, but the misguided amateur gardener as a rule despises it. The plant known as the churchyard geranium is also one marked out by Providence for the amateur, as is also cosmea, a plant that comes up year after year when once planted. In creepers, bignonia and lantana will hold their own under difficulties perhaps as well as any that can be found. In trees, the Port Jackson fig is a patriotic plant to grow, and it is a fine plant to provide exercise, as it sheds its leaves unsparingly, and requires to have the whole garden swept up every day. Your aim as a student of Nature should be to encourage the survival of the fittest. In grasses, too, the same principle holds good. There is a grass called nut grass, and another called Parramatta grass, either of which will hold its own against anything living or dead. The average gardening manual gives you recipes for destroying these grasses. Why should you destroy them in favour of a sickly plant that needs constant attention? No. The Pparramatta grass is the selected of Nature, and who are you to interfere with Nature?

Having thus decided to go in for strong, simple plants that will hold their own, and a bit over, you must get your implements of husbandry. A spade is the first thing, but the average ironmonger will show you an unwieldy weapon only meant to be used by navvies. Don't buy it. Get a small spade, about half-size — it is nice and light and doesn't tire the wrist, and with it you can make a good display of enthusiasm, and earn the hypocritical admiration of your wife. After digging for half an hour or so, you can get her to rub your back with any of the backache cures advertised in this journal and from that moment you will have no further need for the spade.

Besides a spade, a barrow is about the only other thing needed, and anyhow it is almost a necessity for removing cases of whisky into the house. A rake is useful sometimes as a weapon, when your terrier dog has bailed up a cat, and will not attack it till the cat is made to run. And talking of terrier dogs, an acquaintance of ours has a dog that does all his gardening. The dog is a small elderly terrier, whose memory is failing somewhat, so as soon as the terrier has planted a bone in the garden the owner slips over and digs it up and takes it away. When the terrier goes back and finds the bone gone, he distrusts his own memory, and begins to think that perhaps he has made a mistake, and has dug in the wrong place; so he sets to work and digs patiently all over the garden, turning over acres of soil in his search for the missing bone. Meanwhile, the man saves himself a lot of backache.

The sensible amateur gardener, then, will not attempt to fight with Nature but will fall in with her views. What more pleasant than to get out of bed at 11.30 on a Sunday morning, and look out of your window at a lawn waving with the leathery plumes of Parramatta grass, and to see beyond it the churchyard or sinking geranium flourishing side by side with the plumbago and the Port Jackson fig? The garden gate blows open, and the local commando of goats, headed by an aged and fragrant patriarch (locally known as De Wet from the impossibility of capturing him), rush in; but their teeth will barely bite through the wiry stalks of the Parramatta grass, and the plumbago and the fig tree fail to attract them; and before long they scale the fence by standing on one another's shoulders, and disappear into the next-door garden, where a fanatic is trying to grow show roses. After the last goat has scaled your neighbour's fence, and only De Wet is left in your garden, your little dog discovers him, and De Wet beats a hurried retreat, apparently at full speed, with the little dog exactly one foot behind him in frantic pursuit. We say apparently at full speed, because old experience has taught that De Wet can run as fast as a greyhound when he likes; but he never exerts himself to go any faster than is necessary to just keep in front of whatever dog is after him; in fact, De Wet once did run for about a hundred yards with a greyhound after him, and then he suddenly turned and butted the greyhound cranksided, as Uncle Remus would say. Hearing the scrimmage, your neighbour comes onto his verandah, and sees the chase going down the street. 'Ha! that wretched old De Wet again!' he says. 'Small hope your dog has of catching him! Why don't you get a garden gate like mine, so as he won't get in?' 'No, he can't get in at your gate,' is the reply, 'but I think his commando are in your back garden now.' The next thing is a frantic rush by your neighbour, falling downstairs in his haste, and the sudden reappearance of the commando skipping easily back over the fence, and through your gate into the street again, stopping to bite some priceless pot plants of your neighbour's as they come out. A horse gets in, but his hoofs make no impression on the firm turf of the Parramatta grass, and you get quite a hearty laugh by dropping a chair on him out of the first floor window, and seeing him go tearing down the street. The game fowls of your other neighbour come fluttering into your garden, and scratch and chuckle and fluff themselves under your plumbago bush; but you don't worry. Why should you? They can't hurt it; and besides, you know well enough that the small black hen and the big yellow hen, who have disappeared from the throng, are even now laying their daily eggs for you at the back of the thickest bush. Your little dog rushes frantically up and down the front bed of your garden barking and racing, and tearing up the ground, because his rival little dog who lives down the street is going past with his master, and each pretends that he wants to be at the other — as they have pretended every day for the past three years. But the performance he goes through in the garden doesn't disturb you. Why should it? By following the directions in this article you have selected plants that he cannot hurt. After breakfasting at 12 noon, you stroll out, and, perhaps, smooth with your foot or with your small spade the inequalities made by the hens; you gather up casually the eggs that they have laid; you whistle to your little dog, and go out for a stroll with a light heart. That is the true way to enjoy amateur gardening.

1903

H. E. BOOTE

War and the Devil

When you have learned to identify the Devil, as I have done, you meet him in the most unlikely places.

The other day, for example, I came across him on the Sandhill, gathering wild flowers.

His black clothes shone in the sun with a lustre that a beetle might have envied. His top hat fairly dazzled the eyes with its glossiness. He was stouter and more prosperous-looking than ever.

. . .

'Ah! is it you?' he said, as I drew near. 'I had a notion I should see you here. "Where shall I look for the dear fellow?" said I to myself, and knowing your poetic temperament, the answer came quite pat, "Where else than at the feet of Spring, among the sweet wild flowers." I admire your taste. I share your feelings. Are they not exquisite — these delicate little what-you-may-call-ems? — these beautiful pale blue thingumbobs? I am not strong on geology — or is it botany? Really, I could not tell you; but I love the pretty dears. Is there anyone with a sense of refinement who would fail to be moved by the delicious fragrance they exhale?'

I pointed out, somewhat brusquely, that the flowers on the Sandhill had no fragrance whatever. He was not in the least put out.

'What a keen observer you are!' he exclaimed admiringly. 'I should never have discovered that for myself. Really, I must cultivate your society more, if you will let me. There is so much I could learn from you.'

'This war must leave you very little time for social intercourse,' I said sourly.

He looked at me with an air of pained surprise.

'The war!' said he. 'Surely you don't for a moment imagine I have any business interest in the war! I loathe the thing. There is no greater advocate for peace on earth than I am.'

His fat features assumed an aspect of the most expansive benevolence as he uttered the words. He seemed to literally ooze fraternalism at every pore.

'Ah, my friend,' said he, 'if you but knew how I love peace! If you could only realise how your cruel insinuation hurts!'

He turned his head aside for an instant and dabbed his eyes with a spotless cambric handkerchief, hurriedly extracted from his coat-tails.

It was a nauseating spectacle. The Father of Lies, the Prince of Evil, with a bunch of innocent wild flowers in his hand, pretending to weep because of a reflection on his virtue!

With an exclamation of disgust I turned to leave him.

'No, no, my dear chap!' he said, laying a detaining hand upon my arm. 'You must not go away like that. I am better now.'

'You're a consummate old hypocrite,' said I.

He smiled urbanely, and put the handkerchief away.

'For once,' said he, 'you are mistaken. I am perfectly sincere in this matter. I really DO love peace, but I don't mind admitting — strictly between ourselves, of course — that it's only because it pays me better than war. In the business which I carry on, a dozen years of war is less profitable than a single year of peace.'

'A famous general said that war is hell!' I snapped.

The Devil raised a plump white hand in mild expostulation.

'Now, don't,' he said. 'It really isn't worthy of you. The place you refer to only exists in the imagination of the vulgar. I'm sorry to hear it mentioned by an intelligent person. Were I not naturally of an optimistic temperament it would make me despair of progress.'

'You canting old humbug!' said I, 'spare me this unctuous make-believe. War creates hatred, it incites cruelty, and on the hatred and cruelty of those who should be brothers you have waxed fat.'

'I make my profit out of living men,' said the Devil, 'and war kills 'em. Therefore war is opposed to my interests. Surely you will recognise that that is logic.'

'In the hands of a liar,' said I, 'logic is a knife to stick in the back of Truth.'

The Devil swept off his top hat with a flourish and a bow, and replaced it on the bald patch, jauntily.

'Your compliments have an ingenuous quality which I heartily appreciate,' said he. 'In the same spirit, let us exchange views on this matter.'

. . .

We sat on the sand among the flannel flowers, overlooking the ocean at Bondi. The beauty of the scene affected my companion deeply.

'Lovely! Divine! Quite absolutely nice!' he gushed. 'A humble rose-covered cottage by the sea, and I'd be happy. Awfully impressive, don't you think? A really tremendous quantity of water!'

'Yet not enough,' said I, 'to quench the fires of wrath that war lights in the human heart.'

'I can't agree with you there,' said the Devil. 'Peace is the greatest incendiary on earth. It not only plunges the firestick in, but pours kerosene on the flames. What is the bloodiest war to that process of peace which you call "the struggle for existence"? In times of peace men trample on one another for gain. In times of peace they build the slums, and plant a pub at each corner of Poverty Court. There is more genuine misery caused by the peaceful operations of the payers of low wages than all the depredations of warring armies.

'I am an advocate of peace. I earn my biggest dividends through those who wear, not helmets, but top hats. The mailed fist is no use to me; I prefer the gloved palm. There is the capacity for evil in living men; in dead ones there is none. War, because it kills men, and thus renders them incapable of further mischief, is a thing for which I have no respect.'

'You're an unblushing scoundrel!' I said angrily.

The Devil added a flannel flower to his bouquet.

'A scoundrel, if you like. I should be sorry to limit your freedom of speech. But not an unblushing one. Oh, no! Blushing is an art I rather flatter myself upon, and nobody cares to have his pet accomplishment depreciated. I have made a thorough study of it. I have all the varieties of blushes at my finger-ends, as it were. At a moment's notice I can blush with indignation. I can blush with wounded pride. I can blush with offended propriety. I will give you an example of the last-named blush right now.'

I averted my eyes. The Devil blushing, with a silk tile on his head and a nosegay in his hand, was a spectacle I had no relish for.

'Oh, very well,' said he. 'I've no desire to display my gifts, if it makes you jealous.'

'You were explaining,' I said coldly, 'that war does not profit you.'

'Not in the least,' said the Devil briskly. 'War wipes men out of existence, and I want to keep them with all their delusive senses alert. Every living man is an agent for me. Every living man contributes to my income. Dead men are dead capital. Now do you understand?'

I let him see that I did by edging away from him in disgust. The Devil merely smiled, and went on:

'I love peace. I love everything that stands for peace. I adore these pretty flowers, because they have never known bloodshed. I kiss them. I salute the sweet blue sky, the emerald mead, the shadowy groves, the little singing streams, and — and — all that sort of thing, you know.'

His fat face lighted up with a cunning simulation of ecstacy. Never have I beheld a more sickening sight — a slimy reptile basking on the breast of sleeping innocence. I listened to the sound of his voice as one might listen to the hissing of a snake.

. . .

'I want this war to end,' he continued. 'I want the warriors to knock off, and give the traders a show. I pin my faith to the traders. Civilisation suits me best. Poverty, hard labor, low wages, high rents, overcrowding, insanitary conditions; — give me this social system, under the protection of the Law, with the blessing of the Church upon it; give me this, I say, and crown it with peace, and I come into my own!'

'What you call peace is still war,' said I. 'It is class war.'

The Devil shrugged his shoulders.

'I am not learned in these nice distinctions,' he said smugly. 'No casuist am I, but just a plain elderly gent in business, with esthetic tastes.'

'Socialism will come along, and spoil your villainous game,' said I.

'Socialism will keep men alive,' said the Devil, 'and that is all I ask. Let me have living material to deal with — let me have men with hot hearts and busy brains, and I'm safe from the bankruptcy court. That's why I love peace — it keeps the breath in men's bodies. That's why I don't like war — it piles up the dead, and dead men do no evil.'

'I'll hear no more of such abominable sentiments,' I snarled.

The Devil raised his hat from the bald patch, and bowed with the elegance of a Beau Brummel.

'Good-bye,' said he. 'So glad we met. I always enjoy your conversation.'

. . .

I watched him descend the hillside, sleek and smirking, and resplendent in broadcloth, like a citizen of high repute.

'Surely,' I mused, 'the Devil was never so vile as now, when he has done away with the horns and hoofs that signalled "Danger!" and taken to the shiny tile and patent-leather boots of Respectability.'

1915

A. G. STEPHENS

A Word for Australians

Writing in an English magazine some years ago, a son of Daniel O'Connell told how he was struck by the fact that the universal adoration of Irishmen never seemed to stimulate his father to personal vanity or to disturb his equanimity. To his son's question how this might be, O'Connell answered simply, 'I pray very often.' Nor is it likely that the answer was suggested by a mere religious pose. O'Connell's hereditary piety was sufficiently intensified by life-long habit to make sincere prayer both natural and necessary. And doubtless his character was strengthened by the religious faith which to him meant so much — and to Australians, on the whole, so little.

For even the clerical party is forced to admit that every year religion and religious observances have less hold upon Australia, and exercise less influence upon the development of the national character. Our fathers brought with them the religious habit as they brought other habits of elder nations in older lands. And upon religion, as upon everything else, the spirit of Australia — that undefined, indefinable resultant of earth, and air, and conditions of climate and life — has seized; modifying, altering, increasing or altogether destroying. In the case of religious belief the tendency is clearly to destruction — partly, no doubt, because with the spread of mental enlightenment the tendency is everywhere to decay of faith in outworn creeds; but partly also, it seems, because the Australian environment is unfavourable to the growth of religion, and because there is in the developing Australian character a sceptical and utilitarian spirit that values the present hour and refuses to sacrifice the present for any visionary future lacking a rational guarantee.

O'Connell prayed, and was benefited by prayer, because prayer belonged to his temperament — he was fitted to pray. Doubtless there are still in Europe many similar individuals in whom heredity has not yet been ousted by the progress of thought. But, except as adherents of O'Connell's creed, or among women — with minds more slowly moving, there are very few of his temperament in Australia. In the religious sense, probably nineteen-twentieths of Australians are heathen. In this country the rudiments of religious faith have been uprooted or were never rooted; we cannot, if we would, derive from daily prayer O'Connell's daily stimulus and solace. Our fathers went regularly to church and chapel as a matter of conscience, and were none the worse for it; we go chiefly as a matter of custom, and are none the better for it in any vital sense; most of us do not go at all. The holy Sabbath, degenerated to the formal Sunday, has become the weekly holiday in city and bush. Beyond the perfunctory observances associated with it, the day is meaningless: it has lost for us the essentially sacred character which it had for O'Connell — which it still has for men of O'Connell's temperament. No one who knows Australia can doubt that these statements are generally true. Our fathers, or their fathers, or some of them, had the kernel of religion: we in Australia have little more than the husk, and we shall have less and less of the husk as the years go by.

The loss of religion is not a thing to deplore, yet it may seem sometimes a thing to regret. With Emerson,

'I like a priest, I like a cowl,
I love a prophet of the soul:
And on my heart monastic aisles
Fall like sweet strains or pensive smiles:
Yet not for all his faith can see
Would I that cowled churchman be.'

The downfall of geocentric philosophy necessarily implies the ruin of geocentric religions. If their relics linger for a thousand years or five thousand, that is little more than a moment in the probable history of the human race; and assuredly humanity will find a rational stick to replace the irrational crutch.

Our present difficulty, and it is not Australia's difficulty alone, is that for many people the influence of reason upon character is not yet so potent as has been the influence of faith.

'We stand between two worlds, one dead,
The other powerless to be born.'

We have lost religion, and we have not yet adapted ourselves to the loss. Like a drunkard suddenly deprived of his dram, we are ill at ease, unready for emergencies. Whether religion did or did not do more harm than good is a profitless question. The religious stage was one stage in human evolution, as natural as the irreligious stage that is superseding it. Religion gave to all men what they were in their day and generation fitted to receive. To the weak it was an opiate or a maddening draught, but to the strong a magnificent stimulant. In many of the most memorable episodes of history it infused into the veins of nations a courage and a strength that we have not yet quite attained without it. For the Covenanters, for the Puritans, for the little Dutch republic fighting for its life against overwhelming Spain as for that other little Dutch republic recently fighting for its life against overwhelming Britain, it edged the sword of patriotism and sharpened the pike of liberty. Lacking religion, one cannot but think that some of the most inspiring national contests and resistances of the past would not have been continued quite so strenuously or quite so long. Horatius fought all the better for the ashes of his fathers because he had a sincere reverence for the temples of his gods.

And here in Australia, we have no temples, no ashes worth the name. We have still to make the history and create the legendary associations that are such a powerful binding force in national life. The Murray to Australians is still only a geographical label; but think what the Thames means to an Englishman! Think how Nelson was nerved by the thought of Westminster Abbey; of how his sailors were nerved by the signal '*England* expects…'! What a mass of record and tradition, of song and story, of memorable life and love and death, presses behind that *England*! *Australia* is meaningless by comparison, lacking the inspiration of the past. But is it not possible to catch meaning and inspiration from the future? Is it not better to be of those who make St Crispin's day worthy remembrance than of those who look back to remember it? This country has still for us few hallowed associations; but if we choose it may have them for our children. If we are not History's legatees, it is because we have the chance to be History's founders and stablishers. And, even already, there are many who see in this vast virgin land a brooding charm not to be exchanged for England's chequered story. There is even already a nostalgia for the breadth of the bush and the breath of the gums that yields nothing in intensity to the nostalgia for the green turf and the hawthorn-buds in pleasant Warwickshire lanes. Even already, how few Australians would exchange for England's glowing national sunset — or if you will, her splendid noon — our own intimate and fragrant dawn?

It is the duty and should be the pride of every father and mother and teacher of Australian children to intensify the natural love of Australia, and to point out in how many ways Australia is eminently worthy to be loved — both the actual land and the national ideal. Good and evil are mingled everywhere; but there is no land with more beautiful aspects than Australia, no ideal with greater potentialities of human achievement and human happiness. Australia may never be a great country; yet it will be the fault of the people, not of the land, if it is not one of the best countries in the world to live in and die in — given that we are free from foreign aggression until we are able to resist foreign aggression.

'But you have no great rivers.' Well, there have been great nations without great rivers, as there have been great rivers without great nations. Probably, if the Eastern Dividing Chain could be bodily shifted five hundred miles westward, extending the coastal rainfall to the interior, and sending a score of considerable rivers and their tributaries tumbling to the sea, Australian development would be easier and Australian prosperity more assured. Practicably, were Lake Eyre connected with Lake Torrens, Lake Torrens with Spencer Gulf, and the ocean restored to its old home in the central basin of Australia, the clouds evaporated from a vast inland sea might rise to increase the interior rainfall and permanently mitigate the severity of summer climate. But, leaving the impossible and the dubious, what is the measure of national greatness? A vast population or an extended empire does not necessarily make a great nation. 'The great city,' says Whitman, 'is the city with the greatest man or woman'; and the great country is not that one where millions of people toil squalidly in order that comparatively few may live in idleness and luxury. With a bare ten thousand families, or less, Australia might still be the greatest country in the world, if only every individual had the opportunity of living the best and most enlightened life that was possible to him — of fulfilling to the utmost his capacities for development and happiness.

It is the false standard of 'greatness' that vitiates many published inferences from the decreasing Australian birth-rate. The European nations desire to increase their birth-rate because they are military nations, and because every son is a potential soldier, every daughter the potential mother of a soldier. And, until our numbers are such that we can defy attack, similar reasons have weight in Australia also. But they are not the only reasons that have weight. One may point out that, in the struggle for national ideals, the quality-standard is by far the most important, national existence being once assured. There is no national profit in the multiplication of children destined to live and die miserably. And the decreasing Australian birth-rate might be as much the token of a wise restraint as of a weakening national vitality. Probably it is not; but it might be. We have little occasion for anxiety if the criminal aggregation of the people in the coastal cities were ended. It is in the cities, not in the bush, that the national fibre is being in a hundred ways slackened and destroyed. No one, acquainted with the every-day heroism displayed by our agricultural and pastoral and mining pioneers, can have the least doubt of the stability of the nation if the Men on the Land are helped and encouraged as they deserve to be helped and encouraged.

The making of Australia proceeds, according to the previous argument, without the binding influence of religion. All the more reason, then, to encourage the growth of nascent patriotic sentiment, and to pay attention to the development of individual character. Patriotism may have little or no logical warrant, but while it remains a natural instinct it justifies itself. Yet the future of Australia depends in the last resort neither upon the lessening religious force nor upon the increasing patriotic force: it rests upon the character of Australia's inhabitants. If it be the pride of every Australian boy to become a better man than his father, of every Australian girl to become a better woman than her mother, of every Australian father and mother to rear children better than themselves, both the individual and the nation will surely have their reward.

1899

HENRY LAWSON

If I Could Paint,

And were still an Australian, I don't think I'd worry too much about old masters, sunset studies, or even horses; you can study and enjoy real sunset effects any day and from almost anywhere — University Park for preference and convenience; and Australia is already smothered by the horse. Sunlight and scenery endure, and there are plenty to paint them, but types and classes are passing away or changing rapidly in Australia. I'd be prouder of a picture like 'Breaking the News' than of a hundred exquisite alleged studies in the nood, which, as they are, are rather less satisfactory than a study in the latest Paris fashion would be. (The most beautiful studies in the nude are of children; but go to Manly Beach any summer day for the real thing — with the moving grace and laughter thrown in.) I'd long to be able, and give many years if need be, to learn to set the miner's table as it is in the picture. To lay the coarse cloth, the common knife and fork and cottage crockery, put the miner's meal (for he is late) between two plates on the white hob, keep the kettle 'on the bile', make the young wife start out of the canvas as she meets the blow — catch up the child — Oh! that first gesture and cry of the widowed: 'My child! my child! your father — ' The startled, painful, suddenly wild and entreating look in her eyes, that read the worst, like a flash, in the eyes of the other, ere the other can speak. The hand thrust forward as to ward off a blow and entreat mercy (as a young wife might throw her hands forward when a husband, drink-maddened, raises his hand to her for the first time) while the heart jumps from its place to settle back slowly with a chill empty life-long heartache in it — or never to beat again. To paint the old bearded digger as he is, to put the catch in *your* throat, as it is in his; to make *your* 'cynical' mouth twitch as his does under his grizzly beard. To lay his big, rough, clay-stained hand on the poor girl-widow's shoulder, gently as a sister's but with the great heart of a man trembling in it. Such a scene as the man who saw it first, or conceived it, *had* to paint or write, were he artist or no. To show the world how it suffers, that it may not eat its own heart so much in fancied grief.

A picture has a greater holt and a more lasting impression on the mind of the people than printed words, especially in these days, when picture printing has been brought to such perfection and copies of a great painting can be scattered broadcast. A painting is dumb, but type is dumber as far as speaking to the heart of the people is concerned.

My ambition would be to paint Australia as it is, and as it changes: pictures that Australians could look *through* — and through a mist of tears, perhaps — back into their pasts: pictures that Australians could look through onward to a brighter and nobler future. Pictures that the 'careless' joker might stand in front of and chuckle comfortably to himself, and feel less lonely and cynical in his heart than careless jokers are apt to feel. Pictures that might soften hard eyes and mouths, and so ease hard hearts. Pictures showing the best and noblest sides of human nature, so that the world might keep its faith in it, and love it, or, failing that, be more charitable and tolerant towards it. Pictures showing the worst side of humanity, the poverty, misery and squalid vice, that men might hate the greed and selfishness that causes it all. Pictures that would bring hot tears to the eyes and fire the hearts of men. And pictures that would make men laugh more and be cheerful in our time.

And if I went to Europe it would be to learn to paint Australian, not old-world, scenes — the old-world born can do that better than we. A Dutch tavern scene looks picturesque to us — probably on account of the costumes mostly — and is restful to our eyes and therefore good to have in our galleries. A real Dutch tavern scene mightn't be any more picturesque otherwise than our own haggard threepenny bar, but — Anyway, Van de Velde can paint all our Dutch tavern scenes for us.

Pictures of our threepenny bars might set men wishing for a different style of pub, and a different fashion in drinking. The narrow bar — for most things made by men are narrow and haggard in this thin-faced time of ours; no seat, except perhaps a ledge under the window (for seats also, like verandahs, have narrowed and disappeared) for it is only intended that men should stand in front of a bar, and drink as long as they can pay for it, and then go away; the dingy little 'parlours' are for the accommodation of 'molls' and their acquaintances. The unpicturesque, unredeemed guzzling on one side and undisguised 'business' on the other.

And the humorous side of it, 'Breaking the Law', for instance: a group representing or, at least, suggesting as many sorts and conditions of ordinary sinners as possible, by a side entrance of a cross-street hotel on Sunday or after hours; one stooping down to listen or speak through the keyhole, or giving the knock; make a study of his face — the face of a born leader in mischief or otherwise. The atmosphere of school-boyish guiltiness and watchfulness, with something of the uneasiness born of mature caution or experience. The two or three interested casuals — without the knowledge of the 'lay of the country' or, maybe, without the pluck to 'battle' for themselves — hanging about the opposite corner with a poor show of neutrality, and ready either to stroll on with an assumption of indifference at the sight of a policeman, or to slip across and in after the bolder spirits as soon as a breach is made. The population of the alley in sympathy, and aiding and abetting, maybe, with advice and signals. All human in our times. And, as a companion picture, the bar dimly lighted by a point of gas, or in the dusk behind drawn blinds. An air as of schoolboys safe in hiding and enjoying stolen fruits after an orchard-robbing expedition, yet alert and ready for a surprise; the irrepressible wink and the soulful grin of the jokers. The one or two dead-earnest, matter-of-fact characters — generally small contractors or bosses, who take everything (drink included) as seriously as they do their jobs and the 'men'.

All human.

The Saturday afternoon drunk who gets drunk by accident — as we all do if we do it at all — who has lost his mates, or is temporarily parted from them, and has passed the point when he'll either go home with the bulk of his wages or make a night of it; see him with his back to a support, solemnly arguing or putting the case to himself, and striking off the main points (for or against) with one fore-finger across the other. The boozers' boat on Saturday night. And — well, it's a pity that there is so much humour, wit, and sympathy in drinking. Isn't it? …

Paddy's Market, Saturday night — a world of types, humour, pathos, and tragedy there. The usual haggard-featured, temper-and-voice-spoilt mother, going from one entrance to another of the markets: a boarding-house keeper, with two or three grown-up, white-shirted, stand-up-and-turn-down-collared (mother does all their linen herself) straw-hatted, cigarette-smoking sons (boarding at home and paying twelve or fifteen shillings a week), aping men-about-town in King Street to-night. She has the ordinary load of Sunday-dinner stuff on one arm, and a great, peevish brat on the other, two or three trailing behind, or hanging on to her skirts. She turns sharply, at last, goaded to it, and says: 'Be quiet, blast yer! (that I should say such a thing) where am I to get hokey-pokey money from?' I'd like to paint her and the children — and the 'nan-nan' sons — hurrying past in the background. I'd call it 'Nit! There's Mother.' Where was she to get hokey-pokey money from? … And in the face of Mother Grundy and to the advancement of Australia, the slums — there are miles of 'em now — and the poor of Sydney; the interiors of brothels (where little girls keep the door when 'Aunty' is at the pub, or too drunk), and Chinese dens (for European and Australian types as well as Chinese — the variety of types and feminine beauty would surprise you a bit, I reckon). The Patrol of the Prostitutes at night in Elizabeth, Bathurst, College, and Hunter Streets; splendid types, some of them, and there is plenty of street light to allow of effect. Our civilisation has advanced so that these are no longer shy of light and crowds.

And I would, in all probability, be called liar on canvas and hounded down all my days, and die in abject poverty, to be famous hereafter when the same wrongs, greed, poverty, squalor, and vice are hidden under a different fashion in clothes, and therefore the city is supposed to be pure compared with what is was in my time — as it is now compared with what it was in the days of Hogarth, when folk were not so particular about adjusting their dress before leaving.

The drovers, the teamsters, the shearers, the station hands, the cockies, the diggers — and the acts and scenes of their lives — what place have these in our galleries? I would paint the shearing-shed as it is, the swagman tramping through the heat, and the swagman tramping through the rain (paint, but not 'hang' in Australia); the swagmen's camps and selectors' homes; the bushwomen; the drovers riding home with their dogs and pack-horses after a long trip — on wiry, ungroomed stock-horses and burned brown, and ragged and dusty, and with the patient weariness of five hundred miles of Dry Country in their eyes....The selector — take a scene at random, 'The Last Tree on Our Selection': a great gum grubbed out and that moment fallen; the cloud of dust from the branches: the hard, caked clay flying from the butts of the roots; the great tap-root cut through; the rush of dogs into the head of the tree after a colony of possums long left undisturbed in the hollows of the branches. The selector standing back, leaning on his axe and wiping his forehead.

...A long-ago abandoned goldfield in the rain, and with the spirit of the past haunting it....Two old diggers working the old field over again, pegging out old claims anew (as they would have been pegged out in the first place had diggers been able to see through the ground) jabbing down shafts and following workings with their index fingers on the table — Gulgong...or any of these in the Roaring Days. We have the dresses, tents, cradles, etc., ready to our hand in crude but faithful old water-colours done on the spot. And wild and strange and mixed and 'foreign' enough for anything such a scene would look. Do you know that men wore hats with ribbons to them, and capes, and other outlandish things in those days in Australia? And well-greased ringlets and earrings were common. And stockmen wore strapped trousers. Do you know what strapped pants are? Well, rip the side and 'tween-leg seams of a pair of pants, take the back out altogether and put a new one in of a different colour; that will give you some idea — no, it's not that; get on a horse, draw a chalk-line in curves all round the spaces of contact between you and the saddle and the horse, get a woman to cut out and sew neatly over the spaces enclosed, a length of good saddle tweed, taking care that the colours are something in harmony. Then you'll have a pair of strapped trousers, and if you've got good legs and the trousers fit close, as riding pants should, very natty they'll look. What were they for? Why, for riding in, of course. The old poverty-advertising ashamed patch carried to extremes and made fashionable. Would be a grand thing nowadays when a well-made pair of jeans go behind prematurely, through too much thinking.

Do you know that chignons and hoops are to be met with way out in the bush? Do you know that shearers at a shed, to eyes used to cities and scraped chins, look foreign and brigandish at first sight — principally on account of new, short beards? Do you know — Do you know anything at all about the bush? If all these things were painted and set before your building-blinded eyes labelled: 'Backwood and Prairie Life and Scenes', would you know the difference?

The 'Rescue Party' 'packing water' and fighting out across the plains in the furnace-blast of the terrible drought. The 'Death by Thirst' for the sake of Wool, Tallow, Hides & Co.

'The Ride for the Doctor'. Take an ordinary plain bushy girl — the brave mother-sister of the family, riding (man's saddle, perhaps — shabby, old apology for a riding-skirt) on a rough track through the lonely bush, under dark brooding ridges, on the 'old grey horse' — broken-winded, but settled down to it and running bullock-like; the girl's face drawn and haggard through anxiety and want of sleep, and all but hopeless — whiter in the ghostly daybreak, but brave! and in it the fixed purpose of unconscious heroism. Thin lips dry and set, great tears of fear, bodily pain and weariness dropping from wide-open eyes that seem to have lost the power of ever closing in sleep again, fixed on the distant ridge beside which lie the town, hope, and the doctor. Forty miles from home. Paint that picture! ... 'The Bush Doctor' in the hut....'The Crisis'....The parting between the bushman and the doctor after the danger has passed.

And a picture that should be painted. Plain girl again: 'Sweet ugly woman of the past'. The only one with a trace of refinement in a rough bush family; too proud or too sensitive to live at home, she studies at night-school; she is slave to the brats, cows, 'poddy calves', and selection generally all day, and eventually she is appointed teacher to some out-back State School, or two half-time schools maybe, and 'boards' in such homes as I have sketched, where every sight, smell, sound — every word almost — is repellent to her nature. This girl, by a slab school-house in a dusty patch in the eternal, God-forgotten, body-mind-and-soul-destroying scrub, 'marking-time' before a row of half-savage children, of whom the youngest might be as tall as herself. Paint her in school; paint her at home — and the surroundings! Paint her kneeling by her bed, or in school after hours, arms thrown out on the desk, aching head down, in utter loneliness, hopelessness and weariness of life.

The angry diggers and the soldiers face to face on Lambing Flat, and Commissioner — on the stump speaking to those diggers *after* the first shot has been fired! ... Way back of it all the Roll-Up! on Ballarat. Lalor asked to take command. 'The Night before Eureka'; the diggers kneeling under the flag. The day-dawn fight at Eureka Stockade. Vern ('to whose being conspiracy was essential') marching (some say dancing) at the head of his men, in the night-storm, from Creswick, flourishing his sword, singing a wild rebel hymn in a foreign tongue, marching to battle and fighting in imagination, no doubt, for Italy, and striking, indirectly, the grandest blow that was ever struck for Australia. The meeting called 'to strengthen the hands of the Government', and the doom of bad governments written in stern faces. The scene outside the courthouse where justice was done.

And, for scenery, the lung-filling depths and distances of hundreds of unknown places like M'Donald's Hole and Capertee Valley. 'Grim grey coasts and sea-boards ghastly'. The Darling River rising from far-off Queensland rains;

drought blazing down to the narrow dark band of soakage between the water and ashen banks. The yellow water rising in the branches of trees, and over high levels — where the grass will sprout fresh and green — phantom or unreal-looking sheets of water spreading through the broiling scrubs. ... A camp on the sea-beach, jagged edges and gums softened in the moonlight, mountain stream running down and spreading over the sands, sea mystical — all the world far and faint — faint and far, mates dreaming, smoking and yarning lazily round campfire. And — rest and peace for a while.

1899

SIR ERNEST SCOTT

The Flinders's Centenary

Just one hundred years ago, on 19 July, 1814, there lay a-dying, at 14 London Street, Fitzroy Square, London, a man who deserves to rank among the foremost of the world's great explorers. We cannot consent to relegate Matthew Flinders to any subsidiary place. Judged by the sum and quality of his achievement, by his historical importance, by the spirit in which his work was done, he challenges and invites comparison with some about whom libraries have been written. Concerning him, it is true, the mass of published material of consequence is not very considerable. He is far from being one of the spoiled darlings of Fame. Rather, indeed, has the measure of appreciation of him fallen short of his deserts. But the man who was the first to circumnavigate this continent, who completed the discovery of its coastline, and who gave to it the name it bears — the name which is music to the ears of those who love it — Australia — that man, if there were nothing else to be said of him, would surely have a claim to affectionate remembrance in this, the centenary of the year of his death.

He died, broken — broken — before his time. He had much more to say and to do; it was cruel that he did not live a little longer to round off his work, so splendidly performed to the point where the inexorable hand snatched him away. If anyone should make out a speculative list of books which ought to have been written, but were not, the book which Matthew Flinders had it in him to write should occupy a place in it. We know from his associates how he sparkled in talk. He had lived a life of exciting adventure from his boyhood. He had fought in a great historic battle. He had shared the dangers of attacks by savages, had endured shipwreck, had voyaged incessantly, and was a shrewd observer, with an eye that brightened to the humour of a situation. His friends delighted to set him going, and he could hold his company spell-bound. A book from him, written with a free hand — not an official work published under authority, like his *Voyage to Terra Australis* — a book, giving the racy flavour of his talk, would surely have been a classic of British adventure literature.

But, alas, even the book that he did write, he never saw in the completed form. His own copy of it came from the publisher on the day before he died; but he was then unconscious. It arrived too late for him to know that the record of his labours was at last before the world. His wife unfastened the packet, and laid the two quarto volumes on the bed, so that his hands might touch them. But his eyes and his understanding were by then curtained by the everlasting dusk; and he never knew. There needs no art of narrative to heighten the pathos of that end. It is relieved by the knowledge that in the delirium that preceded the final moment his vagrant dreams were not all grievous. Surely there was a fleeting recollection of joy in the scene that flitted before his mind when he murmured the words which were heard to come from his lips some little while before the finger of death touched them: 'But it grows late, boys, time to dismiss.'

Perhaps the most salient characteristic of Flinders was initiative. From his early youth he saw clearly what he wanted to be and to do; and, taking his life into his own hands, he shaped it to the realization of his designs. He went to sea, 'against the wish of friends', because he perceived that only on the sea could he do the work that lay nearest his heart. He equipped himself for service by teaching himself the principles of navigation, from textbooks, in the little Lincolnshire fen-town where he was born. He himself planned the discovery voyages on which he did such memorable things. Even the *Investigator* voyage was a project emanating from his own suggestion. Banks, it is true, aided him nobly; and the Admiralty listened readily to his proposals. But those proposals were entirely his own. He never waited for Fortune to open opportunities before him. Rather did he force her hand. He had no powerful influences in his favour. He won his way to the front by sheer dint of enterprise, originality, courage, and by his power of impressing those in authority with his signal capacity for doing the things which, he showed, required doing.

And then, a task taken in hand, he carried it to consummation with unsparing personal application. No man on a ship commanded by Flinders worked as he did. When he was discovering the coasts of southern Australia he charted every league himself. He was ever at the masthead by day; and at night in his cabin, he laid down on the large sheets the material he had carefully gathered while the sunlight lasted. Naval men of his period called him 'Flinders, the Indefatigable', and the name was well-earned. With the same intensity of ardour he worked at his book and his great folio atlas of charts, after his return to England in 1810. He toiled from early morning till late at night. His life might have been prolonged had he spared himself, and attended to the warnings which nature gave.

He commanded not merely the confidence and respect but the affection of his men. His letters to his friends and relatives reveal the exceeding tenderness of his nature; and that quality in him is conspicuously evident in incidents affecting his handling of those under him. Friendliness was natural to him. When he commanded, though the service might be strenuous, his men felt that he was their comrade. John Whistle, who was with Bass on the celebrated whaleboat voyage to Westernport, and was promoted from A. B. to master's rank, returned to England only a few days before the *Investigator* sailed, and joined her at once, glad of the prospect of serving again under Flinders. There are features on the Australian coast which bear to-day the names of seamen who sailed with Flinders. During his long imprisonment in Mauritius, his servant, John Elder, remained with him long after the date when he might have returned home, refusing to leave him, until his own mind showed signs of collapse, and he had to be sent away. Some of the best friends Flinders made during his whole life were amongst the French in Mauritius, who esteemed him exceedingly. Throughout his career, this compelling power of personal affection is strikingly apparent.

Yet, in a self-critical mood, he expressed the fear that he had often been too imperious. In one of his letters to his wife from Mauritius he alludes to the habit of mind which the exercise of unrestrained power is apt to inculcate. 'I shall learn patience in this island,' he said, 'which will perhaps counteract the insolence acquired by having had unlimited command over my fellow men. You know, my dearest, that I always dreaded the effect that the possession of great authority would have upon my temper and disposition. I hope they are neither of them naturally bad, but when we see such a vast difference between men dependent and men in power, any man who has any share of impartiality must fear for himself. ... My mind has been taught a lesson in philosophy, and my judgment has gained an accession of experience that will not soon be forgotten.' There is absolutely no ground for believing that the exercise of necessary authority by Flinders on any occasion ever exceeded the limits of just consideration; and the attitude of mind presented in this remarkable piece of self-revelation is to be taken as indicative of that real delicacy with which Flinders habitually viewed his relations with subordinates.

The Flinders's centenary, synchronizing with the visit to this country of the British Association for the Advancement of Science, makes a reference to him as a scientific navigator peculiarly appropriate. His work throughout was informed with the true scientific spirit. He experimented constantly to improve the conditions under which voyages were conducted, to make them safer, and to render life aboard ship more wholesome. Every well-equipped steel and iron ship in the world to-day carries attached to her compass a small vertical rod of soft iron called the Flinders's bar, the use of which is to negative the deflection of the needle caused by the proximity of the steel. Flinders invented that device as the result of observation made principally on the Australian coast, and of experiments conducted on ships of the navy after his return to England. He taught the Admiralty, through a vigorously drawn memorandum, the importance of providing for the proper inspection, storing and testing of compasses, which before his time were so carelessly handled that very often they were rather instruments of delusion than of safety. He showed, from experiments conducted on his voyages, how the barometer could be employed to foretell changes of wind; an important function still, but of vital consequence in the days of sailing ships. He wrote elaborately on the theory of the tides, and demonstrated several methods of determining longitude. There are aspects of his activity which are very little known, even amongst well-read seamen to-day, but which should be remembered when we are paying our tribute to him in this, his centenary year.

The same scientific zeal, passion for accuracy, aspiration after improvement, marked his work in the construction of his charts, and the writing of the history of his voyage. There is in his letter-book a letter which he wrote from Port Jackson in 1802 to the Naval Hydrographer, who, he believed at this time, would superintend the publication of his charts. Probably it was never despatched, as Flinders had drawn his pen through it; he saw a chance of superintending publication himself. But it is worth quoting (it has not hitherto been published) to illustrate the care he bestowed upon small points, with a view of making his charts thoroughly and at a glance informative:

To Alexander Dalrymple, Esq.,
Hydrographer to the Admiralty, London.

H.M.S. *Investigator*,
July 1st, 1802,
at Port Jackson.

Sir,

Having transmitted to my Lord's Commissioners copies of the charts which I have made of the south coast of New Holland, which I apprehend will come into your hands, I think it necessary to write you a few particulars of them, hoping that the occasion of the intrusion will be an excuse for it.

It has been a principal object in the construction of the charts to make them contain as much as possible every information which is necessary to the knowing and safe navigating of the coast; and also to be in themselves a journal of the *Investigator's* voyage as far as relates to nautical remarks. With these views there are a good many remarks scattered upon the charts, mostly explanative of the appearance of the coasts and of particular points and capes. These will in some measure answer the purpose of views of the land, and they appear at once upon each chart in their proper places.

In the track a distinction is made between that at night, or in such weather as nothing could be seen, and the day track, and in convenient places are marked arrows showing the direction of the wind, and by the feathering of the arrows I have endeavoured to express the quantity that prevailed at the time....

To express the weather concisely I have adopted the following mode:

Fine needs no explanation.

Hazy or cloudy: when distant objects cannot be distinctly seen;

Hazy or cloudy: when distant objects become invisible;

Hazy or cloudy: when distant objects are totally invisible and near objects become indistinct;

making the line under the word hazy or cloudy to express the second degree of hazy, or cloudy weather; and the double line the third degree. The word 'squally' is also used in the same way. When near objects become invisible the track is dotted at night; in which case I do not hold myself answerable for the non-existence of rocks or dangers, even close to the track. A few examples of these modes of expression when combined follow.

Another of his letters (also hitherto unpublished) may be quoted here, as indicating the small administrative details to which close attention had to be devoted on the *Investigator* voyage, which added so large a stretch of freshly discovered country to the map of the globe. It is not unamusing. The men of science who sailed with him studied and worked in their cabins at night. That involved a consumption of candles beyond the regulation allowance; and these candles had to be accounted for when the accounts of the voyage were overhauled ten years later:

London,
7 Nassau Street, Soho,
Jan. 31, 1811.

The Commissioners for victualling His Majesty's Navy,
Somerset House.

Gentlemen, —

I beg to call your attention to a hardship I labored under as purser of His Majesty's sloop *Investigator* with respect to furnishing the cabins of the men of science, borne as supernumeraries during the voyage, with lights.

In addition to an uncommonly large proportion of officers for a complement of 83 men, I had six men of science, occupying five cabins, and four servants, in the first part of the voyage, the five scientific men in four separate cabins, with three servants, in the latter part. The consumption of candles in the cabins of studious men constantly employed cannot be (as you, gentlemen, will readily conceive), and was not, less than four pounds per month; so that at the least estimate the consumption in four cabins, was 40 pounds per month. The price at which candles were bought in England in 1801, when I sailed, was 11½d. per pound; but at Port Jackson I was obliged to replenish my large consumption at 20d. per pound; so that, at the average price, the expense to me of five men of science, with three servants, was more than £1 per month for lights alone, whilst the whole necessary money allowed is no more than 4s.

My request therefore is that your Board will be pleased to take this peculiar case of a voyage of discovery into your consideration, and be pleased to make me, in the passing of my accounts, such an allowance of extra necessary money for the men of science as in your wisdom and justice may seem meet; but that if nothing more adequate to the expense can be allowed, that you will order the supernumeraries of the *Investigator* to be put upon the same footing, in point of necessary money, as the officers and men who composed the complement of the ship.

A certificate from the men of science, showing that their cabins were supplied with lights in the same manner as those of the officers of the ship, was transmitted to your Board from Port Jackson.

I have the Honor to be, Gentlemen,

Your Most Obedient Humble Servant,

MATTw FLINDERS,

Late Commander and Purser of H.M. Sloop, *Investigator.*

The pathos of the life of Flinders centres round his imprisonment for six and a half years in Mauritius. I fear that very much of the ink that has been spent in denunciation of General Decaen, for his supposedly-tyrannical part in these misfortunes, has been occasioned by insufficient acquaintance with the real facts of the case. The full story cannot be traced in an article with the dimensions prescribed for this; but it may at least be said that the blame for the long detention of our navigator does not lie entirely with Decaen. His first intention was to punish Flinders for what he regarded as an affront to his dignity as Governor of Mauritius, by detaining him until a report could be sent to and instructions received from Paris. Decaen thought that it would probably mean holding Flinders for about a year. But the stormy circumstances of the time were responsible for stretching out the period from one year to six and a half. The suffering endured by Flinders during this unfortunate time was very largely due to his chafing anxiety to complete his work on the discoveries he had made, and to enter upon a fresh sphere of investigation. He had a keen desire to undertake the inland exploration of Australia. But it must not be supposed that the detention in Mauritius was attended by physical hardships. For the greater part of the time Flinders was living under exceedingly pleasant conditions. He never, during his whole mature life, enjoyed so restful an existence as in the years of his detention at Wilhelms Plains, in the centre of the island. His letter-book, containing copies of letters written after his liberation, furnishes abundant evidence of the charming hospitality which he received from the French people at Mauritius, and for which he was ever grateful. He never lost an opportunity after his return to England of using his influence with the Admiralty to render a service to those of whose kindness he cherished the fragrant recollection.

A wide and detailed survey of the events of Flinders's career disposes one to emphasize less the much-misunderstood romance of its later phase than the usefulness, the courage, the resource, the intense application, the unsparing devotion of his principal life's work. It is that for which he is so eminently worthy of being remembered; for which, one feels sure, Australians will celebrate his second centenary a hundred years hence with at least as much appreciation as we celebrate the first to-day. The literature of maritime discovery does not contain the name of a better man, or of one whose work was illuminated by richer gifts, highly trained and scientifically directed, than Matthew Flinders.

1914

EDWARD S. SORENSON

Christmas in the Bush

Though lacking the attractions, variety of sights and entertainments, the festivities and general gaiety that the cities offer, Christmastide brings good cheer to the denizens of the ranges and forests, and is looked forward to and enjoyed in the humblest places.

It is a time when the scattered flocks foregather from far and wide under the old roof-tree. There are innumerable homes from which many have gone out to battle with the world, as shearers, drovers, carriers, fencers, tank-sinkers, station hands, prospectors and miners, stockmen, and bush rouseabouts, leaving only the old couple, and probably one or two of the youngest members of the family. The boys may be working within easy reach, and they may be hundreds of miles away. In either case 'mother' expects them home.

Preparations are made weeks beforehand; Willie and Jim and Bob are daily discussed, and surprises are planned for them. Their rooms are done up and readied, and the old paddock is made doubly secure for their horses, which, being strange, 'are sure to try to make back'. The chips and bones, leaves, and pieces of paper are raked up and burnt in little heaps; the garden is trimmed up, the house is painted or whitewashed outside, the steps and fireplace receive similar attention, and the inside walls are papered, if only with newspapers.

The sentiments and predilections of the old people in this respect are shared to a great extent by the young, whose thoughts turn now to home and kindred ties more than at any other time of the year, and some will bridge the gulf that lies between them in spite of all obstacles.

One Christmas Eve a girl who had been at service in Winton (Queensland) started by coach for Boulia, where her parents lived. There had been heavy rains on the way, and on reaching Caddle Creek it was found impossible to cross the flood by vehicle, and the horses were taken out. But the girl was determined not to turn back, and she was equally resolved not to remain on the bank. She won the sympathy of the driver and a male passenger by telling them that she had never missed a Christmas dinner at home, and she did not want to miss this one. The men then fastened a strap round their bodies, and, with the girl clinging to it between them, successfully negotiated a seventy yards' swim. At Middleton, some miles farther on, she swam another flooded creek on horseback, and, drenched and mud-covered, she eventually reached Boulia in time to participate in the all-important function.

One of the principal features of the time is the gay array of bushes that deck the veranda-posts of the houses. In towns men go round with drayloads of green bushes, selling them for sixpence or a shilling a bundle; but outside they are cut and dragged home by the children. A big armful is lashed to each post till the veranda is hidden behind a wall of greenery. Even the selector's hut, standing alone in a wilderness of trees, is annually decorated in this way, and the prospectors' camp, pitched where no one passes, and where the usual greetings are exchanged only between the two mates, sports an emerald cluster on the pole for 'auld lang syne'.

Another custom favoured by those who still cling to Old World associations is the hanging of the mistletoe from the centre of the ceiling. Any bush does for a mistletoe in Australia; but the shy young bushman seldom takes advantage of the privilege it gives him when some pretty little creature he admires stands defiantly under it. He knows nothing of the old traditions that enshrine the bough; in his home it is suspended mainly to minimise the annoyance caused by flies settling on the table.

More important than the mistletoe to him and his sister is the Christmas mail, which brings the pictorial annuals, seasonable presents, cards, and letters from far-off friends and relatives. The arrival of the mailman, jogging along lonely tracks, is at all times welcome, but now he comes under the halo of a bushified Santa Claus. The annuals are more appreciated by bush people than by city folk; the whole family will gather round, with heads clustered together, peering over one another's shoulders, while one turns the pages.

On the goldfields the miners take delight in surreptitiously introducing a few small nuggets into the plum-duff — and they do not go round the table after dinner collecting them as some women do the coins. The gold becomes the property of whoever finds it, and it is made into pins, rings, and brooches. This habit of salting the pudding induces a good deal of prospecting, and as the prospectors have to eat up the tailings, it is probably the reason that so many people don't feel very well after the Christmas gorge.

Hop-beer, ginger-beer, and honeymead are also made, and stored away in kegs and bottles. 'Sugarbags' are plentiful in many parts of the bush, and a good nest or two is usually left for December, when the trees are felled and the bees robbed. The beer is made from the comb after the honey has been drained out of it. Sarsaparilla is another extensively-made drink, the vines growing plentifully among the ranges. The women and children are fond of these home-made drinks, but father is not always so enthusiastic.

A day or two before Christmas the wanderers return. First comes Jim, cantering up the track with a valise strapped in front of him and a smoke-cloud trailing behind, while the old folks and the little ones are watching with glad faces from the veranda. Towards sundown Bill appears on the hill in another direction, and comes jogging along quietly with a well-loaded pack-horse, and quart-pots, bells, and hobble-chains rattling and jingling to every stride. The children run shouting to meet him, and some ride back behind him and some perch on the pack. They help him to unsaddle and carry his pack-bags in; they take his tired horses to water, and lead them through the slip-rails, and let them go in the paddock with a gentle pat on the neck. The sun is down, perhaps, when Bob comes plodding slowly along through the trees, carrying his swag, and swinging a billy in one hand, while he shakes a little bush before his face with the other to keep the flies away.

'Poor old Bob!' says mother, 'still walking!' The youngsters race down the road again, and they carry his billy and tucker-bag for him and hang on to his hands as though helping the tired traveller home. They all talk to him at once, their eyes dancing with excitement, telling him that Jim and Willie are home, and that Strawberry has a young calf and the speckly hen has ten chickens. Bob listens with a dry smile as he plods along, recalling when he, too, was interested in Strawberry and the hens. When he reaches the door the smile broadens, and he says, 'Merry Christmas!' and throws his swag down against the wall. They crowd round him, wringing his hands till he feels tired, and ask him how he's been getting on. 'Orlright,' says Bob simply.

Though Bob has 'humped bluey' home, he has probably as many pound notes in his pockets as those who come in creaking saddles, and he feels well repaid for his long tramp and his many months of hard work and battling in the back-blocks when he observes the pleased look on his mother's face as he hands her the bulk of his savings.

The brothers swop yarns till late at night, telling of their experiences and adventures by flood and field; and each has some curiosity to show, brought home as a token or keepsake from strange and far-off parts of the bush. The old home, which has so long been dull and quiet, now rings with merry laughter and glad voices, and when Bob does a jig in his clod-smashers the very roof shakes and the crockery rattles loudly on the dresser. There is an hour or two's dancing, maybe, to the strains of the violin. Then somebody goes off for the Jackson girls, and the Maloneys, and the Andersons, and old acquaintances are renewed — likewise the dancing.

On Christmas Eve the boys go out with guns for scrub turkeys, pigeons, and ducks. Often they spend the whole day shooting in the scrubs, and round the swamps and lagoons; and they come home well laden with game. All hands and the cook turn to after tea and pluck the birds. The bushman's table is very rarely without game at this time.

Christmas Day is quiet, and generally dull — a day of rest; but Boxing Day makes up for it with a quantum of sport and excitement. There are usually horse-races somewhere in the vicinity, or a cricket match between Wombat Hill and Emu Creek. A cricket match isn't very sensational, except when the ball lodges in the hollow spout of a tree or gets lost down a rabbit-burrow and has to be dug out. A kangaroo hunt is more exhilarating. A dozen girls and young men ride out in the morning, and when the game is sighted the whole cavalcade starts off at a gallop, with the dogs in the lead. The mob breaks right and left, and when the dogs separate there is often a split in the pursuing party, many of whom do not meet again until they return home.

Sometimes a horse comes down, or a lady rider, more enthusiastic than prudent, parts company with her mount in the thick timber, or loses her seat in jumping logs and water-courses. Sometimes a dingo is brought to bay in a reedy swamp, or he darts into a hollow log, and has to be smoked, prodded, or chopped out. The kangaroo, too, after a long run, will occasionally spring into a waterhole and fight his assailants. When the whole party have gathered round him with sticks, however, he has but a small chance of victory.

There are many persons in the bush every year to whom the festive season is only a memory. These are men camped in lonely parts, batching at station out-camps or boundary-riders' huts. Some of them have been so long alone that, though they know that Christmas is somewhere near, they could not tell you whether it is two days ahead or two days past. I have often found men keeping up Saturday or Monday for the Sabbath, even within a few miles of a town. The majority of bush workers who have no homes of their own, and no kith or kin within reach, spend their Christmas at an hotel, mostly drinking. I remember one man who rode into a western town to enjoy himself, and got drunk the first night; and it was nearly a fortnight afterwards before he properly recovered his senses. Then he asked the publican how many days it was to Christmas.

'About three hundred and fifty-seven,' said the publican. 'Yesterday was New Year's Day.'

The man from Farther-Out thought hard for some seconds; then he said, still hopefully, 'Did I keep up Christmas?'

'You did,' said the publican. 'You had a roaring time.'

'That's orlright, then,' was the rejoinder. 'S'long's I kep' up Christmas, 'm satisfied. Let's 'ave a drink — and a 'Appy New Year to yer, an' many of 'em.'

1911

CHRISTOPHER BRENNAN

The University and Australian Literature

Jubilees differ, like most things. Thus, to go to history for famous examples, the first jubilee of Queen Victoria was but a small affair beside the second; the colonies were lukewarm — we even hear of disloyalty openly vociferated in an Australian city; whereas the second has become historical for its pageant and sacrament of imperial union, a fitting prelude to those generously conceived, magnificently planned, and superbly executed schemes for 'cleaning the slate', which were presently to be the admiration, envy and terror of an onlooking world.

Well, looking back from our present vantage on earlier celebrations — the Centenary of 1888, the Commonwealth Inauguration, or the first jubilee of our own University — we smile, though not unconscious of their pathetic side. It seems as if Australia were thanking Heaven for having survived the measles and praying that she might not be carried off by the whooping-cough.

But if jubilation was anywhere superfluous, fifty years ago, most certainly was it ridiculous in that matter of our 'national literature'. For here, surely, the phrase was fully applicable which I find penned by a French writer in that year 1902: 'Australia, though scarcely formed, is already degenerating, through lack of a foreign leaven.'

It would be impossible to state cause and effect more concisely. For all purposes of art and culture Australia was a suburb of that provincial town, London. London possessed the finest opera in the world: the greatest singers in the world were Patti and Albani — or our own Melba, just because she caught on in London: the greatest actors, Irving and Ellen Terry: the greatest painters, those belonging to the Royal Academy; the greatest dramatist was — but I have forgotten his name.

An absolute dependence like this was in itself bad, even given a general high standard of taste in London. But when London had degenerated, as it did in the eighties and nineties, Australia was bound to touch shuddering depths of vulgarity. Its culture was a wonderful kind of high life below stairs, where the high life imitated had beforehand modelled itself on the below stairs. Its picture galleries were filled with the dregs of the Royal Academy, stuff which even the Chantrey Fund had passed by; its theatres were given up to Gaiety farces and adaptations from 'the French' (a 'foreign leaven' this, at least!); its bookshops —

no, I must draw the line somewhere. The degeneracy was more marked in this, that whereas twenty and thirty years previously there had been a small group of cultivated men, capable of some action and influence upon public taste, now there was no group at all, only a few scattered individuals anxiously keeping their heads above water.

Such was the nation — be it understood that I would not vainly seek to tarnish the glorious Constitutions or the famous deeds in battle done by the sons of the Commonwealth: I speak merely of art and culture — such was the nation in which a 'national literature' was to arise. And now, what had been done in that respect?

For the twenty years preceding our first jubilee, Australian literature had received decided encouragement on all sides to go ahead and be Australian. It was supposed that you could improvise yourself Australian and a man of letters by simply following your native genius. The writers who devoted themselves to this worthy object could certainly not be charged with dependence on the degenerate culture of London, just as they carefully guarded themselves against all chance of an accusation of going after strange gods — I might explain that this means any 'effete' literary traditions. As Nature had not been good enough to hurry up and fashion a race pervaded with the spirit of the soil, the Australianity of this literature, which largely dealt with and was mainly addressed to mythical individuals called Bill and Jim, was painted on, not too laboriously, from the outside. What ruined the school was that it forgot its main (and only) object after all and took to celebrating imported fauna, such as the horse and the jackeroo.

Side by side with this school was a smaller one, the 'literary' school, as we might call it, which, looking back to the spacious days of — I have again forgotten whom — maintained, in our ruder land, the glorious traditions of Bohemianism, and proclaimed the sovereignty of the Poet. Finally, in a corner, there was a most ridiculous little 'school', which we must call a school in order to distinguish it, seeing that it was often confounded with the Bohemians. It was, as a matter of fact, just a heterogeneous collection of a few gentlemen, solemn cultivators of the Muse, who were forced into the semblance of a school by the need of some audience for their productions. The latter have not been read yet and gather dust among the appalling collections of early Australian literature in our public libraries. A certain presumption in their favour exists, owing to the tradition that they were, at the time, accused, by some very respectable persons, of immorality.

Now, what had our University to do with all this? Nothing of course; you could not expect it otherwise, could you? And even if the University had desired it, yet it could not have had any influence on our 'literature'. For that had been entirely 'corralled' by the *Bulletin*, a paper grown old and hidebound in its convention of aggressive irreverence, and jealously maintaining its monopoly by the artful diffusion of a prejudice against our Alma Mater as a home of pedantry and formalism, and a refuge for causes that were never worth even losing.

Well, all these are old, but not too unhappy, far-off things, and we may now take a rapid survey of the principles which are the roots of our present growth, without imitating our predecessors of half a century ago in their slightly amusing self-adulation.

That Australia became a nation, that a spirit was breathed into the dry bones of politician-made Constitutions, that an energy suddenly awoke in the people and manifested itself in a hundred different transformations — this was, fortunately for us, no merely local portent, but part of a world-wide human revolution. We have got rid of the so-called nineteenth century. In that abominable age the life of man was artificially divided, and not merely was it divided, but one separate and lifeless aspect was forcibly made lord over all the rest. It was as if the shoemaker had determined to make all leathern — a German synonym, as we know, for deadly dull. So low had man sunk in his own estimation at the beginning of this century that he had come to regard his whole life as a mere anxious avoidance of hunger. But all that is dead and rotten and we need not beat the bones of the dead. We have come to a fuller appreciation of life, understanding that the greater the variety of forms in which it manifests itself, the greater the harmony, and the more perfect the expression of the single divine principle manifesting itself in life — an expression of which we do not too selfishly ask the end and aim, being satisfied to know that it exists.

So, as we reverence, with the real democratic instinct, every variety of human expression, be the variety that of the people or of the individual, and arm ourselves only against those who would fanatically subject all to a starved and narrow uniformity, out of harmony with the subtle laws by which we live, we have restored the poor wanton Art to her proper place in the national life. [...] The nineteenth century, for ever aching, in spite of its self-glorification, with a sense of its maimed and divided life, suffered from a bad conscience, and was stern in demanding a moral purpose and a 'message' from art. No back-blocks debating club would today dream of starting the question of the morality of art, any more than that of the relative importance of form and matter — dear old childish puzzles of the decadent intellect. For all these have vanished in the restoration of the old and only true religious institution of art, as at once a pledge and a portion of that perfect world that shall be, when the divine leaven, now working in this crude lump of us and our world, shall have spiritualized the whole dead mass.

Sadly grey and commonplace, I fear, do these principles, thus stated, appear, which thirty years ago, and more, set us all on fire: but who can bring to his daily bread from heaven the same craving, the same keen gust that he had when he escaped from the prison of his famine? The deeper reverence which comes from true familiarity forbids us to speak too openly of the simple secrets of life, and would we, after all, speak, our speech is turned to a babbling. It is not the child that celebrates the mother's breast.

So let us turn, knowing, all of us, well enough what it is that these dull words have failed to express, to our subject of the moment. What has the University done for our now flourishing national art and literature?

Well, to look first at the most obvious aspect of the question, how many writers of genius or talent it has produced, I don't think we can charge it with doing less than might be demanded. In fact, I think we might say, using the phrase as a seemingly paradoxical eulogy, that it has done less than might be expected. The capacities of a university for turning out poets are generally limited to a rudimentary sense of the verb; and our University has certainly not spoiled as many as it might have. But it has done noble and appreciable work in preparing the soil, the light, the atmosphere in which a literature might most favourably develop; in creating a community pervaded with a living sense of spiritual values, of the deeper unity of culture in all its forms, and carrying that sense into every daily act of its life, so that no corner is left for barbarism, vulgarity or materialism. Everyone who has graduated from our University, we might say without much exaggeration, has become a centre of such enlightenment for all about him; carrying away with him from his academic days something more than a mere improved capacity for earning his living, and a gift of platitude.

For this we have to thank both the governing and teaching bodies of our University, past and present.

The governing body, perhaps, most of all: for in their hands lay most power for good or evil. Never have they been seen to despair of the University. Never, even in the muddiest flow of the nineteenth century, have they sacrificed the idea of a University, saying 'Go to, we are modern men: what have we to do with these phantoms? Let us make veterinary surgeons, and, when horses are superseded, let us turn out automobile-engineers: for a new dispensation is come upon us, and these things alone are of value.' No: remember how they dared, under the leadership of him who will always be known as the Great Chancellor, to stem the current that howled about them, saying steadfastly, 'To our keeping has been entrusted an idea, *Universitas* — the unity of human culture throughout all its bewildering phases. Let these new developments be welcome; let them enrich us; but let them not seek to oust the ancient treasures; let them not claim to usurp the place of the idea which is more than they or any other temporal form, old or new. Let us feed the lamp and hand it on undimmed: in honour we can do no less.'

Thus were the vital interests of the institution protected by men of broad outlook and generous courage. And in the more formal and special work of instruction, has not our teaching staff nobly and effectually seconded them? Here, in this University, has a stand been always made against that 'specialization', in a narrow sense, which was one of the symptoms of the nineteenth-century disease. True, every student has had to restrict himself to some branch of learning, since Nature has not given the capacities (or the life-time) demanded by them all: but he has had developed in him, what Nature gave him along with the capacity for his special subject, the sense of its deeper relations. The student of literature is invited to perceive it as a total expression, in each people, of some mood of the world-spirit; he is warned against confounding national life with the institutions it leaves as milestones along its way; above all, he is encouraged to notice the beauty of the subject with which he deals. If we have a national literature worth speaking of, is it not largely due to the fact that literature has here been taught always as an organic unity, without hostile frontiers of country or language, and without artificial chasms in time, so that the writers — the good writers, of course — of ancient and modern days are regarded as being equally alive for the student? The student of philosophy is not asked to accept a system in lieu of experience: he learns that philosophy is just such another medium of expression as literature, the 'highest music'. As for the student of science — you would in vain search, among the graduates of our University, for an example of that theoretic arrogance or that practical unculture which were so rampant in the palmy days of 'Science' with the capital S and the inverted commas.

Enough said, I think: and as one cannot close without a more or less formal phrase, it remains then for me to congratulate our country on its literature and our University on its regents and teachers. I would also congratulate myself on being able to lay down my pen, and wish that I may find it possible to congratulate those who imposed this subject on me, sorely against my inclination, on their thorough satisfaction with the manner in which I have treated it.

1902

CHARLES MacLAURIN

Death

When William Dunbar sang, 'Timor mortis perturbat me,' he but expressed the most universal of human — perhaps of animate — feelings. It is no shame to fear death; the fear appears to be a necessary condition of our existence. The shame begins when we allow that fear to influence us in the performance of our duty. But why should we fear death at all? It is hardly an explanation to say that the fear of death is implanted in living things lest the individual should be too easily slain and thereby the species become extinct. Who implanted it? And why is it so necessary that that individual should survive? Why is it necessary that the species should survive? And so on — to name only a few of the unanswerable questions that crowd upon us whenever we sit down to muse upon that problem which every living thing must some time have a chance of solving. The question of death is inextricably bound up with the interpretation of innumerable abstract nouns, such as truth, justice, good, evil, and many more, which all religions make some effort to interpret. Philosophy attempts it by the light of man's reason; religion by a light from some extra-human source; but all alike represent the struggles of earnest men to solve the insoluble.

Nor is it possible to obtain help from the great men of the past, because not one of them knew any more about death than you do yourself. Socrates, in Plato's *Phaedo,* Sir Thomas Browne in the *Religio Medici* and the *Hydriotaphia,* Shakespeare in *Hamlet* and *Macbeth* and many other plays, St Paul in various epistles, all tried to console us for the fact that we must die; the revolt against that inevitable end of beauty and ugliness, charm and horror, love and hate, is the most persistent note in literature; and there are few men who go through life without permitting themselves to wonder, 'What is going to happen to me? Why should I have to die? What will my wife and children do after me? How is it possible that the world will go on, and apparently go on just the same as now, for ages after an important thing like me is shovelled away into a hole in the ground?' I suppose you have dreamed with a start of horror a dream in which you revisit the world, and looking for your own house and children, find them going along happily and apparently prosperous, the milkman coming as usual, a woman in the form of your wife ordering meals and supervising household affairs, the tax-gatherer calling — let us hope a little less often than when you were alive — the trams running and the ferry-boats packed as usual, and the sun shining, the rain falling sometimes, Members of Parliament bawling foolishly over nothing — all these things happening as usual; but you look around to see anybody resembling that beautiful and god-like creature whom you remember as yourself, and wheresover you look he is not there. Where is he? How can the world possibly go on without him? Is it really going on, or is it nothing more than an incredible dream? And why are you so shocked and horror-stricken by this dream? You could hardly be more shocked if you saw your wife toiling in a garret for the minimum wage, or your children running about barefoot selling newspapers. The shocking fact is not that you have left them penniless, but that you have had to leave them at all. In the morning joy cometh as usual, and you go cheerfully about your work, which simply consists of postponing the day of somebody else's death as long as you can. For a little time perhaps you will take particular note of the facts which accompany the act of death; then you will resign yourself to the inevitable, and continue doggedly to wage an endless battle in which you must inevitably lose, assured of nothing but that some day you too will lie pallid, your jaw dropped, your chest not moving, your face horribly inert; and that somebody will come and wash your body and tie up your jaw and put pennies on your eyes and wrap you in cerements and lift you into a long box; and that large men will put the box on their shoulders and lump you into a big vehicle with black horses, and another man will ironically shout Paul's words, 'O death, where is thy sting? O grave, where is thy victory?' And in the club some man will take your seat at lunch, and the others will say you were a decent sort of fellow and will not joke loudly for a whole meal-time. And ten years hence who will remember you? Your wife and children, of course — if they too have not also been carried away in long boxes; a few men who look upon you with a kindly patronage as one who has fallen in the fight and cannot compete with them now; but otherwise? Your hospital appointments have long been filled up by men who cannot, you think, do your work half so well as you used to do it; your car is long ago turned into scrap-iron; your little dog, which used to yelp so joyously when you got home tired at night and kicked him out of the way, is long dead and buried under your favourite rose-bush; your library, which was your joy for so many years, has long been sold at about one-tenth of what it cost you; and, except for the woman who was foolish enough to love and marry you and the children whom the good creature brought into the world to carry on your name, you are as though you had never been. Why should this be? And why are you so terrified at the prospect?

During the past few years we have had ample experience of death, for there are few families in Australia, and I suppose in England, France, Germany, Italy, Russia, and Europe generally, which have not lost some beloved member; yet we are no nearer solving the mystery than we were before. We know no more about it than did Socrates or Homer. The only thing that is beginning to haunt the minds of many men is whether those gallant boys who died in the war were not better off than the men who survived. At least they know the worst, if there be anything to know; and have no longer to fear cancer and paralysis and the other diseases of later life. Many men have written in a consolatory vein about old age, but the consolants have in no way answered the dictum that if by reason of strength our years exceed threescore and ten, yet is our strength but labour and sorrow. No doctor who has seen an old man with an enlarged prostate and a septic kidney therefrom, or with cancer of the tongue, can refrain from wishing that that man had died twenty years sooner, because however bad the fate in store for him it can hardly be worse than what he suffers here on earth. And possibly there are worse things on earth even than cancer of the tongue; possibly cancer of the bladder is the most atrocious, or right-sided hemiplegia with its aphasia and deadly depression of soul. Young men do not suffer from these things; and no one can attend a man so afflicted without wishing that the patient had died happily by a bullet in Gallipoli before his time came so to suffer. Yet as a man grows older, though the likelihood of his death becomes more and more with every passing year, his clinging to bare life, however painful and terrible that life may be, becomes more intense. The young hardly seem to fear death; that is a fear almost confined to the aged. How otherwise can we explain the extraordinary heroism shown by the boys of every army during the late war? I watched many beautiful and gallant boys, volunteers mark you, march down the streets of Sydney on their way to a quarrel which nobody understood — not even the German Kaiser who started it; and when my own turn came to go I patched up many thousands who had been shattered: the one impression made upon me was the utter vileness and beastliness of war, and the glorious courage of the boys in the line. Before the order went forth forbidding the use of Liston's long splint in the advanced dressing stations, men with shattered lower limbs used to be brought in with their feet turned back to front. High-explosive shells would tear away half the front of a man's abdomen; men would be maimed horribly for life, and life would never be the same again for them. Yet none seemed to complain. I know that our own boys simply accepted it all as the inevitable consequence of war, and from what I saw of the English and French their attitude of mind was much the same. The courage of the boys was amazing. I am very sure that if the average age of the armies had been sixty instead of under thirty, Amiens would never have been saved or Fort Douaumont recovered, nor would the Germans have fought so heroically as we must admit they did. Old men feel death approaching them, and they fear it. We all know that our old patients are far more nervous about death than the young. I remember a girl who had sarcoma of the thigh, which recurred after amputation, and I had to send her to a home for the dying. She did not seem very much perturbed. I suppose the proper thing to say would be that she was conscious of her salvation and had nothing to fear; but the truth was that she was a young rake who had committed nearly every crime possible to the female sex, and she died as peacefully and happily as any young member of the Church I ever knew. But who is so terrified as the old woman who trips on a rough edge of the carpet and fractures her thigh-bone? How she clings to life! What terrors attend her last few weeks on earth, till merciful pneumonia comes to send her to endless sleep!

[...]

Probably what most men fear is not death but the pain and illness which generally precede death; and apart from that very natural dread there is the dread of leaving things which are dear to every one. After all, life is sweet to most of us; it is pleasant to feel the warm sun and see the blue sky and watch the shadows race over far hills; an occasional concert, a week-end spent at golf, or at working diligently in the garden; congenial employment, or a worthy book to read, all help to make life worth living, and the mind becomes sad at the thought of leaving these things and the home which they epitomize. I remember once in a troopship, a few days out from an Australian port, when the men had all got over their seasickness and were beginning to realize that they really were started on their Great Adventure, that I went down into their quarters at night, and found a big young countryman who had enlisted in the Artillery, sobbing bitterly. It was a long time before kindly consolation and a dose of bromide sent him off to sleep. In the morning he came to see me and tried to apologize for his unmanliness. 'I'm not afraid of dyin', sir,' he explained. 'I want to stoush some of them Germans first, though. It's leaving all me life in Australia if I 'appen to stop a lump of lead, sir — that's what's worryin' me.' Life in Australia meant riding on horseback when he was not following at the plough's tail. It was the only life he knew, and he loved it. But I was fully convinced that he no more feared actual death than he feared a mosquito, and when he left the ship at Suez, and joined lustily in the singing of 'Australia will be there' — who so jovial as he? He got through the fighting on Gallipoli, only to be destroyed on the Somme; his horse, if it had not already been sent to Palestine, had to submit to another rider; his acres to produce for another ploughman.

[...]

To sum up, death probably does not hurt nearly so much as the ordinary sufferings which are the lot of everybody in living; the act of death is probably no more terrible than our nightly falling asleep; and probably the condition of everlasting rest is what Fate has in store for us, and we can face it bravely without flinching when our time comes. But whether we flinch or not will not matter; we have to die all the same, and we shall be less likely to flinch if we can feel that we have tried to do our duty. And what are we to say of a man who has seen his duty, and urgently longed to perform it, but has failed because God has not given him sufficient strength? 'Video meliora proboque, deteriora sequor,' as old Cicero said of himself. If there is any enigma at all, it lies in the frustrated longings and bitter disappointment of that man.

Probably the best shield throughout life against the atrocious evils and injustices which every man has to suffer is a kind of humorous fatalism which holds that other people have suffered as much as ourselves; that such suffering is a necessary concomitant of life upon this world; and that nothing much matters so long as we do our duty in the sphere to which Fate has called us. A kindly irony which enables us to laugh at the world and sympathize with its troubles is a very powerful aid in the battle; and if a doctor does his part in alleviating pain and postponing death — if he does his best for rich and poor, and always listens to the cry of the afflicted, — and if he endeavours to leave his wife and children in a position better than he himself began, I do not see what more can be expected of him either in this world or the next. And probably Huxley was not far wrong when he said: 'I have no faith, very little hope, and as much charity as I can afford.' It is amazing that there are some people in the world to-day who look upon a man who professes these merciful sentiments as a miscreant doomed to eternal flames because he will not profess to believe in their own particular form of religion. They think they have answered him when they proclaim that his creed is sterile.

1923

SIR WALTER MURDOCH

Bad Language

A few weeks ago, you may have noticed, an Anglican clergyman was suspended for two years on account of his addiction to bad language.

The vocabulary of the clergy is not, however, the subject of this essay — it is a subject about which I am too ignorant even to write an essay, — but I may observe, in passing, that clergymen might reasonably be expected to be, of all men, the most proficient in the use of strong language. All true profanity is connected with Theology; in all countries and in all ages men have sworn by gods, angels, devils and the sacred mysteries of religion. As it needs a sober man to get drunk, so there is a sense in which it needs a religious man to be profane. Blasphemy, as Mr Chesterton has pointed out, depends on belief. 'If any one doubts this, let him sit down seriously and try to think blasphemous thought about Thor. I think his family will find him at the end of the day in a state of some exhaustion.' Of course, you must not carry this to extremes, and conclude that the next loud and fluent bullock-driver you may overhear is necessarily a strict churchgoer. Still, it remains true that blasphemy depends on conscious or subconscious reverence. 'Holy Moses!' is now a perfectly innocent expression of surprise; it was once regarded as a wicked blasphemy. The change is due to the fact that we no longer venerate the lawgiver as our ancestors did. I remember, as a child, being rebuked for saying something frivolous about Noah, on the ground that the names of 'these sacred personages' must not be taken in vain. Why that enterprising navigator should be regarded as a sacred personage was not explained.

In the past, swearing has often become such a nuisance that it has attracted the attention of legislators. In ancient Athens, for example, there were certain prohibitions: boys, we read, were not allowed to swear by Hercules, unless they did it in the open air. (This distinction between indoor and outdoor profanity seems strange to us; but there may be something in it. If, every time you broke your back collar-stud, you had to run out into the garden before saying what you wanted to say, the probability is that you would never say it.) In classical Rome, again, custom allowed the men to swear by Hercules and the women by Castor. (It is castor oil that both men and women swear by in Rome to-day.) If any such attempt were in our time made to discriminate between the sexes in the matter of swearing, what an outcry there would be! What denunciation of man-made laws! And quite justly so, for if swearing is right for a man it is equally right for a woman; although, as a matter of fact, a woman who swears always does it amateurishly, with a certain comic self-consciousness; as the schoolboy swears to show how manly he is, a woman swears to show how advanced she is.

Speaking of Rome, I am reminded that the present Italian Government has embarked on a great campaign against blasphemy. 'For the honour of your country, do not blaspheme,' is a notice you may read in every tram-car and in countless public places throughout Italy. I do not know what Signor Mussolini's motive may be; perhaps he suspects that, if his people swear, it will probably be at him; anyhow, he has shown a praiseworthy courage in ordering the Italians, of all people, to stop swearing — for they possess a language which is, next to Spanish, the finest language in the world for this purpose. I hope the campaign may succeed, and I am not at all sure that the time has not come for a similar campaign in Australia. I am not sure that profanity has not become a national Australian disease, like drink, gambling and high tariffs.

Notice, however, that there is a great difference between Australian swearing and Italian or Spanish swearing. A Spaniard, when he is really irritated, will curse you for three hours by the clock without once repeating himself; he will curse you, and your remotest ancestors and your remotest posterity, with an astonishing ingenuity, volubility, and vigour. You may object to profanity on principle, but you cannot fail to admire his wonderful mastery over all the resources of his rich, expressive tongue. The Australian is not a bit like that. He shows no ingenuity. He uses vain repetitions. He is nothing if not reiterative. He is probably quite as intelligent as the Spaniard, but you would never guess it to listen to him. He reveals a singular barrenness, a most limited range. He repeats, endlessly, some half-dozen nouns, adjectives, and verbs. You feel inclined to cry out to him, 'For heaven's sake, either reform your swearing, and put some intellect into it, or drop it altogether! This eternal drumming on the same few words is merely bestial.'

A friend of mine, knowing — I cannot guess how he knew — that I was interested in the subject, lent me the other day a book by an American psychologist, Dr G. T. W. Patrick, on *The Psychology of Relaxation*, containing a chapter on 'Profanity', which is the best scientific study of the subject I have ever read; the best answer to the questions, Why do men swear? and, When they swear, why do they use the words they do use?

Dr Patrick distinguishes two kinds of swearing, asseverative and ejaculatory. (These awe-inspiring words are enough, of themselves, to make the subject respectable.) The first kind includes, of course, the swearing which is required of us in the courts of law; compulsory profanity, so to speak. It includes, also, the profanity you use when you wish to impress upon your hearer that you are telling the truth. There is not much to be said of this variety, except that it fails of its purpose, and is therefore rather silly. When a man has to swear in order to convince you that he is not a liar, you are apt to suspect that he is telling you a particularly thumping lie. Even when the man who tries to sell me a vacuum cleaner prefaces his wildest flights with the word 'honestly', I at once jump to the conclusion that his vacuum cleaner will not clean. The honest man is accustomed to being believed, and takes for granted that you will believe him. When he has to swear about it, he shows that he is accustomed to being doubted, probably with very good reason.

The commoner kind of swearing is the ejaculatory, and about the origin of this the psychologists are disagreed. Some hold that it is an outlet for pent-up emotion; and this is also the popular view. When you are trying to drive a nail with a heavy hammer, and hit your finger instead, the short, sharp monosyllable which you employ — and which I strongly suspect that even the Archbishop of Canterbury would employ in the like painful circumstance — comes of an instinctive desire to relieve the over-burdened soul. There is a sudden flame of anger, an inner excitement which calls for an outlet; profanity is the only outlet available, since you cannot fight the hammer. You are like the sailor in Byron's poem: 'He knew not what to do and so he swore.' Profanity is a kind of safety-valve. It is the relief of a central stress; it relieves nerve tension. It has a pacifying and purifying effect on the soul.

Dr Patrick makes short work of this story, which is based, it seems, on false psychology. Ejaculatory swearing, according to him, dates back to a time before language had been invented. In ages when articulate speech as yet was not, man, in common with other animals, made certain sounds when he was angry; the purpose of these sounds was to frighten the enemy. The dog shows his teeth and growls, the lion roars, the cat makes his hairs stand on end so as to look bigger than he really is, the turkey-cock ruffles out his feathers for the same reason — all to overawe the foe. In the same way prehistoric man made alarming noises, and when language came to him he used words connected with alarming ideas — such as the infernal regions, eternal torments, and gods and devils. Even when you say so mild a thing as 'By Thunder' you are reminiscent of a time when thunder was one of the most terrifying phenomena in nature. The French try to make the expression more alarming still by the simple method of multiplication: they say 'a thousand thunders'. The Germans have carried still further this quantitative method, which has never appealed to the Anglo-Saxon temperament. Where the English-man, annoyed by the painful accident above alluded to, utters a monosyllable so expressive that it sounds as if it had been made for such an occasion, the German will say things like 'Alle Weltkreuzmohrentausendhimmelsternundgranatensakrament,' which is certainly an alarming word. In either case, you are using a word for a terrifying idea, to terrify the enemy. The old instinct is too strong for you, and you forget that the hammer is not an animate enemy and is not amenable to terror. Such is Dr Patrick's explanation of profanity, which, he says, can be explained only from the standpoint of phylogeny. As I do not know what phylogeny means, and have no dictionary at hand, I shall not presume to criticize the statement, but it sounds all right.

What I wish to point out, however, is that there is a third kind of profanity which Dr Patrick does not mention, and which, at least in Australia, is the commonest of all. This may be called decorative profanity; the profanity which Australians weave into their conversation like a sort of embroidered pattern. Of this kind of profanity I declare myself heartily sick and tired. If its original purpose was, as I suppose, decoration, it has lost its pristine beauty, and has become merely ugly, barbaric, and disgusting: it is beginning to make us a byword among decent nations. I fancy it is high time we took a leaf out of Signor Mussolini's book. We might start a 'Yea Yea League', sworn to dry up this murky stream which threatens to inundate our daily speech; or, if we cannot hope to dry it up altogether, we might at least, by resolute, concerted effort, dam it.

1939?

C. E. W. BEAN

The Legacy

They gave it into your hands, Australians, when the bullet took them. It lies in your hands now — you, the younger generation of Australia; you, the men of the A.I.F., most of whom are still young Australians; even to the young Australians still at school. Australia lies in your hands now, where those men, dying, laid her. This is not a mere fancy — it is the simple, splendid truth. You have a much bigger task facing you than the Australian Force in France and at Anzac had. It is the same great task really; but the A.I.F. only began it.

The men who would have won through it so splendidly — the men who could have fought it with a certainty of winning — they started out on it with such pride in their country and what they were going to do for her. Perhaps you may remember the early days when they trained — and went away. When they reached the front they led the first stages of the fight, and grandly they led it. They stood where others crouched; they were up and over the top when others hesitated; they went straight for the machine-gun when others planned or thought or questioned.

They began the fight grandly. They established the name of our country amongst the foremost of all brave nations. They made our people a famous people, though it is only a small people; they made it so famous that every Australian is proud for the world to know that he is an Australian. That was what these men did for you — all in three or four years.

But, one after another, we who watched saw them fall and lie there motionless while the attack swung on and forgot them. The great fight went on for Australia — rolled over and beyond them. And they, who could have led it, lay under the moonlight, on the wan brown moorland battlefield. The shellbursts, the smoke and dust and noise moved away into the far horizon. But they who could have fought that battle as none of us could — and we know — they lay far behind, face upward under the stars. Some good friends of the platoon, of the company, came back afterwards and placed a little cross made of biscuit-box above the body, or carried it gently to one of our crowded graveyards. But they had passed out of the great fight for Australia. They had given everything.

And why did they do it? Why did they enter that service? What were they aiming to obtain? What were they fighting for? Not themselves, certainly. No man, unless it be the Kaiser and the great German Staff, ever entered this war for himself. It was different from any private business — no man entered this war to make money out of it.

They entered it and they fought to keep the world (and Australia above all the world) a free place, where men have the right to live according to their lights, provided those lights involve no harm to others, without being dictated to by others who happen to be stronger than they. They know that if the rule of Might over Right became the order of the day, then Australia was not safe — and they wanted Australia to be the sort of place which we think ideal to live in. They wanted to make her a great and good country — yes, the greatest and best country in the world. That is what Australia was to them. That is why they fought.

I don't suppose that one of those men ever died without thinking of those behind him in Australia. They liked to think that Australia was as proud of them as they were of her; that Australians were watching their deeds as anxiously and proudly as a mother watches her sons. When things were really bad — in the clinging, orange Somme mud, when the fatigue of dragging one foot after another out of that morass became almost unbearable on the march; when the cold stopped all circulation and actually bit the flesh from the bone so that many men had to have their feet cut off despite all precautions; when men were almost at the end of their tether and would have welcomed death certainly — the one consolation was to think: 'If those in Australia knew, how pitiful and how proud they would be.' Many a man lying out there at Pozières or in the low scrub at Gallipoli, with his poor tired senses barely working through the fever of his brain, has thought in his last moments: 'Well — well — it's over; but in Australia they will be proud of this.'

It is the loss of those men, beyond all question, that is Australia's loss in this war. The money — the material — is nothing, simply nothing. With a trifling effort we can replace all that — if we did not we should scarcely miss it. But we can never bring back those 60,000 men. In the midst of the work which they began so grandly they were cut off — the very best men our young country had; these that we could so ill spare — the sort of men of whom this vast Australia, with its tiny population, wanted all that it could possibly get. Australia wanted all its population to be of that kind — and more. And it lost them when their work was only begun. Who is there to go on with their work and to give them what they died for?

Only you — the younger generation of Australia. No one else can do it. If there is to come about what they fought for, you must do it. Otherwise they will have died in vain. They handed that work on to you; when they fell dying they left it in your hands — yours and ours who survived them. What are you going to do about it? You will put up a memorial to them — a memorial which will enclose for ever the sacred relics of their fighting and the treasured, precious pictures of their sacrifice. A history of it will be written to crystallise for all time the greatest incident in Australian history — this first revelation of the Australian character. But their work — the work they left unfinished; the making of Australia into such a place as they would have wished to make it; the making of Australia, this country that they died for — who is going to do it? They cannot do it now — the home return that they looked forward to will never come; they will never see the smiling faces, the bright cities, the laughter, the cheers, the gay hand-waving which they pictured to themselves again and again in their yellow, soppy, muddy, shell-hole trenches. Those things are not for them. They will not return to help to make up the country which they loved and longed for. Who is going to make of it the country they wished to see?

It is you — the younger Australians — even the boys and girls of Australia. You or no one.

I know that they often dreamed and dreamed of the country that they would make of her. For example, there was one youngster who was a very, very fine platoon commander. He knew his men through and through. And the more he knew them the more he was filled with the same idea which has impressed hundreds of Australians here: that anything could be made of Australia.

He used to dream of what he could help to make of Australia. In the long hours of the night at Fleurbaix, when the white flares shot from behind the German parapet opposite and stooped like graceful, glinting lilies over No-man's-land, it was not these that he saw.

A patch of unkempt white wet grass was vignetted for twenty seconds till the thing fell smouldering into it, half extinguished. It lay there a few instants and died. The sandbags sprang into glaring white against the sky, and then the deep shadow of the trench rose as the flare fell and consumed them; but his eyes saw only a land of sunshine — of green and gold. A German machine-gun and then another chirruped out like a pair of canaries, ran along in step for a minute, and then died in a few resentful outbursts. The night was quiet again. And all the while this boy leaned against the parapet and thought: 'What can we make of Australia? When we get back…? What cannot we make of Australia?'

When he went on his short leaves from the front he used to go to any place where he thought he could pick up knowledge which would be useful for Australia — to Bournville chocolate works to find out how a factory could be run; to Liverpool to see how great mail steamers could be received; to model villages, model houses, model gardens, to see how his country and its homes might be made beautiful.

And then a German machine-gun laid him low, near Passchendaele. The head that held all that knowledge for Australia lay in the vile mud of a Broodseinde shell-crater. In the dawn, like thousands upon thousands of others, with the glowing light under the yellowing sky and the ragged grey clouds just showing through the cold vapour of vanishing dusk, that bright life with all its plans for Australia flickered out.

That is the loss to Australia. Who is going on with that work for her? Who is going to finish the fight which he began?

You — the young people of Australia. You, or no one.

1919

FREDERIC WOOD JONES

Of a Horse Muster

There is a peculiar quality in vast open spaces. When at sea we are used to seeing the same scene all round us, we are accustomed to the line of the horizon completely encircling us. As one would say in more accepted fashion, the sky meets sea all round. But we are not so familiar with the landscape in which sky meets earth all round. We do not often wander in places where great stretches of the earth's surface are as level as the sea. One traveller in desert places has described the effect produced by a completely encircling land horizon as the feeling of being in the centre of a vast gramophone record. For me the presence of a complete land horizon has always produced the feeling of being on the very top of the earth. It ever seems that beyond the line at which earth meets sky all round, the earth sloped downwards on every hand. This impression begets another. There is always the feeling that by journeying one will certainly see something different beyond the line at which the view ahead is arrested. When travelling across Illusion Plains on the Birdsville track there is an ever-present longing to get beyond the next ridge, for on the other side will surely be a change of scene. But the ridge is never passed — it is the rim of the gramophone disk which moves with us — and the longed-for change of scene does not come until the whole great pilgrimage of the Plains is done.

Exploration has its romances in every land; but the terrors of the jungle, the danger of wild beasts and the perils of mountain peak and flooded stream seem to me as mere exciting experiences in a sporting adventure compared with the horror of the endless journey towards the land horizon, faced by Australian pioneers. Treeless, waterless, pitiless and seeming unending are these gibber plains. Without incident, without stirring experience, save a constant aching uncertainty as to what lay beyond that line ahead; such was their exploration. Of all flat solitudes I think the gibber plains have precedence in terror. The hot and shining gibber stones packed close like an uncemented mosaic pavement, the water mirage which the fierce sun calls forth, and in which great lakes of glistening wave-stirred water are ever waiting at that deadly line ahead; that is the picture which may make real to anyone what the verb 'to perish' meant to the pioneers. The gibber plains, the seeming top of the world, are still terrible. Even the motor cannot deprive them of their desolate awfulness.

There is another type of plain which gives an encircling land horizon, but wears a far more kindly aspect, since it produces vegetation instead of that unending series of small flat stones laid in the haphazard, but regular, pavement known as gibber. To the cattle man, if to few others, the blue bush plains mean much. Endless miles of a restful misty blue, the blue of lavender bushes knee high, a sea of peaceful bloom which rests upon the inhospitable floor of sand and stone — such are the blue bush plains.

Far away across the blue bush there is a little cloud of dust. To a townsman's eye it is nothing more. To those who live upon the plains, and have the long sight of folk who live in wide spaces, it means the advent of a mob of horses rounded up from the three thousand square miles of Australia, which compose one great unfenced cattle-run. Three thousand square miles of country is large as a farm is reckoned in other lands, but it is not large for a holding in the land of blue bush. Over these wide plains roam cattle and horses. Beef is the product of the blue bush, and cattle are the first consideration; but horses run on all the wide limits of the plains, and from the run they must at intervals be rounded up and mustered and brought in to the stockyards. The little cloud of dust in the distance heralds the advent of a mob of bush horses, born and bred in the wild, and which have not yet dreamed of bridle or bit, or thought to have man as a master. Before long, the cloud of dust is seen to be definitely towards us, and in front of the dust there may be distinguished, every now and again, a man on horseback who leads the mob. Later, upon either side of the cloud, other figures may be seen as they wheel this way and that as some horse attempts to break from the mob and return to the wild. Five hundred bush-bred horses, led by a man on a horse, flanked by two more men, and pressed on by other two, come neighing and nervous across the plain and to the stockyard. A moment or two, and all is noise and neighing and dust. The whole mob has swept across the plains and is upon us, for although the dust-cloud seemed to move so slowly when first we saw it, it has taken form and enveloped us while we are still debating as to who is in the lead and who is behind with the pack-horses. All the animals in this moving, sounding mass must be brought to face the stockyard rails; they must be rounded up and held outside the yard before the more leisurely, but even more exacting, business of yarding and drafting is done. But most of the horses are wild animals, and the stockyard is to them a threat and a danger. There is an incessant neighing and whinnying; every horse is vocal, every neigh is answered, and it is easy to see that the whole mob is actuated by impulses initiated and correlated by the voicing of emotions present in them all.

In the whole excited mass there are five hundred horses which until now have known no restraint — their restraint now consists of only four mounted men. They may fidget, and kick, and bite, and neigh, but they are held — held by nothing more than four of their own kind each with a man astride. But they are held only until some psychological thing runs as a wireless message through the mob, and with a neighing and a kicking the whole dense mass breaks. It refuses to face the rails; a something is communicated to the whole packed mass of horses, and in a moment there is a break for the open plains.

Now watch the progress of this instantly communicated determination to dash for liberty. The mob breaks, and as it breaks the watchful men on its flanks turn their horses towards the quarter whence the trouble comes. There is a flying of dust, and a wild rush directly for the open and away from the stockyard rails. On the one hand are wild, fit, untrammelled bush-horses dashing for liberty, on the other there are trained men mounted on, maybe, tired station-horses. There may be a wide stampede. Dust flies far over the plain, but the result is ever the same — the station horse with the man astride outwits the wild-horse leader, and the mob is pressed together again, once more to face the stockyard rails. Surely this is a wonderful thing. The finest stallion in the mob will lead the whole crowd of horses straight for the open — one horse will be the instantly recognized leader of five hundred. He is unimpeded by a rider, he is perhaps a far superior horse to the one on which the man rides, and he may have a good start and a wholehearted desire to be away.

The chase may be a long one; but the man on the horse will head him and turn him back. The performance may be repeated many times — the result is always the same: the horse, handicapped by the weight of a man, but urged on by a man's will, and guided by a man's brain, will win. What the horse with the horse's brain can get out of its body is not so good as that which a man with a man's brain can get out of a horse's body, even though the horse has to carry the dead weight of the man. A horse with a man's brain, one thinks, would be a great racer, and the sons of Ixion, maybe, were such.

Evidently even the merest physical abilities of an anatomical body are not to be measured in terms of muscle and bone and tendon. What we *can* do is what we *will* do. And perhaps we can do better than that. A man's brain can make a horse capable of better action than that which its own brain can call forth. In some ages philosophers have fancied that man himself is capable of better things than those his own immediate and unguided dictates prompt. And it may be that it is so.

1924

NORMAN LINDSAY

The Question of Ned Kelly's Perfume

As I live outside the postal delivery area, which also includes delivery of the daily newspaper, I rarely see one, unless it arrives as tradesmen's wrapping paper. It was, therefore, only by the courtesy of my butcher that I read of Mr Sydney Baker's stigmatisation of Ned Kelly as a homosexual which so justly outraged the citizens of Jerilderie, a township which reveres Ned as its national hero.

I have not read Mr Baker's work on the new Australian Language, which contains his assumptions of Ned Kelly's homosexuality, but if, as I understand, it is based on the use of perfume by Ned; and that the Gang was given to selecting each other as dance partners, then Mr Baker is accusing a very large section of the male population of the Kelly era as homosexuals.

I was born in that era, being, I think, about the age of eight when Ned was hanged, but I am not to be relied on in respect of dates. And I don't think any trial at law, before or since that of Ned Kelly, has taken possession of the Australian people with such a passionate intensity. It touched on a content of the national ego which is as potent today as in Ned Kelly's time, and that is the amalgam of reckless man and dangerous man, which becomes heroic man when a people is threatened by war or conflict with other nations. This is in part the theme of Douglas Stewart's superb verse drama *Ned Kelly*.

And no section of the population of this country was more obsessed by the exploits of the Kelly Gang than the small boys of my generation. With us the eternal game of cops and robbers became that of Police and Bushrangers. We played it to the exclusion of all other diversions, though with considerable grudging from the junior members of my nonage, of which I was one, for we were forced to sustain the role of police, while our elders took over that of the Kelly Gang, who, with the unerring marksmanship of cork-popping pistols, shot down the ignoble police to a man.

We had the whole saga of the Kelly Gang from my father's groom, Dennis Denny, who claimed to possess Dan Kelly's saddle, though how he came to inherit this historic relic was not revealed. I see him now, seated on the chaff bin, surrounded by an admiring group of small boys, while he recounts to us how the police would have had Kate Kelly for what that era solemnised as a fate worse than death, and of how Dan Kelly, nobly defending his sister's honor, shot a policeman in the arm. Or was it that the policeman shot himself in the arm in order to prove a case of criminal assault against Dan, forcing him to take to the bush and join his big brother Ned, who had already fled there to escape a pumped-up charge of horse-stealing by the malignant police?

I have reverted here to the biographical, as it is essential to refuting the charge against Ned Kelly of homosexuality because he used perfume. Nearly all men of that era, irrespective of class, used perfume. My father, an Irishman, a horse and buggy doctor, and as dominant a male as ever wore whiskers, always finished off his morning toilet by dabbing his handkerchief freely with perfume. When my parents gave a dinner party it was the men guests who loaded the atmosphere with perfume and hair oil. It was, in fact, almost a male prerogative, for women, or those who classified themselves as ladies, used very little perfume. At most, a lady dressing for any social event dabbed a little eau-de-cologne behind her ears. A woman who overdid the use of a scent bottle was considered 'fast'.

Men had other rituals which if practised today would make them suspects of a sexual kink. They wore a considerable amount of jewellery, heavy signet rings, jewelled tie-pins, watch-chains form which dangled lockets, medals, charms, and other trinkets. Also they wore flowers in the button-hole, nosegays they called them, and some perfectionists, to keep the flowers fresh, had their stems inserted into a small bottle of water fastened by clips under the lapel.

Here I have dealt only with the gentry. Let me turn, then, to the toilet of one of our many grooms, for, like most tolerable decent small boys of that era, the stable was for me a chosen domicile within the home and the company of grooms preferable to that of other members of the home circle. The groom I have in mind was a notable member of the local football team, and, in his own estimation, an amorist of distinction among the professional tarts from Ballarat who frequently weekended at a sort of bordello run by old Jimmy Ah Wah at our Chinese camp. Herewith is his Saturday night's toilet, for that was the week's gala night, when shops and pubs remained open late. It began with a stiffly starched white shirt, a polo collar, and a narrow, red tie fastened to his shirtfront with a brass clip. He then inserted his stockinged feet into a pair of bell-bottomed pants which were too skintight at the knees to permit the passage of boots. His boots were very elaborate, with high heels, decorative toecaps, and brass lace-up tags. His coat was of the flash pattern known as a ducktail, because it had two buttons designed to cock its tail upwards, while its very small lapels made another class distinction from the long-tailed coats of the gentry with their wide spread of lapels. But the culmination of his toilet was the way he brushed his well-oiled hair. This was parted at the side and brushed down in a curve over his forehead. With that he placed a forefinger about midway on the curve and brushed the ends of the hair upwards in a curve over his finger. When this was adjusted to his satisfaction he carefully inserted into the curve the tail feathers of a drake to preserve its upward curl. His high-crowned boxer hat was adjusted about an inch above it so that the brim should protect this final perfection of his toilet. It need hardly be added that the perfume bottle was up-ended on his handkerchief that he might go forth imposing on all noses an aroma of the barber's shop.

I am not implying a lack of erudition in Mr Baker that he failed to discover that perfume was a property common to all men of the period he deals with, because I had forgotten it myself till he called it back to memory. When digging up material about any past period the hardest data to unearth is that of the trivialities which writers in the period rarely record, because they are conventions accepted as understood by their readers. The reason for a lavish use of perfume all through the Victorian era is not far to seek. Anyone who reads *Bleak House* or Henry Mayhew's documentation of London life during the 'fifties will realise how much the squalor of the slums impinged on all main thoroughfares. Even in those the open drains were clogged with refuse, so that the whole atmosphere must have been equally clogged with stenches, carrying with them the germs of typhoid and cholera. In such a miasma men, hurrying about their affairs, had no other resource but to clap a handkerchief loaded with perfume to their noses.

In answer to Mr Baker's other inference of homosexuality in men dancing together, I have appended to this article a woodcut of the 1870s of men dancing together at a pub. How else could they work off the exhilaration of liquor, lacking women to dance with?

The use of perfume by men petered out with my father's generation. The custom had been inherited from England and the generic cause for it forgotten, since there were no city stenches in Australia to demand a prophylactic against them.

1967

NETTIE PALMER

On Surfing

Have we a characteristic national sport, with all our notorious passion for sport in general? Some would say it was cricket, some horse-racing. Taking Australia all round, though, especially all round the edge, surely surfing is our inevitable pleasure. It comes from the very nature of the continent. Tennyson's hackneyed line, quoted so often because of its wild-watery sound, suggests not one but a hundred of our places convenient and perfect for surfing:

And the long wash of Australasian seas.

Many are the mile-long beaches, dancing every summer with the coloured flowers that are jovial bathers. Many more of these beaches have never yet been marked off as the bathers' prey. There they stretch, ten miles perhaps of long rollers spreading themselves forward over white, gleaming sands. Almost one could say there that the stage was set and there were no actors. Someone else might suggest that the eternal tides have had other objects in view through all their centuries. Humanly speaking, though, they do seem made for surfing, here in Australia more than anywhere else in the world.

On the north coast of France there are occasional smooth bays, shapely as a pearl-shell. These are crowded with neat, bright bathing-boxes, and their languid, lovely waves are enjoyed for two or three months in the year. Between these infrequent bays are miles of every sort of coast — green, sheer cliffs, harbours, honeycombed with little islands, everything in fact except surf-beaches.

Take another place, the Canary Islands. Somehow you would expect the Atlantic to deal handsomely with Teneriffe. But no; although the water is beautiful enough, the beaches are impossible — all steep shale and shingle. It seems that Mount Teneriffe's past was not all it should have been. And there is the Mediterranean, that brimming lake, almost tideless, where a poet can write:

I swam far out in to the bay
Where the waves laughed warm and clear.

It has bays and crags of every sort of loveliness, with no deep-sea dangers as of sharks: but it has none of what we mean by surf.

Surf-beaches of any size are rare in the world, and on the whole it seems to need the Pacific to make them. It has to be the sheer, unhindered Pacific. All the miles inside the Great Barrier Reef, for instance, we cannot hope for surf, even in wild weather. There remain the true surf-beaches of our great littoral. It seems queer to think that it is only recently that we have come to use them for what is obviously their manifest purpose. A century ago we would have had to make quite a mental and moral effort before we could venture far into the water. The seafaring nations of Europe, in fact, did not begin to think of bathing in the open sea until some time in the eighteenth century. The sea was there, and they used it to sail upon, but they rarely went into the water except to be drowned.

Then some intrepid persons suddenly decided to see what would happen if they plunged in and let the breakers roll them about a little. It may be imagined that for this experiment they chose some secluded bay. Nothing happened, and gradually the idea spread, until beaches became known as watering-places.

Oh, the waterings that took place, the gingerly, delicate management. You had to undress in a shed, which was called a bathing-machine, there being, in our sense, no machinery about it. You entered it from the dry beach, and then a man and a horse towed it into the sea — not far, of course. Then, if you had changed by this time, you bathed. No, I am wrong. You usually were bathed, by the bathman or bathwoman. It is hard for us to understand what this meant, but it seems that the bathing-machine had a sort of veranda-top in the front, and you could descend into the sea under this cover; and there you were bathed.

Perhaps you had water poured over you from a can: perhaps you were dandled up and down in the water, being held under the arms. Is there anyone alive who remembers the process? All I know is that the daring persons who 'bathed themselves' paid a little less for the use of the machine than if they had been bathed. As far as the women were concerned, they were probably too helpless and hampered by their vast, full bathing-gowns for any more exertion than was forced on them by the gentle lapping of the waves.

We need not stop, though, to giggle over our ancestors. Our posterity will doubtless grin over us, though not, I really think, at our bathing-costumes, which supply little material for a joke. Meanwhile let us surf — dressed now in less than twelve yards of serge. The chief difference, the entire difference between our days and the bathing-machine days, seems to me to lie in the social nature of our present doings in the water. The old method was simply a way of getting wet with the greatest possible privacy. The present method is for all sorts and conditions of men, women, and children together to be 'hopping through the frothy waves' or dealing in a more expert way with the breakers.

Was there ever a sport that gave such a play for all temperaments? One and the same short stretch of surf (for it is usually marked off short to give the life-saving patrol a chance of handling the crowd) will provide scope for the expert swimming on the very high seas and 'coming in' on a breaker; scope for the expert's mother to have a quiet, refreshing bathe among the smaller waves near the shore, even chatting to her friends of the same type; scope for the smallest youngsters to dabble at the edge and get used to the idea of sharing the ocean.

And there is the sheer beauty of the scene. How many sports are there that leave nature as lovely as they find her! Surfing leaves the ocean unspoilt. The beach is hardly broken by a few large, bathing-sheds tucked against the cliffs, while the tides erase even the crowded footmarks from the sand. Then the human beauty is added. We may be a little tired of pretty-girl contests and set scenes of Beauty-on-the-Beach, but hardly of the Egyptian contours suggested by bronzed life-savers in their drilled teams. And there remains the grace of springing forms whirled among the waves. The costumes have never been so natural as now: the bathing-caps, even, look like something made by the sea itself. I seemed to see a mermaid fashion-expert making notes on a shell the other day.

Even the comic (usually elderly) silhouettes that will sometimes emerge have a jolly grotesqueness in harmony with the slapping waves. Altogether a surf-beach is a marvellous pageant of abundant life. To see a human being caught up and glimmering like a whiting through a wave! To see children inventing new ways of tweaking Father Neptune's beard! There is no end to these glimpses. No end except to tramp home along the sands, eyes dazzled, shoulders burning a little, feet light, mind in a sling, and heart — well, perhaps a little more human than before.

1932

VANCE PALMER

The Spirit of Prose

Prose is the language of civilisation — that is, of the three-fourths of life that we spend in intercourse with our fellow-beings. Poetry is, in its nature, a solitary thing. It is not absolutely dependent on an audience. You can imagine a man writing it on a desert island, in the sheer exaltation of being alone. In our desert island of Australia, where there is no audience to speak of, many people do write it: they write it in increasing quantity. And though they would probably like to have an audience to buy their little books, that is not their first concern in writing.

Prose, on the other hand, is dependent on an audience, on civilisation. You can hardly imagine a man writing prose on a desert island for the sheer joy of individual expression. 'To write great poetry you must have great audiences, too,' said Whitman, quite mistakenly, for he was really thinking about the subject matter and the spirit of prose. It is quite certain that neither Milton nor Dante had any illusions that they would have good audiences in the immediate and direct sense, quite certain that they drew no inspiration from them. But prose always draws inspiration from its audience; it will develop when the audience is best. It will thrive in those countries where there is delight in the play of wit and ideas, where there is good conversation. For prose is good conversation brought to its highest pitch. …

The spirit of prose, then, is one of balance, proportion, reason, humour. It looks on with a detached, critical smile at the divine transports of poetry or the more facile emotionalism of mob oratory. It diffuses light without heat. Perhaps humour — that great beast Humour, as Yeats called it once — is its most unvarying quality. That does not mean that good prose should be always seeking to provoke a grin or a guffaw, but that it should show a twinkle in the mind's eye. …

Coming to Australia, it must be admitted, I think, that we have a poor record in prose. The conditions were more favourable for poetry. Or that is putting it too strongly. The conditions were not favourable for prose. We have not yet created the atmosphere in which it would find root. Can anyone believe, for instance, looking back over the past few years, that any Australian Academy would have given Henri Barbusse's novel, *Le Feu*, a prize in 1917? Even if it had, there would have been hysterical letters in the newspapers, and the judges would have had to apologise or resign. Does that seem exaggerated? Well, let it be recalled that Barbusse's novel, crowned in France by the Goncourt Academy, was censored by some Jack-in-office in Australia, and that no one protested …

I have all along been asserting the dependence of good prose upon civilisation, but perhaps that is a one-sided way of putting it, for it may be that civilisation is dependent on good prose. The only thing that can prevent a nation from being a muddle of blindly conflicting creeds and classes, each shouting its war-cries at a top note, is the presence of some medium for a rational interchange of ideas. Not poetry. Poetry is related to the war-cry, coming as it does largely from the emotional side of man. Only good prose (of which drama may be considered a branch) can achieve the work of unity. Through it man is reminded that he is a creature of intelligence, after all, not merely the plaything of passions and emotions; his reason and judgment are restored, and find a neutral region cleared for them, where they can live and move freely.

To cultivate the prose spirit, then, is the work of civilisation. In Australia it hardly exists. There is a lot of political writing, of course, but it is conceived in the spirit of hysteria, not of prose. Take the *Argus* and the *Worker*, for instance. No one would ever accuse them of appealing primarily to the intelligence. Their happy hunting-grounds are the emotional prejudices of their readers, and their functions are those of drums. Drums are all very well in their place, but any barbarian can use them to stir up emotions for his tribal dance. This degradation of the forms of prose is an unhappy thing, and destroys all sense of community. We have the spectacle of a lot of wordy combatants, uttering a jargon that the others do not understand nor want to understand. There is no interchange of ideas, not even a conflict of ideas, for the political writers move in circles that never touch. As for the general public, we have reached a stage when a man would much sooner be accused of heavy drinking than of reading a leading article in the newspapers.

Criticism, too, is in nearly as degraded a state. It has come to be an affair of concern. This is bad for both the writer and the public, for the writer doesn't get the benefit of impartial criticism, and the public loses all sense of proportion. Anything that is less than a puff is considered an attack, for a public unused to criticism can't conceive of a critic caring about literature too passionately to ladle out indiscriminate praise. Twenty years ago there was the Red Page of the *Bulletin*, with its thousands of readers all over Australia. Whatever its faults, it certainly did keep criticism alive, forming a court where books were judged with some semblance of impartiality; it also reacted on the other newspapers, as may be seen by reading the reviews at the back of the books published in those days. But to-day there is merely silence — silence or the megaphone of the publicity agent.

I believe that some sort of civilisation will have to be built up in Australia if we are not to remain a meaningless jumble of incoherent creeds, cliques, classes. At the present time we are living intellectually in a state of barbarism. Poetry is not enough to alter our condition — a poetry that is read only by a small circle. We want a social life created through prose and the drama, both to satisfy our own instincts as reasonable beings and for the sake of the country as a nation. I would say that the foremost civilising agency in Australia up to the present had been — no, not the Ford car — but Lawson's short stories. Here you have something created where all sorts of people can meet on common ground — the artist and the miner, the bushman and the lawyer. No one has the right to ask that all stories should be as general in their appeal as this, but when they happen so they are a lucky accident for all concerned.

The spirit of prose, though, is not an accidental gift to a country. It is a trained poise of the mind. And it is valuable, not only for what it creates itself, but for what it saves from destruction.

1921

ARTHUR PHILLIPS

The Cultural Cringe

The Australian Broadcasting Commission has a Sunday programme, designed to cajole a mild Sabbatarian bestirment of the wits, called 'Incognito'. Paired musical performances are broadcast, one by an Australian, one by an overseas executant, but with the names and nationalities withheld until the end of the programme. The listener is supposed to guess which is the Australian and which the alien performer. The idea is that quite often he guesses wrong or gives it up because, strange to say, the local lad proves to be no worse than the foreigner. This unexpected discovery is intended to inspire a nice glow of patriotic satisfaction.

I am not jeering at the ABC for its quaint idea. The programme's designer has rightly diagnosed a disease of the Australian mind and is applying a sensible curative treatment. The dismaying circumstance is that such a treatment should be necessary, or even possible: that in any nation, there should be an assumption that the domestic cultural product will be worse than the imported article.

The devil of it is that the assumption will often be correct. The numbers are against us, and an inevitable quantitative inferiority easily looks like a qualitative weakness, under the most favourable circumstances — and our circumstances are not favourable. We cannot shelter from invidious comparisons behind the barrier of a separate language; we have no long-established or interestingly different cultural tradition to give security and distinction to its interpreters; and the centrifugal pull of the great cultural metropolises works against us. Above our writers — and other artists — looms the intimidating mass of Anglo-Saxon culture. Such a situation almost inevitably produces the characteristic Australian Cultural Cringe — appearing either as the Cringe Direct, or as the Cringe Inverted, in the attitude of the Blatant Blatherskite, the God's-Own-Country and I'm-a-better-man-than-you-are Australian Bore.

The Cringe mainly appears in an inability to escape needless comparisons. The Australian reader, more or less consciously, hedges and hesitates, asking himself: 'Yes, but what would a cultivated Englishman think of this?' No writer can communicate confidently to a reader with the 'Yes, but' habit; and this particular demand is curiously crippling to critical judgment. Confronted by Furphy, we grow uncertain. We fail to recognise the extraordinarily original structure of his novel because we are wondering whether perhaps an Englishman might not find it too complex and self-conscious. No one worries about the structural deficiencies of *Moby Dick.* We do not fully savour the meaty individualism of Furphy's style because we are wondering whether perhaps his egotistic verbosity is not too Australianly crude; but we accept the egoistic verbosity of Borrow as part of his quality.

But the dangers of the comparative approach go deeper than this. The Australian writer normally frames his communication for the Australian reader. He assumes certain mutual preknowledge, a responsiveness to certain symbols, even the ability to hear the cadence of a phrase in the right way. Once the reader's mind begins to be nagged by the thought of how an Englishman might feel about this, he loses the fine edge of his Australian responsiveness. It is absurd to feel apologetic towards *Such is Life*, or *Coonardoo* or *Melbourne Odes* because they would not seem quite right to an English reader; it is part of their distinctive virtue that no Englishman can fully understand them.

I once read a criticism which began from the question 'What would a French classicist think of *Macbeth*?' The analysis was discerningly conducted and had a certain paradoxical interest; but it could not escape an effect of comic irrelevance.

A second effect of the Cringe has been the estrangement of the Australian Intellectual. Australian life, let us agree, has an atmosphere of often dismaying crudity. I do not know if our cultural crust is proportionately any thinner than that of other Anglo-Saxon communities; but to the intellectual it seems thinner because, in a small community, there is not enough of it to provide for the individual a protective insulation. Hence, even more than most intellectuals, he feels a sense of exposure. This is made much worse by the intrusion of that deadly habit of English comparisons. There is a certain type of Australian intellectual who is forever sidling up to the cultivated Englishman, insinuating: '*I*, of course, am not like these other crude Australians; *I* understand how you must feel about them; *I* should be spiritually more at home in Oxford or Bloomsbury.'

It is not the critical attitude of the intellectual that is harmful: that could be a healthy, even creative, influence, if the criticism were felt to come from within, if the critic had a sense of identification with his subject, if his irritation came from a sense of shared shame rather than a disdainful separation. It is his refusal to participate, the arch of his indifferent eye-brows, which exerts the chilling and stultifying influence.

Thinking of this type of Australian Intellectual, I am a little uneasy about my phrase 'Cultural Cringe'; it is so much the kind of missile which he delights to toss at the Australian mob. I hope I have made it clear that my use of the phrase is not essentially unsympathetic, and that I regard the denaturalised Intellectual as the Cringe's unhappiest victim. If any of the breed use my phrase for his own contemptuous purposes, my curse be upon him. May crudely-Dinkum Aussies spit in his beer, and gremlins split his ever to be preciously agglutinated infinitives.

The Australian writer is affected by the Cringe because it mists the responsiveness of his audience, and because its influence on the intellectual deprives the writer of a sympathetically critical atmosphere. Nor can he entirely escape its direct impact. There is a significant phrase in Henry Handel Richardson's *Myself When Young*. When she found herself stuck in a passage of *Richard Mahony* which would not come right, she remarked to her husband, 'How did I ever dare to write *Maurice Guest* — a poor little colonial like me?' Our sympathies go out to her — pathetic victim of the Cringe. For observe that the Henry Handel Richardson who had written *Maurice Guest* was not the raw girl encompassed by the limitations of the Kilmore Post Office and a Philistine mother. She had already behind her the years in Munich and a day-to-day communion with a husband steeped in the European literary tradition. Her cultural experience was probably richer than that of such contemporary novelists as Wells or Bennett. It was primarily the simple damnation of being an Australian which made her feel limited. Justified, you may think, by the tone of Australian life, with its isolation and excessively material emphasis? Examine the evidence fairly and closely, and I think you will agree that Henry Handel Richardson's Australian background was a shade richer in cultural influence than the dingy shop-cum stuffy Housekeeper's Room-cum sordid Grammar School which incubated Wells, or than the Five Towns of the eighteen-eighties.

By both temperament and circumstance, Henry Handel Richardson was peculiarly susceptible to the influence of the Cringe; but no Australian writer, unless he is dangerously insensitive, can wholly escape it; he may fight it down or disguise it with a veneer of truculence, but it must weaken his confidence and nag at his integrity.

It is not so much our limitations of size, youth and isolation which create the problem as the derivativeness of our culture; and it takes more difficult forms than the Cringe. The writer is particularly affected by our colonial situation because of the nature of his medium. The painter is in some measure bound by the traditional evolution of his art, the musician must consider the particular combinations of sound which the contemporary civilised ear can accept; but ultimately paint is always paint, a piano everywhere a piano. Language has no such ultimate physical existence; it is in its essence merely what generations of usage have made it. The three symbols m-a-n create the image of a male human being only because venerable English tradition has so decreed. The Australian writer cannot cease to be English even if he wants to. The nightingale does not sing under Australian skies; but he still sings in the literate Australian mind. It may thus become the symbol which runs naturally to the tip of the writer's pen; but he dare not use it because it has no organic relation with the Australian life he is interpreting.

The Jindyworobaks are entirely reasonable when they protest against the alien symbolisms used by O'Dowd, Brennan or McCrae; but the difficulty is not simply solved. A Jindyworobak writer uses the image 'galah-breasted dawn'. The picture is both fresh and accurate, and has a sense of immediacy because it comes direct from the writer's environment; and yet somehow it doesn't quite come off. The trouble is that we — unhappy Cringers — are too aware of the processes in its creation. We can feel the writer thinking: 'No, I mustn't use one of the images which English language tradition is insinuating into my mind; I must have something Australian: ah, yes — ' What the phrase has gained in immediacy, it has lost in spontaneity. You have some measure of the complexity of the problem of a colonial culture when you reflect that the last sentence I have written is not so nonsensical as it sounds.

I should not, of course, suggest that the Australian image can never be spontaneously achieved; one need not go beyond Stewart's *Ned Kelly* to disprove such an assumption. On the other hand, the distracting influence of the English tradition is not restricted to merely linguistic difficulties. It confronts the least cringing Australian writer at half-a-dozen points.

What is the cure for our disease? There is no short-cut to the gradual processes of national growth — which are already beginning to have their effect. The most important development of the last twenty years in Australian writing has been the progress made in the art of being unself-consciously ourselves. If I have thought this article worth writing, it is because I believe that progress will quicken when we articulately recognise two facts: that the Cringe is a worse enemy to our cultural development than our isolation, and that the opposite of the Cringe is not the Strut, but a relaxed erectness of carriage.

1950

LENNIE LOWER

Learning the Facts of Life

Even when I was very young I had a strong suspicion that there was something wrong with our education system. Sitting right at the back of the class, I could never hear anything, and the teacher had a nasty habit of springing questions on me just when I was halfway through a green quince or fixing the handle of my all-day sucker.

Now, I'll bet you eight to one you can't remember the date of the Battle of Blenheim. ... Thought you couldn't. That's what makes me mad with our present system of so-called education. If I was Minister for Education things would be altered a bit.

There would be none of this business of being sent to the bottom of the class and having children growing up with inferiority complexes as big as a cathedral. That's what's held me back in life. Just because a man's not too strong on his arithmetic, there's no reason for the Income Tax Department to put that stuff over in the assessments. They ought to know I don't know what it's all about.

My school would equip a child for its journey through life in a sensible manner. Who cares a hoot if the Battle of Trafalgar was fought in 1066, or whenever it was? On the other hand, isn't it better for a child to know the difference between a bad shilling and a good one?

Now, listen-in to my ideal class-room. You sit there and be a pupil. I'm the teacher.

'Well, girls and boys, I hope you've all brought your *Turf Times* with you?'

'Yes, teacher!'

'Well, now, can anyone tell me the past performances of Ooopadoop King at Rosebery during March?'

'Yes, teacher. Third in the Welter Handicap in March, beaten by a short head on the same course in April. Won at the next meeting and was odds on. Looked a lay-down misere from the start. Hopped out from the tape and was never headed.'

'Good! Now, if I had ninepence each way on a horse which won at six to four on, how many taxis could I take home at the rate of one shilling a mile? You can do that for your homework.

'Now, you girls, what is the correct thing to say when a man rings the front doorbell savagely and you rush to the door wondering whether anyone has been killed or the lottery ticket has romped home by a nose and the gentleman at the door wants to sell you knife polish?

'Well, I can see that question doesn't call for an answer. Now, are there any questions you'd like to ask, children?'

'Please, sir, is that right that you embezzled the Sunday school money to have a crack at the chocolate wheel last week and let the poor heathens whistle for their beads and mirrors what the missionaries give them?'

'You stay in after school and, what's more, you get eighteen lashes across the back, you pimp. Any more questions?'

'Please, teacher!'

'Yes, my boy?'

'If A has three Kings and B has three Kings and two Queens, what should B do?'

'That question is a bit moot, my boy. Who dealt in this case?'

'Please, sir, it was B.'

'In that case B should shove a couple of Kings down his sock, declare the hand a misdeal and try again. Now, children, we will go through our limericks. No! One moment. Have all your girls done your homework?'

'Yes, teacher!'

'Gertie Hansen, read out your recipe.'

'Take one measure of gin, sir, half of white curacoa, one cupful of brandy, a heaped teaspoon of good rum, equal parts of French and Italian vermouth and garnish with small pieces of gelignite.'

'Very good. Now what have you done, Doris Duncan?'

'Sir, you take a gallon of absinthe with a pinch of caustic soda, a handful of brandy and one kettle full of the best chablis. Add a little molasses a drop at a time, stirring thoroughly the while, then you pour in the gin gently, a bottle at a time. Shake well and swerve.'

'You're going to make a wonderful hostess when you grow up, Doris. Take a month off. Cedric Bowker! What are you doing there?'

'Please, sir, I was only rolling the bones with Joe Hennessy.'

'What did you throw?'

'I threw a seven, sir.'

'Hop out here and be thrashed. How do you expect to get on in life if you throw sevens?

'You can all go now and don't forget I want everyone to know the Stock Exchange reports off by heart tomorrow morning. Beat it!'

I don't care what anyone says, that's my idea of a decent modern education. And I'm sticking to it.

1940?

BRIAN PENTON

It's Too Hard to be Free!

I've just been reading an article of Thomas Mann's on the coming triumph of democracy. He believes in it. He believes that a great revolt of reason is about to break upon the world. I wish I could believe it too. But I'm damned if I can. That's *my* weakness, I admit. But there you are — I just can't accept the first premise that human beings want to be decent. Even that they want to want to be decent is too much for me to swallow. Yes, I know that's as much a comment on me as on human beings — more, if you like. I'll admit anything, but don't ask me to believe in the essential goodness and beauty of the human heart. I've had a few glimpses of my own. And that, of course, is where fascism begins — in the human heart, the weak, timid, perverse, gullible, miracle-provoking human heart.

Don't blame Hitler. Blame yourself. You're the fascist-monger. You're the one who is crying out for a dictator. Oh yes, you are. 'Let this cup pass from me', you cry — this bitter cup of reason, personal responsibility, judgment.

All right, I may be wrong, but it's the way I see it. I see this ideological war as the effort of the human heart to slough off the too busy burden of being civilised. 'Off with our heads!' That's the cry. And the liberals, the rationalists, are yelling as loud as the rest — for bonfires to burn the books and bodies of the anti-liberals. What a muddle. You talk to a man about the pogroms in Germany, the war in Spain, and think you're getting along fine — twin souls — until it dawns on you that he wants a pogrom too. He wants to beat up all the fascists. You go away wondering what he's got against the fascists then.

Here's an example. A Sydney newspaper published an interview with a young German who'd just arrived. He said Germany was a pretty awful place, otherwise he wouldn't have left it. But, just the same, he said, Australia wasn't perfect. We oughtn't to fool ourselves, when we made jokes about the gestapo, that we were living in paradise. We banned books too, didn't we, and invented a hundred and one puerile restrictions on individual liberty, some of them too puerile even for Germany? A salutary reminder.

You'd think that the people who made jokes about the gestapo would have been the first to appreciate it. My God no. What an uproar. 'Kick him out. Send him back to Germany.' One man, a friend of mine, quite an intelligent chap, said: 'The paper oughtn't to publish things like that. It's an advertisement for Germany.'

'But it's true, isn't it?'

'Maybe it's true. But it's not the time to say anything even inferentially good about Germany'.

A liberal, too.

A group of liberals called on the young German and said: 'You'd better clear out of the country if you're going to say things like this. You're in a land of liberty now. We won't stand for it.'

Funny, but oh how depressing! Like in the Wwar, when you didn't dare to say that you thought it would be pleasant to hear the Beethoven late quartets again.

It's the picture of the human mind deteriorating which depresses you. All over the world you can see it happening — the human animal getting down into the muck again, bawling with intolerance and hatred, bawling for violence to cure violence. And of course it won't cure anything. Really, in our hearts, we know that. We can wipe Hitler out and Mussolini and all the rest of the gang, but what will we do to ourselves in the process? Will we stimulate reason, tolerance, individual liberty? No, really — you haven't forgotten the last War for democracy, have you?

We'll have the war all right. We'll fight for democracy again — under a dictator. We'll churn out the propaganda about corpse factories. We'll get hysterical about the defence of reason. We'll kick conscientious objectors to death in the name of tolerance. We'll ban Wagner and Beethoven and Schoenberg and Strauss and Goethe and Nietzsche in the name of civilization. Whooppee! What a holiday.

Be honest now, there's something attractive about this programme, isn't there? It's a break in the monotony of living by reason — that narrow, disenchanted circle of living where miracles never happen, dreams are frustrated, only the commonplace and hard work are your lot.

A hell of a thing this civilization which liberals like Thomas Mann and Bertrand Russell exalt — I'm the first to admit it. They demand that you should be realistic, rational, free, tolerant, detached. What a business. It requires such an effort. To be realistic — to face the facts — to admit that the world's a round little microscopic pin-point in space and you a momentary cosmic accident upon it — that you've got one chance in a hundred thousand of winning the lottery — that picking up pins or bowing nine times at the new moon won't alter your destiny: what a chilly outlook. And freedom — oh that's all right, if only it was something you were born with, and kept till you died, like your liver. But damn it, as Goethe says, you've got to win the thing afresh every day. And tolerance, detachment, rationality — more bugbears. What does Bertrand Russell say about them? — that they depend on your ability to dominate your reflexes. Really, now, who could be bothered? A man comes into the room and slights you — perhaps by the way he looks at you or doesn't look at you (your heart is so susceptible to hate) and your reflex action is to dislike him at once and everything he believes in.

The man's a bolshevik, a liar, a wife-beater, an embezzler. There's nothing you won't believe. It's easy. It's not so easy to say: 'Hey, wait a bit. He might be more intelligent, more kindly, more honest than I am — *although* he doesn't like me.' Damn it, the liberals ask too much. They expect you to say: 'This man believes exactly the opposite from what I believe, but he may still be human.' How much simpler to say: 'He's a swine. Hanging's too good for him.'

You see, civilization is a devil of an effort. You have to keep up the struggle for twenty-four hours out of the day. You've got to keep a sceptical eye on yourself all the time, on the tricky, lazy, deceitful devils that intelligence has outlawed in the obscure corners of your heart. Even your dreams are suspect.

Let us be honest again and admit that we often wish — not explicitly, if you like, but with a great weariness at the prospect of a lifetime of struggling to be intelligent, tolerant, and free — that we could find some bosom on which to lay the burden of living, of judgment, of personal responsibility, of choosing between good and evil and accepting the consequences of the choice we make. Ah, the State! Let it take over the burden. Let it decide for us. The State and the Dictator. He offers to take it all on his own shoulders, like the church. Give up the struggle for personal responsibility, and in return he will give you peace of mind. It is more precious to you than honour, far more precious than bread. To rest in the bosom of the dictator! At last — sleep.

Can you deny that the prospect allures you? No, don't mouth phrases at me — liberty, freedom of speech, freedom of thought. You don't want them. You don't even trouble to define them. Remember the Grand Inquisitor's tale in *The Brothers Karamazov.* Christ turns up in Toledo and the Grand Inquisitor burns him. 'I know you're Christ,' he says. 'But confound it, if I let you go about telling people that they have to make the choice between good and evil themselves, have to assume the burden of judgment and personal responsibility, where's it going to end? In misery. You'll make everybody unhappy. Here now, we've got everything nicely organized. We do the choosing. We carry the burden. You're really an enemy of human happiness, you know, telling them they ought to want to be free, from mumbojumbo and priest-craft and a thirst for miracles. You never really understood human beings. They don't want to be free. And they want miracles — not hard work. You made a big mistake that time you refused to turn the stone into bread. That's what they want, poor devils — stones turned into bread. You know you really hate human beings. You want to make them into gods. It's too much, dash it all. Tomorrow I'll burn you.'

An instructive parable. Not the whole truth, perhaps, but a pretty big slice of it.

1939

SIDNEY J. BAKER

Language and Character

Visitors to this country from abroad rarely fail to feel (although they may be too polite to declare in so many words) that, although we are hospitable outdoor types, we live in what is tantamount to a cultural concentration camp. To which, of course, there is no adequate reply. Hence, perhaps, the Australian's enthusiasm for journeying on the face of the earth, especially in the direction of Places Where Things Happen, and his sneaking reverence for collections of old rocks such as Pompeii and the venerable piles that litter the landscapes of England and the Continent.

Whatever else they may be, Australians are certainly great travellers, and this is often their redemption. For the fact is that the Briton and the American rarely fail to recognise an Australian if he chances along, and when he returns to this country (if he ever returns) it is usually with a belief that there must be something recognisable as an Australian character and that, as a corollary, there must be at least the faint hints of an Australian way of life.

We have been assured by some observers at close hand that these things exist. Many writers — among them Thomas Wood, Professor W. K. Hancock, that indefatigable word-spinner A.G. Stephens and his *Bulletin* successors — have found occasion to expatiate on the Australian character and on what they deem to be developing facets of an Australian way of life. But since they have spoken intuitively rather than scientifically, their documentation has been sparse. Not until the 1950s, when Professor O. A. Oeser and his colleagues in the Psychology Department of Melbourne University launched an inquiry into Social Structure and Personality in Australia, was a frontal attack made on the accumulation of evidence. This investigation was of great value, but since the fieldwork was confined to Victoria we cannot be sure that the findings apply to Australia as a whole.

There is, however, one branch of inquiry which has reached into the far corners of Australia and been pursued back to our earliest days. Perhaps in no other field of sociological investigation in Australia has the documentation been more thorough, or, at this stage of our history, anyway, more instructive. Inquiry shows not only that Australians have invented thousands of new words and given new meanings to countless expressions which originated in Britain and America, but that, in the process, they have developed a recognisable pronunciation of their own.

It is justifiable to ask, of course, whether this development reflects the nature of either an Australian character or an Australian way of life. In short, is there any demonstrable link between Australian dialectal developments on the one hand, and an Australian character or way of life on the other? It is a matter on which philologists are more ready to commit themselves than sociologists. The philological view is that, of all the manifestations of human behaviour, nothing reflects more accurately both the individual personality and the collective character of a society than the words used in that society and the way those words are used. The sociological view is that such dialectal habits may serve as a loose sort of guide, but lack of statistical evidence puts the issue on a non-scientific basis. And, of course, this is true, because you cannot factor-analyse a dictionary.

But until such time as a national survey of our social structure and personality is conducted along the lines of that undertaken at Melbourne University we are entitled to see what language can tell us about our collective character and way of life.

Australian English tells us many things. In the first place, it makes it quite evident that our environment is vastly different from that of Britain. As we etch in the details of this environment with words that Australians have either invented or borrowed from abroad and converted to their own use, we become aware that a distinct picture is emerging which has no more than a vague English counterpart: *bush, outback, backblocks, never-never, gibber plains, gully, scrub, creek, station, run, billabong, bombora, channel country, Red Heart* and so on. Against this background stand many people pursuing tasks that are as intimately a part of our unique environment as the maruspial. We have found special names for many of these people, either concocting new words to describe them or filching terms from overseas and giving them new applications: *squatter, pastoralist, jackeroo, ringer, boundary-rider, rouseabout, bullocky, stockman, cow cocky, poddy dodger, overlander, bushwhacker, digger, fossicker, sundowner, swagman, hatter, black tracker* and scores more.

These words are memorials to the fact that environmental influences have forced us as a nation to give special emphasis to certain tasks. If we are inclined to forget how unique these environmental influences are, we have a strong reminder in the vast number of words used to describe our flora and fauna. For example: *dingo, kangaroo, koala, wallaby, wallaroo, wombat* (animals); *brolga, budgerigar, currawong, galah, kookaburra* (birds); *barramundi, mulloway, nannygai, tabbigaw, wobbegong* (fish); *boree, brigalow, coolibah, geebung, jarrah, karri, kurrajong, mallee, mulga* (trees); and words such as *cobra,* a marine worm, *joey,* the young of a kangaroo, *taipan,* a type of snake, and *witchetty grub.*

All these words are taken direct from the Australian aboriginals. Our borrowings from the natives go far beyond this. They include *billabong, boomerang, bunyip, cooee, corroboree, didgeridu, dillybag, gibber, gin, humpy,* and *waddy.*

The variety of these words reminds us of an important statement made by the lexicographer Noah Webster in the preface to his *American Dictionary of the English Language* (1828). He wrote: 'Language is the expression of ideas; and if the people of one country cannot preserve an identity of ideas (with people of another country), they cannot preserve an identity of language. Now, an identity of ideas depends materially upon a sameness of things or objects with which the people of the two countries are conversant. But in no two portions of the earth, remote from each other, can such identity be found. Even physical objects must be different.'

The material differences marking Australia as distinct from England are so varied that only the misinformed or the wilfully blind can ignore them. In so far as those differences are reflected in the things we do and the way we do them, we are clearly entitled to feel that we have at least the beginnings of a way of life of our own. Since behaviour patterns are inextricably woven into character, we become aware that this way of life is inevitably contributing to the development of an Australian character.

What are some of the facets credited to this national character of ours? First of all, a to-do is usually made about the accent placed on mateship in Australia, on our egalitarianism, on our tendency to gravitate towards the lowest common denominator in thought and action, on our low tolerance to personal inconvenience in contrast to our extraordinary capacity for collective sacrifice. Then we hear a great deal about the Australian's fanatical absorption in sport, his low-browism, his resentment of authority, his willing acceptance of the near-enough and the fair-average. To my mind, all these alleged aspects of our collective character hold together. They are certainly reflected in our linguistic habits.

To begin with, those linguistic habits are spread with great evenness over the whole of Australia. There is little difference, for instance, between the expressions used and the pronunciation of Western Australia, the eastern states, northern Australia and Tasmania. Minor differences exist, it is true, but for a country of Australia's size they are extremely few. So here is preliminary evidence of an egalitarian levelling. When a person in Albany speaks of *bludging, cobber, furphy, pommy, larrikin, ratbag, ropeable, rort, sheila, wowser, zac* and *ziff*, the gold fossicker on Cape York and the cow cocky in the Mallee knows what is meant. And when the Sydneysider mentions *S.P. betting, drinking with the flies, whingeing, swy, no-hoper, Buckley's chance, hard case, offsider, game as Ned Kelly, full as a goog, drunk as Chloe, whipping the cat, putting the acid on, dropping one's bundle* and *cracking hardy*, there is probably not a single Australian who does not understand immediately. The most important thing to note about these terms is that they are Australian; they do not belong to the language of either Britain or America.

Since we may find some difficulty in understanding how environmental influences can have shaped the development of these expressions (and many more like them), we are confronted with an interesting problem. For some reason, the Australian seems to have a notable capacity for linguistic invention.

I believe that this flair tells us quite a lot about the Australian character. Not only does it assure us of the Australian's sharp-witted innovation and adaptability, which have been features of his life since the earliest days of settlement in this country, but it betrays his restless discontent with the orthodoxies of the English language. This latter point may well be one of some significance, for it is quite clearly a rebellion against established authority. Innovation is justified (and inevitable) when the environment of one linguistic community differs from that of another, but here we seem to be confronted with novelty for novelty's sake.

This word-making exuberance extends into many remote corners of our speech. Consider, for example, such common expressions as *stockwhip, stock route, tucker, pigroot, bushranger, duffing, southerly buster, dinkum, brumby, bowyangs, barracking, googly, guiver, nitkeeper, shanghai, smoodge, bombo, slygrog, skerrick, waltzing Matilda, Rafferty's rules* and *johnhop*. And such phrases as *to poke borak, bald as a bandicoot, no good to gundy, put the hard word on, home on the pig's back, to go hostile, do a perish, rough as bags* and *send her down, Hughie!*

It is important to remember that these expressions are not casual neologisms, used once and then forgotten. Most of them have been long-established as part of the linguistic currency of Australia. Not only do they remind us that in spite of English and American influences, we have preserved an identity of our own, but they suggest that the spirit of linguistic rebellion runs deep. If we suspect that this rebellion is not altogether unrelated to the Australian's contempt for authority, his resentment of discipline, his lowbrowism, we shall probably not be far astray.

Where some observers (particularly Pure-Well-of-English addicts) go wrong is in mistaking the Australian's readiness to pull a forelock when reproved with an equal willingness to abandon his viewpoint. The Australian has often been accused of possessing a national 'inferiority complex'. One of the main reasons is because, in his relative isolation at the end of the world, he has lacked standards of reference, and, because of this, he has been none too sure whether he has any right to justify his habits, his opinions, his way of life. Not far beneath the surface of his uncertainty, however, there is an arrogant and unshakeable conviction that what he has is worth keeping. Upon this rock, the surf of critical opinion from without breaks with little effect. And well it might. For our egalitarianism is not merely a defensive levelling; it is a formidable and aggressive unity that refuses to wilt under condemnation. If the dinkydi Australian uses such terms as *plonk, shickered, ridge, grouse, kidstakes, blue, stoush, wog, Aussie, Tassie, possie, fair cow, willy willy, barney, dingo on, wowserism, digger, good sort, sool on, old identity, hoot, ready up, go crook, do one's block* and *whacko!* he does so with the perfect confidence that, among fellow Australians, anyway, he will be understood. No matter how doggedly attempts may be made to ignore Australianisms out of existence, they continually break through, just as the Australian character continually breaks through. The reason is that both the Australian character and the Australian language are strong enough and vital enough to survive in spite of all the pressures that seek to quench them.

1956

PATRICK WHITE

The Prodigal Son

This is by way of being an answer to Alister Kershaw's recent article *The Last Expatriate*,* but as I cannot hope to equal the slash and dash of Kershaw's journalistic weapons, I shall not attempt to answer him point by point. In any case, the reasons why anybody is an expatriate, or why another chooses to return home, are such personal ones that the question can only be answered in a personal way.

At the age of 46 I have spent just on twenty of those years overseas. During the last ten, I have hardly stirred from the six acres of 'Dogwoods', Castle Hill. It sounds odd, and is perhaps worth trying to explain.

Brought up to believe in the maxim: Only the British can be right, I did accept this during the earlier part of my life. Ironed out in an English public school, and finished off at King's, Cambridge, it was not until 1939, after wandering by myself through most of Western Europe, and finally most of the United States, that I began to grow up and think my own thoughts. The War did the rest. What had seemed a brilliant, intellectual, highly desirable existence, became distressingly parasitic and pointless. There is nothing like a rain of bombs to start one trying to assess one's own achievement. Sitting at night in his London bed-sitting room during the first months of the Blitz, this chromium-plated Australian with two fairly successful novels to his credit came to the conclusion that his achievement was practically nil. Perhaps significantly, he was reading at that time Eyre's *Journal*. Perhaps also he had the wind up; certainly he reached rather often for the bottle of Calvados in the wardrobe. Any way, he experienced those first sensations of rootlessness which Alister Kershaw has deplored and explained as the 'desire to nuzzle once more at the benevolent teats of the mother country'.

All through the War in the Middle East there persisted a longing to return to the scenes of childhood, which is, after all, the purest well from which the creative artist draws. Aggravated further by the terrible nostalgia of the desert landscape, this desire was almost quenched by the year I spent stationed in Greece, where perfection presents itself on every hand, not only the perfection of antiquity, but that of nature, and the warmth of human relationships expressed in daily living. Why didn't I stay in Greece? I was tempted to. Perhaps it was the realisation that even the most genuine resident Hellenophile accepts automatically the vaguely comic role of Levantine beachcomber. He does not belong, the natives seem to say, not without affection; it is sad for him, but he is nothing. While the Hellenophile continues humbly to hope.

So I did not stay in my elective Greece. Demobilisation in England left me with the alternative of remaining in what I then felt to be an actual and spiritual graveyard, with the prospect of ceasing to be an artist and turning instead into that most sterile of beings, a London intellectual, or of returning home, to the stimulus of time remembered. Quite honestly, the thought of a full belly influenced me as well, after toying with the soft, sweet awfulness of horsemeat stew in the London restaurants that I could afford. So I came home. I bought a farm at Castle Hill, and with a Greek friend and partner, Manoly Lascaris, started to grow flowers and vegetables, and to breed Schnauzers and Saanen goats.

The first years I was content with these activities, and to soak myself in landscape. If anybody mentioned Writing, I would reply: 'Oh, one day, perhaps.' But I had no real intention of giving the matter sufficient thought. *The Aunt's Story*, written immediately after the War, before returning to Australia, had succeeded with overseas critics, failed as usual with the local ones, remained half-read, it was obvious from the state of the pages, in the lending libraries. Nothing seemed important, beyond living and eating, with a roof of one's own over one's head.

Then, suddenly, I began to grow discontented. Perhaps, in spite of Australian critics, writing novels was the only thing I could do with any degree of success; even my half-failures were some justification of an otherwise meaningless life. Returning sentimentally to a country I had left in my youth, what had I really found? Was there anything to prevent me packing my bag and leaving like Alister Kershaw and so many other artists? Bitterly I had to admit, no. In all directions stretched the Great Australian Emptiness, in which the mind is the least of possessions, in which the rich man is the important man, in which the schoolmaster and the journalist rule what intellectual roost there is, in which beautiful youths and girls stare at life through blind blue eyes, in which human teeth fall like autumn leaves, the buttocks of cars grow hourly glassier, food means cake and steak, muscles prevail, and the march of material ugliness does not raise a quiver from the average nerves.

It was the exaltation of the 'average' that made me panic most, and in this frame of mind, in spite of myself, I began to conceive another novel. Because the void I had to fill was so immense, I wanted to try to suggest in this book every possible aspect of life, through the lives of an ordinary man and woman. But at the same time I wanted to discover the extraordinary behind the ordinary, the mystery and the poetry which alone could make bearable the lives of such people, and incidentally, my own life since my return.

So I began to write *The Tree of Man*. How it was received by the more important Australian critics is now ancient history. Afterwards I wrote *Voss*, possibly conceived during the early days of the Blitz, when I sat reading Eyre's *Journal* in a London bed-sitting room. Nourished by months spent traipsing backwards and forwards across the Egyptian and Cyrenaican deserts, influenced by the arch-megalomaniac of the day, the idea finally matured after reading contemporary accounts of Leichhardt's expeditions and A. H. Chisholm's *Strange New World* on returning to Australia.

It would be irrelevant to discuss here the literary aspects of the novel. More important are those intentions of the author which have pleased some readers without their knowing exactly why, and helped to increase the rage of those who have found the book meaningless. Always something of a frustrated painter, and a composer *manqué*, I wanted to give my book the textures of music, the sensuousness of paint, to convey through the theme and characters of *Voss* what Delacroix and Blake might have seen, what Mahler and Liszt might have heard. Above all I was determined to prove that the Australian novel is not necessarily the dreary, dun-coloured offspring of journalistic realism. On the whole, the world has been convinced, only here, at the present moment, the dingoes are howling unmercifully.

What, then, have been the rewards of this returned expatriate? I remember when, in the flush of success after my first novel, an old and wise Australian journalist called Guy Innes came to interview me in my London flat. He asked me whether I wanted to go back. I had just 'arrived'; who was I to want to go back? 'Ah, but when you do,' he persisted, 'the colours will come flooding back onto your palette.' This gentle criticism of my first novel only occurred to me as such in recent years. But I think perhaps Guy Innes has been right.

So, amongst the rewards, there is the refreshed landscape, which even in its shabbier, remembered versions has always made a background to my life. The worlds of plants and music may never have revealed themselves had I sat talking brilliantly to Alister Kershaw over a Pernod on the Left Bank. Possibly all art flowers more readily in silence. Certainly the state of simplicity and humility is the only desirable one for artist or for man. While to reach it may be impossible, to attempt to do so is imperative. Stripped of almost everything that I had considered desirable and necessary, I began to try. Writing, which had meant the practice of an art by a polished mind in civilised surroundings, became a struggle to create completely fresh forms out of the rocks and sticks of words. I began to see things for the first time. Even the boredom and frustration presented avenues for endless exploration; even the ugliness, the bags and iron of Australian life, acquired a meaning. As for the cat's cradle of human intercourse, this was necessarily simplified, often bungled, sometimes touching. Its very tentativeness can be a reward. There is always the possibility that the book lent, the record played, may lead to communication between human beings. There is the possibility that one may be helping to people a barely inhabited country with a race possessed of understanding.

These, then, are some of the reasons why an expatriate has stayed, in the face of those disappointments which follow inevitably upon his return. Abstract and unconvincing, the Alister Kershaws will probably answer, but such reasons, as I have already suggested, are a personal matter. More concrete, and most rewarding of all, are the many letters I have received from unknown Australians, for whom my writing seems to have opened a window. To me, the letters alone are reason enough for staying.

*Also reproduced in this collection. I. S.

1958

MANNING CLARK

Rewriting Australian History

It would be appropriate to begin an essay on such a young subject as the writing of Australian history by quoting a powerful passage from one of the oldest faiths in the world. This is from the first book of Samuel: 'And it came to pass, when the *evil* spirit from God was upon Saul, that David took an harp, and played with his hand; so Saul was refreshed, and was well, and the evil spirit departed from him.'

True, in comparison with religion and music, history has not been one of the great comforters of mankind. But our ideas of the past are part of that great enormous attic of the mind which devours everything which looks as though it might help us to achieve what we are all after — 'to be there when everyone suddenly understands what it has all been for'. And of course these ideas have a big influence on the way we think and even the way we behave.

One of the convictions of the majority of educated people in England or Australia is that British political institutions and the Protestant religion were the creators of political liberty and material progress. It was because Macaulay persuaded teachers that the seventeenth century was the decisive period in the moulding of both British political institutions and the Protestant religion that the study of the seventeenth century became the centre of courses of history in the English-speaking world and all those areas which came under British influence in the nineteenth century. So men and women studied that era not as a discipline or diversion for the mind, but because such a study would reveal to them the secrets of political liberty and material progress. Men, then, are refreshed, comforted, and instructed by their ideas of the past.

This study of British political institutions and the Protestant religion seemed worth while only so long as people believed strongly in political liberty and material progress. When such beliefs perish people still involved in the old mental habits seem to be 'darling dodoes'. This is the situation we are now in in Australia. Our ideas of the past are those of preceding generations. They are not a response to the problems and aspirations of this generation. I believe that the task of the historians for this generation is twofold: to show why the comforters of the past should be dropped, and to put forward new ideas for this generation.

First, let us drop the idea that our past has irrevocably condemned us to the role of cultural barbarians. The past, it is said, has made us resourceful, good improvisers, but not made possible the cultivation of the things of the mind; it has left us coarse and vulgar, forced us to accept the second-rate — more, given us a taste for the second-rate, and a rather perverse pleasure in taking down the mighty and talented from their seats, what Howard Florey called 'the apparently endless nagging at anyone who pokes his head slightly above the ruck'. So we can never become cultivated, graceful Europeans; we must remain well-fed barbarians forever.

Our ancestors took a terrible drubbing on this score. As early as November 1835 a writer in the *Van Diemen's Land Monthly Magazine* was chiding the locals for their 'too engrossing pursuit of riches', a habit which he said was 'prejudicial to the cultivation of science and literature'. The English historian Froude was still harping on the same theme in 1880, reminding Sydneysiders of the lack of 'severe intellectual interest'.

'They aim,' he wrote, 'at little except what money will buy: and to make money and buy enjoyment with it is the be-all and end-all of their existence.' In January 1921 Sir Arthur Conan Doyle, who, of course, could claim to speak with peculiar authority on the things of the spirit, made this terse comment to an *Age* reporter: 'It is the unliveliness and spiritual deadness of the place which gets on my nerves.'

It was left to D. H. Lawrence to go the whole hog. After a quick look at Perth, Sydney, and the south coast of New South Wales, he dashed off this account to his sister-in-law in 1922:

> This is the most democratic place I have *ever* been in. And the more I see of democracy the more I dislike it. It just brings everything down to the mere vulgar level of wages and prices, electric light and water-closets, and nothing else. You *never* knew anything so nothing, Nichts, nullus, niente, as the life here. They have good wages, they wear smart boots, and the girls all have silk stockings ... That's what the life in a new country does to you: makes you so material, so *outward*, that your real inner life and your inner self dies out and you clatter around like so many mechanical animals.

Although a few of our ancestors made rude replies such as that of the bullock driver in *Such is Life*: 'But what — good does that do to the likes of us?', the majority were all too willing to confess their unworthiness. Oddly enough, at the same time as Lawrence was fulminating against our lack of an inner life, Henry Handel Richardson in *The Fortunes of Richard Mahony* was pouring out on paper how her father had been tortured by this lack of refinement and things of the spirit in Australia. With more urbanity, Martin Boyd raised the same sort of problem in *The Montforts*, but it was left to Keith Hancock to borrow this idea from the creative writers and circulate it among the historians. In 1930 he wrote in his *Australia*:

> This middling standard is characteristic of democracy in Australia...they [i.e. the Australians] have accepted the 'middling standard'. They have been willing to water good wine so that there may be enough for everybody. Their democratic theory asserts that the divine average has, potentially, a cultivated palate.

We now no longer need to use cheek and ridicule, or to clutch convulsively on that broken reed that history explains everything, or to pitch our tents in the camp of the philistines. Europe is no longer the creative centre, the teacher of the world. Today the English send their observers to China. Is it not time for our historians to abandon their preoccupation with causes and effects of the Australian Cultural Desert?

For one thing, this harping on our pursuit of material gain and indifference to the things of the mind, and our satisfaction with middling standard, creates the idea that there were no differences in the past — that there is, as it were, a dull and depressing sameness in our history — no great issues, no differences of principle, but always the same pursuit of filthy material gain and only a sordid struggle for power between various groups believing they could show us how to achieve it.

The trouble is that this view encouraged the historian to look in the wrong places for difference, i.e. in politics. There they saw none, and complained about sameness, middling standards, and mediocrity. Actually there have been big differences. Consider the difference in values between the following two statements. The first is from the *Hummer*, a newspaper published in Wagga on 16 January 1892.

> Socialism...is the desire to be mates, is the ideal of living together in harmony and brotherhood and loving kindness...if things were once fixed right we should no more need laws to make healthy men good mates than we need laws to make healthy women good mothers. It is diseased, vicious, evil conditions that breed infanticide and competition, which to me are each about as bad as the other — no better, no worse. Neither of them are being MATES!

That was the faith of one socialist in 1892.

In the same community there were people with quite different opinions on human behaviour and human destiny. Below is an extract from the sermon preached by Cardinal Moran in St Mary's Cathedral at a mass for the repose of the soul of Cardinal Newman:

> In many respects it is an age of ruins, and amid these ruins false scientists will set before us a phantom temple of socialistic atheism, or infidelity, or pantheism, in which selfishness and pride, the idols of a corrupt heart, demand our homage and worship. It is otherwise within the domain of the Catholic Church. She gathers her children around the altar of God to impart to them a divine life, to instruct them in heavenly wisdom, to unfold to them the secret of true happiness, and to lead them to their eternal destiny.

Today there are only two great beliefs in Australia — two tremendous utopias. There are those who believe in that dream sketched in the Communist Manifesto. Then there are those who believe in the last paragraph of the Apostles' Creed. Earlier generations worried themselves sick trying to explain why in Australia there was what A. D. Hope has called an 'Arabian desert of the human mind'. This generation has to worry out this question of fundamental faith. That is one of the great differences today — and I suggest that one of the great tasks of our historians is to explain how it came about.

Another significant difference they missed was and is the difference between the Catholic and the Protestant view of the world. I will illustrate this with an example from the history of political liberty — a subject highly coloured in our history books by the Protestant and secular view of liberty. To these historians liberty was a frail but precious bark nosing its way between the Scylla of economic privilege and the Charybdis of the tyranny of the majority. The attitude of the church was severely snubbed by this school, that is, they did not even deign to mention it. Yet in fact the attitude of the Catholic Church to liberty illuminates two of the great events in the last 100 years: the education controversy and the conscription crisis. There really were big differences. Below is an example of a pronouncement by the bishops of the Roman Church on liberty. It is from a pastoral to their priests commanding them to forbid their parishioners to read a Church of England periodical.

> These roaring lions [they are referring to the Church of England writers] in their audaciousness, usurp everything to themselves; everything must be examined; everything must be weighed by minds, perhaps but lightly imbued with Catholic truth and discipline; and nothing at all reserved for episcopal authority and the loving obedience of the faithful and confiding soul. Wherefore, most beloved brethren, we, whom the Holy Ghost has appointed to rule the Church of God, cannot in so great a corruption and blindness, do otherwise than arouse, as far as in us lies, the spirit of your devotion...to unite with us...for the same end. You having been made dispensers of the mysteries of God, be careful that the sheep entrusted to your care, and redeemed with the blood of Christ, be kept from such poisoned pasturage as just alluded to.

That pastoral was issued in Melbourne on the occasion of the feast of St Barnabas in 1858 — one year, by the way, before the publication of Mill's essay on *Liberty*.

This was not the Protestant conception of liberty. As an all too brief example of their view we have the brilliant judgement of Mr Justice Windeyer in 1888.

> The time is surely past when countenance can be given to the argument that knowledge of the truth either in physics or in the domain of thought is to be stifled because its abuse might be dangerous to society ... Ignorance is no more the mother of chastity than of true religion.

It was partly because they were not prepared to run the risk of exposing the children of the faithful to teachers with such a conception of liberty that the Catholic Church used extreme measures to force its members into the Catholic school. This meant, of course, that one set of values was taught to the Catholics and another to the Protestants. For the former, education was a preparation for eternity: for the later, the aim was more mundane. It meant, as well, two different views of history. The minds of the Catholic children were steeped in the wrongs of Ireland and the injustices of English domination: the minds of the Protestants with such works as *Deeds that Won the Empire.* Compare, for example, the attitude to the war of 1914: 'At the beginning of the war,' said Archbishop Mannix, 'I made up my mind that the recruiting platform was not the place for a Catholic priest or Catholic bishop.' By contrast, in September 1916 Dr Leeper told the Anglican synod in Melbourne that the war was a religious war. The synod then carried without opposition a resolution in favour of conscription. The *Age* account ends: 'The National Anthem was then sung.'

By 1919 the *Argus* was warning the Protestants that the real grievance of the Irish Catholic was that the empire was a Protestant empire with a Protestant monarch (*Argus,* 4 November 1919). And in November of 1919 an elector wrote to the *Argus* urging every returned digger and every Protestant to vote for the Nationalist Party, because the Labor Party would increase the power and the prominence of the Roman Catholic Church (*Argus*, 8 November 1919). Surely, by now, it has become urgent for the historians to explain why there is a close association between the Catholic Church and the Labor Party, and to remind us that there are two traditions in the community with different conceptions of liberty, of equality, and of democracy. So let us drop the talk about middling standards, mediocrity and sameness, and have a look at these differences.

The next comforter I want us to drop is the one about our convict origins. This was created to heal the wounds about the 'birth stain'. Let me remind you of the picture of transportation designed to comfort such diverse groups as the humanitarians, the Australian nationalists, the radicals, and the old Australian families with a skeleton in the cupboard from the convict era. First we were told that economic changes in England in the eighteenth century forced large numbers of respectable breadwinners and their dependants to choose between starvation, the humiliation of poor relief, or theft. Then we were given a harrowing account of peasants crushed by cruel landlords and a monstrous criminal law, transported to Australia for minor offences against property, and there forced to associate with the dregs of humanity from the underworld of the towns. The heroes of this melodrama, the middle-class politicians, then entered on the scene to rescue the victims of such a vicious system by making the criminal law more humane and abolishing transportation. The extreme view was put by the late G. A. Wood: 'The atrocious criminals remained in England, while their victims, innocent and manly, founded the Australian democracy.' There is only one trouble with this opinion. It is just not true. You will notice one thing about this approach — you are never shown a convict. Instead you are reassured with generalizations such as 'innocent and manly' or 'village Hampdens' or some other high-flying phrase. Yet the facts were there, if they had wanted to see them. The great majority of the convicts were professional criminals. So instead of stirring up pity for the victims of enclosure, the rise in prices, the inadequate system of poor relief, and instead of castigating the savagery of the English criminal law, let us rather examine the habits and values of the criminals.

That, I can assure you, is far more illuminating, for there you will find the germ of some of the great themes in our history: the attitude to work as well as the curious paradox of the warm embrace for members of the same group but a snarl for the rest of the world. It is just as illuminating to examine the habits and values of the Irish thieves, partly because their contempt for all the laws of the Anglo-Saxon gave, as it were, a flying start to building up a tradition of lawlessness in Australia, but mainly because they were the cause of the coming of the Roman Catholic Church to Australia. This meant not only the Irish brand of Catholicism, but also the close association between that church and one section of the working classes in Australia. In fact, if one dropped the habit of dismissing the whole convict question after due censure of the English governing classes and some quivers of horror at the vices of convicts, one would have time to acknowledge their contribution. I am thinking also of our extreme good fortune that they did the pioneer work without leaving an ugly social problem for after-generations — as, for example, did the Negro in the USA and the Kaffir in South Africa.

My next suggestion is that we should drop the idea of the past created and used to support the political and cultural movements at the turn of the century, say, to be safe, 1880–1920. First let me show you how this idea came to birth. There were three movements which were sometimes identical, sometimes separate. First, there were the nationalists. What they were after was put simply by W. J. Sowden:

> It had become the fashion to belittle everything Australian. Our wealthier men boasted, when they gave a dinner to their friends, that there was nothing 'Colonial' upon their tables. Colonial wine was sour, Colonial ale was watery, Colonial cheese was rancid … Colonial waiters were clumsy; the Colonial sun had a sickly glare; the Colonial firmament was an exceedingly poor and shockingly burlesqued copy of the dear old original heavens canopying the dear old original Mother Country!

Like most nationalist movements they were quite impressive when putting their claim for recognition, but often ludicrous when they talked about what they would put in place of the habits of the 'dear old mother country'. For instance, this same Sowden suggested that the old world 'three cheers' be replaced by an Australian 'three cooees'. Then there was the movement for political democracy, supported by the Liberals and the new political labour movement. I imagine some of the Liberals, and even the prosaic labour leaders must have been embarrassed by the language used to describe their creed. Take this piece of doggerel from the *Bulletin* of 8 November 1890:

> *Down with old world race dissensions,*
> *Truth and Justice leads the van.*
> *Creed and hate are hell's inventions,*
> *Trust the brotherhood of man.*

This was put more soberly in the labour paper, the Brisbane *Worker*, on 5 January 1901, but you can see the idea developing: 'Australia has ever been an exemplar to the old lands ... By a happy fortune it sprang up free of most of the superstitions, traditions, class distinctions and sanctified fables and fallacies of the older nations.'

Notice how this writer is beginning to sketch an idea of the past to fit in with his political aims — to justify and sanctify them. The mundane journalists had their eyes on the present, and were prepared to use the past. The poets went on with astonishing pictures of the future. Do you remember the coy question in Bernard O'Dowd's 'Australia'?: 'Or lurks millennial Eden 'neath your face?'

I should like, by courtesy of the work of Vance Palmer, to resurrect from the past O'Dowd's 'Lyceum Tutor'. The prophet is asked: 'Peer into the future and tell me what you see there.' He replies: 'The spectacle of a United Australia! Free from all connections with old world tyrannies, rich in possession of a glorious race, free from religious tyranny as from political.' In a moment I will show you how the poets built up an idea of the past to persuade people that history too was on the side of democracy.

But first a word on the third strand in this movement — the creed of the bushman. 'A gambler and a nomad' *The Times* correspondent in Australia called him in an article in *The Times* of 31 August 1903. And he went on:

> in such surroundings he remains perpetually a child ... And he is especially like a child in this, that his code of social ethics is based on the family. The bush folk are of his family, every one of them *ipso facto* a mate of his, to be welcomed and treated as such unless some meanness demands expulsion; outsiders are for that very reason to be suspected — people to whom he owes few or no duties except that of hospitality — though the best of them may, after due trial made, be admitted among his comrades. Within that family it is the cardinal virtue to be 'straight', and property is shared to an extent that might almost be called communism.

He went on to point out shrewdly that the bushman's politics were those of a child, that he felt misunderstood, and was therefore inclined to accept the advice and friendship of anyone who was sympathetic.

All three trends are anti-English: the last two believe in brotherhood, in being mates, and in equality. Gradually the men holding these opinions built up their own idea of the past. You can see this beginning during their campaign for more political democracy. Remember those words of the Brisbane *Worker:* 'Australia has *ever* been an exemplar to the old lands.' The poets were not slow to take up the hint given by these working journalists. So Victor Daley in 'A Ballad of Eureka' written in 1901 went further and began to create a pantheon of democratic victories in the past. He settled on the Eureka rebellion in 1854:

> *Yet ere the year was over,*
> *Freedom rolled in like a flood:*

They gave us all we asked for —
When we asked for it in blood.

By 1904 the prose publicists were popularizing the idea, for example Robert Ross' pamphlet *Eureka: Freedom's Fight of '54*. The historians were late into the field, but quickly filled in the details left blank by the poets, and industriously dug up an array of evidence to support their view. So 1850–54 became the great watershed in Australian history, the start of a crusade for the victory of political democracy and equality in the constitutions of the colonies, the ownership of land, education, and social conventions. In fact, by 1948 the idea became so safe, so respectable that the Labor Party, with great daring, climbed on the band-waggon and decided to name a Commonwealth electorate after Lalor, the diggers' leader. A Labor minister justified this by showing that he too accepted this idea of the past: 'Democracy in this country began at Eureka.'

That is the great Australian illusion: the idea that we were pioneers of democracy, that while Europe reverted to the blackest reaction after the abortive revolutions of 1848–51, Australia was the political and social laboratory of the world with her experiments in democracy, equality of opportunity, and *material progress*. And, it is argued, we owe this distinction to the diggers, to Eureka, and to a delightfully vague movement called 'Chartism'. It is time to prick the bubble of this conceit.

First, it ignores the contribution of the period before gold; a great pity, because there, rather than on the goldfields, is the germ of the belief in equality. It was the labour shortage in country districts, rather than imported social and political ideals, which eroded the centuries-old belief in inequality. Second, it over-emphasizes the degree of political democracy introduced after the gold rushes. Third, it concentrates attention on the political achievements in the period of gold and thus loses sight of two of the central facts of the period. This was the great period of the squatters — up to 1890. It was also the great period of bourgeois civilization in our cities, the period in which cathedrals, town halls, universities, schools, banks, and pastoral company buildings were put up as symbols of its faith. There has been nothing like it since. That is the sort of picture one begins to build up once one drops the idea that the past is a mirror of Australia's radical tradition and that if one looks very closely one can find reasons for believing that Australians, unlike Europeans, can build heaven on earth.

[...]

So much for the way in which this illusion of a radical tradition distorts and warps our idea of the past. I doubt, however, whether one would have much success in persuading people to drop it just because it is not true. The truth about the past excites a tiny minority — it is their spiritual pleasure and their bread and butter. There are, however, more compelling reasons for dropping it. Take, for example, one of the strands in the creed: the ideal of mateship. This was the great comforter of the bushman:

They tramp in mateship side by side —
The Protestant and the 'Roman' —
They call no biped lord or 'sir'
And touch their hats to no man!

So Lawson. It was their holy of holies — the last disgrace was to be proved unworthy of 'mateship'.

I doubt whether it is wise for us to treat this ideal with such awe and veneration. Like most groups living in conditions of material hardship they built up a code of love and fellowship for each other and damnation for the rest of the world. This is an all too frequent feature in schemes of brotherhood. You will remember the Jews made this sharp distinction in their version of harmony: 'The wolf,' wrote the prophet Isaiah, 'shall also dwell with the lamb; and the leopard shall lie down with the kid...They shall not hurt nor destroy in all my holy mountain.' That was, however, reserved for the Jews. As for their neighbours: 'Their children...shall be dashed to pieces before their eyes; their houses shall be spoiled and their wives ravished.'

You will find it too in a less exalted form in the ideals of the costermongers of London. The members of society outside their own circle were described with one term of contempt: 'bloody aristocrats'. The Australian ideal had this same taint of xenophobia: they were contemptuous of Englishmen and savage on money-lenders and Jews. That was baed enough, but they reserved their bitterest bile for the one group we can ill afford to offend. So the high priest of mateship, William Lane, warned his fellow mates and 'dinkum Aussies' about the 'piebald brats'. And the bushman's staple reading matter, the *Bulletin,* sneered at Edward VII's stupendous nigger empire — 'the greatest nigger empire in the world' (22 February 1902) — and reminded mates of the blessings of a White Australia: 'A White Australia will never have to fry a nigger at the stake' (25 November 1906). Instead of worshipping at the altar of mateship we may find ourselves making expiation and atonement for such arrogance, for are we not that third and fourth generation on whom the sins of the fathers are to be visited?

Nor is that the only reason for jibbing at their ideal. Mateship was the product of a way of life: a mate was a bulwark against loneliness, a help in time of sickness and accident. There was no attempt to make mateship universal in application — to extend it from the people they knew to all people — nor was there any attempt to find universal reasons for believing in it. You do not find them putting forward any metaphysical or religious reasons for their belief. In fact, in comparison with the questions raised by another group of semi-nomads, their questions seem shallow and trivial: 'If a man die, shall he live again? All the days of my appointed time will I wait, till my change come.' And: 'What is man that he should be clean? and he which is born of a woman, that he should be righteous?' Beside such questions, the Lawsonian precept to 'call no biped lord or "sir"/And touch their hats to no man' is rather small beer.

[...]

So the first move to be made in the rewriting of Australian history is to drop the ideas of the past which have comforted and instructed earlier generations. What then shall we put in their place? To that question I have only given snatches of an answer for the simple reason that the whole answer has so far eluded me. But I do believe that it is a great and noble task to answer that question, and that what I have discussed is a necessary preparation for it.

I do not believe that this rewriting will come from the universities, though they will greatly assist the work of the creative writer. It will not come from the universities because they, instead of being the fiercest critics of the bankrupt liberal ideal, are its most persistent defenders. Then too they have been made afraid by the angry men of today with their talk about 'corrupters of youth'. It will not come from the measurers, for they hold the terrible belief that measuring will show there is no mystery. It will not come from the radicals of this generation because they are either tethered to an erstwhile great but now excessively rigid creed, or they are frightened by the self-appointed inquisitors of our morals and political opinions.

History, to be great as history, must have a point of view on the direction of society. It must also have something to say, some great theme to lighten our darkness — that, for example, the era of bourgeois liberalism, of democracy, and belief in material progress is over, and that those who defend such a creed are the reactionaries of today. To be great as literature — the aim of all historians — it must be written by someone who has something to say about human nature, but, above all, it must be written by someone who has pondered deeply over the problems of life and death. Like the fox in the Greek fragment, the historian must know many things, but like the hedgehog, he must know one big thing — and feel it deeply.

While I believe that Australians should drop the comforters of the days of their youth and innocence, I believe even more strongly that the historians should come back to the great themes they abandoned when they joined in the vain search for a science of society.

1954

JAMES McAULEY

Poets Anonymous

It is strange that decline in the reading of poetry has not been accompanied by a decline in writing it, or at least attempting to write it. Literary editors begin to suspect that almost everyone is seized with the delusion that they can write poetry: turn but a stone and start a wing. Many of these would-be practitioners obviously have read very little poetry themselves. They know little of the tradition, and have no idea of what has been going on in the present century. It really does not occur to them that poetry is an art and that it has 'professional' requirements.

Certainly, poetry is different from the other arts. If you look at the history of music or painting, for example, it becomes evident that virtually all significant developments and all outstanding achievements are the work of full-time professionals. It may be my ignorance, but I can think of no amateur painter of importance. One eighteenth-century composer whose work has been recently and deservedly revived, Frantisek Mica, was by profession a lawyer. He was the Emperor Joseph II's favourite composer, and his work was appreciated by Mozart. Perhaps there are other examples of good composers who were not full-time professional musicians, but none comes to my mind.

Another point that strikes one about composers and painters is that they can turn out work of a good standard more or less on demand or at will: a portrait, a landscape, a quartet, a song.

The case is otherwise with poetry. In the first place, even the best poets cannot produce a good poem on demand or at will. They can turn out some sort of a text, put together with skill and ingenuity, but poetic success is the result of rare and happy conjunctions which cannot be predicted or controlled. One can go through the work of many poets who once had some reputation and find scarcely a line, let alone a whole poem, of poetic value.

In the second place, in the history of poetry, amateurs — meaning people who are not full-time professional writers — have played an important part in the development of form and style, and the composition of poems of lasting value. In English poetry one can think of Wyatt, Surrey, Sidney, Greville, Ralegh and Donne for a start. It remains true, of course, that writers who were dedicated to poetry as their main vocation form the great mountain chain: Chaucer,

Spencer, Shakespeare, Jonson, Milton, Dryden, Pope, Wordsworth, Keats, Tennyson, Browning, Yeats.

. . .

One is forced to use the terms 'amateur' and 'professional' in a different way if they are to be useful in describing poets and their poetry. No-one can live by poetry today. The real distinction is between those who are seriously dedicated to the practice of poetry as an art and can be thought of as truly 'professional' in their work, and those who indulge in some sort of verbal daubing which is incorrigibly amateurish because they really don't see that the practice of poetry as an art is an immensely demanding and difficult thing.

Why can't they see this? I think the amount of blindness and self-delusion is much greater than it used to be, and that there are two reasons for this.

One reason lies in the education system. Once upon a time everyone knew that poetry was a kind of patterned language, and everyone with a minimum education easily learned about the technical aspect of poetry such as metre, rhyme, stanza form. Many people had an elegant skill in handling these elements and could turn out light verse or *vers d'occasion* which was agreeable and which no-one, including the author, mistook for more than what it was. No-one had yet heard of 'creative writing'.

Today in schools 'creative writing' is being used to obliterate the distinction between poetry and non-poetry. 'Take a sentence and dribble it down the page', recommends one Australian guide to 'creative' expression. As practised, 'creative writing' involves the subordination of literary — and also scholastic — values to other ends such as self-expression, self-discovery, 'adventures in...' all summed up in the ruling slogan: 'Growth through English'.

It is possible that 'creative writing' may have some pedagogic or therapeutic value in special cases. When installed as a general method, the danger is that students and teachers will fail to recognize the difference between the verbal activity thus elicited and the writing of real poems: I mean the sort of thing Keats was doing when he wrote 'To Autumn', or Hardy when he wrote 'Beyond the Last Lamp', or Yeats when he wrote 'Lullaby'. The difference is radical, but it can become obscured because both kinds of writing use words and images and personal experience. There is doubtless some degree of overlapping, but any real poet would want to say that 'creative writing' is not the same, in process or result, as *the making of a poem as a work of art,* and schools should not be used to obscure this.

The differences are hard to specify precisely. No-one has ever satisfactorily described what is involved in writing a poem. The most obvious difference is relatively superficial but important: there is a disregard of formality which is characteristic of the educationists' approach to 'creative writing'. Many English teachers today have acquired a horror of anything that is formal, and they pass this on to their students: indeed, anti-formalism in regard to *all* the arts is positively and wilfully inculcated in schools — in defiance of everything that a knowledge of the history of the arts and of cultural anthropology must inevitable suggest to the contrary.

This takes me on to the second and more general reason why would-be poets today find it harder to see why their amateur verbal daubs should not be published. The rejected poet must often wonder what is so different in kind and quality between his work and many poems that are published. And well he might wonder. In many cases there is a little enough difference; a vast confusion reigns in the lower reaches of modern poetry, and though people find it hard to admit the fact, the question of formality has much to do with it.

. . .

The ordinary notion of a poem is that it involves some sort of patterning of language, which is enjoyable in itself, and seems to support a heightening or intensification of emotional expression or verbal interest. Principles of formality alternative to the standard metrical patterns have been tried out from time to time. Classical quantitative verse has been tried; also verse measured solely by the number of syllables. When Robert Lowth in the eighteenth century demonstrated at last the formal principles governing Hebrew poetry, this gave a new impulse to experiment in English poetry. Hopkins in the nineteenth century tried an accentual system which remained peculiar to him. No alternative system to the standard one has established itself, though some interesting results have been achieved.

Finally, the abandonment of any principle of regularity had to be tried. Free verse has been written now for over a century. It seemed to be on the decline, but at present it is dominant and even regarded as essential for truly contemporary poetry.

It is highly deciduous stuff. Virtually none of it has managed to enter into the received body of English poetry. By this obvious empirical test, free verse is just a goer. Each generation produces its crop in great quantity; the practitioners seem to be encouraged rather than warned by the rapid disappearance of last generation's crop. The lesson is not drawn, as it should be, that some principle of formality is a necessary preservative; and I mean a real principle, not a bogus one like breath-lengths.

Such free poems as have temporary success depend heavily on content. There is no reason why a well-written account of some significant moment should lose all literary value because the writer has broken it up into irregular lines on a page. But the value it has is as a disguised prose paragraph. D. H. Lawrence's free-form 'Snake' which often appears in school anthologies is such a piece of writing: it stays in the mind and has some power, though it is not as good as some of Lawrence's earlier formed poems, which are often overlooked.

In contrast to the dependence of free poems on content for whatever interest they might offer, one of the notable things about genuine poetry is that it can often succeed with very little weight of subject matter, by sheer compelling artifice. Campion once likened his song-lyrics to a goldsmith's book of gold-leaf sheets which can be gently separated by a breath: 'such are light ayres'.

In Australia, egalitarianism and bureaucracy have combined to encourage would-be poets in their delusions. Public money is handed out to all sorts of writers without any odious prying into whether they are any good or not. It has not been explained why the recipient poets need the money: they seem to exude words readily enough without subsidy. Money has even been offered to poets who haven't asked for it, and in some cases, to their credit, they have refused it. One can see why the writing of major prose works, or the maintenance of theatre, film, ballet, music, need public financial support. One can also see the case for supporting publication in book form or in journals. It is not clear, however, why a poet cannot manage without a grant of money to write in a year a dozen or so short poems worth preserving. If he averages more poems than this he is probably writing badly and on his way to becoming a public nuisance.

. . .

Some years ago I predicted a scheme for an organization to be called Poets Anonymous, on the analogy of Alcoholics Anonymous. It was on the occasion of a dinner in celebration of Australian Literature in Townsville in 1968, presided over by Lord Casey and in the distinguished presence of Douglas Stewart. Lord Casey agreed to become patron along with Dame Ethel Malley, surviving sister of one of Australia's best-known poets. Douglas Stewart, having had long experience as editor of the Red Page of the old *Bulletin,* was sympathetic to any attempt to alleviate what has become a major social problem. Poets Anonymous is based on the principle that poetry-writing is merely a psychological addiction. It is possible to give it up without severe physical withdrawal symptoms. If the craving recurs the sufferer can hold out against it with the fraternal help of those who have succeeded in shaking off the habit. The essential thing, however, is that one must have reached the point of really wanting to give it up.

At one stage I raised with Mr McMahon when he was federal treasurer the possibility of a tax rebate if one could show that, as a certified previous offender, one had neither published nor attempted to publish a poem in the past three years. We were making some progress, I thought, when the political winds started to change, and eventually Mr Whitlam came in and ordered a hundred, nay a thousand, flowers to bloom. Nevertheless I think the problem deserves the attention of the Literature Board. Why should financial assistance be confined to those who want to go on writing? Why should it not be also available as an encouragement to those who have become convinced that they can and must give it up for their own good as well as in the public interest? Let us hope that the next list will contain grants to a number of authors who have undertaken not to produce any work for the period of the grant and at least two years following, the money to be repayable if there is any breach of this undertaking. I would be glad to act as referee on behalf of a considerable number of applicants.

1976

ALISTER KERSHAW

The Last Expatriate

New Australians — so why not new Europeans? Why are expatriates in one direction virtuous and discerning fellows — in the other, renegades and *ratés?*

This business of expatriation — *towards* Europe — awakens a fanged resentment in the stay-at-homes, a raucous defensiveness in the expatriates. It is very odd.

You're supposed to 'lose your roots' — whatever that may mean — as soon as you overstay a sabbatical year. What *does* it mean — this losing of roots?

Apparently it's only the 'artists' who suffer from this humiliating deprivation, the poor brutes. Soldiers can be posted overseas for most of their careers, engineers can spend ten years on projects in Assam or the Trobriands: when they get home no-one seems to suspect them of being rootless. It's the painters, the musicians, the writers — especially writers — who occasion such concern, such melancholy head-wagging: every tuppeny-halfpenny critic can always fill up his column in the local paper with sage frettings over the rootlessness of his expatriate betters, shedding goanna tears over the sterility, alcoholism and disillusion ahead of them.

Well, well. Perhaps it's no more than envy, envy and gutlessness. It must be a bit depressing to hang abjectly on to your wretched secure little job year after year, inwardly hankering after St Germain and never having quite enough nerve to get further than Eltham.

Only isn't it time that the consolatory legend was looked at a trifle closer? Most modern writers, at any rate, have been expatriates, from Byron to D. H. Lawrence. And after Lawrence, Roy Campbell lived (past tense now, alas) in Provence and Spain for most of his adult life: it would take a Cyril Connolly to detect his rootlessness. The fact is that he was as much at home in Provence or Spain as in his native South Africa. Is that rootlessness? Or the reverse?

Personally, I've always felt that 'nationality' — the quirks and ties and prejudices and, no doubt, virtues which one picks up from one's early environment — must be pretty damned tenuous if it's endangered by going outside territorial waters.

And, equally, there's something suspect about self-identification with one's native land when accompanied by such very vociferous insistence on one's possession of a passport. A while back I was introduced to a gentleman in Paris who, in a turgid German accent, talked about 'us Australians' for several hours on end. Rarely had I heard so many references to billabongs, waratah, the Nullabor Plains and Tasmanian Devils — with U-modified cropping up as regularly as clockwork and the verb at the end of every sentence. I wondered who or what it was he reminded me of: suddenly I remembered: twenty years ago in Australia there was — is there still? — a school of poets which held that good poetry — good Australian poetry — required at least three strictly antipodean allusions per stanza: Hiawatha in the pidgin English of Arnhem Land,

Where poets kiss away the abos' cares
And dream of wombats and koala bears.

Getting back to the expatriates ... They become 'decadent' along with everything else. This is like rootlessness — ducdame — with nobody caring to be too precise as to what it means: but the decadence of expatriates is an article of faith with all the homebodies. You become decadent, it seems, by sheer contagion: all foreigners are decadent; if you live among them long enough, you, too ...

An Australian communist stepped off the plane at Orly, the first instant of his visit to France, sniffed deeply and told a waiting compatriot: 'You can smell the decadence, you can smell the decadence!'

This is where all foreigners come together — communist, businessmen, bureaucrats: they all share the marvellous antique idea of 'the Frenchman' as a bibulous, gesticulating clown, an aura of ornate garters and hurriedly vacated bedrooms always around him. And 'the Italian', 'the Spaniard' of their imaginings not so very different.

Percipient visitors. In France, they drink a few aperitifs in the vicinity of the place de l'Opéra, hustle unhappily through the Louvre, take in Versailles (with a bit of organising they can manage both in the same day), spend an evening at the Moulin Rouge and take off for the Côte d'Azur. By the time they're back from Nice or Cannes, they know France like an open book. And, by God, it's decadent — take it from me, Mac, I've *been* there.

As a matter of fact, the expatriates, most of them, don't run much risk of infection. It's a mystery, if you come right down to it, why the hell they live outside their native lands, they're so careful to insulate themselves. They are registered at their ridiculous embassies and wait palpitatingly for the big day each year when they'll be invited to drink a glass of cheap 'sparkling wine' with the bureaucrats. They patronise one particular café where the entire clientele is English, Australian, or American, and where even the barman has an Australian accent. They have never set foot in La Roquette, say, or Villejuif, but they tell each other that they've just found a wonderful place 'where the foreigners don't go'. It usually turns out to be the Dôme.

And after a few years, suddenly, in spite of all their precautions, it breaks sickeningly in on them — the unfamiliar language all round, the bizarre food, the unaccustomed drinking hours, the menacing *foreignness* of it all; and hurriedly drawing their cash from the bank — for these daredevils have always got a bit tucked away for an emergency — they tear round to Thomas Cook and buy a one-way ticket home.

Once there, what luxury to drop casual allusions to 'one evening in the Deux Magots…' or to 'an amusing little boîte in the rue de Seine…'. But, all the same, what a comfort to be back, what a relief, nuzzling once more at the benevolent teats of the mother country!

Within six months they're writing sombrely about the dangers of rootlessness.

What about the few who really go native? It's not easy to generalise since, obviously, they tend to avoid each other; but one can make a reasonable guess or two. I'd imagine that one reason why certain people prefer living in France, for instance, rather than Australia is quite simply that France feels as though it were *meant* to be lived in. Whereas in Australia it was somehow as if one were hanging precariously on a cliff edge, with the Genius Loci stamping on one's finger tips.

There's a point of contact with the mass of Frenchmen, maybe with all Europeans, so that the chances are you — a poet, a painter, or whatever — can pass a pleasant hour or so with a truckdriver, the local cop, the greengrocer. In Australia, I seem to recall, artists huddled uneasily together, only leaving their garrets in order to visit friends at the university.

No! None can break the umbilical cords
Which join these poets to their mortar boards.

But what the devil does it matter why this one or that may choose to live in France or Spain or Germany or Greece? What is of much more interest is why there should be such ardent opposition to their doing so. Envy, I've suggested; but that can only apply in specific individual cases. Then there may be those who genuinely believe that a writer who produces great prose in Mildura will go to hell if he sets foot in the Carmargue.

Only is it really so simple? There is a grisly consistency in the cult of stay-at-homism and a sinister vehemence. What does it signify? But what else? It fits in with the ugly slavery of our epoch. Governments like to keep their property close at hand where they can watch it and control it. Only the bureaucratic trusties and the businessmen on safari after profits can safely be permitted to roam the world. The rest must be subtly (and not too subtly) discouraged from travelling until the happy time when they can be *compelled* to stay put. Hence the grotesque currency restrictions, passports, visas, clearances, and the other impudent impediments to free movement. And hence the propaganda whereby the artists — traditionally suspected of rebellious tendencies although, these days, how unfairly! — are to be convinced that their paint will flake and their lines no longer scan if ever they cross a frontier.

It's gloomily diverting to see so many of them yelping for their own final enslavement.

1958

CHARMIAN CLIFT

Images in Aspic

There has been a lot of interested, if not quite animated, talk lately in our Alice in Wonderland film circles (shrunk-and-still-shrinking: oh *why* did they eat the wrong side of the mushroom?) about the two big foreign feature films to be made here soon. The one about drovers. The other — still in the stage of preliminary reconnaissance — about a kangaroo.

Oh dear!

I knew a funny story once, which (mercifully) I have forgotten. Only the tag-line seems appropriate here. 'Hang on to your beaver hats, kids! Here we go again!'

Not that one has anything against drovers, or kangaroos either for that matter. The lean man on the big horse gazing out through sun-creased eyes across the spinifex is a romantic image, and home-grown rather than imported, which is something, and our furry marsupial friend is quaint enough to warrant even enhanced celebrity overseas. But when did *you* last sit loosely in the saddle? And what do you keep in your pouch, anyway? I am Australian born and bred, and I can't ride a horse at all. And I've never seen a kangaroo outside a zoo.

Eighty-two per cent of the population of Australia lives in cities or towns. Surely that suggests an alternative national image, or even images, not *instead* of the drover one, but as well as. I am not necessarily thinking of a paunchy man with a briefcase (although according to the statistics he would be a far truer image than the man on the horse), but of the unique aspects of Australian life that could be so excitingly dramatised.

Nobody yet has exploited cinematically our stupendous beaches, or sought to portray the neo-paganism of the surf cult, which is utterly contemporary, utterly Australian, and so very intriguing with its rituals and hierarchies, its austerity of physical discipline, its more-than-liberal morals, the orgiastic quality of its songs and dances, the physical beauty of its devotees. The bronzed man on the surfboard is at least as authentic an image as the bronzed man on the horse, and much more familiar to most of us.

Neither has anybody touched upon our particular contemporary problem of the integration of hundreds of thousands of Europeans into our communities. There is yeast enough there to ferment a dozen films, without formula or cliché.

We have the strongest trade union movement in the world. Our industries are expanding at a fantastic rate. Every element of drama is present, not American drama, not British drama, but Australian drama, as the story of Mount Isa so dramatically illustrates.

And on the heroic scale, what stories might not be dug out of the grand conception of the Snowy Scheme, or the Ord, or the Cape York peninsula? Or for glamour take the jazzy Gold Coast, or the romantic islands of the Great Barrier Reef. And haven't we tuna fisheries, giant meat-works, enormous road trains, gem-fields, wharves and shipping, whale-spotters, a rocket range, radio telescopes?...the possibilities are endless. Above the Nullarbor there are small groups of hunters who live in isolation for months at a time, filling up modern freezer-trucks with the carcases of rabbits they shoot at night from Landrovers. It is a strange country, an exciting country, an original country, from the stupefying immensity of its scale to the most delicate of its particular nuances.

Ever since I have been back here I have been conscious that Australians, caught in international cross-currents of ideas and manners and fashions, twisted about by reassessments of their own old myths, bewildered by elusive and changing standards, are desperate to be redefined.

But it is for us to define ourselves, to reveal ourselves unself-consciously in our many facets, before the aspic of the overseas conception sets firmly around the jolly swagman and the overlander and condemns us to be served up forever in jellied garnish. Because one thing is certain: if we are incapable of presenting ourselves in our own true image and images the huge overseas companies, on whom we seem to be relying rather optimistically to do it for us, will carry on with the safe cliché that conforms so glibly to the prefabricated notion.

Lately I have been talking with film people, or listening to them, rather, and one particular conversation was a striking illustration of this very point. A British film director, a good one, and a perceptive sensitive man, was advising an American director, newly arrived and scouting locations for his kangaroo film. The British director strongly recommend a location (quite remote) which I swear not one per cent of Australians have ever seen or are ever likely to. The British director had himself made a film there. So had an earlier American company. You couldn't go wrong, said the Britisher. He strongly recommended it for the American's purposes, even though the story would certainly have to be altered a little to fit the locale. It wasn't perfect, he said, but it was quite the closest thing he had been able to find to what he had imagined Australia to be like *before he came here.* And he thought that it was most important to portray that preconceived idea as nearly as possible. After all, he summed up, that's what people overseas *expected* to see.

And another highly successful American script-writer, again a sensitive, intelligent (although disenchanted) man, came here looking for Australian material and went back to Hollywood empty-handed. He said, with a little deprecating grin, that what his company really wanted was another Australian 'Western', and it wasn't much good presenting them with anything more subtle. It makes one wish, he said, that you had a film industry of your own. There is so much you could do here on a modest scale in that intimate and wise way the Italians have. And what is so sad, he said, is that you have the people here, and all the technical equipment and the technical knowledge to do it.

It's true too. The studios, the equipment, the labs, the cameras, the cameramen, who must long to do something bigger than TV and film commercials, or even the quality sponsored documentaries that seem to be the only hopeful thing happening here in the film industry.

There must be an answer somewhere. Even in the depressing realities of finance and distribution and profits and markets and all the reasons put forward by the people who should be making the films as to why it is absolutely impossible to do anything at all. In my ignorance of big business and high finance I tend to believe that image-making could be more important than profit-making. Perhaps I am wrong.

In Sydney recently a taxi-driver asked me what I thought of the Opera House, glimpsed just then with the gaunt framework of its skeletonic sails fantastic against the water. If they could finance such an undertaking by means of a lottery, he said, why couldn't someone start another lottery — a more modest one perhaps — for the benefit of a native film industry. It wouldn't cost anybody anything, would it? And then we could get the industry back on its feet again without begging the Government for subsidies.

'What makes you so interested in the film industry?' I asked curiously, and in the driving mirror he gave me a small, lenient smile. 'I'm an actor,' he said. 'Resting.'

1964?

FRANK KNÖPFELMACHER

The Threat to Academic Freedom

Recent events at some Australian universities have led to discussions on the rights and duties of academic teachers. Yet even before occasional remarks on this topic could be found in some quarterly journals. Frequent, if somewhat confused, statements on the subject are now being made at public and formal as well as at private and informal gatherings of Australian academics. Unfortunately most participants in these discussions, particularly at meetings of University Staff Associations, play a rather passive role, restricting themselves to mere voting or, at best, to cautiously qualified utterances of assent or dissent. Thus it comes about that the field is given over to a small but noisy minority, whose record in matters affecting cultural freedom is, to say the least, very ambiguous. As everybody knows, serious accusations are currently being made, directly in private and by innuendo in public against the State as well as against other powerful groups with regard to their attitude towards the universities. Some accusations are concerned with the poor financial situation of the universities. These are often quite just and have been substantially borne out by the findings of the Murray Committee. Yet there are other accusations: Freedom is in peril. The Catholic Conspiracy and the Security Service are stalking the Academy. They silence the heretic and bar the man of the 'Left' from his well deserved access to academic platforms. They do, or at least plan to do, all this by administrative violence well disguised and cunningly exercised. On hearing this it is only fair to assume that some members of the academic community suffer or pretend to suffer from dread of actual or impending persecution. The situation ought to be examined even if the simile that where there is smoke there must be fire is clearly inapplicable: the other simile relating to smoke, the one on smokescreens, perhaps is.

In nine cases out of ten people complaining about breaches of academic freedom emerge with an assertion that an academic has been penalized because he was an alleged or actual Communist. The story is often amplified by historically imprecise references to such diverse things as the Spanish Inquisition, the late junior senator for Wisconsin and the NSW State Security branch, yet curiously enough, while no limit is being placed on the distance of the adduced evidence in time and space, the Iron Curtain is never crossed to provide what must surely be the most scandalous as well as the most numerous examples of cultural terror against academics. On closer examination the complaints boil down to the following simple facts: (1) in some universities and research establishments there is now considerable reluctance to employ open members of the Communist Party; (2) not all fellow-travellers get all the jobs for which they apply; and (3) support for the Stalin–Mao type of horror is no longer taken as an unmistakable index of intellectual brilliance and moral rectitude. In all this two very important issues are clearly involved — directly and by implication: first, the political relations between the State power and the universities, and, second, the problem of totalitarian groups in a university. Both issues should be removed from the reach of mere whisper and the sly innuendo and discussed widely, intelligently and publicly. In order to make a rational discussion at all possible, certain general principles must first be explicitly stated, and some order introduced into the dense network of pseudo-liberal verbiage of people whose interest in freedom is nil, yet who never miss an opportunity to pull a fast one on behalf of totalitarian despots and their agents in Australia.

Like Great Britain or the USA, Australia is a multi-centric and multi-institutional Open Society. The State is only one among many powerful and genuinely independent institutions, of which business corporations, trade unions, churches, political parties and universities are some others. The governing élites of many institutions interlace into more or less discernible cliques and interest groups, which sometimes form their own organizations, but there is no evidence of a closely knit and co-ordinated 'power élite' in the sense in which Communist bureaucracies in Communist countries are 'power élites'. Hence the severely restricted, federalized and liberal state power of the Commonwealth is not and cannot be a mere instrument of the 'ruling class' as the Marxists claim, and it in no way approximates the totalitarian Leviathan. The university is a self-governing institution in a multi-centric Open Society maintained from public funds to provide facilities for research and instruction in ideas and skills, of science, scholarship and technology. One of its tasks, which is of fundamental importance for all institutions, including the State, is the education of élites. In addition to purely vocational training universities are expected to inculcate the belief that certain principles of conduct are valuable: the requirements of intellectual honesty, the courage to criticize venerable doctrines and influential authorities, tolerance towards the antagonist who defends his views openly and honestly, and the courage to defend the institutions of the Open Society against subversion by usurpers. It stands to reason that without acceptance of these principles by most members of institutional élites an Open Society such as ours could not function effectively. Universities are governed by statutes and by certain unwritten principles which are perhaps of even greater importance than the statutes: the right of the university teacher to teach his doctrine without extra-mural or intra-mural interference, provided the doctrine is openly and honestly imparted, and based on principles of evidence and testing which are publicly defensible before the international community of the teacher's professional peers. The duty of selection committees to make appointments on academic and pedagogic merit and their equally important duty to make their principles of selection in each particular case potentially accessible for scrutiny and constructive criticism by members of faculty. Implied by all this is the obligation not to discriminate against candidates for academic appointments on religious or political grounds, provided that political, religious or any other affiliations are not detrimental to the exercise of their profession. And university élites have a professional obligation to defend the integrity of their institution against subversion.

The term 'subversion' has been used loosely for so many things by so many people that it now means very little. For our purposes we shall define as subversive any attempt to divert an institution by conspiracy or violence from its appropriate purpose. A university is being subverted if an individual or a group use guile or pressure to divert the university's resources for purposes other than teaching and research. Thus, if a business corporation used pressure or if it engaged in intrigues to prevent the appointment of a socialist to a teaching position it would be acting subversively. Or, if the State attempted to influence the appointment, say, of history teachers so as to force the teaching of history into conforming with national mythology or foreign policy, the State would be acting subversively. And members of university élites were they to yield to subversive pressures would themselves become accomplices of subversion. On our definition of the term no teaching of doctrine as such *can* be subversive, since the free pursuit and proclamation of truth are the main legitimate purposes of a secular university. From what has been said it is quite obvious that the State may attempt to subvert universities but that organizations other than the State may also attempt it. From time to time almost any group may be tempted to extend its power by permeating institutions for the purpose of using them as instruments of expansion. Yet most people in most groups in Australia, including members of institutional élites, accept at least implicitly the principles of the multi-centric Open Society. Thus they accept at least tacitly the view that to subvert a university by conspiracy or pressure is not right, and hence their efforts at subversion, if at all made, will bear the hallmark of half-heartedness bred of guilt or at least of a feeling of impropriety. Not so the Communists. For them the plurality of institutions is just a sham which hides and diversifies the grip of the 'ruling class'. Themselves addicts of totalitarian despotism, the Communists cannot conceive that any other type of social organization is really possible. For a Communist our universities are at best sectors on the ideological front between 'capitalism' and 'socialism' and at worst machines for churning out the more ornamental bits of capitalist 'ideological superstructure'. Subversion by conspiracy and guile whenever necessary, and by open violence wherever possible (as in Prague in 1948), are pursued as a matter of course, systematically and with a perfectly good conscience. For the Stalinist a university is just another 'mass organization', to be permeated, captured, and eventually merged into the amorphous plasma of the totalitarian mass-society.

There is overwhelming historical and factual evidence to show that Party members in universities *on both sides of the Iron Curtain* are officially instructed to use their positions primarily and overwhelmingly in the interest of the Party. This includes, apart from open indoctrination, systematic political corruption of appointments and examinations, the use of organizational manipulations and systematic calumny against selected opponents and in rare but significant cases espionage. In all this Party members enjoy the conscious support of fellow-travellers and the unconscious support of the new amorphous mass, men in academic positions whose new religion is 'personal adjustment' (by implication, to anything with everybody) and who by their sheer unwieldy presence block the forces of principled resistance to subversion. Australia is, of course, no exception to all this. The only *significant* threat to academic freedom in Australia today does not come from the State in its present form or from any other group, e.g. the Catholic Church, the Trade Unions or the Freemasons, which accept at present and for the foreseeable future the principles of the Open Society, but from the *only* totalitarian organization in this country — the Communist Party and its open and secret accomplices. This would be so even if the Communist Party were not, as it plainly is, an agency of a mighty and implacably hostile power-bloc, a clear and present danger to the security and welfare of the community. Many liberals do not see this because their thinking about totalitarianism is based on a fundamental misconception. They believe that totalitarianism is the mere result of state-supremacy — 'statism' as the right-wing protagonists of the fallacy are in the habit of calling it. Consequently any attempt of the non-totalitarian state power to assert its authority is denounced by liberals as a 'step towards totalitarianism', and the 'right' of totalitarian conspirators to undermine and destroy the Open Society is defended in perfectly good faith by people who in doing so believe that they are in fact protecting the Open Society against the growth of totalitarianism. [...]

Totalitarian subversion of academic freedom is of considerable topical interest at present in Australia. Despite the fairy-tales of professional optimists it is becoming more and more obvious that Australia, like the rest of the non-Communist world, will be subjected to increasingly ferocious assaults from the Communist power-bloc which has now dramatically demonstrated its achievements in military technology. The usual 'mixed' tactics of external pressure and internal subversion will grow in scope, boldness and malignancy but there are signs of a change in emphasis and direction. Events during the last two years have demonstrated to practically everybody that the lot of workers in the Soviet orbit is appalling. This cannot remain without influence on Communist positions in the Trade Unions. On the other hand Soviet scientific achievements have had a favourable impact on institutional élites here and elsewhere and have enhanced prospects of subversion among members of the managerial intelligentsia. [...] Educational institutions in which the attitudes and values of future institutional élites are being shaped will probably increase in importance as target areas for totalitarian penetration, overshadowing even the Trade Unions. Defenders of freedom in Australia would be well advised to take stock of the new situation, and to realize that *far from being an auxiliary operation, the subversion of institutional élites may become gradually more important than the subversion of Trade Unions.* Despite 'Hungarian' defections, the Stalinoid Left is still one of the most powerful forces in the intellectual life of Australia. This fact must, of course, be reflected by conditions at the universities. [...] Thus it will happen that the Party satellite or the pliable fool will gain undeserved and unnoticed precedence over the better man who stands by the principles of the Open Society. In this unhealthy atmosphere it is somewhat comic to hear the Stalinoid intellectuals referring to themselves as 'non-conformist'. Among the highbrows at present, particularly at universities, the surest way to social acceptance and respectability is either an attitude of political know-nothingism, or one of moderate fellow-travelling. The fully-fledged Party member is still 'respected' even if his company is not particularly sought. The only person likely to incur hostile social pressure with concomitant damage to status and career is the defender of the Open Society who lets his values influence action and who is consequently an anti-Communist. He is at present the true non-conformist at Australian universities, alas only too rare. All the spurious noise about the impending terror against the 'Left' is probably calculated to hide this state of affairs. It also reflects a justified fear that one day the hallowed principle of 'jobs for the boys' may be effectively challenged by its victims. Meanwhile, however, unconditional opposition in Australian universities to the most inhuman system of social organization ever devised by man entails social and economic penalties. This fact is scandalous.

[...]

Attempts to obtain help from outside against subversion may be effective in the short run but it is injurious to long-term fundamental interests of the Open Society. State interference in university administration should always be regarded as dangerous. The only effective *long-term* antidote to totalitarianism in universities as elsewhere is firm, militant and intelligent adherence to humanism and to the principles of the Open Society. Yet militant defenders of humanism must have a chance of stating their case which they do not get if totalitarian groups succeed in preventing or breaking their influence by organizational manipulation and slander. Covert totalitarian attacks on individuals can be effectively neutralized by exposure of their sources but only if university élites are prepared to co-operate. Whispered slander campaigns particularly those conducted by members of staff among students must be tracked down and answered by firm disciplinary measures. Stealthy organizational manipulations must be answered by principled organizational resistance. Appointment committees should participate fully in the selection of candidates for all academic appointments including the appointments of lecturers and tutors. The current practice of reducing the function of appointment committees to a formality and leaving matters by tacit agreement to heads of departments is both morally vicious and politically dangerous. [...]

Needless to say, any attempt to combat totalitarianism through judicial or semi-judicial boards or committees of inquiry at universities or elsewhere is, under present conditions, worse than useless. Totalitarian organizations with their inbuilt, very effective defences against action by 'bourgeois' courts would come out of it with flying colours. The disastrous American experience in combating large-scale racketeers, crime syndicates and the spy-rings through boards of inquiry, and our own experience with the Victorian Royal Commission on Communism, should serve as a warning. There is no legal or juridical substitute for political sophistication and for shrewd and resolute politically motivated action. In a multi-centric society such as ours which is threatened by totalitarian subversion, no judge and no policeman can relieve the citizens who are in positions of leadership of the responsibility which is irrevocably theirs.

1958

ALAN DAVIES

Small Country Blues

We need a term like 'the illusion of completeness' to catch the way people in small countries blot out the recognition that their society lacks differentiations, complexities and competencies vital to the functioning of major powers. Its nearest analogue in social psychology would be the 'illusion of knownness', which psychoanalytically aware observers have discovered to be characteristic of the culture of poverty, a refusal to contemplate an external society richer in any detail than the known small world. Cultural deprivation is clearly often handled in like fashion, with disparaging denial of superiority past one's own level of desire and ability masking philistine envy of cultivation. As part of their training as citizens residents of small countries seem to imbibe from their political cultures, not only specific ambitions and ideals and a sense of the relevant shaping of talents, but this general blindness to lack and the compensating illusion of comprehensiveness. This piece is an experiment in looking at Australia without the recommended shades. What are the discomforts of smallness? Are there any comforts?

First, and most obviously, a small social system implies a strained and probably under-equipped élite. However small the society, it must, if it wishes to perform at an advanced level, fill out a fairly complex system of leading roles. In each social realm there are institutional tasks to be performed according to quite exacting standards, roles that must be manned by people who at least purport to be capable of carrying out their specialised tasks effectively. There must, so to say, be a conductor of the Darwin Symphony, head of the fraud squad in Perth, chief rabbi of Tasmania. In a large society, we find queues up behind leading posts that are long and thick, much competition for the chance of a turn at the wheel, intense scrutiny of the performance of the incumbent by well-informed peers and rivals, and an urgency (with often brief terms) to leave some clear mark of one's incumbency. In a small society there are unfillable posts, tasks here and there that go by default, many posts filled only by over-promotion or very approximate fit — serial fraudulence, as it were. And there are one of two extreme patterns of recruitment: either unusually early instalment and long, leisurely incumbency; or selection relatively late in careers, from peers indistinguishable in merit, on the basis of seniority or the like; and lax standards of criticism and weak sanctions against poor performance.

Individual ambition thus takes rather different forms. The large society demands fine specialisation, constant evidence of current fitness; the small offers the luxury of unimpeded scope: each person, 'professing' from the start a territory much more loosely defined, indeed, in large part unfenced, can wander off their speciality into something else for years at a time, or run a double career, for example as city solicitor and international relations consultant (Eggleston), as central banker, administrator of the ballet and Aboriginal welfare reformer (Coombs). We even see, too, here and there an endearing pattern of self-nomination for posts *by thesis*: in technico-administrative fields especially, it has often seemed enough to declare an interest in something to be given immediate care of it.

[...]

A second source of small country discomfort lies in the imbalance and tension between imported and local ideas. Cultural rifts of portentous depth and sharpness open up between a corps of importers of ideas, who live like merchants exacting their percentage from the knowledge products they bring in and render fit for local distribution, and a corps of loyalist protectionists, who buy the locally made for preference and mock their adversaries' abject 'cultural cringe'. 'Australian life is too lacking in tradition, and too confused' to support an Australian literature, the professor of English at Melbourne University wrote in 1935, a remark that ignited P. R. Stephensen's rousing polemic, *The Foundations of Culture in Australia*. The dispute is perennial — indeed, was recently rehearsed again, as if obligatory, in perfectly standard form (though with unusual decorum) early in the career of *The Age Monthly Review*. 'Patriots', it seems, currently tangle less with 'Anglophiles' than with 'internationalists', who do not mind continuing to live at home, but wish to do so as in a suburb of world culture and who actively resent whatever looks like emphasis on (or indulgence to) local cultural production as a separate and especially valuable project. And, indeed, an amusing figure can be constructed of 'discoveries' over the last two generations by local pundits that Australia has 'come of age', each coinciding exactly with their authors' own emergence from adolescence.

However, a genuine pathos lies behind the ritual jousting, a chronic and painful doubt about the achievable quality of life in the small country. In part this is just the modern burden that Simmel detected in the 'over-growth of objective culture', the oppressive weight of the sheer mass of cultural objects and artefacts already in existence set against our limited capacity to learn about, master, or meaningfully assimilate them. So each new generation everywhere — and not merely the small country's — finds itself torn between an 'empty too much' (a wild dash to crop; hurried, skewed choice; an inability to say 'no' to any new fad) and a 'pure too little' (hanging back; staying loose; resignation to one's restrictive niche and its harsh filters). But small country morale is sapped additionally by one apparently specific remedy for the ailment — expatriation. The steady trickle away of those believing this is no country for people of refinement, and/or that their own talents are such as can only find full scope in a metropolitan centre, shapes as a standing cultural reproach (and therefore tends to be strenuously denied). The depth of the wound, of course, varies over time and with the classes of promise lost, and many would like to think the whole problem in Australia slight since, say, the late 1960s. At present, at any rate, the modal expatriate seems to have become the 'underfunded' scientist or technologist with highly defined and portable skills and a narcissism certainly no less than the pre-war artist's.

[...]

Thirdly and more cheerfully, visitors from the metropolitan centres have lately taken to suggesting that small countries may in the nature of things have a better chance of solving their problems. With quite small numbers, they remark, the scale (and cost) even of 'drastic' solutions need never be prohibitive, and, from the other side, the contriving of the necessary consensus for innovative turns of policy should come more easily with the manageably small sets of authoritative actors in play. It may be that what is really new here is the frustration, pessimism and despair in these large country policy professionals themselves, for whom small has suddenly become beautiful, but the sense that problems increasingly loom out of scale with the political units they present to goes back some way. 'The average nation state,' Daniel Bell wrote in 1979, 'has become too small for the big problems of life and too big for the small problems of life...The problem, sociologically, for the end of this century and the next, is the matching of scales. What is the proper size and scope of the approximate social unit to handle what kind of problem? ... What kinds of institutions can best meet the kinds of values that people want, to be able to express those needs most freely and fully?' The particular problems recently at the top of the political agenda — social integration, poverty, unemployment, economic stagnation — have, of course, powerfully abetted this sense of large-nation impotence (though small country performance during this time has hardly been notably superior). Yet hopefulness about future possibilities may still have a separate dynamic; and it is certainly interesting that when quizzed about the likelihood of solving its current most pressing problems by the year 2000, a substantial sample of the Australian organisational élite expresses firm confidence.

That smallness of scale may enhance the quality of public decision-making has, of course, been a commonplace at least since the advocacy of Rousseau and Hume. New Zealanders have long been justly proud of their citizens' 'right' of personal interview with the responsible government minister; and an ability to get all those politically concerned with a problem together in one room — even if quite a large room — and on first name terms, has smoothed much in Australian administrative practice well before current fashions in 'summitry'. Political leaders, indeed, will boast that their main strength is exactly in having known for a long time their counter-players in government and the economy, and having earned their good opinion and trust. But bitter and irreconcilable rifts may divide people in groups of hundreds or thousands as deeply as in groups of millions, and smallness cannot of itself guarantee a 'people so fundamentally at one that they may safely afford to bicker'. And, looking back, Australia cannot be said to have contrived, any more often than the France of Durkheim's solicitude, moments of creative efflorescence and collective renewal, when the alien unresponsiveness of social institutions is overcome, structures dissolve or are disregarded, rigidities break down and people come alive and experience their society as excitingly *constructable* and their individual existence as thoroughly social.

Fourthly, to follow out a little the converse of our last hypothesis: that if small countries may at times seem to move forward more easily, they may at others prove more vulnerable to small shocks (especially demographic ones). Some examples will help shape the point. The number of the Australian dead in the First World War was twice that of the American dead (from a population one-sixteenth the size). It is hard to detect any lasting American consequences. But the impact of this loss on Australian life runs deeply across the inter-war years — from the large number of women of the generation born before 1900 who never married, to the sheer lack of lustre and leadership in politics, the economy and culture in the two following decades. Again, to dive back a century, the attractive radical–nationalist tempered polity centred on Sydney in the 1840s, energised by its fifty different newspapers and its tri-denominational school system, was ripe for independent nationhood, when it was suddenly swamped by the gold rushes, relations with Melbourne became more absorbing than relations with London, and 'cutting the painter' lost its urgency till in due course the number of native-born came at last to outstrip the immigrants — and refloated it. There is still some sense of mystery about the lack of direct impact on the political system of the doubling of the Australian population between 1946 and 1976, and, with the steady decline of the British intake, the raising to one in seven the ratio of those wholly or partly socialised outside the culture. But there is no denying the wasting away of the narrow preoccupations and clannish allegiances of pre-war Little Australia. The same years saw a further significant change, a ten-fold increase in the annual crop of university graduates, which not only opened professional careers to individuals in a steadily rising curve but thickened the whole texture of the culture, making it possible, for example, to have a graduate press; for women to give up conservative politics; and providing perhaps at last the extra protective crust that Arthur Phillips thought necessary for the insulation of local creative talent.

If there is anything to these arguments one inescapable conclusion is that we should spend less time in awed upward contemplation of the great metropolitan centres and a good deal more looking sideways at the experience of like small nations, whose solutions should be better scaled to our problems, and whose very definitions of their problems are more likely to help us understand our own. [...] One certain early lesson if we turned to a serious contemplation of New Zealand, for example, might be that Australians' neurotic superciliousness and guiltless ignorance of, and incuriosity about, our neighbour is needed under our illusion of completeness to preserve us from acknowledging our own smallness and insignificance.

It is not always easy to disentangle the effects of smallness from those of remoteness or peripheralness — or from those of newness. It may not, in the end, be specially profitable to try to do so. Would we wish, for example, to claim that we have now outgrown Walter Bagehot's observation that nation-building in new countries like ours inevitably develops 'a prosaic turn of mind', a literal 'bare-mindedness', a 'worship of visible value' and 'ostentatious utility', all of which culminates in a politics of 'pitiless realism'? Certainly it is fascinating to see how quickly intellectuals in the early settlement became impressed with several of the themes we have judged currently salient. In his anthology of 'voices from the chorus' in the middle third of nineteenth-century Australia, George Nadel has people, for example, observing: 'If we have not a division of labour, we have a more varied development of the individual.' Again, 'In a limited community like this...each of us, in our individual capacity, has greater opportunity of impelling the onward march than individuals in densely populated countries.' There is a gratitude at having 'escaped from the lostness in crowds of the old countries', and the lostness in custom and habit; and a sense of freedom to choose prudently in social arrangements, avoiding the mistakes of the old world and immediately adopting the best new thinking. There was even a sense, as in dreams of eerie lucidity, of being privileged to 'observe the growth of our society as plainly as the operations of bees through a glass hive'. That sense we have certainly lost somewhere along the way, and even our heavy investment in the social sciences in this generation has hardly compensated. And, though it may just be true, as Conor Cruise O'Brien has suggested, that small countries draw on and digest their recent past better than large ones do, we may also have lost that initial pride, because of 'greater individual influence over events', in a capacity to 'make our own history'. We could surely put up with many assorted discomforts of smallness, if only this pristine illusion could be restored to us.

1985

VINCENT BUCKLEY

Intellectuals

It would be as well to apologize at once and say, with Kingsley Amis, 'On the whole I may seem to have shown a certain amount of acrimony towards the intelligentsia, which is rather unfair, because some of my best friends are intellectuals.' Almost everyone in our society who writes about *the* intellectuals succumbs to the tendency to dissociate himself from them; and this fact in itself suggests something about the status which the title has in our society. Not only in ours, however. The same note of ambiguous dissociation from their subject sounds unmistakably in a French work like Raymond Aron's *Opium of the Intellectuals* and in some of the contributions to the symposium *America and the Intellectuals*, which the editors of the *Partisan Review* published a few years ago. For my part, I think the title of intellectual an honourable one, though less honourable than that of poet; yet I am sure that an alert listener will be able to hear me busily dissociating myself just as everyone else does.

It is interesting that Amis make the collective noun 'intelligentsia' and the term 'intellectuals' interchangeable. This seems to me misleading. Most of the active and influential intellectuals, in our society at any rate, do not compose an intelligentsia in anything like the original sense: 'The scribbling set', as the Duke of Wellington called them; a group of thinkers who were freelance, under-employed, to a considerable degree alienated from the sources of social power or personal stability, and who virtually composed a world of their own. Alienated from the 'normal' institutions, they composed an institution of their own. They were on the whole literary intellectuals, eternal students, subversive if not revolutionary in spirit; and they lived a night-world life in which, as Dostoevsky shows, conversation often sounded like nothing so much as an exchange of manifestos.

The few small Australian groups whose way of life resembles theirs are not intellectuals but artists. An intellectual in the Australian context is something quite different. For one thing, most intellectuals here work at least eight hours a day in jobs which society agrees with them are socially useful.

But after all, how are we to decide who are the intellectuals in a society which puts pressure on educated men to deny that *they* are intellectuals? Or, to put it in another way, an educated man who behaves and thinks much like everyone else is pretty deliberately defining himself out of the class or group which we should want to distinguish by some such title. The question, 'Who is an intellectual?' is very similar to the question 'Who is a Jew?' — a question to which some writers return the answer, 'A man who is conscious of his Jewishness'. I think I am an intellectual, therefore I am. By this criterion almost nobody in Australia merits the title, because almost nobody claims it; and I know that, by agreeing to use it in a simply descriptive way, I am laying myself open to the charge of presumption: a fact which in itself carries a certain significance for my analysis.

To begin, then, by using the word in its widest connotation: In the first instance I will mean by 'intellectual' all those who would not be irretrievably astonished (though they might blush) to hear the word used of them. Such an amorphous group is hard to characterize, but if we take university teachers as typical representatives of it and generalize from them, we can locate four outstanding characteristics: they are institutionally absorbed and job-conscious, they are suburban, they are ideologically unsophisticated, and they are very little concerned with the more intense manifestations of our culture.

[...]

Since there is virtually no free-floating intelligentsia here, our intellectuals are institutionalized. Their intellectual energies are profitably *used* by our society, and are dedicated to use in practical affairs. There are very few who would not define their intellectual role in social terms. There is no nonsense about an intellectual's existing to think and to make other people think; on the contrary, he exists to 'work' in a 'job'. Most university lecturers, for example, would think of themselves as teachers merely, or as scientists merely, or as technologists merely. An historian would be generally perceived as a man who taught history to students, with perhaps a little 'private research' on the side, often undertaken to keep himself entered in the academic stakes. As one lecturer in literature (of all subjects) has said, 'The only sensible thing is to see it as a nine-to-five job.' In all this, there is not much suggestion that most academics or other intellectuals see it as their task to think and speak about human destiny, or even about the actual present human condition. All such tasks have been subordinated to, and eventually absorbed in, the 'job'; and thinking about the great issues is at best a spare-time activity, like pruning the rose-bushes, or going to a symphony concert.

The effects of this conception on the cultural tone of Australian society and on the spiritual morale of the intellectuals themselves is obviously very large. So far as cultural tone is concerned, the reduction of the intellectual life to the doing of a job, the occupancy of a niche, prevents our society from becoming familiar with the very notion of an intellectual as that word would be understood in Paris. Professor X in a charcoal-grey suit briskly telling people about foreign affairs on television presents an image of the intellectual very little different from that presented by a business consultant or, indeed, a racing tipster. All three are brainy blokes and knowledgeable men, and all three perform the useful function of producing and manipulating facts, which, if they are not useful at the moment, may become so some time. In the images presented by all three of them informedness and efficiency are the keynotes. It would be as disconcerting in the lecture theatre as on the television screen to have a man present himself simply as someone who thought hard about the fate and destiny of his fellow human beings and who did so because not to do so would be as intolerable to him as the loss of a lung. Yet many men have thought this even in our century.

Far worse, however, is the effect of such a conception on the morale of the intellectuals themselves. As every idealistic school-teacher knows, a man who lets his life-work be reduced to the status of a 'job', with increments, working conditions, and all the rest of the weary defensive mechanism, soon becomes cynical about the very job he has been so avid to fill. Australian intellectuals in general are highly conscientious about their jobs, but do not appear to see them as something capable of expanding the personality, of other people as well as of themselves. Consequently, they seem to have little conception of a world-wide and centuries-deep intellectual community, composed of and contributed to by all those who have struggled consciously to increase human understanding. An Australian biologist may feel that he has something in common with biologists the world over, since they are all engaged in a common job; and he may have a proper pride in that job, and a proper respect for those who join him in doing it. But he would usually be surprised to be told that the fate of Boris Pasternak concerned him as intimately as it concerned Pasternak's fellow-poets; for he would never have learnt that the people who threaten intellectuals in a far-off country are not merely threatening a few unfortunate individuals but are undermining a corporate enterprise for the understanding of the human condition and the enchantment of human life. The biggest staff meetings at Australian universities are held on the question of salaries and although there is much indignation over the disgraceful events in South Africa, expression of it tends to be confined to the morning-tea breaks in the common-room; there it attains the status of a conversational topic alternative to the inflationary spiral or the latest film; and it remains a topic only so long as it remains topical, only so long, that is, as the newspaper headlines provide the necessary stimulus.

The state of institutional security goes with the second characteristic — a way of life based on suburbia and lived, so far as the 'job' allows, in a surburban mode. The intellectual is generally attached very firmly to his home, and that home is generally a solid unit in the vast suburban complex of which all Australian cities, with the possible exception of Sydney, are composed. In this, as in their concern to be thought of as practical men and their lack of concern for the great tissues of human destiny, Australian intellectuals are typical of their society. Very few of them would think of 'the city' as the venue for an intellectual life intensely led and intensely shared; and up to date our actual city-centres are so insubstantial as to make such a thought rather unrealistic. The Middle-European notion of a café-culture which is closely linked with the very existence of a freelance intelligentsia is quite unfamiliar here; and the pubs are no substitute, although both in Sydney and Melbourne there are famous pubs which cater for the arty trade. In fact, there is little notion of the Being-an-Intellectual as a corporate way of life or an almost unquestionable value. Thank God, one breathes, remembering the sort of existence which is given its drab celebration in Simone de Beauvoir's *The Mandarins*: the pointless relationships, the parasitism, the use of the world as a great elongated mirror, the lax insistence on 'writing' as a therapy or an inevitable fate, the polemics which are as habitual as a nervous tic. But then one remembers that our way also has its disadvantages; if there is a refreshing absence of narcissism and cant, there is also a depressing absence of any sense that intellectuals may have a corporate existence which represents and ultimately serves the corporate existence of all men.

At 'work', one sticks to the 'job'; the rest of the time is for genteel living. The Smiths visit the Joneses at predictable intervals, drink a little red wine decanted from a flagon, eat French salad off wooden platters, chat about the car and the kids and the holidays. Then — the men talk one kind of shop and the women another. Socrates, stay in your grave, you won't be needed for a long time yet. And all you great writers, stop fooling round with our nervous systems.

At the occasional parties, sophisticated gossip goes the round — an addiction learnt, perhaps, in Oxbridge; shop once more but this time under its prurient aspect.

Certainly, there is a steady drift from suburbia, in one sense. In Melbourne, the young married lecturer who ten years ago would have considered it inevitable to go to a six-roomed timber villa in Cheltenham or Box Hill might now think first of Carlton, Parkville, or even North Melbourne, places which in time may even become the suburban fringes of the university. But in this, too, they are not untypical of the society as a whole; the slow drift back towards the city has been joined by a variety of middle-class types. The fact is that these inner-suburban areas are ceasing to be industrial centres and slums. So a preference for Carlton over Kew may be as bourgeois a piece of conformism as any other. In either place his neighbours are likely to think of the university man as very much like themselves — engaged in a different 'job', certainly, and doing it in the uniform of tweed jacket and slacks rather than a dark suit which is mandatory elsewhere but giving himself no airs and pretending to the appropriate trade-skills rather than to any special sources of enlightenment. Obviously there are advantages as well as disadvantages in this conformity to national habit; but one cannot be expected to welcome the phenomenon with much enthusiasm.

If our intellectuals are job-absorbed and suburban, they are also — to come to the third characteristic — ideologically unsophisticated. They do not move with much freedom or subtlety among the ideas which have motivated men in this century; and they have the sketchiest idea of where these ideas tend in practice. If one seeks an easy answer to the question why so many of them think that, although of course it would not suit us, the Russian or the Chinese 'solution' is at least 'efficient', and why a surprisingly large number of them are still, vaguely, fellow-travellers, it will surely be found in an ignorance which in turn is grounded in a failure to see that the recent massive insults offered to the human person by totalitarian regimes are any of our business. But such a blindness is impossible to anyone who, however unfettered his own thinking, sees that questions of ideology matter, and that one of the tasks of an intellectual is to discuss them. Australia has never had an atmosphere of discussion anything like that of post-war Paris or even pre-war New York. Both of those cities are, of course, closer to the centres of ideological disturbance; and both have been blessed with an influx of ideological refugees from Nazi and Communist power. Both, too, are familiar with the phenomenon we may call the intellectual colony, whether it exists with or without a café-culture.

The practical-man syndrome which affects our intellectuals is surely relevant too. Where everyone is concerned not to step outside his own 'field', we are likely to find that there are some 'fields' which nobody considers it his business to occupy. Whose field is totalitarianism for example? The statement that it is everyone's might be greeted by Australian intellectuals as a piece of posturing or a piece of fanaticism. Like the Romantics in Matthew Arnold's account, they simply do not know enough; and they have not sufficient impulse to find out. Of course, most of them could honestly say that they dislike Communism; but one has the uneasy suspicion that the reasons for their doing so are the sort which melt away under a certain kind of propaganda heat. A businessman who dislikes Communism only because it threatens his business may begin changing his mind as soon as he begins to trade with Communist countries. An intellectual who dislikes it only because it denies free discussion is likely to begin losing his dislike as soon as he has been persuaded that Russia is being 'liberalized'. Such assurances are very soothing; and a man who is impatient with the very need to be concerned with international issues ('politics', after all, are only marginally his business) is likely to accept them without looking too closely into what the process of liberalization consists of. Refugees' tales show him a world so remote from the one which usually preoccupies him that he will turn away from it with an uneasy impatience; or it may be that a friend of his has lately 'been there' and found things not too bad. It is possible that, in a society like ours, only a frightened man or an existentialist can adjust himself to thinking about the appalling challenges of our century. And Australian intellectuals don't include many frightened men or existentialists.

The naïveté does not come out, of course, only in matters of international tension. Insofar as there is a typical congeries of attitudes, it would be something like the following: a vague animosity towards the right wing, an aesthetic distaste for the commercial ethos, a deep-rooted distrust of Catholicism, a slightly contemptuous unease with Protestantism, a rejection of McCarthyism (which for some people means saying that a known Communist is a Communist) and a reaction from censorship, the police force, eminent administrators, anti-Semitism, party politics, poets, socialists, licensing laws, and the Royal family. Not a bad bag, when all is said and done; but an extremely untidy one. And a man who carries his life-work in it is not likely to have a very subtle understanding of the great religious and philosophical issues which I thought as a boy preoccupied intellectuals. Perhaps it goes without saying that only a minority of our intellectuals belongs to a church; it may be more surprising that even fewer belong to any political party or grouping. A refreshing scepticism about prefabricated answers to the most important issues often has as its underside a refusal to see that those issues are really important or even discussible.

The fourth most noticeable feature of this barely identified group is that its members are not very much concerned with ventures of the sort the promoters of which would describe as 'cultural'. An honest intellectual tradesman is of course preferable to a dilettante; and it is consoling to think that the *promotional carry-on* which some people confuse with culture absorbs very little of the energy of Australian intellectuals. But it has its disheartening side as well. The fragmentation of intellectual life caused by the occupancy of fields which are never to be stepped outside can be overcome only by the existence of organs for the discussion of those issues which we might call socio-cultural and which affect the whole pattern of our society. And any Australian starting a journal devoted to such concerns might well wonder where and who his audience was. The vigorous condition of *Nation* and the new *Bulletin* may be a sign that the situation is changing, and that, whether or not the audience can be identified, at least it is now known to exist. But the fragmentation still seems alarmingly permanent; and even the men with whom one would most like to discuss a philosophical or social or theological problem might be embarrassed if one introduced questions of poetry or painting. They would be more likely to be at home with music, which has an enormous vogue, and which is generally supposed to be more relaxing than the other arts.

There is a tendency, in other words, to see *haute culture* not as a body of shared experience but as somebody else's 'field'. This was inevitable, of course, as soon as the arties laid claim to it, and pretended that it *was* a field like any other; and it is certainly not an aberration unique to Australia. But it is particularly noticeable in Australia; where there is no free-floating intelligentsia, there will be few men of general culture, and the whole notion of a culture will suffer.

[...]

When I say that, until very recently, the intellectual climate was surprisingly amiable towards the Communists, I am pointing to a very peculiar paradox. For, on the one hand, the Communists and their cultural allies have for a long time carried a great deal less intellectual weight than their careful self-advertisement laid claim to; but, on the other hand, it has always been disarmingly easy for the determined anti-Communist, however good his arguments, to be isolated and rendered ineffective. Only some basic inadequacy in our intellectual habits could produce this anomaly. And yet my generalization still holds good, at least for Melbourne. For local reasons, it has not held good for Sydney during the past thirty years.

The two cities, so dissimilar in many other respects, also produce very different attitudes to life. For sixty or more years Melbourne, so staidly provincial in its demeanour, has been the home of radicalism and of activity in the higher journalism. In Sydney, if you have something to say you hold a party; in Melbourne you start a journal. The 1920s, which saw the Socialist poet Bernard O'Dowd flourishing in Melbourne, surrounded by other socialist writers like Vance Palmer and Furnley Maurice, produced in Sydney a new breed of vitalist poets around that very odd prophet, Norman Lindsay. In Melbourne of the 1930s and early 1940s, everyone was writing a novel of social destitution, and even the painters argued about Marxism; but in Sydney, the poets created myths of adventure and struggled to affirm the basic energies of life, preserving either a conservative attitude or a disdain for political action of all sorts.

Commentators are apt to explain the difference by mentioning the name of John Anderson, who was Professor of Philosophy in Sydney University for three decades. And, as a partial explanation, this will do. It is possible that Anderson's temper responded unusually well to the mood of that turbulent city; but it is certain that he in his turn has had more direct influence on its intellectual temper than any other single man has had on an Australian centre. Anderson was free-thinking, libertarian, sceptical, 'realist', and anti-Communist. Now, in the 60s, so is Sydney's intellectual community, by and large. Melbourne, on the other hand, has been influenced by the History School of its University as well as by its own radical past. Melbourne intellectuals tend to be earnest, do-gooding, voluble, assertive, preoccupied with 'McCarthyism', and avid for printed opinion, and, where Sydney has most of the better poets, Melbourne has most of the overt formers of opinion — though soon it is likely to be rivalled in this by the intellectuals of the national capital, Canberra. (Many of them, it hardly needs to be added, were originally Melbourne men.)

It will not be surprising that, in such a situation, the basic ideological issues have some trouble in emerging very clearly, and that the writers in the competing journals seem to be not so much engaging in a dialogue with one another as issuing manifestos into a void. These men often cannot see who their natural allies are; for they work in an atmosphere where differences of terminology and of immediate allegiance loom larger than they should, and in which it is therefore dangerously easy to convert intellectual disagreements into matters of personal or social acceptability. This is the only respect I can think of in which Melbourne or Sydney or Adelaide resembles that other centre of elevated gossip, Dublin.

Obviously Australian intellectual society cannot stay in this state forever. A certain provincialism, a certain hesitancy, are inevitable from our very geographical isolation; but each year this isolation comes to seem less and less crippling. Any intellectual, for example, who becomes urgently concerned with Australia's position in Asia, will have a certain ideological sophistication forced on him by the sheer brute facts; and after a while he may even come to welcome it. Then, too, many of the European migrants who work stoically in manual or clerical jobs in the Australian cities were once intellectuals; and as soon as they master the local idiom they are sure to make their voices heard. Migration, in fact, is altering the whole social environment in a number of ways; a Europeanizing tendency races along, keeping pace with the American which is affecting Australia as much as it affects Europe itself. [...]

With surprising rapidity, the environment into which the majority of Australians wake every morning is being jazzed up and internationalized. Even the senses are taught to respond daily to a world which is no longer felt to be a drably provincial, a cosy and unexacting antithesis to that bright remote world where crucial decisions are made and the fairy stories begin. Perhaps it will quicken the intellectual's pulse; at least it should lessen his feeling of loneliness and isolation, by providing him with an external surface adequate to symbolize the possibility of his belonging. [...]

1962

DAVID STOVE

Cricket versus Republicanism

It passes my understanding how anyone with even a grain of sense can feel pleasure at the prospect of a republican Australia: an Australia, that is to say, even more 'base, common and popular' than it is now. Anyway, I am myself for the British connection. In my World XI, Britons — Shakespeare, Purcell, Newton, Hume and Darwin — would be the first five picked. Either to the British exclusively, or to them more than to any other nation, the world owes, and Australia especially owes, whatever it has of scientific knowledge, sober philosophy, stable government without oppression — and cricket.

Only the British, and indeed, to tell the truth, only the English, could have invented this game. It requires gentlemanliness, and teaches it. This sounds like headmaster's talk *circa* 1938. It is, too. It is also true. I have seen cricket make gentlemen out of the most intractable Australian materials, at least for four hours on Saturday afternoons, more times than I could count. It doesn't *always* work, of course; that would be unreasonable to expect.

But the fact remains that the game, as it required a ripe civilisation to invent it, is also a means of transmitting civilisation to others. Of course I do not mean to suggest that this is why it is played. It is played because playing it is a pleasure beyond price. The cricketer, even the humblest village player, when he reflects on his life, can recall very few things so deeply delightful as the time he caught so-and-so at short forward leg ('off a full-blooded drive, mind you'); or the time he smashed so-and-so's bouncer through point for four ('*and* along the floor all the way').

> *Old men forget; yet all shall be forgot,*
> *But he'll remember, with advantages,*
> *What feats he did that day.*

Just because cricket is so civilised and subtle a game, 'an essence almost too fine', it might have been expected that it would never take root in this harsh country. And in fact Australian barracking, by its quantity and overwhelmingly stupid quality, seems to testify to a residual antipathy to any problem more complex than can be solved by the sturdy republican method of everyone immediately having a go.

But the book before me is a reminder, not only of how widely and deeply the game has taken root here, but of the fact that at cricket the Australian is a Pom-beating animal. The margin of superiority is slight, but it is consistent, and therefore calls for explanation. I have heard dozens of theories advanced to account for this. My own belief is that it is due to a difference in attitude towards the opponent: that whereas the Australians hate the Poms, the Poms only despise the Australians. I was very interested therefore, when Neil Harvey, during the wonderful centenary test just ended, said something similar only in politer words: that Australians always *want* to win more than their English opponents do.

But Australia, unlike England, has no literature of cricket. We have nothing to put beside the very beautiful chapter called 'The Flower Show Match' in Sassoon's *Memoirs of a Fox-Hunting Man*; nothing, even, to put beside Hugh de Selincourt's novel *The Cricket Match*, which, though good, is far inferior to Sassoon. We have only cricket journalism. Ray Robinson's book [*On Top Down Under: Australia's Cricket Captains*] is a very favourable specimen of this class. It is vilely written, but it is an extraordinarily rich collection of stories, jokes, statistics, facts of every kind, bearing on Australian test cricket under every captain from the beginning to Greg Chappell.

The circumstances here and now are obviously far less favourable towards a literature of cricket than they were, say, for Sassoon in the Weald of Kent in 1903. Still, I cannot help thinking that there are the seeds, in Australian temperament and Australian wit, of such a literature; though it would of necessity be a less gentle literature than the English one. There was, for example, a severe kind of poetry in what Greg Chappell said to Terry Jenner when the latter fell, bleeding from the head, hit by a short ball from Snow at the SCG a few years ago, and the ball careered away unregarded. Unregarded by everyone, that is, except the non-striker Chappell, whose only comment to Jenner was, 'There was a single in it.' Has not that the real Duke-of-Wellingon touch?

And again, the Sydney Hill every now and then produces wit of a quality which no English crowd *ever* produces. Not in this book, but in Alan Davidson's cricket autobiography, is the best example I know. The Rev. David Sheppard, having allowed yet another playable ball to go unattempted outside the off stump, was admonished in clerical tones from the Hill: 'And it came to pass — '. Such a thing gives me hope for my fellow-countrymen; and the joke was only made possible, I might point out to my anti-British friends, by the 'peculiar institution', the Church of England.

1977

BARRY OAKLEY

Meeting the Great

It is impossible to be humble and famous, especially if one is a writer. Fame corrupts, and absolute fame corrupts absolutely. In society, away from the typewriter, the famous writer is passive, resting between great works. Others have to keep the conversation going, worry about whether they are being witty and making a good impression. The famous are above all that.

Take the television personality, critic and versifier Clive James. Yes, we were going to meet him at the invitation of a North Sydney publisher friend. Poolside, on a sunny Sunday afternoon.

Was the white wine cold? The epigrams crisp and ready, hot from the oven? I was bristling, on my toes, as before a 100-metre sprint or an important tennis match. I needn't have bothered. The personality lay in a deck chair, in bathers, comatose and boneless, as if it was his turn next to be spitted on the barbecue coals.

The great intellect was at rest, ticking over in neutral. He was in the Antipodes and he was relaxing and he was not to be disturbed. Though he would go back to the real world and tell them how hedonistic we all were, he was to absorb, in the next hour, as much sun, swimming and steak as possible.

Eventually, social intercourse became unavoidable. We sat at a table over a salad. He spoke.

His long comic poem about Prince Charles was doing famously, he confided, and the great German writer Hans Magnus Enszenberger was going to run it in his literary magazine.

Once the Germans think you're funny, I ventured, you're done for.

The sally bounced harmlessly off him. Soon they rose to go.

Had his wife met with an accident? We were presented with a hand so limp and vertical I suspected a wrist fracture.

On another occasion at the same hospitable publisher's home the leading Canadian novelist Margaret Atwood put me in my place. I was sitting next to her on a couch. Conversation hummed all round, but between us there was complete silence. The Principle of Celebrity was operating: she was famous, so she was resting. It was up to me.

'I was one of the judges in the Canada/Australia Literary Award,' I offered. She sat on, pale-faced and unmoved. Fame had sedated her. I blundered on. 'We've chosen the novelist Leon Rooke,' I said.

She regained consciousness and turned her head in my direction without actually looking at me. 'A good choice for a Canadian award, considering that he was born in South Carolina,' she said. 'We love Americans.'

'But surely his readers regard him as Canadian by now,' I said, forced on to the back foot. 'He is regarded by very few readers at all,' she answered, helping herself to salted peanuts. 'You mean he's not known in Canada?' I defended, snicking the ball towards slips. 'I mean' — she was looking at me! At last I registered! — 'that if being known by Canadians was measured in points out of ten, I would rate ten — and Leon Rooke about four.'

I have sat next to the literary greats from a number of countries. In Toronto once, at an international festival, I had on one side Alain Robbe-Grillet of France, the inventor of the new novel, and on the other Sir Angus Wilson of England, the refiner of the old.

Though the three of us sat quite close, I was struck by the way each great ignored the other. I was a provisional buffer state between two proud and mutually hostile cultures. It was hard to believe that the high-nosed man with the Gauguin profile and the claret-faced, silver-haired old gentleman in the grey suit came from countries only 35 kilometres apart at the Straits of Dover.

Robbe-Grillet sniffed at the excellent French-Canadian wine as if it were insecticide, while Sir Angus downed it with relish. If Robbe-Grillet's English was broken, my French was fragmented. But, true to the Celebrity Principle, the onus was on me.

I asked him, in slow English, about Levi-Strauss and Barthes. His look suggested he regarded these French thinkers as more or less on a par with the wine. He retaliated by sketching a crude map of Australia on a saucer and asking me to mark in the cities. The map looked more like a sclerotic dog, so I added legs and a tail.

'C'est un chien,' I experimented, 'ce n'est pas l'Australie.' He started laughing — not at my observation but my accent, and kept muttering the sentence to himself the way I'd expressed it, obviously intending to dine out on it back in Paris.

Opposite at this international gathering was a Bulgarian poet with a long beard shaped like a spade. He was staring at the blond Canadian girl beside him. Then he turned and said something to the lady interpreter on his other side. 'He is saying,' she said, leaning across to the blond girl, 'that the whiteness of your smile is the Toronto memory that will never die for him.' From then on, his eyes gleaming as he moved in for the kill, came a series of similar compliments that sounded like a cross between Algernon Charles Swinburne and a toothpaste commercial.

I have read on the same platform as J. P. Donleavy, author of *The Ginger Man*: sad-faced, like so many comic writers, he was layered in thick grey tweeds. He was aquiline, white-bearded and slightly stooped — a combination of Jewish pawnbroker and Irish country squire. We were photographed together after the reading, but I never got the picture. But I like to think of us on some Toronto darkroom shelf, linked together forever.

I have met the great on my home ground. At Kallista once, in the Dandenongs, out of Melbourne, a group of Australians conferred with a group of German writers for a very long weekend. It was frightening. We sat around a large table facing microphones, so that no banality went untaped.

The clown was a round, unshaven Swiss dramatist who, about 11.45 every morning, would say, 'Yess, I haff a question. Ven is lunch?' The prince was Hans Magnus Enszenberger, to whom the other Germans deferred in a way the egalitarian Australians sometimes found embarrassing.

Enszenberger, a slim, elegant, charming man, had a minor disagreement with another German poet. It flared up sharply for a second, and then the poet went strangely limp and crestfallen, and said something in German to Enszenberger in a plaintive, abject murmur. 'What's he saying?' one of the Australians asked. 'He is saying,' said Enszenberger with some embarrassment, 'that he is not worthy to undo the straps of my sandal.'

The late Nobel Prize winner William Golding was a pleasant man. After a literary conference in Exeter, my wife and I did a tour of the region with Ian Turner, who knew him. We drove, on a perfect English summer's day, to the village of Broadchalke, where he lived in a house of rose-red brick.

The Goldings had prepared a nice lunch for us. The food and wine were good, the conversation lively, but I was suffering more and more from a stomach upset I'd picked up on the way. When Mrs Golding went into some detail about the vomiting and dysentery they had endured during a recent trip to Egypt, I had to get up and hobble at embarrassing speed to the lavatory.

I had ruined the image of the tough Australian, tall and lean in the saddle, for good. To make it worse, my wife was harsh as we drove away. 'You were jealous,' she said. 'You weren't getting enough attention, so you got sick.'

I sometimes used see Patrick White in Oxford Street, in gumboots and knitted beanie, looking like a retired dairy farmer. Occasionally he nodded to me — only, some mutual acquaintance told me, because he thought I was Robin Lovejoy.

The poet Ted Hughes once said hello to me. I have shaken the epic novelist Xavier Herbert by the hand, which agitates him as if his arm had been a lever and he a poker machine, and starts him talking in a continuous tumbling flow. Dorothy Hewett once accused me of being scared of her and of women generally. Alex Buzo once ordered me to put out my cigarette when I was fielding for his cricket team. Jack Hibberd, another playwright, has written me illegible prescriptions for valium. I have picked up Laurence Ferlinghetti's black gaucho hat and passed it to him, noting the vastness of its circumference.

I have argued abut the place of women in Australian drama with Germaine Greer and survived without a tetanus injection. I have criticised the screenplay of the movie *Reds* to Trevor Griffiths, who wrote it, and he took it like a lamb. I have stood in a foyer with David Williamson and Bruce Spence and felt five feet tall.

And — the great novelist John Updike and myself were once close. It was in Adelaide, during Writers' Week. Updike was to give the keynote address in the Festival Hall. A quartet of local writers was required to decorate the stage, like literary potted palms.

The hall was packed. The audience stretched into the distance in an infrared haze. Updike and I peeped through the curtain. Jesus, he said, either to Him or to me. Then he asked me where the men's washroom was. And, weighing every word, I told him. What directions! They were terse, they were pithy, they were publishable.

Afterwards there was a party at someone's house. He was surrounded by admirers. Did my directions still linger? Was the haiku I had made out of turning left then right still in his head? It seemed, from the number of women around him, unlikely.

The party's conviviality was shattered suddenly near the end of the evening. The hostess, carrying a tray of drinks, crashed through a glass door, not realising it had been closed. She made it through to the patio, shocked but unhurt.

It seemed an effective image for what great writers do. They break through an impalpable glass, reality's transparent pane, into some other region, whence they return with gifts. Read them, enjoy them, admire them, but don't, whenever possible, sit next to them.

1984

DAVID MALOUF

A First Place

My purpose is to look at the only place in Australia that I know well, the only place I know from inside, from my body outwards, and to offer my understanding of it as an example of how we might begin to speak accurately of where and what we are. What I will be after is not facts — or not only facts, but a description of how the elements of a place and our inner lives cross and illuminate one another, how we interpret space, and in so doing make our first maps of reality, how we mythologise spaces and through that mythology (a good deal of it inherited) find our way into a culture. You will see, I hope, how a writer might be particularly engaged by all this, and especially a writer of fiction; and you will see too why any one man might have only a single place he can speak of, the place of his earliest experience. For me that was Brisbane. It has always seemed to me to be a fortunate choice — excect that I didn't make it. But then the place you get is always, in the real sense of the word, fortunate, in that it constitutes your fortune, your fate, and is your only entry into the world. I am not suggesting that Brisbane is unique in offering the sort of reading I mean to make. The city is unique, as all places are, but the reading, the method I hope, is not.

To begin then with topography.

The first thing you notice about this city is the unevenness of the ground. Brisbane is hilly. Walk two hundred metres in almost any direction outside the central city (which has been levelled) and you get a view — a new view. It is all gullies and sudden vistas. Not long views down a street to the horizon — and I am thinking now of cities like Melbourne and Adelaide, or Manchester or Milan, those great flat cities where you look away down endless vistas and the mind is drawn to distance. Wherever the eye turns here it learns restlessness, and variety and possibility, as the body learns effort. Brisbane is a city that tires the legs and demands a certain sort of breath. It is not a city, I would want to say, that provokes contemplation, in which the mind moves out and loses itself in space. What it might provoke is drama, and a kind of intellectual play, delights in new and shifting views, and this because each new vista as it presents itself here is so intensely colourful.

The key colour is green, and of a particular density: the green of mangroves along the riverbanks, of Moreton Bay figs, of the big trees that are natives of this corner of Queensland, the shapely hoop-pines and bunyas that still dominate the skyline along every ridge. The Australian landscape here is not blue-grey, or grey-green or buff, as in so much of southern Australia; and the light isn't blond or even blue. It is a rich golden pink, and in the late afternoon the western hills and the great flat expanse of water that is the Bay create an effect I have seen in other places only before or after a storm. Everything glows from within. The greens become darkly luminous. The sky produces effects of light and cloud that are, to more sober eyes, almost vulgarly picturesque. But then, these are the sub-tropics. You are soon made aware here of a kind of moisture in the air that makes nature a force that isn't easily domesticated — everything grows too fast, too tall, it gets quickly out of control. Vegetation doesn't complement the man-made, it fiercely competes with it; gardens are always on the point of turning themselves into wilderness, hauling down fences, pushing sheds and outhouses over, making things look ramshackle and halfway to ruin. The weather, harsh sunlight, hard rain, adds to the process, stripping houses of their paint, rotting timber, making the dwellings altogether less solid and substantial, on their high stumps, than the great native trees that surround them.

I'll come back to those houses in a moment. It is no accident that they should have invaded a paragraph that is devoted to nature, since they are, in this place, so utterly of it, both in form and substance. Open wooden affairs, they seem often like elaborated tree-houses, great grown-up cubby-houses hanging precariously above around.

Now what you abstract from such a landscape from its greenness, its fierce and damply sinister growth, its power compared with the flimsiness of the domestic architecture, its grandeur of colour and effect, its openness upwards to the sky — another consequence of all those hills — is something other, I would suggest, than what is abstracted from the wide, dry landscapes of southern Australia that we sometimes think of as 'typical'. It offers a different notion of what the land might be, and relates it to all the daily business of life in a quite different way. It shapes in those who grow up there a different sensibility, a different cast of mind, creates a different sort of Australian.

So much then for the lay of the land; now for that other distinctive feature of the city, its river. Winding back and forth across Brisbane in a classic meander, making pockets and elbows with high cliffs on one side and mud-flats on the other, the River is inescapable. It cuts in and out of every suburb, can be seen from every hill. It also keeps the Bay in mind, since that, clearly, is where all its windings, its odd turns and evasions, lead. But this river does not have the same uses for the citizen as the rivers that flow through other towns.

We think of the Thames, or the Seine or the Tiber or the Arno, and it is clear how they are related to the cities they have growing up on their banks. They divide them, north and south. They offer themselves as a means of orientation. But the river in Brisbane is a disorienting factor. Impossible to know which side of it you are on, north or south, or to use it for settling in your mind how any place or suburb is related to any other.

So the topography of Brisbane, broken up as it is by hills and by the endless switching back and forth upon itself of the river, offers no clear map for the mind to move in, and this really is unusual — I know of no other city like it. Only one thing saves you here from being completely mapless, and that is the net — the purely conceptual net — that was laid down over the city with the tramline system. Ideally it is a great wheel, with the business centre as the hub and a set of radial spokes that push out into the suburbs. The city is conceived of in the minds of its citizens in terms of radial opposites that allow them to establish limits, and these are the old tram termini: Ascot/Balmoral, Clayfield/Salisbury, Toowong/the Grange, West End/New Farm Park, to mention only a few; and this sense of radial opposites has persisted, and continues to be worked with, though the actual tramlines have long since been replaced with 'invisible' (as it were) bus routes. The old tramline system is now the invisible principle that holds the city together and gives it a shape in people's minds.

But that wheels-shape, as I said at the beginning, was ideal — not actual. I lived at Ascot. I have always thought of Balmoral as being at the other end of the city geographically — say, an hour's tram journey or twelve to fifteen miles away. But when I looked at a map recently I discovered that it is, in fact, only half a mile away on the opposite side of the river. Space, in this city, is unreadable. Geography and its features offer no help in the making of a mental map. What you have to do here is create a conceptual one. I ask myself again what habits of mind such a city may encourage in its citizens, and how, though taken for granted in this place, they may differ from the habits of places where geography declares itself at every point as helpful, reliable, being itself a map.

I have already referred briefly to the Brisbane house, setting its insubstantiality for a moment against the solidity the big local trees, evoking the oddness with which it places itself, reared high on tree-stumps, on the side of its hill.

The houses are of timber, that is the essence of the thing, and to live with timber is to live with a material that yields at every step. The house is a living presence as a stone house never can be, responding to temperature in all its joists and floorboards, creaking, allowing you to follow every step sometimes, in every room. Imagine an old staircase and magnify its physical presence till it becomes a whole dwelling.

Children discover, among their first sensual experiences in the world of touch, the feel of tongue-and-groove boards, the soft places where they have rotted, the way paint flakes and the wood underneath will release sometimes, if you press it, a trickle of spicy reddish dust. In earlier days they often made themselves sick by licking those walls and poisoning themselves with lead.

You learn in such houses to listen. You build up a map of the house in sound, that allows you to know exactly where everyone is and to predict approaches.

You also learn what not to hear, what is not-to-be-heard, because it is a condition of such houses that everything can be heard. Strict conventions exist about what should be listened to and these soon become habits of not-listening, not-hearing. So too, habits grow up of not-seeing.

Wooden houses in Brisbane are open. That is, they often have no doors, and one of the conventions of the place (how it came about might be a study in itself) is that doors, for the most part, are not closed. Maybe it is a result of the weather. Maybe it has something to do with the insistence that life as it is lived up here has no secrets — or should have none. Though it does of course.

Whatever the reason, bedroom doors in a Brisbane house are kept open — you get used to that. Even bathroom doors have no locks and are seldom closed. The proximities are dealt with, and privacy maintained, by just those subtle habits of not-seeing, not-hearing that growing up in such a house creates in you as a kind of second nature. There is something almost Indian about all this. How different from life as it is lived in solid brick houses, with solid walls and solid doors and the need to keep them sealed against the air. Brisbane houses are unsealable. Openness to the air, to the elements, is one of the conditions of their being — and you get used to that too.

So there it is, this odd timber structure, often decorated with wooden fretwork and scrolls of great fantasy, raised on tree-stumps to leaf level and still having about it some quality of the tree — a kind of tree-house expanded. At the centre a nest of rooms, all opening on to a hallway that as often as not runs straight through from front to back, so that when you step up to the front door of the house you can see right through it to trees or sky. Around the nest of rooms, verandahs, mostly with crossed openwork below and lattice or rolled venetians above; an intermediary space between the house proper, which is itself only half closed in, and the world outside — garden, street, weather.

Verandahs have their own life, their own conventions, but serve, for the most part, to make the too-open interior seem closed, therefore safe and protected. Weather beats in on the verandah and the house stays dry. Hawkers and other callers may be allowed up the front steps on to the verandah, but the house, utterly visible and open right through, remains inviolate. There are conventions about this too. You develop a keen sense, from early on, if you grow up in such a house, of what is inside and safe and what is out there at the edge, a boundary area, domestic but exposed.

Inside and out — that is one aspect of the thing: the nest of rooms at the centre and the open verandah. But there is also upstairs and down, and this doesn't at all mean the same thing here as in the two-storeyed terrace, where upstairs means sleeping and downstairs is public life. Upstairs in the Brisbane house is everything: the division between night and day might at the very least be established as one side or the other of a hall. Downstairs here means under-the-house, and that is in many ways the most interesting place of all.

It comes into existence as a space because of the need to get those houses up on stumps, to get them level on the hills it might be, or to keep them cool by providing a buffer of cool air underneath. There are several explanations, no one of them definitive.

So the space down there may be a cube, but is more often a wedge of deepening dark as the high house-stumps at the back diminish till they are as little at the front as a metre or half-a-metre high.

The stumps are capped with tin and painted with creosote against termites. The space they form is closed in with lattice, sometimes all the way to the ground, sometimes to make a fringe a half-metre or so below floor level. The earth is bare, but flooring boards being what they are, a good deal of detritus falls down there from the house above: rusty pins and needles, nails, tacks, occasionally a peachstone or some other rubbish where a child has found a crack big enough to push it through. And a good deal of what the house rejects in other ways also finds its way down there: old sinks or cisterns or bits of plumbing, bed-frames, broken chairs, a superannuated ice-box or meat safe, old toys.

It's a kind of archaeological site down there, and does in fact develop a time dimension of its own that makes the process of falling below, or sending below, or storing below, a passage out of the present into limbo, where things go on visibly existing as a past that can be re-entered, a time-capsule underworld. Visiting it is a way of leaving the house, and the present and daylight and getting back to the underside of things.

It's a sinister place and dangerous, but you are also liberated down there from the conventions. It's where children go to sulk. It's where cats have their kittens and sick dogs go. It's a place to hide things. It is also, as children discover, a place to explore; either by climbing up, usually on a dare, to the dark place under the front steps — exploring the dimensions of your own courage, this is, or your own fear — or by exploring, in the freedom down there, your own and other people's bodies. There can be few Brisbane children who do not associate under-the-house, guiltily or as a great break-out of themselves, with their first touch or taste of sex.

A landscape and its houses, also a way of life; but more deeply, a way of experiencing and mapping the world. One of our intellectual habits, it seems to me, is the visualising, in terms drawn from the life about us, of what is not visible but which we may need to see. One such entity is what we call mind or psyche. One observes in Freud's description of how the mind works how essential architectural features are, trapdoors, cellars, attics, etc. What I mean to ask here is how far growing up in the kind of house I have been describing may determine, in a very particular way, not only habits of life or habits of mind but the very shape of the psyche as Brisbane people conceive it, may determine, that is, how they visualise and embody such concepts as consciousness and the unconscious, public and private areas of experience, controlled areas and those that are pressingly uncontrollable or just within control — and to speak now of my own particular interest, how far these precise and local actualisations may be available to the writer in dealing with the inner lives of people. What I mean to suggest, at least problematically, is ways in which thinking and feeling may be intensely local — though that does not necessarily make them incomprehensible to outsiders, and it is the writer's job, of course, so long as we are in the world of his fiction, to make insiders of all of us.

We have tended, when thinking as 'Australians', to turn away from difference, even to assume that difference does not exist, and fix our attention on what is common to us; to assume that some general quality of Australianness exists, a national identity that derives from our history in the place and from the place itself. But Australians have had different histories. The states have produced, I would want to claim, very different social forms, different political forms as well, and so far as landscape and climate are concerned, Australia is not one place. It might be time to forget likeness and look closely at the many varieties of difference we now exhibit, to let notions of what is typically Australian lapse for a time while we investigate the different sorts of landscape the country presents us with, the different styles social, political, educational of the states, the different styles of our cities, and even of suburbs within cities, and for those of us who are concerned with literature, for example, to ask ourselves how many different sorts of Australian writing there may be and how much the differences between them may be determined by the particular social habits and physical features of place. Is there, to come back to the present occasion, a Brisbane way of experiencing things that we could isolate in the works of writers who, even if they have not spent their writing life in the city, grew up there, and were in their first experience of the world shaped by it? Is there something in the style of mind of these writers, even in their use of language, a restlessness, a delight in variety and colour and baroque effects, in what I called earlier 'drama' and 'shifting views' that we might trace back to the topography of the place and the physical conditions it imposes on the body, to ways of seeing it imposes on the eye, and at some less conscious level, to embodiments of mind and psyche that belong to the first experience, and first mapping, of a house?

1985

CHRIS WALLACE-CRABBE

Swaying in the Forties

Ration books, whatever became of ration books? Those little brownish pocket-books, the coloured tickets and a neat pair of scissors tied to the shop counter, these are so deeply ingrained in my childhood as to seem inevitable, not memorable. They have a routine quality, like *Champion* or 'The Search for the Golden Boomerang' or visits to the flicks on Saturday arvo, hoping against hope for a film marked out by June Allyson's distillation of sweetness. And opposite the deep naturalness of all these — in the mind's other eye — are to be found the forties' inherently surrealist artefacts: gas producers on the left front mudguards of cars, slit trenches in front lawns, gas masks and midget submarines, all worthy of the starkly graphic imagination of an Eric Thake.

When, a few years ago, I cobbled together a series of reflections on 'my' 1930s the job was easy, the problems of selection few, for my best-loved screen memories were just sitting up there like Jacky, waiting to be made use of, waiting to be strung together. The forties come harder, since in dealing with that faraway but far larger memory-field I have to take account of questions of causation and chronology.

They have their music too, their distinctive flavour, none the less. At one end of the dial sound the sweet beguiling strains of 'Lili Marlene' and 'The Lady from Twenty-nine Palms' (or was it Forty-nine?), familiar occasions for escape. At the other end were darker musics which I did not yet know how to hear. Like this, for instance:

Nietzsche respected the great god Plumb
That lays his pipes in a baby's tum.
Beneath our logic's pure avowals
He heard the murmur of the bowels.

(James McAuley, 'The Family of Love')

Or the fact that another unknown, Judith Wright, was declaring that 'The trains go north with guns'. As a schoolboy I knew nothing of the peculiar utterances of the modern arts; my classmates still called Picasso 'Pig's arse-o' and Dad was to tell me on one occasion that a poet called T. S. Eliot had written that 'The sun was setting like half a tinned apricot into a sea of junket'. And, ah yes,

I did know the private collection of our grandest friend, Hilda (Mrs R. D.) Elliott, a personal gallery which displayed Orpen, Brangwyn, Degas and the wrong John, Elioth Gruner and Blamire Young. Of more interest to me was the fact that she kept kangaroos in her Toorak front garden.

I have on the desk beside me a copy of the *Herald* for Thursday, 4 January 1945. The day was warm, 82 degrees F. — poor old Fahrenheit, I still can't do without it in these diminished Celsian days — and we were probably on summer holidays at Black Rock, now a mere suburb: it was the only place we ever had our holidays, I do not believe we ever said 'holidayed', during the War. But it is the front page of this newspaper which brings rushing back my common childhood terms of reference: 'NEW ATTACK ON NAZI WEDGE', 'ALLIES ON MANDALAY RAILWAY', 'CANADIANS PRESS ON N.W. OF RAVENNA', 'TURKEY BREAKS WITH JAPAN' and 'NEW GREEK LEADER FORMS CABINET AS GUNS ROAR'. No wonder we all knew so much geography in those days; one of my exact contemporaries still remembers the capitals of all the countries in the world, as they were in 1939.

It was not only a World War: it was also a war world. Come August 1945 and the flurry of VJ Day, my main source of puzzlement was to be what on earth they would put in the papers now it was peacetime. You cannot get much media mileage out of the return of Jack Baird's pace bowling to the Carlton team, nor out of such items as 'Mr J. D. G. Medley, Vice-Chancellor of the University, is spending the holidays at Khancoban and will return to Melbourne on January 15'. The editors do not seem to have been troubled: politics is just a way of continuing war by other means.

Let me place a figure in the picture, my own. I begin the decade as a small boy going off with his mother and younger brother to share an aunt's timber house at the seaside because Dad has sailed away to the impending war in Malaya and will not be back — except for one brief compassionate leave — for five years; I end it as a lumpish youth of sixteen scraping through a science Matric by the skin of my teeth and finding a job as Junior Technical Officer at the Royal Mint, William Street, Melbourne, there to work amid the buying and smelting of gold, the smelting and stamping of bronze or silver coinage. The intervening period is stuffed full of schooldays, full of sustained routines, inkblots, nicknames and only rare showings of memorabilia. I begin by going from one small school, Yarra Bank, to another, and then on to another, where we start French at six, Latin at seven. There's history for you. I move to a very large school indeed ('The biggest boys' school in the southern hemisphere'), where one and a half thousand boys could be loosely deployed in picturesque landscape settings, and stay there for eight years and more. For nine years, after Black Rock, we are crammed hugger-mugger into a tiny flat, just off Toorak Road. Only reffos or bachelors are meant to live in flats; ordinary people have, or rent, houses. My mother ignores this palpable fact, willing to put up with being a sardine for the sake of a toffy address. Having no garden, we play in the street. An old tennis ball bounces interminably against brick walls.

It was my mother who had some awareness of what moved artistically. Before the war her friends had included pianists, potters, painters and printmakers, but that global melodrama and the need to look after two boys had switched off her cultural input. Once he had escaped from the jungles of Burma, a thousand miles on foot, lost for much of the time, Dad had it much easier. Stravaging around India, Persia and Lebanon, he could wallow in costume drama and ruined temples, devour exotica, imagine the sweep of tribes, peoples, dynasties through the Krac des Chevaliers or the Red Mosque, and keep alive in his heart the ideals of Norman Lindsay and the great illustrators. Fortified by a century of illustration, his response to most modern painting was an easy one: 'The bugger can't draw.' But I was only to hear this line in the latter half of the decade. Until then my father was the faraway source of photos, flimsy airletters rich with oriental travel details and curvilinear gifts from China or India. He was geography personified: already I could see how he idealized Ptolemy the Great, Asoka the Furious, Alexander — not the British field marshal but Iskandar himself.

History diffuses as much as it classifies; indeed, it dissipates aura because it classifies things and places them in sets or boxes. It is mute household objects, humble tastes and modest smells that by their maverick or mongrel qualities retain their eloquence. So the 1940s are for me still encapsulated in chops, cauliflower cheese and the sparsely fluted metal containers in which were served the chocolate malted milks I loved so well; in the wooden grid that floored the central area of trams; in the smell of a summer northerly bearing malthouse and Rosella tomato sauce flavours richly over from Richmond; in dust and fallen tickets by the wicket gates on railway platforms; in thin, flat wafers of beechnut chewing gum, the currency of our American invaders; in aeroplane scrapbooks; and in the prickly feeling of grey worsted suitpants against my sweaty legs after a lunchtime spent playing some hectic game in the school grounds. Zinc, chromium, manganese — in those lost days I became obsessed by the chemical properties of metals.

It was a time of displacement and imaginative subversion as well as of common participation in that abstract solidarity which we called 'the war effort' or, later, 'reconstruction'. People were moved from place to place in oddly random ways. Not only was Nolan sent off to the Wimmera, there to discover newly expressionist landscape images; not only were Harold Stewart and McAuley sent south to Victoria Barracks, St Kilda Road, there to give birth to that gaudy bellwether, Ern Malley; not only was Patrick White sent to the Aegean and Slessor to the Western Desert. Whole schools went up country to escape from incipient Japanese bombs. Whole industries changed their identities. And many familiar products vanished from daily life. Most surreal of all, there were a few years in which, for the first and last time, it was patriotic to be a Communist.

Whatever the war effort was doing, it was also peeling back piecemeal the sunlit surfaces of daily life, revealing mental flora as bizarre as Albert Tucker's *Images of Modern Evil* or such lines as these, hatched from A. D. Hope's usually Parnassian imagination:

Full sail the proud three-decker sandwiches
With the eye-fumbled priestesses repass;
On their swan lake the enchanted ice-creams freeze,
The amorous fountain prickles in the glass
And at the introit of this mass emotion
She comes, she comes, a balanced pillar of blood

('Morning Coffee')

But nothing of this was visible to a boy growing up, quietly enough, reflectively enough, sportingly enough, through the bipartite forties. The only real artistic flurry I can dredge back from those years was the journalistic brouhaha over the Archibald Prize for 1943. For my rapid-reading machinery it was a span of time that began with William, Biggles and *Puck of Pook's Hill* and ended with an undifferentiated mishmash of Mark Twain, Keats, mathematical puzzles, Neville Cardus, *Eyeless in Gaza, The Rape of the Lock* and *Ulysses.* The one thing I was clear about was that all nineteenth-century prose was unreadable, an extended hoax foisted upon us by adults: well, by some adults.

By the end of 1950 habit-sets were slipping and sliding. I went for the first time to surf beaches instead of the flat, tepid waters of the Bay. I had sharpened up my net game, but my backhand was still my weakness. The local municipal library — for we had changed to an outer suburb — proved to be marvellously rich in Bloomsbury colorations, Gide and Stendhal; I not only read *Aspects of the Novel* but excitedly followed up all Forster's tips, nothing but the bulky *Moby Dick* failing to make an impression. Summerily suntanning daily, I waited for news about my impending job. Communists were bad once again, Korea improbably offering itself as a potential flashpoint. My father was now working for General Motors-Holden while remaining a steady advocate of the Chinese communists against 'that bastard, Kai-Chek'. I and my peers knew all the models of shiny Yank-tanks while our hearts burned for natty little English sports cars. England still produced quality products and the Japanese cheap, tinny junk. I bought a brown pork-pie hat and some army disposals shirts. It was time at last to start working in the city: all those marvellous hours of reading on the train.

Soon, for the gap before night school, I discovered the Hoddle, a basement eating house with a studenty queue all the way up its terrazzo stairs to Little Collins Street. It was the first Italian trattoria I had ever encountered. It had an aura, a very modest aura, which remains with me still, as clear as day and as thick as evening. Thick white table-cloths, thick white china, thick white bread with hard crusts and, it goes without saying, densely brown minestrone for starters. I was now fairly launched in the city. The National Gallery and the Public Library waited under their flat grey dome, prepared to swallow me up.

One summer's afternoon I went to visit Jack Bellew and his daughter June in their modern house on Banksia Street hill. On their living room wall there hung a most arresting image. Queerly simplified, done in shiny enamels, it depicted a dark Ned Kelly with his tincan head, riding across flatness towards the viewer. It was impossible actually to like this painting, but I soon came to realize that it was the most extraordinary, the most unforgettable picture that I had ever seen. Somehow it hacked an icon out of real life. It had to do with life, but was more than it. And, miracle of miracles, here was modern art which actually had an Australian subject.

At this, my whole understanding turned over.

1990

PIERRE RYCKMANS

An Amateur Artist

No sensitive and reflective artist can approach China without being profoundly affected by the experience. Fairweather was certainly no exception to this rule and, for all his reticence and elusiveness, he left convincing evidence that China had played an important role in his artistic and spiritual development.

After a first stay (1929–33, Shanghai and Beijing), he felt the need to return for a second visit (1935–36, Beijing). Although, later on, he occasionally alluded to the discoveries which he made during these years (in some respects, China remained for him a recurrent source of inspiration), one should naturally not expect from a man like him many personal reminiscences or aesthetic statements: the fact is that Fairweather seems always to have abided by Matisse's precept: 'A painter should cut his tongue.' Still, a few points should be noted.

Chinese calligraphy was for him a momentous revelation. He repeatedly acknowledged the fascination which this unique art exerted on him. 'Unique' should be understood here in a most literal sense: with their calligraphy, the Chinese actually possess one more major art. It has no equivalent in any other culture — a fact which is obscured by the unfortunate choice of the word 'calligraphy' to translate a term that simply means 'writing'. In a western context, 'calligraphy' signifies, by its very etymology, 'beautiful writing', and indeed, when we speak of 'gothic calligraphy', 'Arabic calligraphy', and so on, we think of a form of writing that has been 'embellished' by the addition of decorative elements. But in so-called 'Chinese calligraphy', it is the writing itself which is the art, and one could no more think of 'embellishing' it than one could conceive of an 'embellished' form of painting.

As he himself recalled it, Fairweather was especially impressed by the experience of watching calligraphers at work. This is indeed the best way to approach their art, as calligraphy is first a performance — it is a graphic dance, the dynamic trace of a gesture, the translation into two-dimensional space of a fluid sequence of movements unfolding in time.

Chinese painting must obviously have provided Fairweather with another great artistic stimulus. Unlike calligraphy, however, which can be seen and enjoyed everywhere in China, even at street level (commercial inscriptions and sign-boards of shops can sometimes be of remarkable quality), good paintings, as a rule, are not normally put on public display, and it was especially difficult for foreigners to gain access to valuable collections. Still, Fairweather was lucky in this respect, and had the rare opportunity to contemplate a selection of masterpieces from the Ancient Palace Museum which were displayed together in Beijing prior to their great exhibition in London in 1936.

What his reactions were to such an encounter can only be guessed at: once more, we must deplore the extreme paucity of our information on the events of his inner life. The problem is not only that he was reluctant by nature to communicate his deeper thoughts and feelings, but also that the few people who occasionally had the chance to come in closer contact with him appear almost invariably to have shown a lamentable lack of intellectual and artistic curiosity. It is difficult to read the very rare interviews, which he grudgingly granted, without experiencing acute frustration: it seems that none of the questions that really mattered, none of the issues that now fascinate us most, were ever raised by his interlocutors.

Early in his life Fairweather developed a strong interest in Chinese language and culture. How exactly he pursued his intellectual investigations remains largely a mystery: we only have the impressive and enigmatic fruit of his efforts in the form of a book, *The Drunken Buddha*, which, in 1965, he entrusted for publication to the University of Queensland Press. This highly original and beautiful volume (it is enriched with Fairweather's own illustrations: twelve colour plates reproducing large paintings) is the translation of a traditional Chinese novel, *Ji gong zhuan*. The story, which is very popular and has a certain Rabelaisian pungency, deals with the eccentricities and wisdom of a legendary 'Zen' monk, who — in a way — embodied in traditional China the sort of counter-culture which came to flourish in the modern West with the advent of the hippie movement. Fairweather's competent translation reflects a remarkable degree of familiarity with written Chinese (encompassing both literary and colloquial usages). How did he acquire such an ability? How did he originally manage to solve the numerous problems posed by the Chinese text? Why did he choose this particular novel? What attracted him to a work which, in the eyes of traditional Chinese critics, does not have much literary merit? The only thing we know is that he based his translation not on the usual version (which is very long), but on an abridged edition from the late nineteenth century. Unfortunately, the editors and scholarly advisers of the University of Queensland Press do not seem ever to have bothered to seek more information on the exact background of Fairweather's intriguing enterprise.

Finally, a full survey of Fairweather's experience of China should, I suppose, also include a search for Chinese clues in his paintings. Yet, I shall gladly leave this task to others. This may not be pure laziness on my part — the fact is that I must confess to some scepticism regarding the usefulness of such an investigation. Fairweather was an artist of fierce and irreducible originality: whatever inspiration or stimulation he found outside himself, he always 'metabolised' into his own substance and, in the end, what he produced always turned out to be pure Fairweather. One could of course identify in various paintings a certain number of Chinese *motifs* — a pavilion here, a *pailou* there, or again some city walls or gates — but these elements are, after all, merely of anecdotal interest, and I doubt if there would be much point in hunting systematically for them. (This sort of exercise reminds me of the efforts of well-meaning teachers, who, trying to introduce schoolchildren to the joys of classical music, make them recognise, in Beethoven's Sixth Symphony, cuckoos and thunderclaps.)

What I would like to propose here is not an examination of biographical facts, or a critical analysis of works (on both grounds, anyway, it would be difficult to find points not already covered by Murray Bail's definitive study), but rather a *philosophical* approach (I call it thus for want of a better word — or, perhaps, just to hide the essential flippancy of these reflections).

My contention is that Fairweather presents a riddle which remains opaque as long as we keep it in a western perspective, yet reveals transparent coherence once we try to translate it into Chinese terms. In some respects, it seems that Fairweather's eccentricity bordered at times on the suicidal, the inhuman or the insane; and yet, what is remarkable is that his behaviour, even at its most bizarre, shocking or incomprehensible, would always have made perfect sense to a Chinese classical aesthete. Just as a coded message will yield its secret content if one fits it into the right grid, Fairweather's attitude becomes easier to interpret once we adopt as our reading key the ethical model of traditional Chinese painters.

Do not misunderstand my intention: I certainly do not believe that Fairweather ever attempted deliberately to emulate any Chinese stereotypes — even if he knew about them (which is quite possible), it would have been most unlikely for a personality of such radical originality and independence ever to indulge in what would have amounted to a form of theatrical pose. Actually, had Fairweather never been involved with China, I would still trust that my Chinese key could be of some assistance here, just as, in some respects, it could equally help us better to understand painters as utterly diverse as — let us say — Victor Hugo, Cézanne or Morandi. Again, the relevance of the Chinese paradigms is totally unrelated to the question of whether these various individuals had any awareness of China. Similarly, if a Chinese acupuncturist can cure your migraine, this does not mean that you are blessed with particular Chinese affinities; it merely means that, in some cases, acupuncture can provide a valid reading of human physiology.

Fairweather's life was ultimately commanded by one single-minded compulsion: the absolute need to paint. To this pursuit he sacrificed all normal human relations and material comforts — he cared for nothing else, he demanded nothing else. The example of artists driven by a relentless, all-consuming passion for their art is certainly not uncommon in our culture, yet the form it took with Fairweather was most unusual and intriguing. Actually, it would seem that he lodged his passion more in the activity of painting than in the paintings themselves, which he often treated with savage indifference. Rats gnawed at them; humidity and haphazard storage made them rot; when he had to send them away, the dispatch was usually effected with shocking negligence. Insufficient drying and inadequate packaging frequently caused irreparable damage to paintings which, anyway, were often doomed from the start, since he worked with cheap and foul materials, inferior paints applied on makeshift and fragile surfaces scavenged from dumps: broken crates, discarded cardboards, old newspapers.

He was not desirous to show his work; he did not care for the reactions of the connoisseurs, the critics and the public; he would certainly never have bothered to organise or attend exhibitions of his works. He had no interest in whatever comments were passed on his paintings; in the end, whether he was being appreciated or misunderstood became largely a matter of indifference to him. If he finally agreed to send regularly part of his production to an art gallery, it was simply because this arrangement could conveniently solve the problems of his livelihood; these amounted merely to securing a modest supply of tinned food and beer, and occasionally to mending his leaky shack. Had he disposed of any other income to keep himself fed and sheltered, he would probably never have taken the trouble to sell even one painting. Fame and wealth were nothing to him; besides his frugal diet and frightfully primitive hut, he had no material needs. Celebrity was a nuisance, as it could only draw more intruders to his island-hermitage, disrupting his concentration and disturbing him in the only task that mattered: painting. He needed to paint like one needs to breathe; had he dropped his brush, he would have suffocated.

It is precisely on this type of attitude that the reflection developed by classical Chinese aesthetes can shed a useful light.

The theory of Chinese painting is based upon a fundamental distinction between amateurs and professionals: only the art of the former is deemed to possess true value, as they alone are individual creators, whereas the latter are mere artisans who practise their craft on the same footing as carpenters, potters and other anonymous manual workers. No amount of skill and beauty can redeem the paintings of the professionals and make up for the spiritual deficiency that taints their origins. Actually, technical virtuosity and seductiveness in a painting are considered vulgar as they precisely suggest the slick fluency of a professional hand answering a client's commission, and betray a lack of inner compulsion on the part of the artist. The professional works for an external reward, whereas the amateur seeks self-cultivation; to the former, painting is only a trade; to the latter, it is a spiritual discipline. Therefore, it was hardly a paradox if, for instance, a great painter of the Qing period could inscribe on one of his masterpieces the defiant calligraphic statement: 'What I fear most of all is that my painting may look competent.'

A certain form of clumsiness was indeed valued by painters, as it clearly established the non-professional character of their work and vouched for the purity of their inspiration. A famous Ming painter, who was copying again and again an archaic masterpiece from the Tang, was asked why he was still dissatisfied with his copy, even though it already looked much more beautiful than the original. 'It is precisely for this reason,' he replied, 'that it is still inferior to the original.'

Naturally, complex historical and social factors also intervened in the progressive elaboration of these conceptions; yet, at the heart of this extraordinary valorisation of the art of the amateurs was the view that painting is first and foremost an operation of the mind, and thus should remain the exclusive preserve of a small elite of contemplative souls — monks, scholars, hermits — who could nourish their inspiration with philosophy, poetry, calligraphy and music. These spiritual exercises were obviously beyond the reach of barely literate professional craftsmen, whose understanding of art was limited to technical recipes. The aim of a true painter was to attain a state of harmony with the vital rhythm of the universe; he sought to achieve a communion with the ultimate and invisible 'Oneness' that underlies and pervades the visible metamorphoses of the 'Ten Thousand Creatures'. Therefore, in the art of the amateurs, the primary objective was not to reproduce natural forms (as was the case with professional painting), but to duplicate the activity of the Cosmic Creator. For this reason, the actual process of painting was, in a sense, more important than the finished works themselves. (A Chinese painter of the eighteenth century even developed the habit of destroying his paintings as soon as he finished creating them, as if he wished to emphasise that they were merely a coarse residue, the material left over from a mystical experience which alone mattered.)

In the western conception, 'amateurism' usually entails a connotation of superficiality and frivolity, a lack of commitment and seriousness; 'professionalism' on the contrary suggests dedication and thoroughness. In Chinese aesthetics, it is exactly the reverse which is true, and for a reason that actually recoups common experience: we attach a positive value to professionalism only in matters that require specialised technical competence and narrow expertise; in the great issues where fundamental values are at stake, or which should involve the totality of the human person, the very idea of a merely 'professional' approach has a ring of farce or fraud, as it implies an attempt to shrink life and to distort humanity. Thus, for instance, the emergence of a class of professional politicians usually signals a perversion of politics and the death of democracy; professional love pertains to the brothel; professional philosophy is a form of intellectual corruption; professional soldiers are mercenaries; professional patriots are scoundrels; professional preachers do not believe in God — for no one can be paid to love, to think, to have faith, to sacrifice his life, to offer his soul; morality is never a sound business proposition; whatever has value cannot be bought: it is arbitrarily given, or freely received.

By excluding true painting from the range of professional activities, the Chinese sanctioned its sacred nature and equated aesthetics with ethics. In traditional Chinese criticism, the artistic quality of a painting always mirrors the moral quality of the painter. This notion, which was fundamental in China, is not entirely ignored in the West, though, when it is formulated here, it is usually with a disconcerting or paradoxical twist; thus, for example, when talking of a writer whom he admired (such as Tolstoy), Wittgenstein used a striking standard: 'This man had a right to write.'

One can often experience this strange phenomenon when visiting art galleries in this country: whenever a Fairweather is being displayed among various other contemporary works, even though the latter may sometimes look more brilliant at first, or more attractive, or more approachable, after a while it is as if the Fairweather were slowly undermining these other paintings and, in a way, invalidating them all — and Wittgenstein's criterion then comes irresistibly to mind: this man had a right to paint.

Fairweather once said: 'Painting is a personal thing. It gives me the same kind of satisfaction that religion, I imagine, gives to some people.' From his point of view, this was merely the terse acknowledgement of a sober fact. In traditional China, the rich and splendid theoretical literature on painting is essentially a development of the same conception — but, among contemporary western artists, how many could make such a statement without giving the impression that they are uttering intolerable cant?

In his solitary and uncompromising stand, what Fairweather keeps reminding us of is this: in the end, the only art that really matters is the art for which the artist can vouch with his whole being.

1994

LES MURRAY

The Trade in Images

Making images of Australia is arguably something we do too much of. Making images of themselves is something very many countries do too much of, even Old World countries you would think should by now be secure in their identity. America does far too much of it, though we have to remember she is a Noble Experiment in human self-government. Here in Australia, the making of national images is a major journalistic and literary industry. It has been a growth industry for at least two generations, if not longer. *The Australian Emptiness, The Australian Ugliness, The Lucky Country, The Land of the Long Weekend, The Great Australian Stupor, The End of the Dreamtime*: along with all the coffee table books and treatises on every facet of Australiana, we have had a seemingly insatiable appetite for those often tartly hectoring sociocultural studies of our country. We have indulged gluttonously in mirror staring and navel gazing, avid for more and more angles on our own fascinating image. Other countries have learned the hard way the terrible dangers inherent in out-and-out nationalism; it is a Moloch which can swallow incredible amounts of tormented human flesh. We have, thank God, largely been spared an education in this at first hand, but perhaps that very fact has stunted the growth here of a genuine humility. We have got carping instead, which differs from humility in not including oneself. It can sometimes seem that the note of denunciation in most of our serious studies of Australia is a dash of bitters, put in to disguise the sweet taste of endless self-regard and persuade us we are consuming adult beverages. Harsh strains of criticism, of our sloth, our indifference, our unsexiness, our slowness to take up the latest and most refined items of High Culture, these serve as a guarantee that our indulgence in national narcissism is respectably intellectual. If capitalism tends to turn all things into consumer goods, and radicalism tends to turn all things into inquisition, the commerce in Australian images contrives to reconcile the two rather marvellously. The standard paperback study of Australian mores really has it both ways, at once commanding respectable sales and allowing the author a generous measure of self-righteousness and hectoring zeal.

Someone, somewhere, is eventually going to suggest that much of this image-mongering is rather transparently late-colonial (cf. late adolescent) and parvenu. That person is going to make themselves very unpopular, especially with the writers of the sort of books I'm talking about. Maybe not with the readers of them, but definitely with the writers. And especially perhaps, with those writers who have only a polemical point of view to offer, and not some properly grounded new perspective, some genuinely fresh discovery. They will also make themselves an odium to publishers, for the formula is such a sure-fire seller that it has tended to crowd out most other sorts of non-fiction writing here. Who wants to take a risk on an Australian book about universals when there is easy money to be made from a mix of photogenic Australian Views and denunciations of the Myth of Mateship? If you doubt what I'm saying, ask yourself how many Australian philosophers you can think of, working and publishing here. Or how many Australian historians with original and cogent theories about some supra-national question or other. I can think of a few of the latter, just a few — but they didn't publish in Australia. They published overseas, in that big outer world where we are still led to believe all truly original thinking is done. That's the traditional division of labour: new ideas are imported, and it is our part to re-jig them for local use, applying them to the benefit and the apathetic backs of our fellow citizens.

A good many of the images we make are graven ones. Firmly inscribed, in hard prose, they are meant to be admired, to become the touchstones of debate, to be influential. They are tokens of power, sometimes effective in bringing about changes, including changes their proponents may come to regret. Blessed, at least initially, are those whose cause they further, and woe betide those who stand inconveniently in their way. If you suffered under White Australia, you may yet be maladroit enough to get run over by Multiculturalism. Or by the Creole idea, which I predict will be its successor. Some of these images last longer than others, but all eventually pass away. Few, in Australia anyway, now remember the workingman's paradise. And the empty continent that we had to populate or perish has suffered a complete reversal. As we leave late colonial reality, more of these formulations get invented. Merely as crutches for lazy minds, these successive conditioning visions are the blight of quality journalism and dinner parties alike, though they do power a busy commerce in conferences; as climbing ladders seized and set up by aspiring politicians, though, they can cause havoc not only to the subtler weave of difficult truth, but to actual human lives. An image, we should remember, is a description shaped by an inner intent. Damage to human lives and communities is likely to happen when one image is being more or less forcibly replaced by another.

I learned this law (we may call it the Law of Loaded Descriptions) the hard way when I came to the city from the bush. I came along just at the moment when the bush was beginning to plummet out of favour and become very unfashionable. Australia had become Urban, and it behoved her to get Sophisticated as quickly as possible, casting off all earlier Dad-and-Dave simplicities and even much of the romance of the Outback. The complex, time-layered realities of the bush hadn't been fully explored or described, but suddenly they were impatiently 'understood' and dismissed. We had become obsolete, just as individuals now do before they die. In a decade or two, the whole of the bush, including the Outback, would become the Environment, which all but its earliest inhabitants had despoiled, and in which nothing more should ever be built. I had also made the mistake of coming from the world of struggling small farmers, a caste our elites have loathed from the start. Epithets such as hick from the sticks, peasant, rural idiocy, and pejorative uses of that pretentious belch-word 'bucolic', these helped me to find my own identity and even lent my writing some of its impetus, so I guess I have something to thank our image-makers for. Many of my relatives would have less reason for gratitude, as a bitterly engineered diminution of sympathy with their struggles against a difficult continent slowly robbed them of government services and self-esteem alike, and eroded any willingness to alleviate the very social deprivations they were derided for. Paradoxically, the perennial attractiveness of the bush for many Australians has not gone away, despite the propaganda. We are now getting a new settlement pattern in the country, partly made up of the holiday houses and hobby farms (the Soviet term is *dachas*) of privileged urban people, but more typically a pattern of disguised unemployment, by which the bush absorbs, as it has always done, some of the strain of industrial restructuring. People from the city sell their one large asset, their suburban house, and move on to a few acres in the country, where they build often quite handsome houses for themselves. It takes a while to realise that in those houses many are living quite precariously on savings or superannuation, on expedients or pick-up work or the dole. They are less productive in volume terms than farmers were, but they do bring variety: of genetics, of social experience and ideas, as well as new crops and occupations. They also bring an attractive innocence about the wellsprings of ancient community friction, in long-settled places. And since the bush is a great and powerful spirit, many of them, if they last long enough, eventually become country people themselves, and join the rest of us in the sorrow of watching our children sucked out of our communities into the cities, where the Action is supposed to be and where most wait around in vain for some worthwhile slice of it. This last, of course, is part of a vaster worldwide pattern, in which the ethic of the Interesting wins out over the ethic of the Good, but we have been slow to discern any but a fairly standardised range of worldwide trends operating in our society.

If much of the foregoing sounds like the soured confessions of a reformed image-monger, I have to plead guilty. I have done my bit of prose image-making, in the past, though I've only been polemical in essays, never in a full-length book. By the time I reached the stage of writing a prose book, I had grown very mistrustful of the conceptual poverty and stereotyping that bedevil the Australian Identity industry, and tried as far as possible to steer clear of any sort of predictable polemic. Even when the game had seemed fun, I was always uneasily aware of something our religion gets itself hated for reminding people of: that every proposal is likely to have its dark as well as its bright results, just as every criticised reality is likely to have its hidden virtues and rationales as well as its vices. It may represent the decay of some initially noble impulse, or the deposit of some formerly pressing need. In Australia's case, the escape of many of the poor from the conditions of the Industrial Revolution, or of the terrorised from the power imagery of tyrannical governments, have been supremely powerful motives — just as, in the case of the bush, we have seen the power of a simple longing to escape even the most honoured and politically romanticised servitude and be one's own boss, at almost any cost in poverty and deprivation. If the suspiciously free-flowing afflatus of polemical argument didn't remind me of these things, my other and true vocation of poetry did. Poetry has a way of reminding us, through its very inexhaustibility, that there are always more sides to a thing. You can't be in its presence long without feeling the pull of that.

Another thing which kept tugging me away from national image-mongering was its pervading acrimony, its frequently dismissive and contemptuous tones, its readiness to bury things before they were dead. If, as our religion teaches, the spirit is inseparable from the body, there seemed ample reason to be worried by the tone of social criticism here. The tone in which a thing is proposed may easily become the atmosphere of its realisation, and the spirit in which it is enforced. I would add, not entirely as an aside, that our Church is partly to blame for this. By abandoning the field of higher intellectual life in Australia, or being browbeaten out of it, and not even having a high-quality magazine in which Catholic and Christian perspectives could be published, it left some of us either silenced altogether or forced to slip our thinking into journals highly antipathetic to it. By electing not to have an intellectual presence in the society, the Church removed its people from the sphere of intellectual debate, because no one else was going to give them more than the barest sufferance. As a result, no criticism of the tone and style of Australian polemic has been possible, and no alternative spirit in which to describe our society has had a natural home. The position is the same in book publishing. A Catholic press for books now barely exists, except as a few tiny operations with no access much to distribution or review and certainly no mainstream influence. I know from hard experience the short shrift which serious Catholic manuscripts usually get from secular publishers. None of what I've been saying is meant to denigrate the few small Catholic magazines and book publishers that do exist in Australia. The pity with these is that they are in-house, not equipped to challenge the wider society. Also, they are apt to be riven by the internecine battles of left wing versus right wing, that desolating alien terminology which an intellectually vigorous Catholic culture should have been to the fore in opposing.

The theology of the commandment against graven images is fascinating but utterly remote from most people in the Western tradition; it was thrashed out mainly in the Orthodox tradition over a thousand years ago. But if one is around the arts for a time, one discovers that the commandment contains crucial wisdom. You cannot make an image of any large reality. You can't make an image of Australia and do justice to all its aspects. You will inevitably do great injustice to the parts you think less important, and dismiss or leave out, and you can't even see the reality of the country from all the angles you would need to see it from. The dimensions of the subject are too great to observe, and an accurate report on them would take more time to give than anyone has to give it or listen to it. We can only draw images from the reality, and gradually we find that the number of these potentially there to draw is infinite. The whole can't be described; it can only be *evoked*, which is essentially why our church allows images. What we share in practice (and such sharing is what makes a nation) is a rough but poignant *sense* of the reality we live in, a sort of signature tune only partly in words, made of common experiences and family references. No single part of this tune is likely to be shared by all, but there will be a fairly large degree of commonality overall. One modulation of the Australian tune which used to be shared by a broad majority of us used to be a habit of seeing our society in caricature terms that were a subtle and partly amused reaction to how Britain and Europe saw it, when they bothered to look. We had a liking for slum effects, in part because society had largely escaped from its earlier slums and was good at modulating its nostalgia for them. The modern ocker sensibility is nothing like as subtle or sardonic as that older spirit; it's a parody and a crude take-off of it. The Church understood the society which shared this slum joke, and was well adapted to it. But then the society began to be gentrified, and the Church was left floundering. Gentrification is a morally complex process, with many vehement pretensions, and the Church didn't catch on that the old tune had altered. Getting an intellectual presence now might seem a belated piece of gentrification by the Church itself, but it's something you need in gentrifying times, in order to understand them and comment on them, on the way to being able to minister to those they hurt and neglect and exploit. You can only talk to gentrifying people in terms their gentrification obliges them to respect.

As a native of the old half-mythical Australian slum (rural division), still partly in thrall to the delight and disgust of its tune and unable to make the necessary repudiations of loved things on demand, my position in the image business was always precarious, and now I think I've been dropped from it. Journalists no longer ring me up for my opinions on the Australian republic, possibly because of the puzzlingly spiritual answers I give them, starting from the premise that it has in effect come, at least to the extent we're comfortable with for the moment. I sometimes grow apprehensive, as I know many other people quietly do, as to what sort of an ideological whited sepulchre a fully realised Australian republic might be. What would it draw on for its dimension of vision and public panoply? Whose dreams would it exalt, whose images? Not Catholic ones, we may be pretty certain. An American poet asked me a few years ago a question that seemed to me both simple and crucially difficult. The question was: Why don't

Australians kill each other like Americans? This isn't merely stereotype; the figure of over 20 000 deaths by gunshot per year in America is admitted to be accurate. Our population is about one-fifteenth theirs, and our annual rate of deaths by gunshot rarely exceeds fifty, though it may have begun to climb. I had to ponder the question for quite a while, since it wasn't simply a matter of centralised state police forces versus elected local police forces and a tangle of overlapping jurisdictions. It was a difference in the spirit of the two societies. I finally suggested that it might be because in the past we weren't a republic for bringing things to a head. We weren't actors in a political drama of world significance, in which we felt that what we did counted. We thus lacked the principled American determination to see all conflicts resolved, all questions decided. I don't know whether that is the answer — and I doubt it's the whole answer — but just after I gave it, we had the first of a series of horrific mass slaughters by gunfire. Please God this is not a straw in the wind of the spirit here. Getting back to the image business, I suspect that the only lasting contribution I made to the sociopolitical side of it was to get the Anglo-Saxon altered to Anglo-Celtic, which seemed to me obviously more accurate. There we poor downtrodden Celts were, about to become respectably Ethnic, and Murray has to go and re-yoke us to the Anglos, the dread lords of the Establishment. A strange house, the Establishment: everyone enters it facing backwards. In the longer term, it may prove even stranger than that: it may be non-existent even as it stands there, and someone may show that it was built of nothing but rhetoric.

If I am out of the prose national-image stakes, and perhaps I only think I am, I still draw on Australian imagery for my poems. In a way, I hope this may be more responsible of me. Images are at their least disruptive in art, where they are at their most mysterious and many sided and inexhaustible, food for contemplation rather than precipitate action. In art, imagery and conflict alike are raised beyond embodiment in action to a more perpetual embodiment where their life needs nothing further from the world to feed itself. Art is thus, in Christian terms, effectual but vicarious. It has arrived, without having to find its way there through tyrannies, at the true ambiguity of things, and can let all things, even opposites, be true at once.

1988

GERMAINE GREER

Sex and Society — Whose Rules?

'Sex and society — whose rules?' is the portentous title of a debate in which I am to spar with a well-known churchman on Australian television tomorrow evening. Besides the ominousness of the assumption that present moral conflicts are nothing more than a tussle between would-be rule-makers, there is, I suppose, something engaging in the impression one might derive from this formulation of sex and society as some kind of game. Perhaps it is a choice like the one that various Australian states have made, between Australian Rules, Rugby Union and Rugby League. It might even be supposed that I, as the opponent of the pop preacher on the programme, was about to defend a brand-new set of conventions for the conduct of sex and society; am I expected to outlaw the forward pass by the masculine initiator or to drive the missionary position out of play by heavy penalties?

The fact that I am a law-breaker does not entail the notion that I must be a law-maker. Because I ran away from my own husband and find monogamy the most incomprehensible perversion of all, I am wrongly assumed to order all other women into a life of promiscuity. Because I do not wear a brassière and do not believe that women ought to feel obliged to wear such an unbecoming garment, it is said that I have ordered all women to throw away such underwear, to burn it even. The sorry fact is that I am not so compulsive in my attitudes that I would spurn all forms of breast binding at all times. On horseback, even I wear a tit-bag. Nor do I jeer at my sister who is nursing her infant and must keep her bosom well supported or leak milk all over her clothes.

People like those who devised the title of the debate do not only imagine that I have drawn up the book of rules for sex and society in the future, they are also unfailingly irritated with me, when they find out that I have not. It becomes my responsibility to provide new norms for behaviour in a world where the nuclear family does not exist, where men are not expected to keep families and women to work for nothing, where work and play are no longer distinguished, although no such society exists to be realistically discussed and it is extremely difficult to foresee how it may come into being. It is not enough to argue that hastening the decay of the nuclear family may of itself be a moral activity with a moral aim, and that new values will emerge in response to new conditions that we will encounter as we work towards it. 'That won't do,' I am told. 'What are you going to put in its place?' New straitjackets must be designed to replace the old, otherwise the unfortunate lunatic must remain bound in the current mode. The champions of rules and repressions draw their best hope from the inability of the bound man to adjust to sudden freedom. They see him staggering and flailing his arms, and so he is bound again, possibly more efficiently than before. This is the process that can be seen in all the toing and froing over liberalization of laws against obscenity, marijuana and abortion — even the prohibitions against homosexuality. Now that homosexuals are not afraid to declare themselves and to behave spontaneously in public, we may even find that the reform of the laws against homosexuality between consenting adults is reviewed. Even the most liberal will lament that the extravagant demeanour of extremists has provoked a backlash, and fail to see that we may only have our freedoms in so far as we refrain from exercising them.

It is a common liberal point of view, that most sets of laws and rituals have developed as a response to existing economic and other conditions; what is not so often understood is that as soon as they become codified and cannot bend to accommodate new conditions, the laws become anachronistic, tyrannical and absurd. The Jewish dietary laws made a good deal of sense when they were first distilled from the pooled wisdom of the elders of the chosen people, but when they become mere ritual observance, they also lose their moral function. The process is astonishingly rapid: in order to retain their relevance to contemporary reality, laws must be under constant critical attack.

Morality is essentially connected with choice, with the exercise of will itself responding to information and observation of the consequences and conditions of action. As soon as a rule is invoked in order to short-circuit the process of individual confrontation with reality, morality has been abandoned.

Those people who claim that other people need rules and leaders or else they will behave outrageously and destructively both towards themselves and others, are denying the whole structure of assumption upon which our concepts of democracy are based. They believe that certain sorts of people, priests and pundits, have special moral insight or expertise, which applies perfectly well to circumstances of which they have no direct experience. So doctors, psychiatrists, churchmen, sociologists and law-makers are better able to make the correct decision about the termination of a pregnancy than the pregnant woman herself. They pre-empt her moral responsibility for her own behaviour, even though they may as a result condemn her to a life of guilt, resentment and inadequacy. Although those who took the decision for her are to blame for that, it is she and her kin who must bear the punishment and the compounded guilt. By this spurious assumption of responsibility for an action for which they will never have to pay, such moral arbiters pervert the course of morality, cripple the spiritual life of the whole community.

The imposition of my set of rules would be no less perverting than that of anyone else's. What we need, in order to become morally agile and strong, is to shake off the ruinous carapace of half-believed, ill-remembered and misunderstood religion and its monstrous excrescence of dead and murdering laws, and so free ourselves to grapple with new problems. There is no other way to develop the spiritual muscle which will build a new morality. That morality may very well be neither monistic nor prescriptive.

We will also need to find again the value of doubting, the courage which is required that we may refuse to codify difficult decisions out of their difficulty. How else will we ever know how to act on the issue of one man's kidney machine costing as much to run as wiping out glaucoma in the children of the poor would cost? How else can we develop sensible attitudes to the transplant game?

The development of morality also entails the acceptance of guilt: one may very well see that motives for taking action in a particular case may outweigh the continuing possibility that the act may not be the right one. It is better to recognize the fact, than to pass the buck to an unassailable body which accepts only symbolic responsibility. It might surprise my opponent in tomorrow's debate to learn that I desire free abortion clinics, abolition of censorship, spontaneous sexual relations, in the interests of morality.

1972

CLIVE JAMES

You Little Bobby-Dazzler

When a certain young Australian writer left Sydney for Europe in the early 1960s, the Opera House had barely risen above its foundations. He didn't come back until the building was finished, whereupon, in an article for the *Observer*, he said, among other things, that the Opera House looked like a typewriter full of oyster shells. The Australian newspapers picked the remark up and front-paged it under the headline THE POMS ARE THE WORST KNOCKERS. It was clear and humiliating proof that he was not only unregretted for his absence, he was unremembered for ever having been there in the first place.

The certain young writer was by that time no longer young, and by this time he is not even certain. He was and is, you will have gathered, myself. I don't think that I ever really knocked the Opera House very severely, except by pointing out the obvious fact that a good number of the most important operas couldn't be easily put on in it. To say that it looked like a typewriter full of oyster shells was merely to evoke the appropriate image, that of an old Olivetti Lettera 44 after an office party. But if a carping tone came easily then, it is gush that threatens now. Enthusiasm is the sign of the late convert. I can hold it at bay — the place *still* looks like a broken Pyrex casserole dish in a brown cardboard box — but there are moments when the eye turns dewy, especially on a spring night when one is inside the building gazing out. Seeing the glass wall of the foyer filled with city lights made lustrous by the clean air and the harbour bridge cutting a black lattice out of the starlight, you would need to feel ill not to feel well-being. Somewhere under that wrecked bathroom of a roof, the household gods are having a good time.

The Opera House has its imperfections, but it is perfectly placed. Half the secret of a great building is to be on the right spot. Bennelong Point was begging to have an opera house built on it almost from the time that Bennelong himself was active. An Aborigine who took easily to the white settlers' ways, he would probably be pleased with the building they have now put up on his old stamping-ground, although less pleased that they took his name away to make room for it. There is no Bennelong Point left: between the Botanical Gardens and the harbour there is now nothing but the Opera House. But before the Opera House there was a very ugly tram depot, so there was room for improvement, even if New South Wales's long-term Labor premier Joe Cahill scarcely seemed ideal casting to bring great beauty into being. He had already disfigured Circular Quay with a construction called the Cahill Expressway, a combined railway station and four-lane flyover that preserved the original innocence of Sydney Cove by walling it off behind a towering revetment of raw concrete so solid that a hydrogen bomb wouldn't singe it.

But however suspect Joe Cahill's eye for aesthetic values, his heart was in the right place. He wanted eminence for Sydney, and not just for the usual reason, i.e. to get the edge on Melbourne. He cherished a vision of a great cultural monument, an aim made no less worthy by the consideration that it would be in part a monument to himself. So what the combined wishes of such musical giants as Sir Eugene Goossens could never have brought about was brought about by the man of the people, Joe Cahill. Twisting arms and kicking ankles, he pushed the project through. An international competition was set up, with judges exalted enough to recognise genius when they saw it. Joern Utzon of Denmark was the genius. Eero Saarinen was not alone among the judges in pronouncing Utzon's design a prodigy of the imagination. They all did, and they were right.

Utzon's conception had the stamp of authority. The shells of the roof floated above the Mayan-massive podium with no apparent point of contact. In the throat of each shell, a filmy curtain was draped in art nouveau folds as if glass were water. Anybody who could draw such a thing, it was assumed, must be able to build it. Only slowly did the realisation dawn that Utzon wasn't at the frontier of technology, he was beyond it. King's College chapel and the cathedral of Chartres took a long time to build, but the men who built them began with the advantage of knowing how to do it. Utzon didn't: he merely had faith that he would find out.

Joe Cahill's adroit use of the state lottery system ensured an unlimited supply of funds, which was lucky, because the Opera House shared with its curvilinear friend Concorde a sensational capacity to keep on getting so expensive that it couldn't even be abandoned. In Utzon's original sketches the roof shells had a sexily complex curve rather like a Mucha négligé, an old Paris Métro entrance arch or a full set of false teeth without the actual teeth. The consultant engineers, Arup and Partners, discovered that these curves simply could not be built, whether in concrete or in anything else. All the time that the neo-Aztec sacrificial platform was rising from the ashes of the old tram depot, Utzon and Arup wrestled with the problem of how to build the roof that would echo the yachts in the harbour and the strato-cumulus in the sky. The podium was clad in pink slabs of reconstituted granite quarried from the Blue Mountains. It was impressive, but would mean little if it had to be roofed with corrugated iron. The tiling system for the roof shells was all worked out — a pet project of Utzon's, it would combine ceramic tiles of alternating Swedish buff and high-gloss into a surface that would dazzle without blinding, startle without stunning. But without the shells, there would be nowhere for the tiles to go.

Time went by, the costs went up and Joe Cahill grew older. Finally, it was Utzon himself who hit on the solution. Instead of complex curves there would be only one curve. Every surface of every shell would conform to an imaginary sphere of 246-foot radius. All the ribs could thus be poured in only four moulds, on site. It took three years to erect the resulting ribs, but with a system of error correction devised by Arups the shells clicked together with no daylight showing anywhere. One idea, plus thousands of hours in the computer, had made most of Utzon's dream come true.

Unfortunately there were other parts of the dream for which the elegantly simple idea that might have made them real simply refused to come. Glass, for example, won't drape like that. The completion date receded further into the future, far beyond the fading eyesight of Joe Cahill, who perforce had to depart for the beyond with his Opera House only a spectral shadow compared with the solid magnificence of his beloved expressway. Utzon fell out with the politicians, headed by Mr Davis Hughes, who was cast as the villain, as the realist often is. The Dane might have alienated the politicos and survived. But he also alienated Arups, and that left him without any support inside the project. There was plenty of support outside in the streets, but all it could do was wave placards. Utzon left in a huff for Denmark and a team of locals took over the job, which included the as yet unsolved problem of how to drape the glass.

Cast as betrayers of Utzon's vision but in fact doing their best to keep faith with it, they sweated over the computer until the answer came up. The curtains of glass which now hang in the shells have not quite the Beardsleyesque swirl that Utzon imagined. The metal mullions look heavy individually and when seen obliquely they combine to block the view. But if you stand centrally in the upper foyer and look out through the glass into the harbour at night, you see the splendour of the water-city as Kenneth Slessor first registered it in his poem 'Five Bells'. John Olsen's mural of the same title hangs behind you, but there before you is the miracle itself, an oil-field of light-towers driving down their drills of pastel into the lush dark:

Deep and dissolving verticals of light
Ferry the falls of moonshine down.

Slessor was a great talent finally unfulfilled, and the Opera House — his memorial because he found the words for the spectacle into which it glides — is like him. Too much is made of how Utzon's original conception was distorted. Probably it would have been distorted even if he had stayed on the case, since not even genius can sew plate glass like cloth. But what is really unfulfilled about the Opera House is something more fundamental. It is just not a very good place to put on operas. It is a very good place, but not for that.

As the world well knows by now, Utzon, according to the brief given him, designed two main halls, the large one for opera and the smaller one for concerts. Half-way through construction their designated functions were switched, mainly because the Australian Broadcasting Commission, which had most of the clout, wanted a four-second reverberation time that only the larger hall could give. The opera people were left with the smaller hall. Actually they still would have been in trouble even in the larger hall, because Utzon had not designed any wing space in that one either. Squeezed by the site, he had rethought the conventions of theatrical lay-out and dreamed up some special machinery which would enable the fly-tower to do the work of the wings as well. There is good reason to believe that the conventions of stage management — by which what can't be flown from a bar is pushed on from the side — are no more susceptible of being re-thought than the laws of gravity, but in the event the whole question became academic. The halls were swapped, the hugely expensive stage machinery was scrapped like TSR-2, and the opera and ballet people were left with a small hall almost devoid of wing-space. Sir Robert Helpmann, who later became a valued resident producer, pointed out at the time a truth which no amount of subsequent euphoria has ever quite managed to falsify — that La Scala doesn't look too terrific from outside but it's got everything you want inside, whereas the Sydney Opera House looks like a billion dollars but hasn't got what it takes where it counts.

It has been said that the Opera House should never have been called that in the first place, since it was always meant to be an entertainment complex in which opera would be only one function. In Australia the word 'function' applies to any kind of staged event no matter how grand, but as the Sydney Function Centre the project wouldn't have sold a single lottery ticket. The people, with a sure democratic instinct, know that the Opera House belongs to them. Only the intelligentsia is ever foolish enough to believe that opera is élitist. The common people are well aware that melody is a blessing from Heaven which, although by definition not given to everyone, can be given to anyone. When Joan Sutherland won the Sun Aria Competition and sailed for Europe, she had Australia behind her as if she had been challenging for the America's Cup. The main reason why the Opera House now sells out every seat of the year is the general assumption, which no amount of sophisticated argument has yet contrived to dispel, that an opera consists principally of beautiful sound. In this respect, the smaller hall is as much a success as the larger one, if not more so. Voices sound rich and lift easily, so that in the first row of the circle the ensemble singing will push you back in your seat and a soprano's upper register will massage your scalp.

On my first trip back to Sydney I was depressed to see, from an only moderately angled seat, the *corps de ballet* in *The Sleeping Beauty* queuing up to get off through a doorway in a solid brick wall and the Bluebird trying to achieve, from a standing start, the kind of mid-air entrance that not even Nijinsky could manage without room to run up. You can't, I correctly deduced, swing a cat back there. But by now, several years later, when I have become used to flying home again every so often, the Opera House looks a more and more cheering sight down there on the left-hand side of the sinking 747 as it lines up to land. Visiting the place, one still sees the limitations, but accepts them as quirks. When Wagner is put on, the orchestra can't be the size he specified, there not being enough room in the pit. So in effect you have got a building that does less than Bayreuth at a thousand times the price. But although the cramped working space is a drawback impossible to gloss over, the gifted resident designer Luciana Arrighi has made a virtue of the restricted stage. The current *Trovatore*, with its brooding stage picture of funereal black and impassioned purple, grown strongly on the spot instead of weakly imported, looks both unique and integrated, a true belonging of the house. And on the first night of spring this year the production made a beautiful noise to go with the pictures. Rita Hunter looked as if she had perhaps made the occasional afternoon trip around to Harry's Café de Wheels at Woolloomooloo, but she sounded glorious; the lady singing Azucena had a gold-rush chest-voice like Zinka Milanov; and Manrico, as well as being built like a block of four home units, sang to strip the brushbox plywood off the roof of the auditorium.

As a baby opera house, the opera auditorium within the function centre known as the Sydney Opera House is a place to be glad about. If a full-scale opera auditorium should become an absolute necessity instead of just something regrettable for its absence — if, that is, the world really does turn upside-down and Sydney becomes one of its great artistic capitals instead of just the very pleasant city that it is today — then perhaps another Utzonesque edifice could be built on a nearby headland. There are plenty of prime sites, all the know-how is still in the computer, and the current building is such a living creature that it is sad to see it so alone.

Meanwhile, in addition to its practical capacities, the Opera House admirably serves whatever symbolic functions are imposed upon it. Earlier on, it symbolised local-yokel cultural pretension, which placed the order for a bobby-dazzler of an opera house without stopping to find out whether the actual operas could be put on inside it. Later on it has come to symbolise a new, confident national ability to see a dream through to reality and love the result even for its faults. On a world scale, it symbolises the belated but total rebellion against the doctrinal architectural precept that form must follow function: the shells have nothing to do with the shape of what happens inside them, they are true only to themselves, and to the joy of the spirit. But finally and lastingly the Opera House symbolises the barbarian's thirst for beauty, towards which he sails open-mouthed, breaking everything he touches but bringing a precious gift of his own — new energy.

1983

GRAHAM LITTLE

The Flag My Father Wore

My father was not in the lodge and never sang the Orangeman's song, 'The Sash My Father Wore', and never even marched under the flag because the government dared not conscript in Northern Ireland, where a quarter of the population was Roman Catholic and not exactly pro-British. So he was an air-raid warden and carried a gas mask in blacked-out streets when other people were in bed. He was probably always a man who would emigrate.

I remember the red, white and blue of the flag from the Twelfth — 'The Twalth' it sounded like — when huge Union Jacks, some with golden fringes and some with portraits painted on them, flew over green, treeless fields, and King Billy rode past on a white horse and we had picnics with lemonade and buns, sitting on a blanket. Later, of course, the people of the Bogside in Derry had reason to fear these annual displays of Protestant triumphalism celebrating the victory of a Dutch Protestant king over a Scottish Catholic one at the Battle of the Boyne. People hung flags from their windowsills too, and I suppose I never saw so many flags in what you might call domestic use until I went to America in 1969, towards the end of the Vietnam years.

I don't know how many people grow up already wise to their own country. I'm afraid my mother told us some stirring stories about the B Specials, admittedly mainly about how grand her brothers and her Da looked in their uniforms, and it was a long time before I knew any better about them or even Churchill's Black and Tans. I grew up believing unwillingly but fervently in God as revealed in grainy lantern slides of *Pilgrim's Progress* and at Sunday school twice and church once on Sundays. (My parents were Methodist and Church of Ireland and lapsed soon after marrying, sealing the children's fate as hostages to the afterlife.) I believed more warmly and more hopefully in British justice, I have to say, which compared with God seemed noble and more on the side of the accused and the threatened, especially since the Gestapo was never out of my nightmares.

We took it for granted we were Irish. I did not know then that nationality could be so political. 'The Micks have stolen St Patrick's Day' was my mother's only political complaint about Australia, and indeed she and my father wore shamrock religiously every year we lived in England and made sure the children did too. Green, tediously, was the only colour and my mother would play 'When Irish Eyes are Smiling' and 'The Wearing of the Green' whenever there was a piano and a party. For all that, I think my father was sometimes embarrassed by the Irish need for attention and the stage-Irish role every Irishman seemed unable to refuse.

In Northern Ireland some people feel both Irish and British while for others, to put it mildly, it's one or the other. As schoolboys we felt very superior to the English and the most timid and protected of us thought we were street toughs by comparison, treating them with the pretended tolerance a Belfast Artful O'Dodger would have shown Little Lord Fauntleroy. As a schoolboy in England I was mocked for my accent, quickly learning not to say 'och' and 'wee' and 'mammy'. My father bridled and left the shop when a salesgirl screwed up her face when he asked for chips 'in a poke'. Being Irish meant being straightforward, plain, not trying to be what you weren't.

My parents went on trips to Dublin (they'd honeymooned at the Gresham in 1938), not incidentally bringing back to rationed Belfast those postwar rarities like chocolate and silk underwear we imagined the Free State abounded in. They solemnly told us that Dubliners spoke the most beautiful and the most correct English in the world, and they spoke of Dublin and the South almost as if they could agree that this was where Ireland seemed most itself. They were never treated as anything but Irish themselves. A bit later I saw them laughing and crying through John Ford's *The Quiet Man*, which for a long time was their favourite film. Maureen O'Hara looking a bit like my mother and my father said they had the same temper. My father didn't get much beyond reading and writing but he ran to school with Victor McLaglen, who was in *The Informer*.

The Roman Catholic Church was another matter. It was the big catch in the enjoyment of the other Ireland. Still, their attitude was more complicated than might be expected, because, like a lot of Ulster Protestants, they had great respect for 'the nuns' and a convent education. I don't know how this could have been, but amid all the suspicion and separation Methodist and Presbyterian and Church of Ireland girls, and some little boys, would be enrolled with 'lovely' Sister Brigid, who was 'just like ourselves', and 'that really saintly one, the mother superior', who was something we'd never be. Above all, it was the kindliness of the nuns that my mother admired, their Irish faces well-scrubbed and red, or pale and visionary, promising to help with daughters it would be nice to raise both good and graceful.

There were good priests too, usually because they'd unbend and have a bit of fun where 'the minister', in his stiff greys, would stand apart and disapprove. A priest could be 'typically Irish' — a term of happy approval — and a bit of a cod, and there were plenty of stories of a priest who'd helped out a Protestant, sick, perhaps and with no one to get a doctor, or a priest who'd talk to you and never so much as mention the Pope, or one with a sad face who never asked for a thing himself and lived to help the poor. The jokes we heard the adults tell had vicars in them riding by with their noses in the air and their bossy wives beside them, while the priests were discovered in betting shops or under beds and in pubs after hours, the jokes Dave Allen has lived off for thirty years. These priests may have represented a hidden side of themselves that my parents and uncles and aunts, as Irishmen and Irishwomen, were delighted to believe in or to be reminded was still there. In every Elder Sibling there is perhaps a Younger, Prodigal one whom even the sternest with themselves want to keep alive.

But the 'RC' as a type was anything but funny, and if anything not quite human at all. George Borrow's *Lavengro* gives the picture of a monstrous organisation using 'mumbo jumbo' — the liturgy and the ornamentation — to enslave good men and women for its own unstated and horrifying purposes.

The most ordinary RC was a figure of mystery: I'm reminded of Hitchcock or *The Invasion of the Body Snatchers* (in which international communism rather than the multi-national church is the object of fear) because nice people, good neighbours and workmates, would be turned into specimens of slavery once you remembered they confessed to a priest and were under orders from the Pope. And of course, the legions of young boys and young girls brainwashed into leaving their families and living an unnatural life were proof positive of the Roman Catholic indifference to ordinary human needs and failings.

There was another Ireland, then, that an Ulsterman felt deeply for and which was at the same time a foreign Ireland, stolen away, as it were, by an alien power, an uncanny force that was as far removed from the friendly priests and kindly nuns as from Protestants and their churches. The point was not that the Pope lived somewhere else; 'Roman' the church was, but that was no mere geographical strangeness. This construction of the Roman Catholic Church in Ireland — a paranoid construction whether it were true or not — has something to do with the Celtic past, with the paganism Protestant experience is so removed from. As we grew up Protestantly individualist, almost Protestantly secular, maybe what troubled us was that the 'other' Ireland, supposedly foreign, was strange only because it was so anciently Irish and deeply familiar, a call to a twilight religion within us.

In Dublin a couple of years ago, I was treated as an Irishman, my being born in the North making no difference at all; indeed I felt Irish as I rarely do in Melbourne, where the world of the Australian-born Irish-Catholic has no clear role for an Australian Irish-born Protestant. At the same time, seeing the mists rise from the Liffey, and watching the people crowding down O'Connell Street in a wintry three o'clock sunlight, something about Ireland frightened me, something both familiar and strange. It was as if Dublin itself were just a promontory of modern life and the ancient bogs were waiting in the gloom. I thought of Joyce's *The Dead.*

[...]

Manning Clark's tricoloured history of Australia counterposes the Protestant, Catholic and Enlightenment traditions, and I had always thought Australian republicanism — Australia's full symbolic independence — would come from the third. Australia was my escape not only from the responsibility of Northern Ireland but also from the sheer impossibility of it. I could hardly return to fight at Ian Paisley's side but by the same token it would take a more heroic person than I am to make myself over and pour scorn on the traditions, however flawed, of my uncles and my sort of Irish. I have been glad, like my father, just to be 'out of it'.

Mannix and the DLP were incomprehensible, though clearly important, the Loyal Orange Lodge never more than an anachronism glimpsed from the tram. Gradually, though, I developed a more positive hope in which Australia would become itself with Whitlamite panache and without any tribalism or harking back to the past. This was how I liked to present Australia to American academics and intellectuals in the early seventies and again during those fateful months in late 1975. I told them our easygoingness was the vital clue to the way we were and the way we would change.

I never thought that the symbolic completion of Australia's independence would come, not from the Enlightenment side, but from the tribal one, that it would be inspired by old enmities belonging to another place, or that it would be driven by the long-held wish to get even and, most surprising of all, by an Irish-Catholic Australian cringe as marked as the Protestant-Liberal Party one it deplored. This is from the *Australian* in May, reporting our distinguished writer Thomas Keneally in New York, in which a great deal depends on the little word 'partly': 'He also managed to put in a plug for an Australian republic, which will come about, he predicted, partly because the case for Ireland's independence from Britain is being strengthened by money from the European Community.'

There is barely one of my seventy political science students who credits Mr Keating with much sincerity on the republican issue (or in anything else, for that matter) but they like his Question Time vaudeville, and when the television news shows Tory twits of no account in their own Parliament scolding our Prime Minister for his manners, there is no doubt whom they barrack for. The debating point about the flag is also obvious. What was one flag is all of a sudden two, ours and a foreign one in the corner. Thus a patriotic *gestalt* falls to ideological analysis and political opportunity.

Even if we put a rein on our cynicism about his motives — though he is a man who openly boasts in the Parliament about his backflips — there is still a question about the kind of republic Keating has in mind. I have been moved and excited by the pleasure Americans take in the diversity their republic is host to. For all its great faults, the American republic has sometimes been as generous as it hopes to be. I am not sure about Keating's republic. Certainly it has started narrowly — provincial, even parochial, rather than generous. 'Oh, God! Surely we're not going through all that again!' was the response of Catholic friends who'd been through it all before at home and at school.

Most of Keating's mileage is from lampooning straw Englishmen and, though he is said to be too smart to need to read books, from rewriting history. In Keating's republican idea there are only two players, the Protestant British and the Irish Catholic, and his method of attacking the issue is the schoolyard taunt he learned in those days of appalling sectarian bitterness. And I cannot follow what being a republic will mean for us if our Prime Minister must first apologise to countries not notably more democratic or generous than Australia for our part-British (and part-Irish) past. Just what are the ideals and the new ideas our new republic is setting sail with — are they more than Up Yours and You Should See Us Now, with French clocks and Italian suits supposed to make the mother country jealous?

A native-born, but not Aboriginal, Australian told me in the middle of the Keating furore that he wanted the flag changed because it made him feel colonised. I respect this greatly, and it led me to think that the native-born Australian should probably have more votes on the matter than an immigrant like myself, even one of nearly forty years standing, whose loyalties are overlapping in the way I've described. On the other hand, some recent migrants would vote for removing all signs of the British past as soon as possible. The problem could be as simple as this, that I was too well colonised in Northern Ireland to be of any use in this debate.

It is tempting to give my qualifications as an Australian and to explain the sort of republican I am. I do not like the passion that seems at once petty and contrived, and the unnecessary polarisation, all the more so because ours can't be more than a storm in a teacup compared to Yugoslavia, the Lebanon or Ireland itself. 'Well, are you a republican or not?' — but can't I march in the body of the column, OK, not in the vanguard (what sort of conversion from my past would that require, and would you trust it?) but not dragging my feet in the rear, either? If I am content when tomorrow Australia is a republic with a President whose powers are no more than those of our present Governor-General (so we preserve the present parliamentary system), and if tomorrow the flag is the Southern Cross on a blue background (but not stylised into the Eureka flag) or ochre-ish like the Aboriginal one, isn't that enough?

The assumption that Australia was moving steadily and calmly towards its future, not stirring old passions and avoiding the muddy malevolencies my father brought his family away from, may have been naive. Nevertheless, Paul Keating — who has never been as interested as a Whitlam or an Evans in our regular constitutional conferences — strikes me as a man too shallow to be playing fast and loose with history. On the matter of Australian identity he is like a boy playing with matches.

Admittedly, politicians are the people we choose to do our dirty work and we have no right to claim we thought matters could be handled more delicately; a dose of us-and-them works wonders for a jaded party facing an election and perhaps may even invigorate a depressed country. But I was hoping not to be made to choose between the two Irelands before I could choose Australia. Australia in fact made the other Ireland accessible to me. Maybe it is usual for migrants to discover that escaping their past is harder than they hoped. If that's so, the quicker Australia becomes itself, uncluttered by the old Irelands or any other foreign tribal disputes, the better.

1992

GERALD MURNANE

Some Books are to be Dropped into Wells, Others into Fishponds

The other day I stood in front of my bookshelves and stared at the spine of *Don Quixote.* According to my meticulously kept records I read that book in 1970, but when I stood staring at its spine I could remember nothing of the book itself or of the experience of reading it. I could remember no phrase, no sentence; I could not remember one moment from all the hours when I had sat with that bulky book open in front of me.

After I had waited in vain for some words from the book to come back to me, I kept a lookout for images. I waited to see some flickering scenes in black and white on the invisible screen that hangs about a metre in front of my eyes wherever I go. But not even the ghost of a scene appeared from the book. For a moment I thought I saw a silhouette of a man on horseback, but then I recognised it as a memory of the print of Daumier's painting of Don Quixote that had hung on the wall in front of where I stood until I had had extra bookshelves built there.

I gave up waiting for *Don Quixote* and performed the same test on other books. From a sample of twelve — all of them read before 1976 and never opened since — I found seven that brought nothing to mind. If this was a fair sample, then of all the books that I had read once and had not read again, more than half had been wholly forgotten within a few years. I wondered whether I was entitled to conclude that the forgotten books had been of no use to me. I wondered whether I might have better promoted my health and happiness by going for walks or doing push-ups or taking naps instead of reading those books that were going to fly away so soon from my mind. I wondered whether I might as conveniently have dropped those books down a well as read them. (Yet how could I have known at the time which books I ought to read and which books make a splash with?)

I could still not believe that so many books had left so little trace behind them. I decided that my memories of them must be buried deep. I decided to poke around in the dark places — the back rooms of my mind. I closed my eyes and said aloud over and over: '*Don Quixote,* by Miguel de Cervantes, is one of the greatest works of fiction of any age.'

While repeating these solemn words I remembered an evening in 1967 when I was a part-time student at the University of Melbourne. A lecturer in English, during a lecture on *Tom Jones,* read out in class a passage from *Don Quixote.* No doubt the lecturer was making a very important point, but I have forgotten the point today. All I remember is that the passage quoted from Cervantes was concerned with a person or persons (I think they may have been aboard a ship) being struck in the fact by a quantity of wind-borne human vomit.

This seemed an odd memory to have been connected with a great work of fiction, but it was the only result of my reciting the mantra about the book. If anyone reading this has a detailed knowledge of *Don Quixote* and has never read in the great book a passage about wind-borne vomit, that person need not trouble to correct me on the point. I am not writing about *Don Quixote* but about my memory of the books on my shelves.

And now I remember one more result of my repeating aloud the words in praise of *Don Quixote*. As I said the words aloud, I became convinced that I had said them on at least one previous occasion — and not to myself, as I happened to be saying the words then, but in company. In short, I became aware that I was a person who sometimes delivered ponderous judgements on books without being able to remember any more than the name of the book, the author's name, and some judgement borrowed from someone else. This awareness made me embarrassed. I remembered people who had agreed with me when I had uttered my judgements — and people who had disagreed. I might have felt urged to seek out those people and to apologise to them. But what saved me from doing this was a suspicion that some at least of the people who had discussed the great books with me might have remembered no more about the books than I did.

Within a few days I had learned to accept myself as a man who could remember absolutely nothing about *Don Quixote* except the name of the author. I even dared to suppose the abyss in my memory might be a sort of distinction. Even the most forgetful among my friends would surely remember one passage at least from *Don Quixote*, but there I was with my memory a perfect blank. I remembered that Jorge Luis Borges had written a story with the title: 'Pierre Menard, Author of the *Quixote*'. Even Borges, with his fertile imagination, could imagine nothing stranger than that a man of our time could *write* the whole of *Don Quixote*; even Borges could never have supposed that a seemingly literate and civilized man could read and then *forget* the whole of the immortal work.

I became interested in the question why I remembered certain books and forgot others. I must emphasise, however, that the books I am writing about are books I have not looked into for at least fifteen years. On my shelves are many books that I read or look into every few years, and some books that I have to pick up and look into whenever I catch sight of them. My memory of these books too is strangely uneven, but for the moment I am writing about the long-forgotten and the long-remembered.

. . .

Some books that I have not read for more than thirty years have left me with images that I see nearly every day. The images are by no means comforting. I can never quite believe those people who write as adults about the joys and pleasures of their childhood reading. As a child I was made restless and unhappy by most of the books that I read. Whether the book was meant to have a happy or unhappy ending, I was always distressed by the mere fact that the book had an ending. After reading a book I would go into the backyard and try to build a model of the landscape where the characters in the book had lived, and where they could go on living under my supervision and encouragement. Or I tried to draw maps of their houses or farms or districts, or to write in secret in the backs of old exercise books an endless continuation of the book that I had wanted not to end. Often I included myself among the characters in these prolongations.

The first book that I remember as affecting me in this way is *Man-Shy*, by Frank Dalby Davison. I first read *Man-Shy* when I was eight. I read it again soon afterwards, but I cannot remember having read it since and I could not say when I last looked between the covers of the book. What I am writing today about *Man-Shy* comes from memory; I am writing about images that have stayed with me for most of my life.

I remember the red cow. As I remember her now, the red cow stands on a hilltop in Queensland in a year not long before I was born. (My father had told me that the book was set in Queensland in the 1930s.) Probably no week of my life has passed without my seeing for a moment the red cow as she appeared in the little line-drawing beneath the last lines of the text of my father's red-covered Angus and Robertson edition. I have never been to Queensland; I have never ridden a horse or seen a sheep being shorn; yet I have remembered all my life an image of a red cow on a hill in outback Queensland.

The red cow is dying of thirst. I am not going to check the text after all these years. I will quote what I have always remembered as the last words of the text. 'She was about to join the shadowy herd that had gone from the ranges forever.'

Even while I typed these words just now, I felt the same painful uncertainty that I used to feel as a child. Was the red cow actual or imaginary? If the cow was actual I could at least be sure that her suffering was over. But in that case I could no longer hope that the cow I had read about would miraculously survive.

If the cow was imagined, then I wanted to ask the author what would happen to her in his imagination. Would she finally die like an actual cow? Or had the author found a way of thinking of her as alive in spite of everything?

The red cow and her calf were dying because their last waterhole had been fenced around. They were the last survivors in the wild of a herd that had been driven in from the bush to a cattle station. The owners of the station had fenced the waterholes, and the red cow and her calf were about to die from thirst.

By the age of eight I had been thoroughly taught in the eschatology of the Catholic Church. Yet nothing I had been taught could help me decide what would happen to the red cow if she died — or what *had* happened to the cow if she had already died. I knew without asking that animals lacked souls. For an animal there was no heaven or hell, only the earth. But I could not bear to think of the red cow as living on earth and then dying forever. I clung to the words on the last page — the red cow was going to join the shadowy herd.

I laid out in my backyard a vast savannah for that shadowy herd. I studded the savannah with waterholes. I reduced myself in size like Dollman in the comic-book. ('By a supreme effort of the will he compresses the molecules of his body and becomes — Dollman!') I led my shadowy herd to the waterholes and watched them drink. I stood beside the red cow while she drank unafraid from the pool at my feet.

Sometimes I left my shadowy herd in a valley while I climbed a hill to look around me. If I saw far away towards the east the cleared land and the ocean, I could still turn towards the west and see my savannah reaching far inland.

. . .

If the red cow had not been dying of thirst, she would have seen from the hill where she stood at the end of the book the edge of the blue Pacific Ocean. In that scene the blue smudge of the ocean has no other purpose than to mark the far edge of the land where the red cow has been driven to her death. For most of my life the ocean has been no more to me than a boundary marker.

Today while I think of the ocean to the east of the red cow, I am reminded of *Moby Dick*.

I have not looked between the covers of *Moby Dick* for nineteen years but I remember rather more of the book than I remember of *Don Quixote*. This need not tell against *Don Quixote*, which I read only for pleasure whereas *Moby Dick* was one of my set texts for English at university — in the same year, as it happens, when I heard about the flying vomit in Cervantes. In 1967 I read the whole of *Moby Dick* twice through with care and some chapters more than twice.

Yet even so, *Moby Dick* has lasted well in my mind by comparison with other set texts from the same years. I can recall without effort today two sentences (one of them is the first sentence, of course), a phrase of three words, and some of the images that occured to me while I read the text twenty years ago. I can recall also the conviction that I had while I read. I was convinced that the narrator of *Moby Dick* was the wisest and most engaging narrator I had met in fiction.

The image that comes to me from *Moby Dick* today is of a toy-like ship on a smooth, green expanse of water. The ship is not a whaling vessel but the 16th century Portuguese caravel that I copied in grade seven into my history note-book from a line drawing in a textbook. On the tiny deck of the toy boat two men stand talking. A few vague figures of other men hang like monkeys in the rigging, but they are there only for decoration — none of them actually does anything. The reason for this is that all my life I have skipped over the technical terms and descriptions in all the books I have read about ships and boats; I have never understood the difference between a bosun and a capstan.

I have only just noticed that the deck of the toy ship is dotted with pots of the same shape and proportions as the pots in which cartoon cannibals cook cartoon missionaries and pith-helmeted explorers. And now, when I look again at the smooth, green water around the toy boat, I am looking not at the Pacific Ocean but at the surface of what might be a kiddies' wading pool. I can see from New Zealand to South America in one glance.

The pots are simmering on the deck because I remember having read in *Moby Dick* that the oil from the catch of the whales was boiled and purified on deck when the sea was especially calm and the weather fine. I could hardly have read that the crew kept a supply of cartoon cooking-pots for this purpose, and now that I have begun this sentence I remember that the fires for heating the boiling-vessels burned in ovens made of brick. The bricks for the ovens, I have just remembered, were laid with mortar on the deck and were afterwards broken apart when they had served their purpose.

Why have I remembered just now the brick ovens on the toy ship, when for the past twenty years I thought of them as cartoon cooking-pots?

. . .

In January 1987 I was half-way through writing what will be my fifth book of fiction. At the time I was not writing well. When I recognise that I am not writing well, I suppose I am staring too hard at what lies in front of my face. I try to stop staring and to notice what lies at the edges of my view. In January 1987 I had been staring for too long at soil. I was writing about a character who was staring at the soil of his native district in order to understand why he always felt drawn to that district. But then I sat back a little and noticed what was at the edge of my view. I noticed a fishpond.

The pond was not one of those bean-shaped ornamental pools overhung with ferns and pampas grass. It was a plain-looking square of bricks rising abruptly from the back lawn behind a house where I had lived for two years as a boy. As soon as I had noticed this pond at the edge of my view I knew I had found the image that would keep me writing until my book was finished. I felt as though I only had to stare at the brick walls rising out of the grass, or at the little grub-shaped bits of dried mortar still sticking between the bricks, or at the dark-green water with the raft of floating water-plants whose leaves were like shamrocks — I only had to stare at these things and all the rest of the story I had been trying for three years to tell would appear to me.

It was a strange experience to discover, half-way through writing what I thought was a story about X, that I had really been writing the story of Y. I had thought for three years that I was writing a book whose central image was a patch of soil and grass, but one day in January 1987 I learned that the central image of my book was a fishpond.

It was also a strange experience just now to discover that I remembered after twenty years the brick ovens on the deck, and to see the ovens as having the shape and size of the fishpond that yielded half a book of fiction six months ago. The American poet Robert Bly once wrote that he learned to be a poet when he learned to trust his obsessions. I trusted my image of the fishpond last January and found in the image of the pond what I needed for finishing my story. I thought when I had finished the story that I had finished with the pond. I had even written into the last part of the story a description of the pond as empty of water and of the red fish that had lived in the pond as drowning in air. But now an image of the same fishpond has appeared on the deck of the *Pequod* — or, rather, many images of fishponds have appeared on deck; and all the fishponds are bubbling like stewpots.

Before I look into the bubbling ponds, I ask myself how I could have lived for more than thirty years without realising how full of meaning my fishpond was. I had never forgotten the pond; I would have thought of my own pond whenever I saw a pond in someone's lawn. But I had not understood how much of meaning was contained in the pond. I was given a hint sometimes, but I failed to follow it up. During most of the thirty-five years after I had left the house with the fishpond on the back lawn, I would become oddly alert whenever I noticed in a front garden a certain small variety of begonia with glossy red and green leaves. I always supposed the leaves themselves would one day remind me of something important; but I was staring at what was in front of me when I should have been watching out for things at the edge of my vision. In the house where I had lived in 1950 and 1951, a row of begonias had grown along the side fence. If I had stood and stared at those begonias I would have seen the pond from the corner of my eye.

The connection between my fishpond of 1951 and the bubbling pots on the deck of the *Pequod* is not only that the pond and the fireplaces were both of brick. The pond and the boiling oil are connected by the fact that the bricks on the deck were laid especially for the purpose and later removed.

Two years after my family had moved from the house with the fishpond, a tradesman left behind in the backyard of the house where we then lived a small heap of bricks and some unused wet mortar. While the mortar was still wet I decided I would build a small fishpond on the lawn. I wanted to have green water-plants and chubby red fish in my backyard again. But after I had assembled the first row of bricks for my pond, my father ordered me to stop.

The boiling that took place in the fishponds on the *Pequod* was for the purpose of refining the substance that the narrator of *Moby Dick* calls mostly *sperm*.

. . .

I wrote earlier that I remembered a sentence apart from the first sentence of *Moby Dick*. As I have remembered it for twenty years and without consulting the text, the sentence is uttered by Captain Ahab to Mr Starbuck not long before the last chase begins. An unfamiliar smell has been wafted into the noses of the two men. In my memory, Captain Ahab does a turn about the deck in the manner of Long John Silver as drawn in Classic Comics, smells the strange smell, and says, 'They are making hay in the meadows of the Andes, Mr Starbuck.'

I happen to have been born without a sense of smell. I can form no idea of the smell of hay being made. When I remember the words that I put into Captain Ahab's mouth just then, I merely see long grass growing in a place such as I have seen in photographs of the *altiplano* of Bolivia. But because I know there is something about the grassy place that I can never experience, I look at it intently, as though I might be allowed to see more in the grass than a person would see who was able to smell it.

Because I have never experienced the smelling of a thing from a distance, I suppose that a person must always be in sight of what he gets wind of. Whenever I see Ahab and Starbuck with the smell of hay in their noses I see them as in sight of land. The two men stand on the deck of their toy boat. The two are alone by now. I see no other men doing pretend-tasks or hanging idly in the rigging. The sea around the toy boat is smooth and green. I can see from end to end of the green water. The world is smaller by far than I had supposed.

Somewhere in his writings, Robert Musil reminds us of how wrong we are to think of the individual self as the one unstable item within a firm world. The opposite is the case. The unstable world drifts like an island at the heart of each of us.

When I look intently at the ocean around the *Pequod*, the green water is the fishpond. At the edge of my vision I see a grassy hill. The world is a small place by now; Queensland and South America are the one grassy hill above the pond.

The red cow smells the water. She goes down from the meadows of hay towards the pool that keeps her alive.

1987

HELEN GARNER

The Fate of The First Stone

Many years ago I came across a remark made by the poet A. D. Hope. He said, 'With hostile critics of my work, I am always scrupulously and cheerfully polite.' Professor Hope's subtle resolution came back to me in March 1995, when my book *The First Stone* finally appeared, and I had to stand up and defend ad nauseam my attempt to discover the truth behind a sexual assault case at one of Melbourne University's residential colleges. I hung on like mad to the poet's tactic, and I'm happy to report that it's possible, in the face of the most intense provocation, to keep your temper for months on end. I bit my lip and gnawed my fist and went on taking deep breaths and counting to ten — partly because I wonder if, when the chips are down, courtesy is all we have left; but also because I knew that, if I waited, a time would come when I could put forward calmly some thoughts about the furore provoked by this book, and about the things I've learnt from the strange experience of publishing *The First Stone*.

Our culture at large is obsessed, at the moment, with matters of sex and power in the relations between women and men. Given this, and given the attempts by the two women complainants from Ormond College to get access to the book in the courts before its publication, I shouldn't have been surprised by the *extent* of the response to the book. But what did astonish me, and still does, is the *nature* of the response — its primal quality. Primal things lie much deeper in people than reason does. People in the grip of a primal response to the very existence of a book like this will read it — and if they consent to read it at all — between the narrow blinkers of anger and fear. I realise now, having had it forced on me by this experience, that there are as many versions of *The First Stone* as there are readers of it. And yet there *are* certain words and sentences on its pages, put there on purpose in a certain order by the hand of a certain person — namely, me. So I'd like to take the liberty, here, of briefly and firmly listing a few of the things I did *not* say.

I did *not* say that the two young women who brought allegations of assault against the Master of their college *ought* to have agreed to be interviewed by me. I was terribly frustrated that they wouldn't, and in the book I often express this frustration, but right up to the end of the book I continue explicitly to respect their right not to speak to me.

I did *not* say that women should 'go back to wearing ankle-length sacks'.

I did *not* say that the correct way to deal with sexual assault or harassment is to knee a man in the balls.

I did *not* say that women are responsible for the way men behave towards them.

And I most emphatically did *not* say that women who get raped are asking for it.

I know it's the fate of all writers to feel themselves misread. I hoped I was writing in such a way as to invite people to lay down their guns for a moment and think again — and not only think, but *feel* again. I wanted people to read in an alert way — alert to things between the lines, things that the law prevents me from saying outright.

The book is sub-titled not 'an argument about sex and power', but 'some questions about sex and power'. There are more questions in it than there are answers. Because it declines — or is unable — to present itself as one big clonking armour-clad monolithic certainty, it's not the kind of book that's easy to review briskly. Because it's a series of shifting speculations, with an open structure, it's hard to pull out single quotes without distorting it. What the book invites from a reader is openness — an answering spark.

But I found that many people, especially those who locate their sense of worth in holding to an already worked-out political position, are not prepared to take the risk of reading like that. Perhaps they can't, any more. What is not made explicit, for readers like these, is simply not there. Being permanently primed for battle, they read like tanks. They roll right over the little conjunctions and juxtapositions that slither in the undergrowth of the text. It's a scorched-earth style of reading. It refuses to notice the side-paths, the little emotional and psychological by-roads that you can't get into unless you climb down from your juggernaut, and take off your helmet and your camouflage gear and your combat boots. It's a poor sort of reading that refuses the invitation to *stop* reading and lay down the page and turn the attention inwards. And it's always easier, or more comfortable, to misread something, to keep it at arm's length, than to respond to it openly.

Thus, several prominent feminists have used the word 'sentimental' to dismiss the scene in the book where the ex-Master's wife speaks, through inconsolable tears, of the devastation these events have brought to her and her family. Less doctrinaire critics have been able to recognise, in this scene, a terrible example of the human cost of political action which narrows its focus to the purely legal, and thus divorces thought from feeling.

Many feminists, even, incredibly, some who teach in universities, have declared it correct line not to buy *The First Stone* or to read it all. This position is apparently quite widespread, judging by countless reports that have reached me of bitter arguments round dinner tables, in women's reading groups, and at bookshop cash registers. This sort of feminist, while refusing to sully her party credentials by reading the book, also knows, however, or has absorbed from the ether by some osmotic process, exactly what the book 'says', so she is able to pontificate freely on how I have 'betrayed the feminist cause', and 'set feminism back twenty years'. One woman, representing the student body of an institution in the town where I was born, wrote to let me know that, the minute she heard I was going to write the book, she had got rid of all my other books off her shelves. She rebuked me for having 'profiteered' off other people's misfortunes, and suggested in a challenging tone that I should donate my ill-gotten gains to a worthwhile feminist organisation. Here I permitted myself the luxury of a coarse laugh.

The question of money in this context is fascinating. The accusation of 'profiteering' is the last refuge of one's enemy — a reproach densely packed with psychic content. If *The First Stone* had been a jargon-clogged pamphlet bristling with footnotes, if it had sold a comfortably obscure, say, three thousand copies over a couple of years, the response to it from feminism's grimmer tribes would have been much less poisonous. But among those who maintain a victim posture vis à vis the big world, where one can earn an honourable living by writing in a language that the person in the street can understand, nothing is more suspicious than a book which appears to have succeeded.

Crudely, there are two possible attitudes that a hostile feminist might take towards the annoying fact that a lot of people, including feminists of broader sympathy, have defied the girlcott and responded favourably to *The First Stone.* The first one is easy: Garner is a sell-out, a traitor to her sex. She's caved in to the patriarchy and joined the other side. This leaves the grim tribes feeling and looking — to each other, at least — squeaky clean. The other alternative is to wonder whether something might have happened to feminism.

Maybe something's gone wrong.

Maybe something good and important has been hijacked.

Maybe the public debate about women and men has been commandeered by a bullying orthodoxy.

My intention has never been to bash feminism. How could I do that, after what it's meant to me? After what its force and truth make possible? But I hate this disingenuousness, this determination to cling to victimhood at any cost.

Why do the members of this orthodoxy insist that young women are victims? Why do they insist on focusing the debate on only one sort of power — the institutional?

Why do they refuse to acknowledge what experience teaches every girl and woman: that men's unacceptable behaviour towards us extends over a very broad spectrum — that to telescope this and label it all 'violence against women' is to distort both language and experience?

The hysteria that this book has provoked in some quarters reveals clearly and sadly that feminism, once so fresh and full of sparkle, is no different in its habits from any other political theory. Like all belief systems and religions and art forms

— like any idea that has the misfortune to have an -ism tacked on to it — feminism has a tendency to calcify, to narrow and harden into fundamentalism. The life spark slips out of it and whisks away, leaving behind it an empty concrete bunker.

To disagree with a fundamentalist feminist, it seems, to question acts carried out in the name of women's rights, is not to challenge her, but to 'betray' her, to turn her into more of a victim than she was already.

One feminist critic in Melbourne put forward the proposition that in telling the Ormond story against the will of the young women involved, I had committed a treachery in the same league as the betrayal of the tribal secrets of the Hindmarsh Island Aboriginal women. The Ormond women, she wrote in the *Australian Book Review*, 'did not want their story told by Helen Garner, writer of fiction making a guest appearance as a journalist. She told their story anyway, has stolen the story that they did not want her to have.'

I find this a piece of the most breathtaking intellectual dishonesty.

In what sense *is* it 'their' story? It is distorting and deeply wrong to bestow on the Ormond complainants the ownership of this story. It could be truthfully called *their* story only if they had decided to keep it to themselves, to hold it to themselves as a private trauma. I don't suggest for a single second that they should have done this. And they didn't. They took their complaints to the police. And the police took them to the courts.

Now the law covering sexual assault may still be seriously skewed against women's interests: it plainly is, and I strongly support the correction of this; but a court in a democratic country like Australia is an open forum. Painful as this might be, a court is open. It is open to the scrutiny of the citizens *in whose names* justice is being aimed at. So, once the complaints reached the courts, the story ceased *of necessity* to belong to the young women, or to the college, or to the man against whom the allegations were made. It stopped being 'their' story, and it became 'our' story — a new chapter in the endless saga of how we, as a community, try to regulate the power struggle between women and men.

I want now to speak briefly about something called eros.

I used the word rather loosely, perhaps, in the book. You could define eros — if it would stay still long enough for you to get a grip on it — as something lofty and mythological, like 'the gods' messenger' or 'the life spirit'. You could call it the need of things to keep changing and moving on. The Jungians call it 'the spark that ignites and connects'. Eros, most famously, comes bounding into the room when two people fall in love at first sight. But it's also in the excitement that flashes through you when a teacher explains an intellectual proposition *and you grasp it* — or when someone tells a joke *and you get it.*

Eros is the quick spirit that moves between people — *quick* as in the distinction between 'the quick and the dead'. It's the moving force that won't be subdued by habit or law. Its function is to keep cracking open what is becoming rigid and closed-off. Eros explodes the forbidden. Great stand-up comics thrill us by trying to ride its surge. It's at the heart of every heresy — and remember that feminism itself is a heresy against a monolith. Eros mocks our fantasy that we can nail life down and control it. It's as far beyond our attempts to regulate it as sunshine is — or a cyclone.

But one feminist, criticising *The First Stone* in the *Australian*, wants us to accept that 'the dynamics of eros', as she puts it, 'are historically produced'. 'We need,' she says, 'to reconstruct eros between men and women *on an equal basis.*'

There will always be these moments, I know, when people who think politically and types like me with a metaphysical bent end up staring at each other in helpless silence, with our mouths hanging open.

It's hubristic to speak of 'reconstructing eros'. The whole point of eros, its very usefulness as a concept, is that it's *not reconstructable.* Eros doesn't give a damn about morals or equality. Though eros moves through the intellect, eros is not intellectual. It moves through politics, but it's not political. It moves between men and women, but it's not in itself sexual. When I talk in the book about eros, I'm trying to talk about that very thing — the thing that's beyond us — the dancing force that we *can't* control or legislate or make fair.

It's an article of faith among some young feminists that a woman 'has the right' to go about the world dressed in any way she pleases. They think that for a man to respond to — and note, please, that I don't mean to threaten or touch or attack — for a man to respond to what he sees as a statement of her sexuality and of her own attitude to it, is some sort of outrage — and an outrage that the law should deal with. I find the talk of rights in this context quite peculiar. What right are you invoking here? You can only talk about rights, in this context, by pretending that it *means nothing at all* to wear, say, a low-necked dress in a bar at two o'clock in the morning, or a pair of shorts that your bum's hanging out of on a public beach. To invoke rights, here, you have to fly in the face of the evidence of the senses — as if they believed that each person moved round the world enclosed in a transparent bubble of rights.

And who's going to protect these notional rights? Which regime will provide a line of armed police to make sure that no bloke looks at a woman's breasts with the wrong expression on his face? I'm inviting these young idealists to get real — to grow up — better still, to *get conscious.* Know what you're doing, what its likely effect is, and decide whether that's what you want. Sexy clothes are part of the wonderful game of life. But to dress to display your body, and then to project all the sexuality of the situation on to men and blame them for it, just so you can continue to feel innocent and put-upon, is dishonest and irresponsible. Worse, it's a relinquishing of power. If a woman dresses to captivate, she'd better learn to keep her wits about her, for when the wrong fish swims into her net.

A woman of my age knows — and it's her responsibility to point this out to younger women — that the world is full of different sorts of men. Many are decent. Some are decent until they start drinking. Many have grown up enough to have learnt manners. Some have taken seriously *their* responsibility to get conscious. Many men like women, and want to be around them. Some men *hate* women, and want to be around them. Many have been taught by imagination, or by reason, or by painful or happy experience, that a woman is a person and not just a clump of sexual characteristics put there for them to plunder.

Some men have learnt to recognise and respect the boundary between their fantasy and what is real. Others, trapped in instinct, have not, and never will — and it's a sad fact that we can't depend on the law to *make* them. Nor will laws alone save us from their depredations, whether trivial or serious. Society makes laws. I am strongly in favour of tough legislation that will give women redress against assault — but around and above and below the laws, for good or ill, there is this fluid element, life. What I'm proposing is that there's a large area for manoeuvre, for the practical exercise of women's individual power, before it's necessary or appropriate to call in the law. And I believe that one of the tasks of feminists should be to expand and develop this area of power.

In the book I describe a photograph. It's a black and white shot of a young woman dressed in an elegant and revealing gown. I wrote, 'It is impossible not be moved by her daring beauty. She is a woman in the full glory of her youth, as joyful as a goddess, elated by her own careless authority and power.' In response to this page of the book there emerged a grotesque distortion of my intent. One feminist critic, for whom perhaps all gods are vengeful, wrote that my admiring description of this lovely, rather wild young woman was in actual fact an invocation, in modern dress, of that monstrous, punitive, man-hating figure of myth — 'vagina dentata in her full glory'.

Other feminists have told me severely that by 'sexualising' young women, I had 'disempowered' them. Leaving aside the hideousness of the language, you don't have to be Camille Paglia to see that this is sick, and mad.

There's been a lot of talk, triggered by the book, about symbolic mothers and daughters. Some feminists have a doom-laden approach to giving maternal advice. The young woman in the beautiful dress is not, they insist, in possession of any power whatsoever, potential or actual, and it is wicked of me to suggest that she might be. For them, only one sort of power is admissible to a discussion of events like these, and that is *institutional* power. This splendid young woman, then, so clever and lovely and full of life, is nothing but a sad victim. These traumatic events, they solemnly assure her, 'will blight her life'.

What sort of a mother, literal or symbolic, would insist to her daughter that an early experience in the rough adult world, no matter how painful or public, would blight the rest of her life? That is not good mothering. That is pathetic mothering. That is the kind of mothering that doubles the damage. A decent mother, when the dust has settled, would say to her daughter, 'Right. It's over. Now we can look at what's happened. Let's try to *analyse* what's happened. See how much of what happened was other people's responsibility, and then try to see how much of it, if any, was yours. Take responsibility for your contribution, be it small or large. You are not responsible for men's behaviour towards you, but you *are* responsible for your own. Pick yourself up now. Wipe your tears. Spit out the bitterness and the blame before they poison you. You're young and clever and strong. Shake the dust of this off your feet. Learn from it, and then move on.'

If all I had to go on, as responses to *The First Stone*, were the critiques of these prominent feminists, I'd be feeling pretty sick by now. But I've had letters, hundreds and hundreds of long, frank letters from strangers. The Melbourne critic (male) who chastised me for writing the book 'to please men' may be interested to know that I estimate the male/female ratio of the letters at about 35/65. I was surprised at how few of them were from cranks or nutcases. By no means did all of these letters — and they're still coming — express blanket approval of the book. But almost all of them were from people who had been prepared to respond to the book in the way I'd hoped — with the defences down — with an answering spark. They're prepared to lay out and re-examine examples, from their own lives, of encounters big and small with the opposite sex, which at the time had bewildered them, or hurt them, or made them angry. I lost count of the people who said, 'I'd like to tell you something that happened to me — of something that I did — many years ago; something that until I read the book I had forgotten — that I'd buried.'

Some of the letters were hilarious. I relate in the book an incident about a masseur at a particular Fitzroy gym who kissed me when I was naked on the table. One woman wrote to me, 'I shrieked when I read about that masseur.' She said the same bloke had kissed *her*, and that furthermore *she'd* paid him too, so I wasn't to feel I was the only mug. A man wrote and suggested to me very disapprovingly that I must have led the masseur on. 'Why did you take your clothes off in the massage room,' he sternly asked, 'instead of in the change rooms? What you did was tantamount to striptease.' A masseur who could see as striptease a middle-aged woman scrambling hastily out of a sweaty old tracksuit in a corner gets my prize for sexualising against overwhelming odds.

Some letters, from both men and women, are full of pain, and anger, and shame. Others tell stories of the patient unravelling of interpersonal and institutional knots, and of happy resolutions.

But the word that crops up most frequently is *relief*. Again and again people speak of the relief they feel that it might be possible to acknowledge that the world of daily work and social life isn't as horrible and destructive and ghastly as punitive feminists insist. People are relieved that it might be possible to admit sympathy in human terms with people on the opposite side of a power divide. They're relieved that ambiguity might be readmitted to the analysis of thought and action. And specially they're relieved that to admit gradations of offence is not to let the side down or to let chaos come flooding in.

A lot of people have asked me if I regret having written this book — and more particularly, if I regret the letter of ignorant sympathy that I wrote to the Master when I first became aware of the case — the letter that got me into so much trouble, and caused so many doors to be slammed in my face. The answer is no, and no.

One thing I do regret, however, is that my publisher's defamation lawyers obliged me to blur the identity of a certain woman who was the young complainants' chief supporter in the college. I did this in quite a simple way: I didn't invent anything, but each time that the words or actions of this woman appeared in the text, I called her by a different name, thus splitting her into half a dozen people. Months after the book came out, the woman identified herself publicly, to my relief, since I had divided her with the greatest reluctance. This is the only ruse I engaged in, but it has given some people the idea that the book is 'fictionalised' — that it's a novel. It is not a novel. Except for this one tactic to avoid defamation action, it is reportage.

I accept that *The First Stone* has caused pain. I know it's no comfort — that it's almost a cheek — for me to say how sad I am about this. But sometimes a set of events erupts that seems to encapsulate, in complex and important ways, the spirit of its time. These are the stories that need to be *told*, not swept away like so much debris, or hidden from sight. My attempt to understand this story was frustrated. My version of it is full of holes. But I hope that these holes might, after all, have a use; that through them might pass air and light; that they might even provide a path for the passage of eros; and that they might leave, for women and men who want to think generously about these things, room to move.

1995

B. J. COMAN

A Short History of the Rabbit in Australia

Wall plaques and friendship cards have changed a lot. Quite often there used to be quotations from the Revised Standard Version but then Christianity fell out of favour and biblical themes were replaced by little extracts from Kahlil Gibran (I see that some plagiarist, a Mr 'Kellogg Allbran', has produced 'The Profit'). But this was still a bit too religious, if you know what I mean — not really the stuff for your modern, comprehensively liberated, multifaceted, multicultural newperson. Even the *Rubaiyat of Omar Khayyam* fell out of favour.

And so it was that Mrs Cottontail arose from the scented pages of Beatrix Potter to overpower the wisdom of the East. She infests the gift shops and knick-knack counters today. You must have seen her a thousand times — an anthropomorphised rabbit-creature with apron and bonnet, extolling the virtues of home and hearth and the Protestant work ethic. Placing her in time is difficult, but she is definitely post-Fowlers Vacola — her fruit preserves are a sight to see — but before Reeboks and Raybans. I have not clapped eyes on Mr Cottontail yet, but I know what he looks like. He wears a vest with a heavy gold watch chain, baggy trousers with bowyangs and heavy boots. He is always out of doors tending his celebrated root crops. If he smokes, it is only the occasional pipe of Longbottom Leaf. If he drinks, it is only the rare jar of scrumpy with his old friend, the Gaffer. Birds always perch on his garden spade and the flowers are always blooming.

For your average city-dweller, this is probably the sort of image associated with *Oryctolagus cuniculus*, the European rabbit. It might be useful to contrast this image, derived from Beatrix Potter, *Watership Down* and various cartoon characters, with the real animal in Australia today.

Poor old Thomas Austin of Barwon Park near Geelong has the dubious distinction of having imported and successfully bred the first wild rabbits in Australia. They arrived on Christmas Day in 1859. What happened thereafter has become perhaps the best-known example in the world of the disastrous consequences that can attend the introduction of an alien animal species into a new and fragile environment. Within little more than a decade, they had become a pest over large areas of Victoria's Western District. In 1866, 14,253 rabbits were shot on Barwon Park. Rabbits released at Kapunda in South Australia in about 1870 also spread rapidly and, by 1880, rabbits from the two release points had merged.

Within the space of another six years, rabbits had spread throughout New South Wales and into Queensland. By the turn of the century, they had crossed the Great Divide to the eastern seaboard and, a few years later, had reached the western shoreline of the continent, perhaps aided by other introductions in Western Australia. Thus, in the space of forty years this small and rather inoffensive-looking animal had occupied the vast hinterland of Australia, achieving densities of such magnitude that the term 'rabbit plague' became commonplace.

It is not that we weren't warned. Strabo, circa 50 BC, was well acquainted with the destructive nature of the animal in Spain and wrote: 'Of destructive animals there are scarcely any with the exception of certain little hares which burrow in the ground and destroy both seeds and plants by gnawing at the roots. It is said that formerly, the inhabitants of the islands of Majorca and Minorca sent a deputation to the Romans soliciting that new land might be given them as they were quite driven out of their country by those animals, being no longer able to stand against their vast multitudes.' The Bible also has a reference to rabbits. In the Authorised Version, the Book of Proverbs speaks of the coneys as a small and feeble folk who make their home among the rocks (a very good defence mechanism). Nonetheless, the translators got it wrong because the Hebrew word *shaphan* refers to the Syrian hyrax, a total different animal, which lives among the rocks much as rabbits might do.

. . .

The economic and environmental damage initially caused by this pest in Australia is now difficult for us to comprehend because Australians have become accustomed to an environment radically altered by two centuries of grazing by livestock and to the changes wrought by the axe and the plough. Some stock runs were made completely barren, often as a combined result of rabbits, overgrazing by livestock and drought. In 1879 at Brim Station in the Wimmera, a total of 670 live sheep were mustered for shearing, where in the previous winter 12,000 shorn sheep had been turned out to pasture. Amongst my collection of historical material on rabbits is a photograph of a rabbit poison trail somewhere in western NSW early this century. The whole landscape is littered with carcases and the caption tells us that some 20,000 dead rabbits were found per mile of trail.

Quite apart from losses caused to agriculture and pastoralism, rabbits continue to have a serious detrimental effect on the regeneration of native plants, particularly shrubs and trees. My colleague and friend Dr Brian Cooke has produced startling evidence of the ability of even small numbers of rabbits to prevent regeneration of sheoaks (*Allocasuarina verticillata*) in the Coorong National Park in South Australia. Earlier studies in the Victorian Mallee during the 1960s showed that, in plots protected from rabbits, seventeen 'new' species of ground layer plants appeared in the space of two years. Particularly in the arid zone, rabbits in uncontrolled numbers continue to cause enormous environmental damage. Some scientists consider that rabbits pose the most significant present-day threat to the integrity of the Simpson Desert.

Rabbits are herbivores, but we should not suppose that the damage caused by them is limited to the destruction of vegetation. It is very likely that this pest competed directly with some rabbit-sized native animals, especially the now rare bilby, *Macrotis lagotis*. Notes dating back well over a hundred years and made by the then Rabbit Inspector at Hay in New South Wales indicate that the myriad numbers of bilby burrows and nests of rat kangaroos made the detection of the first invading rabbits very difficult. Within a few decades, the bilbies had completely disappeared and the whole countryside swarmed with rabbits. The bilby, once inhabiting huge areas of inland Australia, is now restricted to some desert areas in Central Australia, smaller areas in the Kimberley and Warburton Ranges and those areas of south-western Queensland where rabbits are largely absent. The Anti-Rabbit Research Foundation (no, they are not against research on rabbits) in Australia, of which I am proud to be a member, has adopted the bilby as its emblem — Australia's answer to the Easter Bunny. Each year, the foundation raises some cash from the sale of chocolate 'Easter Bilbies'. Power to their cause.

Historically, human efforts to control the rabbit pest in Australia seem to have been only partly effective. Most states enacted harsh legislation compelling farmers to take action, and the farming of rabbits was prohibited. However, the legislators were soon to have a practical demonstration of the biblical maxim that 'faith without works is dead'. Landholders either ignored the 'Rabbit Act' or managed to evade its real intent, either by doing only minimal work or by paying the fines imposed for failure to heed the law. In many cases, it was simply not possible to spend the time and money needed to achieve effective control, particularly in 'light' country. Some states erected long-distance barrier fences but the rabbit had often already penetrated into protected country before the fence was completed. A few landholders in more productive country were able to eradicate the pest from their land, usually by netting their boundaries and always by destroying the warrens.

In my own district, south of Bendigo in central Victoria, several large runs were rabbit-free before the Second World War due to the adoption of this 'island fortress' approach. In 1914, Mr R. A. Barrett purchased Coliban Estate, a large rabbity run near Redesdale. Barrett was a shrewd businessman. When he purchased the property, an extra portion of money was put aside to deal with the rabbits. He let contracts for many miles of netting boundary fence and all gateways were fitted with timber sills underneath to prevent rabbits digging in. In the good old days, rabbit netting was cheap because it was made by the guests at H. M. Prison Pentridge! Gangs of men were employed to dig out the burrows and loose rabbits were hunted down with 'scratch packs' — a motley assortment of mongrel dogs which nearly always included a large hound (called a 'lurcher' in England but more commonly 'kangaroo dog' in Australia) and smaller terriers to penetrate the thick bulrushes and other cover. One summer evening, as Barrett was riding home along the Coliban, he saw a rabbit run into a small hollow log. This was the only rabbit he had seen on the 4500-acre property. He blocked the log, rode home and asked one of his men to chop the rabbit out and bring it to him. Later that night the worker duly returned with the dead rabbit and a delighted Barrett indicated that he could now settle down to sleep!

Barrett, though, was an exception, and over vast areas of Australia, the rabbit remained virtually unchecked until the coming of myxomatosis in the 1950s. Earlier attempts at biological control such as the Rodier method had all failed. (With this method all trapped females were killed and all trapped males were released. The assumption was that the excess of males would harass the remaining females to death.) W. E. Abbott (1913) insisted that releasing cats was the answer and, indeed, a trainload of moggies was dispatched into the bush. Both Rodier and Abbott continued to believe in their systems long after it was obvious that they did not work — another common attitude with rabbit control. Other forms of biological control were promoted — rabbit scab, pasteurella, Tintinallogy disease, bladder fluke, and liver rot. Louis Pasteur tried to claim the New South Wales Government reward of $2,000,000 (today's value) for an effective rabbit control method with his demonstration that chicken cholera would kill rabbits. None of these biological controls succeeded and only the inevitable periods of drought brought the animal to its knees. Banjo Paterson was able to write: 'It's grand to be a rabbit/And breed till all is blue/And then to die in little heaps because/There's nothing left to chew.'

. . .

The story of myxomatosis is immensely interesting and far too complicated to detail in this short account. Interested readers should consult the standard text by Frank Fenner and Francis Ratcliffe (*Myxomatosis*, 1965). Also, Eric Rolls has produced a very readable account (*They All Ran Wild*, 1969). In fact, Rolls' account is required reading for the interested layperson because it is in the language of the poet rather than the stiffer prose of the scientist. Sufficient to say that, in late December of 1950, myxomatosis disease suddenly took off after earlier unsuccessful attempts to produce a widespread outbreak.

My friend B. V. (Bunny) Fennessy was an eyewitness to one of the early outbreaks near Corowa. As a former biologist employed by the CSIRO Division of Wildlife Research, he was sidekick to the then Chief of Division, Francis Ratcliffe. In the first week of January 1951, Bunny (his real name is Bernard but only a few people know that — to the rest of Australia's rabbit biologists and farmers he is simply known as Bunny) received a telegram from Ratcliffe — 'Myxomatosis has broken out spontaneously on Mr P. A. Allen's property Mooratunka Corowa NSW stop please investigate stop' (he still has the telegram). This was near where the CSIRO had been carrying out a field trial to introduce the disease late in 1950.

Bunny duly drove the old Land Rover up from Melbourne and, after seeking directions, eventually found the outbreak. The sight of sick and dying rabbits was, as he told me, something quite new and it took him some time to take in the scene before him. While he was leaning against a gateway pondering this incredible sight, he suddenly became aware of a sunburnt gentleman in shorts and rubber boots — a holiday-maker on the Murray River — walking towards him. 'You looking at those rabbits?' the man asked. Fennessy answered in the affirmative. 'They ought to hang the bastard that done that,' the man said. From that day on, Bunny Fennessy has never underestimated the need for public consultation on issues related to wildlife management!

Myxomatosis changed the rabbit scene in many parts of higher rainfall country. After it, at Kyneton in central Victoria where I was then growing up, you could walk all day without seeing a live rabbit. A year earlier the countryside swarmed with them and an old neighbour of ours declared that 'the varmin are so thick you have to pull a couple out of the burrow in order to get the polecat [ferret] down'. After 'the myxo' my father was convinced that rabbits would soon be extinct. As a very young boy, I was with him once in the Shamrock Hotel after a successful lamb sale. At the far end of the bar was a famous old rabbiter by the name of Boswell whose skill was legend. My father always claimed that Boswell could trap a rabbit in St Paul's Cathedral, even if there weren't any there (St Patrick's was out of the question — we were Catholics). In the course of conversation, he indicated to 'Bossie' that rabbits were a thing of the past. Boswell replied to the effect that rabbits would be urinating on my father's grave. The old warrener has long since died but subsequent history has proved him right.

. . .

Today, the rabbit has hit the headlines again. There is a new disease, rabbit calicivirus disease (RCD), moving through parts of the inland. RCD was originally found in China in 1984, where it devastated the rabbit meat industry. As a result of trading in breeding stock, the disease soon found its way into Europe with a similar outcome. Australian authorities subsequently became interested in the disease as a possible biological control agent and it was imported, under strict quarantine conditions, to the CSIRO Animal Health Laboratory, Geelong. Few candidate organisms could have filled the bill better than RCD. It kills rapidly: within three days of initial contact and within twelve hours of the first outward symptoms. It also appears to produce a fairly humane death; rabbits die quietly and without struggle, probably as a result of massive clotting in small blood vessels. Animal welfare is a big issue today, and rightly so. Still, I find myself having a lot of sympathy with Hilaire Belloc's view — 'He prayeth best who loveth best/All creatures great and small/The streptococcus is the test/I love him most of all.'

[...]

We will never get the last rabbit out of Australia, or even out of Victoria or any other state. We may, however, get rid of the last ones on our farms just as R. A. Barrett did. Even if we don't, it is certainly possible to keep them down to a level where small annual inputs of maintenance control prevent any sudden upsurge. I want to be around when we kill the last rabbit in our little district. We will probably cook it for dinner. But we may not, for I have just read a little treatise on 'cookery of the rabbit' (circa 1900) and it ends by saying: 'Finally, the head is not to be neglected. It contains a variety of delicate picking and gives light, desultory occupation to a wayward appetite.'

I hope we do get the last rabbit out of our district. I won't benefit but my grandchildren will. There is a down side of course. They will never know what it is to keep ferrets or to hear the rabbits bolting underground. They will never know what it is to wake up on a Saturday morning to the whine of Ginger and Spot and Stumpy as they anticipate the day ahead. They will never sit around the open fire on winter's nights knitting up rabbit nets. They will miss those views, early in the cold, autumn morning, when you peep over the hill to see dozens of rabbits sitting on their burrows. They will not know what it is like to come home from the chiller cashed up after the day's haul. That was my happy childhood. I cannot afford to let my grandchildren have the same experiences, because there are other, more important experiences that continuing high rabbit numbers do not allow. A walk in the Australian bush is one.

1996

ROBERT DESSAIX

Nice Work If You Can Get It

'No,' Ania Walwicz said at the Melbourne Festival when asked if she was an ethnic writer, 'I'm a fat writer.' We laughed and applauded.

The multicultural professionals, however, may not let her off the hook so easily. I have in mind that small but eloquent band of people, usually from institutions, who actually have a vested interest in keeping constructs like Anglo-Celtic/non-Anglo-Celtic, English-speaking background/non-English-speaking background alive and functional.

Even as you read these lines, they're out there compiling bibliographies, devising curricula, writing articles for right-thinking journals and editing damning reports, all in ways designed to lock our writers into categories they have willed into existence in the first place. They're out there combing through Edward Said (a favourite), Derrida, Deleuze, Foucault and Althusser in a strenuous effort to make the Australian reality validate French social and literary theory of the 1960s and 1970s.

Well, let's hear it for the fat writers, I say. I'd like to ask (as in fact Foucault did about the sane/insane polarity in earlier centuries) whose actual benefit the polarity works for, because I believe there are winners and losers in the present game. The losers, as always, are the patients, those dubbed 'multicultural writers', while the winners (no surprises) are the doctors who staff the clinics, the academics, the multicultural professionals. I don't think it's a conspiracy, I don't think an ounce of bad faith is involved — I just think that's the way the world (and its institutions) work. 'Multicultural literature', as George Papaellinas has put it, 'has never, as a category, been anything other than a creation of the marketplace'. That's to put it at its simplest.

I don't, by the way, vote Liberal, I live in Fitzroy not Glen Waverley, I don't believe in cutting off immigration, I only read the *Australian* on Saturdays, I don't regard Britain as my motherland and I've read more widely in foreign languages than in English. I only mention this because one of the commonest ploys of those who argue in favour of and promote multiculturalism is to pigeonhole anyone who disagrees with them as 'right-wing' at the very least and at worst racist. [...]

The argument of the supporters of multiculturalism in literature, it seems to me, comes down to this: there is a body of writers in Australia with non-English-speaking backgrounds of one sort or another who have been marginalised into a kind of semi-silence. The finger of blame is pointed in several directions, but most consistently in the direction of people whose background is called Anglo-Celtic and who, in general terms and in many ways, perpetuate the dominance of a monoculture. Steps must be taken to break down the marginalisation and make the monoculture multicultural. There's a general consensus that the most desirable kind of multicultural Australia would be a decentralised one, a culturally pluralistic entity, avoiding the danger of a patchwork of discrete monocultures at one extreme and a kind of well-blended soup of all nations at the other.

Well, that all sounds reasonable enough, doesn't it? If you look through the writers represented in Murray Bail's *Faber Book of Contemporary Australian Short Stories* (1988) or Helen Daniel's highly successful *Expressway* collection (1988), to mention just two very recent prestigious anthologies, you'll find not a single writer of non-English-speaking background mentioned except Judah Waten. All the surnames do indeed seem to come from Cornwall and Wales, England and Ireland. Someone must be marginalising someone, you'd think. Even Pam Gilbert, in her book *Coming Out from Under: Contemporary Australian Women Writers* (also 1988), has written chapters 1 to 9 on people with surnames like Garner and Hanrahan, Anderson and Bedford, and reserves Antigone Kefala for chapter 10, given the unfortunate title of 'Postscript'. Well, you can't get much more marginalised than that. (Mind you, it's a chapter seething with indignation about marginalisation — and not only of Antigone Kefala.)

And so, despite all those bibliographies, anthologies, rectified curricula, conferences on multiculturalism, Australia Council guidelines, government reports and learned articles in respected journals like *Meanjin* and *Outrider* (despite *Outrider*, for that matter), and despite all those academic salaries and fellowships and special project grants (Sneja Gunew's hard-hitting article, 'Denaturalising cultural nationalisms: Multicultural readings of "Australia" ', was written on a fellowship from the Humanities Research Centre at the ANU, for example) — despite all that, those Anglo-Celts just will not sit up and pay attention, apparently. You can see it's a tough nut to crack.

In case you're intending to follow up on some of the theoretical arguments, I should warn you that they're not in the main for the average reader, not even for the educated reader with native English. For a start, they're full of sentences like this: 'Cultural closures are located in natural features and read as paradigmatic classic realist texts.' Now, given her formidable level of linguistic awareness, the author of this sentence cannot be unaware that what she has written will be a totally closed book not just to 99% of the population, but to 99.9% of the population. The dialogue here, if it is a dialogue, is being conducted by design at a level that excludes all those not professionally interested in its continuance.

I don't know how to interpret this use of excluding language (it's not gobbledygook) by institutionally supported writers except as heavily encoded both to warn non-institutional intruders off the occupied territory (to silence them, in effect, and relegate them to the margins) and to attract the admiring attention of other members of institutions. By way of comparison, Stephen Hawking's discussion of infinitely more complex matters in *A Brief History of Time* or Paul Davies' in *God and the New Physics* is informed by a passion to be understood, a delight in making intricate arguments accessible to any educated reader, an almost naive commitment to opening up territory to outsiders and to tearing down the border posts. They're read by millions, of course.

If you do ignore the 'Danger — Keep out!' notices and venture in, you'll be confronted by something almost disarmingly old-fashioned: argument in the canonical style of the preacher. First, close to the top of the first page, you'll find quoted an authority figure, a passage from his canonical writings (it might be Said or Eagleton, perhaps, or Barthes — it won't be an Australian and it won't be a woman). Then it will be suggested to you that the formulation arrived at by this undoubted authority can be applied to Australia and then, in a rush of abstract nouns, it *will* be applied. QED.

An example: '"History", as Salman Rushdie informs us, "has been described as an interview with the winners". Much the same may be said about literary history...' Those are the first lines in an article called 'Multicultural Literature' by Sneja Gunew. The last line reads: 'The interview between winners and losers must metamorphose into a mutually informed dialog in order for Australia to create a more representative national literature.' Note the 'must'. I feel as if I'm in St Swithen's, Glen Iris.However, let's presume you've ventured in, braving the formidable array of imported canons and the assumption of shared (mainly French) cultural values. You'll now find a description of the Australian literary scene as divided into 'centre' (Anglo-Celtic, monocultural, marginalising) and marginalised ethnic fringe.

This quaint description is based on a perception that literary production and distribution in Australia are in the hands of Anglo-Celts who, working from certain culturally imposed Anglo-Celtic assumptions, marginalise writers who do not share those assumptions — publishers reject manuscripts the virtues of which they fail to apprehend, literary editors don't give due attention to books by writers who fall outside recognised categories, reviewers are not equipped to appreciate what they read, book buyers and borrowers are manipulated into reading Anglo-Celtic texts.

To be scrupulously fair, the actual mechanisms for marginalising are rarely, if ever, spelt out, except in one regard of particular interest to the cultural theoretician: the tendency of critics (whether acting as publisher, editor, reviewer or course-setter) to define what is 'good' or what is 'literature' according to culturally imposed criteria. Russians, in other words, think Pushkin the greatest poet who ever lived. English readers can't understand what they're talking about. Writing which isn't seen as 'good' or 'literature' is thus marginalised.

What I would like to argue is that, firstly, the patronising picture of a marginalising Anglo-Celtic centre and a marginalised body of ethnic writers exists only in the heads of the culture doctors and the 'cures' work to their benefit, not the writers'; secondly, that those who uphold it are causing considerable harm to writers of non-English-speaking background; and thirdly, that the true picture contains problems to which the second law of thermodynamics is the only solution.

The idea of a centre is, I admit, immediately appealing. It's simple (good old Occam) and it's French (replace 'centre' with 'middle' and you straight away feel less comfortable with it). It echoes fashionable post-colonial theory about centres and margins and, in a most satisfying way, invites engagement with psychosexual theory about patriarchy and the centralising phallus. It also identifies an 'other' to do battle with. But why is this the chosen model out of all the possible models?

Is it after all supposed to be the centre of a three-dimensional space or a two-dimensional space? Is the space square, rhomboid, circular or camel-shaped? Perhaps it's a tube? Does the centre function as an axis or just a blob, a dot or a spider-web, a conglomeration of dots or a pumping heart? The choice of model does make a difference. Are Anglo-Celts perhaps better described as the rice in the pilau, the meat in the sandwich, the foot in the sock? Are ethnics just the fleas on the dog, the icing on the cake, the fringe on the surrey? Why should our literary culture be described as a space with a centre? Because, unlike camels, cakes and sandwiches, it's a simple image that fits in well with the new imported orthodoxy and, most importantly, it serves institutional purposes by entrenching the deviance it seeks (honestly) to cure. That's how institutions (and fly-spray companies) work. In other words, it keeps the fools on the ship and the doctors on dry land.

As those of us know who work down on the ground in the production and dissemination of Australian literature, there are many modes of influence and power in Australian literature, in publishing, criticism, promotion and the formation of public taste. Most of the surnames of the people involved have their origin in Britain and Ireland, as you'd expect in a country where about 75% of the population (74.6% in 1988, if you want to be pedantic) trace their origins to England, Scotland, Wales and Ireland. There's the odd Polynesian, Mauritian, Frenchman, Canadian, German, Arab, Rumanian, Greek, Italian, Pole, Sri Lankan, Dutchwoman and Austrian (I'm just reeling off nationalities randomly as individuals come to mind) involved in the production of literature and the formation of public taste, but yes, most of the surnames of the people involved at the decisive points in getting books out of heads and into hands will be of English, Scottish, Welsh and Irish origin — and, I hope, native English-speakers.

To describe these people as 'Anglo-Celts', however, is misleading, just as it once was to describe delirium, phobia, depression, hallucination and brain disease as 'madness', a definition that suited the power structure and the medical profession but did little for the 'mad'. If there are Anglo-Celts, there must also be non-Anglo-Celts. Well, yes, and there are, too, in a way, as part of a word game, just as there are one-legged Finns and non-one-legged Finns, but as a description of the Finnish population it gets you nowhere, unless you're an artificial leg salesperson — which, of course, is rather my point.

But if, by dividing the population arbitrarily into Anglo-Celts and non-Anglo-Celts, you mean to suggest that 74.6% of the population share a cohesive set of ideas, a 'monoculture', a 'centralised and stultifying orthodoxy' (to quote Nikos Papastergiadis) about what good literature is, then I think it's supercilious nonsense. Why anyone should assume that, say, John Bryson, Helen Daniel, Jenny Lee, Elizabeth Jolley (or is she ethnic?), Barbara Hanrahan and Marion Halligan, not to mention Gerard Windsor, Kerryn Goldsworthy and Stephen Knight, share anything very much in common at all except the English language and a knowledge of historical and literary canons, I can't imagine. I can't see the point of colouring them red on the basis of their surnames as opposed to say, George Papaellinas, whom you colour blue on account of his father's ethnic background. I think it's patronising humbug. On some questions George may line up with Beverley Farmer, on other with Vasso Kalamaras or Dinny O'Hearn. When you actually talk to individual writers, critics, editors and academics about their tastes, their reading, their criteria, their literary theories, their sacred texts — I mean the actual people who decide what will be published, how it will be packaged and promoted and discussed — the description 'Anglo-Celtic' becomes absurd.

It's a category that exists only in language (like 'mad'). The search for a signified for the signifier ends in the kind of absurdity the Australia Council is saddled with: you're 'multicultural' (and eligible for a grant to revisit your 'homeland') if one of your parents was a non-English speaker!

While so many of our institutional thinkers have canonised a single strain of French social theory to the point of a fetish, there's no evidence at all that those who evaluate literary output in Australia — the publishers' readers, the publishers, the literary editors, the reviewers, the course-setters and teachers — are the unthinking products of a monoculture. What objective data are there to show that people such as Louise Adler of Heinemann, Bruce Sims or Susan Hawthorne of Penguin, William Fraser of the *Sydney Morning Herald*, Philippa Hawker of the *Sunday Herald*, the ABC's Jill Kitson, Martin Harrison or Stephen Muecke of the University of Technology in Sydney, not to mention the hundreds of other men and women who form taste, are locked into some sort of 'Anglo-Celtic' idea of what good literature is? Males with British backgrounds may be prominent in the academy, but the academy is by no means the only site of intellectual nourishment in the community, perhaps not even a very important one, except in its conversation with itself.

Ah, but don't you see, the multicultural professionals say to us, in their best bedside manner, with the best will in the world you're still the Prisoner of Paradigms — unless, possibly, your father was Norwegian or Quebecois. Even Joseph Chetcuti, former President of the Victorian Association of Multicultural Writers, one of the more realistic commentators on the subject, feels obliged in an interview with Rudi Krausmann to allude to a 'problem of paradigms, of what is perceived to be "good" or "bad" poetry or prose' when asked why multicultural writers are underrepresented in anthologies. What are these unidentified paradigms, exactly? Held by which unidentified people, exactly? I mean, who are these people who think Tennyson is 'good' and Tsvetayeva, Cavafy, Rimbaud, Lorca and Sanskrit love poetry are 'bad' and are imposing these views on the general public? Chetcuti doesn't — and couldn't be expected to — say.

Pam Gilbert (with Sneja Gunew's acknowledged help) does have a go at saying in her 'Postscript' on Antigone Kefala. Her point, actually made with reference to another 'marginalised' writer, Faith Bandler, is that our literary culture privileges 'consciously wrought textuality' over plain storytelling, particularly unadorned first-person accounts of life experiences. (Bandler 'describes her work in non-literary terms, thus confirming her own marginalisation'.) Well, naturally, because that's what 'literature' means, as opposed to shopping lists, history books and chats with the neighbour over the fence: the denotational is no longer privileged over the connotational, paradigmatic and syntagmatic semantic structures. The more textuality, the more meaning. That's true wherever people tell stories in their native language — in Iceland, Botswana, Tonga and Arnhem Land.

There's nothing mystically universalist about this. It's just a description of how a certain English word is used to describe a world-wide linguistic phenomenon. Soviet structuralists would go further to claim that by 'good' the speakers of an astonishingly wide variety of languages mean texts that are productive of large, intersecting webs of meaning. The larger the webs, the greater the number of intersections, the 'better' the text — in Japanese, Swahili, English and Estonian. That's why everybody, except an advertising executive, thinks a Beethoven sonata is 'better' than a Kellogg's jingle. That's the way real people, living real lives, open their mouths and speak. Of course it's 'subjective', but the subjectivity is widely shared.

The reason so much migrant writing is 'marginalised' is that, *in this basic sense*, it's often not very good — and for obvious reasons: the author's English simply doesn't allow him or her to produce meaning at the same number of levels — to intersect with the same number of other texts and contexts — as a native speaker's. No matter how good the story, 'literature' demands more — good stories are two-a-penny.

Ania Walwicz and Rosa Cappiello are often held up to us as examples of the kind of marginalised writing we Anglo-Celts would have missed out on if it were not for the efforts of the multicultural activists. Now, I think Ania Walwicz (pronounced Wall-wits, by the way, not in the Polish fashion) is terrific, particularly the first three or four times you hear her prose-poetry read:

> pipe burst call mister plumber he come greek landlord mister next door please come in he tell call greek plumber come they look come go hello go for a look go back yard have see what talk greek i don't understand a word don't understand a word what did come again tell me please he he he landlord is tell me what fix did the greek plumber greek landlord come in to my kitchen . . .

Very funny, multivalent, inventive, transgressive — in a word, very good. But it doesn't actually 'interrogate socio-cultural conventions, notions of linguistic competence and gender certainties', as Sneja Gunew assures me Walwicz's writing does, any more effectively than writing by scores of women and men with Irish and British surnames. Not really.

It's the situation of being a writer from a non-English-speaking background in an English-speaking country that marginalises writers and labelling writers with that background 'multicultural' that keeps them chained to the margins. [...]

It was in the context of the categories created by the multiculturalists that Lolo Holbein, when asked by Rudi Krausmann what possibilities there were in Adelaide for multicultural writers, answered, 'None, since Andrew Deszery's publications are now defunct.' If he'd asked her what the possibilities were for writers in Adelaide, the picture would have been brighter — indeed the next year Lolo Holbein went on to win the ABC's Bicentennial Literary Award for Fiction.

Lolo Holbein's remark appeared in an astounding document, issued by the Australia Council in 1987, called 'Literature' in a series called *Multicultural Arts Today in Australia*. It's written and edited by Rudi Krausmann and consists basically of written interviews with twenty-two 'multicultural writers', overwhelmingly of European origin. [...] Krausmann's questions about the writers these poets and novelists read elicit long, predictable lists of non-Australian writers, with barely a mention of any Australian writer except David Malouf. Tad Sobolewski admits to 'admiring certain Australian writers such as Henry Lawson, Patrick White [and] Katherine Pritchard [*sic*]' but qualifies his enthusiasm by saying 'it is not exaggerating to say that, in matters concerning the mind [Australia] is still a barbaric country compared, for example, to a country like Poland'. 'In Turkey', Nihat Ziyalan tells us, 'nearly everyone considers himself a poet, which shows a general interest that doesn't exist here'. [...] Lidija Simkus-Pocius, who came here when she was seven, when asked how she 'reacts to the Australian literary scene' says, 'My reaction is one of non-reaction'. [...]

This wilful silencing of Australian voices, this declaration of Australia as *terra nullius* 200 years after the British tried the same trick, will certainly lead to marginalisation and deservedly so. These voices from the late 1980s really belong to the 1950s, to the time of *Voss*, when Australia was seen as a spiritual void, removed from a centre of value in Europe, needing to be mapped by Europeans. Well, things have changed.

[...]

Is it not time we, all of us, looked at more helpful, more realistic models for Australian literary life than the institutionalised centre/margins, Anglo-Celtic/non-Anglo-Celtic, monocultural/multicultural ones?

The fact is that there is no such 'group' as multicultural writers. There are writers with little English, writers with native English whose parents spoke Greek sometimes (or all the time), writers whose parents spoke perfect English but who identified with other cultures, writers whose chromosomes are all British who identify with other cultures, writers who had a step-mother who spoke a foreign language and yet who feel Australian, writers who are Russian but feel Jewish. And the Albanian Moslem with working-class English probably doesn't give a fig for what the Vietnamese Buddhist who went to Harvard thinks or writes about anything.

I think we all have to recognise that the *sine qua non* of literature is language. Literature presumes a readership willing and eager to play various kinds of games using language and a readership with a sophisticated knowledge of the language and its history. To 'be an Australian writer' (as opposed to just writing in Australia) you have to have a native's knowledge of English — or your translator does. It's futile to rail against the need for a writer to have this kind of English in Australia — if you don't, hundreds of others do. You can be a Vietnamese Buddhist, a Maltese fork-lift operator, a Bolivian Catholic mother of seven, a French lesbian separatist, an expert in Nigerian oral poetry — anything, but to be taken seriously your English or your translator's must be as inventive, as playful, as historically conscious, as good as a native's.

[...]

It's probably worth our bearing in mind too that, while migrant writers' taxonomies may indeed challenge the dominant taxonomies of the Australian intelligentsia, many of those taxonomies, especially if they have their origin around the Mediterranean basin, will appear to most Australians both sexist and racist. Polarities such as penetrator/penetratee, father/mother, truth/falsehood, believer/infidel, masculine/effeminate, straight/gay, national/non-national and so on, which may be taken for granted in many monocultures and enshrined in their mores, will be looked at askance by the bulk of a writer's prospective readership. You can march through Sydney streets with 'Kill Rushdie!' banners, in other words, but you will be marginalised if you do.

It must also be admitted that, while the 'migrant experience' is of interest to some people, so are many other things — quasars, particle physics, horticulture, Aboriginal bark paintings, Catherine the Great, P. D. James's detective fiction,

Tolstoy's relations with his wife, the theatre of Wole Soyinka, renovating Federation houses, vegetarian cooking, rainforests, Mozart, Hitler, the French Revolution, proto-Indo-European linguistics, sexuality in Ancient Greece, Patrick White, Papua New Guinea, Madonna — any number of things. Readers are not *obliged* (outside institutions) to read what migrants and their descendants write. At the end of the day it's literary skills (and there's no such thing as Anglo-Celtic literary skills) that make the critics and the public sit up and take notice. Up to now, statistically, not many writers from the ethnic communities have had them. Even the multicultural professionals are reduced to examining the same half dozen over and over again.

[...]

As you'll have gathered, I think it's time for the passengers on the ship of fools to disembark, to look around them with interest and a desire to understand, to learn the language — or find a first-rate interpreter — and then to join in some of the myriad conversations already taking place in the country they've arrived in. I think most serious attention will be given to those who seek to interpret, to weave old patterns with new yarn or perhaps the other way around.

And I think it's time our culture doctors closed down their clinics, forgot their definitions about who's mad and who's sane and applied their considerable intellectual skills and financial resources to making their 'fools' feel at home — investigating how a culture can exist, for example, without its material base, the problem of non-convergent cultures, the actual function of bilingualism in an English-speaking country in 1991, ways to professionalise translation (already of interest to some, such as Sneja Gunew), and ways of making Australia's many cultural strands and their histories accessible to those not born here. I think, in a word, it's time our multicultural professionals stopped marginalising multicultural writers.

1991

KATE JENNINGS

Bad Manners

Lest we forget that women writers have legitimate grievances and their anthologies useful purposes, I direct you to George Steiner's musings in *Real Presences*, published in 1990, concerning the poor showing by women in the arts over the centuries. He asks, his tone that of a gentleman taking pains not to be discourteous, 'Is the biological capacity for procreation...absolutely primordial to a woman's being, so creative, so fulfilling, as to subvert, as to render comparatively pallid, the begetting of fictive personae...and of so much representative art?'

Steiner is aware of feminist arguments that posit, in his words, ' "phallocratic" oppression, social constraint, [and] domestic servitude' as the likely causes but gamely insists on there being more to it: 'Can we honestly think further about creation...if we do not consider the essence of form-giving that is child-birth and the abstinence from *poiesis* which this act may entail?' He claims to have come to no conclusions but begins his next paragraph with an odious pronouncement: 'What is certain is that the great artificers...*are* essentially men...'. And this from an author touted on the dust jacket as 'one of this century's most exciting and dramatic thinkers'.

Anthologies of writing by women have been crucial in nurturing creativity in women and promoting a sense of community among them, as well as raising the consciousness of readers, to use nostalgic phrasing. But such anthologies have their pitfalls, the most obvious one being to ghettoise women writers. We are playing, but in a different sandbox from the men, a smaller one, over to the side. And the ascendancy of men remains unchallenged.

Australian women need to be alert to the dangers of ghettoisation because our society has always been segregated, pronouncedly so, the sexes barely tolerating each other. Feminism has not changed this. If anything, it has widened the rift. Women write for, read, review, and debate each other, and men aid and abet the situation; it is less trouble for everybody that way.

When I think about the sexes in Australia, a school dance, circa 1950s, comes to mind. Boys on one side, girls on the other, a mad dash to get a partner, followed by an awkward turn or two around the dance floor. The only difference now is that the 'girls' frequently refuse to dance, or they dance with each other. Although I visit Australia regularly, I have not lived there for over a decade, so it is possible, of course, that things might have changed without me being aware of it. But I wouldn't bet on it. Expatriate Australians who visit home invariably comment on how pervasive sexism still is, how divided the sexes continue to be. Expatriates are held in contempt in Australia, but they have their uses, the main one being an ability to size up their native country with faculties that haven't been dulled by familiarity.

I was particularly struck on my last visit to Australia at the way women had begun to refer to men as 'boys'. As in, 'the boys in the poetry world'. The term was typically spoken in tones larded with hostility and impatience, although sometimes with the head-shaking affection of a mother all too well acquainted with the antics of an unruly son. Now, calling men 'boys' might be a justifiable response to eons of women being called 'girls', but there is something awfully wrong with a society where the sexes find it constantly necessary to infantilise each other.

The chief characteristic of Australian feminism is a proud combativeness, best illustrated by the refrain of a song popular in the first days of the movement: *I'm a shameless hussy, and I don't give a damn.* I used to think that this confrontational mode had its origins in documents such as the SCUM Manifesto, which was read widely by feminists in the early seventies, but now I see it rather as an offshoot of that infamous behaviour peculiar to Australia: larrikinism. In this instance, feminists haven't invented anything new; we are imitating men. And whether we like it or not, it is easier to hurl insults and call for a revolution — heaven knows there is enough provocation — than to do the painstaking and difficult work of changing attitudes, including some of our own.

Early on, in response to criticism, Australian feminists took to circling the wagons. Inevitably, 'us against them' became 'you're either for us or against us', a mentality which has been instrumental in throttling discussion as well as giving rise to rigid codes of conduct. Anyone who disagrees is dismissed for 'selling out' or damned as a conservative. These judgements would be a joke if they weren't so corrosive. I use the word 'joke' because it almost invariably is the case that those who indulge in this sort of condemnatory nonsense wouldn't know a radical thought if it came up and bit them.

To make a bad situation worse, excuses couched in ideology are made for work that is sloppy, ill-conceived, or both. For example, a male editor rejects a poem and is indicted as sexist. Maybe he is, and then again, maybe he isn't. He may have traditional tastes and prefer poems that resemble well-trimmed lawns whereas this poem break-dances. Or perhaps the poet wasn't in top form. She wasn't her usual rigorous self, a banality or two crept in.

African-American college students often have difficulty distinguishing between those situations in which they are truly the victims of racism and those in which they are themselves to blame. Between, say, failing to get a job because of their race, and failing an exam because they haven't studied for it. It could be argued that the whole society is rigged against them, that racism pervades every nook and cranny of their lives, so they should never be held accountable for deficiencies of conduct, just as women sometimes argue that language and thought systems have been contrived by men, with the result that the deck is hopelessly stacked, which leads logically to only one conclusion: don't even consider getting out of bed in the morning.

. . .

Just as feminism in its current incarnation has been around long enough to beget its own traditions, including anthologies of women's writing, so it has spawned its own clichés, one of which is the belief that anger is creative. This mode of thinking is summarised in a letter quoted approvingly in *Angry Women*, the latest entrant in the women's anthology stakes: 'Anger is an amazing source of creative energy.'

Anger can be creative, but it is also an emotion that consumes and blinds. It easily becomes a habit, with nothing to do with the injustice that provoked it, and everything to do with the fine feelings and revolutionary credentials of the person in the throes of it. And too often it devolves into self-righteousness, enabling the one who is in its grip to see everyone's faults in minute detail except their own. Women need to cultivate a sense of outrage over the miserable treatment of their sex; it gets them off their bottoms and doing something about it. But there is a fine line between healthy, appropriate anger and the sort that festers.

When I picked up the *Angry Women* anthology, I thought, Ah, at last these issues are going to be explored in an Australian context. The media release accompanying the book and the introduction to its various sections looked promising, referring as they do in some way or other to the 'complex nature of anger'. Unfortunately, the selections don't deliver. The anger resembles, for the most part, a car that has become hopelessly bogged — engine revving, wheels spinning, mud flying, but going nowhere.

When all else fails, a forceful display of anger can get someone's attention who hitherto hasn't taken you seriously. But it is by no means a sure thing. Phil Donahue did a show recently on the rights, or lack thereof, afforded homosexual couples. Legislators in the United States have been reluctant to give rights to people in long-term relationships and de facto marriages. A lesbian on the Donahue panel was especially furious about the fact that she didn't have access to her partner's company's health plan, something to which a heterosexual spouse would be entitled. She was so furious she was bellowing. I found myself turning away from the screen. The audience were visibly cringing, too. The woman lost their sympathy, even though many of them, judging from their questions, agreed with her position.

A few days later, another Donahue show dealt with the degrading practices typical of stag parties — gang-banging strippers and assorted gross behaviour. On the panel was a feminist from an anti-pornography league, who, given the slightest opening, would spout an unintelligible stream of statistics about rape, wife battering, child abuse, what women earn compared to men, sexual harassment, and so on. Jumping up and down in her seat, she resembled an agitated tree frog. Whenever she opened her mouth, the audience groaned. As with the earlier show, a lot of good points that should have been made weren't.

The *Angry Women* anthology makes me feel like the members of the Donahue audience: hectored and resentful. Good writing invites the reader in, explains, persuades, enlists sympathies, stirs emotions. The more talented and skilled the writer, the more dexterous with language, the more effortless this will seem. Yet the editors who assembled the anthology seem almost to have gone out of their way to feature writers — there are exceptions — whose work is devoid of artistry and whose language is about as fresh as the bread fed to ducks.

The editors want to be democratic, which is praiseworthy, but inclusiveness for its own sake is not always the best guiding principle when it comes to collections of writing. Not all good writing, of course, has technical polish. Some women have deliberately turned their backs on our culture's notion of what constitutes a well-turned phrase and in doing so have produced work that is vital and original. It is also true that women sometimes can bear witness to the horrors of their lives with such integrity that the language they use is unimportant. But raw emotion doesn't always carry the day.

The editors of *Angry Women* claim that an 'ethos' has developed among Australian women writers that 'is characterised in prose writing by tendencies towards using a subjective authorial stance and personal subject matter, both of which assert an anti-authoritarian stance; departing from traditional narrative forms while insisting on the importance of sincerity and integrity. Few feminists go in for demonstrations of superficial virtuosity.' This sounds like an exclusionary party line, but it was the last sentence that caught my attention. It brought to mind the farmers in the district where I grew up, who were distrustful of anyone who had a facility with words, Robert Menzies excepted. They felt that they were being conned.

This attitude is hardly unique. As the novelist Judith Grossman has remarked, 'Style, in England, is usually associated with right-wing tendencies (see Kingsley Amis, Anthony Burgess, and so on)...'. In Australian feminist circles, a woman who demonstrates a concern for craft is likely to be labelled male-oriented or phallocentric. Australian feminism being largely left-wing in character, she will also be thought of as a conservative. In fact, the terms are viewed — woozily, I might add — as interchangeable.

I learned from the *Angry Women* anthology that there is another 'enemy' aside from the patriarchy: 'women who have managed to negotiate success within the system'. That is, middle-class feminists, or as a writer in the Diaries, Letters, Biography section of the anthology describes them, the 'Ms Cocksures' and 'Ms Liberateds'. As the reader progresses through *Angry Women* and finally arrives at the Views and Perspectives section, which is comprised almost entirely of a long essay by Ann Curthoys called 'Women and Class', the not-so-hidden agenda of the anthology, that of championing the working classes, becomes obvious. The average reader might have hoped, however, for a variety of views and more perspective.

The failings of the *Angry Women* anthology need to be taken seriously. As the American poet April Bernard puts it:

> *We seek a slogan, and find only the old ones.*
> *We need a revolution, but settle for bad manners.*

1989

BRENT CROSSWELL

Vinny Catoggio

Vinny Catoggio had been killing them in the seconds, so Carlton took a punt and made him second rover for the big match. He was a lovely little bloke, just a kid, and on top of that it was his first game, but that didn't matter when he failed in the 1973 Grand Final.

When Vinny came into the rooms after that game, he was pale and upset, and he made straight for the showers because his statistics read three kicks and five handballs. It was sad to see his solitary form sitting up in the bath, his arms resting on his knees, his head hanging down, his eyes full of tears.

In the process of playing eighty-eight senior and seventy reserve games with Carlton, Melbourne and the Swans, he became one of the most popular players in the VFL. He was a delightful player to watch, and he loved playing football, but after 1973 he was always struggling for a game. With his afro haircut, his petite appearance, his gentleness and pureness of heart, he seemed a rather odd figure to find in football. If it was necessary for a footballer to have a bit of 'mongrel' or 'dirt' in him to be any good, then Vinny was never going to make it.

At Melbourne he and I would occasionally cut down through the Tan during pre-season training and sit by the lake and practise duck calls. 'This beats training, doesn't it,' he would say, and being bilingual he was a bloody good duck caller, too. That was the thing about Vin, his temperament was in the mould of an amateur, his nature more in harmony with the park than with the stadium. And I suppose that's why it made me angry to see him crying in the bath.

Vinny loved Carlton and desperately wanted to help win a flag, but he had some special problems, as he admitted. 'I was only eighteen at the time — too young to know anything about preparation — the previous year I played in the thirds.' And because he was playing his first full game, and he was sort of cute, he received lots of publicity: telegrams, letters and interviews. One young fan had followed him all her life because as a little girl the first footballer's name she could pronounce was 'Coggio'. On Friday night, Uncle Dominic and Uncle Guiseppi popped around, and Vin started to feel anxious, so he went to Sydney Road and played billiards. In Saturday's press there was a photograph of Vinny running along the beach at St Kilda and by the time he entered the rooms he was 'gone'. 'I was so bloody nervous my legs felt like jelly. I felt crook in the guts. I felt sick.' Looking back he reckoned that he had wasted all his energy before he hit the ground.

Did the club help Vin in any way? They did nothing. No one gave him any advice in the rooms after the game either. 'It was the worst moment of my life,' he recalls. 'I was so upset and ashamed that I didn't want to look up. In fact I remember a committeeman coming along the lockers patting blokes on their heads, "Well done — hard luck," he was saying, but when he got to me he stopped, hesitated, and then moved on and patted the next bloke — that really hurt me so much.'

I tried to console Vin at the time by explaining that football was 'just a bloody game', and telling him about my own experience with failure in a Grand Final. When I came into the rooms at half time, Sergio Silvagni, a player I admired, yelled, 'You weak bastard', and threw an orange that splattered down the side of my face. I, too, went into the shower area and cried. I'm not sure my comments did Vinny much good.

When Vinny got back to the club for a compulsory showing after the Grand Final, no one really wanted to talk to him, so he didn't stay long. 'I walked back from the ground to my home, which wasn't far,' he recalls. 'It was a quiet night — I felt so lousy. When I got home my mum said, "Never mind, Vinny." '

The Grand Final failure was the worst experience of Vinny's life; it coloured the rest of his sporting career. In fact, he did not play a senior game in 1974; he was, in his own words, 'never in contention'. He experienced the Fraser Murphy syndrome and became a professional interchange player. He remembers a journalist telling him after a game that he only played for twenty-eight minutes: 'Eleven minutes in the second quarter, nine in the third and eight in the last.' What hurt Vinny was that although he hardly played that day, he ended up winning a colour television set. 'I played on the interchange bench so much that I used to often think after the match, Will I have a shower or not?' Vinny was always chasing games after 1973.

Throughout his football career, he sought absolution and an opportunity to atone for his failure, but Vinny was not to receive another chance because 1973 was his last Grand Final.

Because of the pervasiveness of the sporting ethic that winning is everything and losing is nothing, in fact, worse than nothing, immoral, Vinny and all those players who fail are made to feel unworthy, or 'shamed'. If winning is all that matters, then any means of achieving that end becomes acceptable. What are the implications of that philosophy for a civilised community? Wouldn't it be more sensible and less dangerous to take the view that losing is simply not winning and leave it at that?

In any event, it seems an indictment of professional sport when the philosophy of winning is incompatible with the character of the Vinnys of this world. When I told him in the bath that football was 'just a bloody game', I wasn't telling the truth.

1986

GIULIA GIUFFRÉ

Who Do You Think You Are?

My father always talked of his Italian birthplace, Salina, as the Island, as though there were no other. Three of my four grandparents came from there. For the first twenty years of my life I had no personal idea of this Aeolian island north of Sicily, a place remote even to Italians. I envied my father his certainty about his cultural identity: he knew he was Italian, he knew he was Australian. He had come to Australia in 1928 as a boy of sixteen, and his had been the story of the migrant-made-good. He could speak quite unself-consciously of 'we', when referring to the ancient Romans! He had that much sense of continuity. He never lost his accent, and he never lost his deep Italianness, despite his complete commitment to his new country.

My mother was born in this country and she seemed Australian by comparison with my father. Beneath her refined manner, though, she has Italian passion, ferocity and *furberia* — quick judgement and street wisdom. She gave me her love for opera. Her parents, the only grandparents I knew, were totally foreign, I now realise, though when I was growing up, they seemed the norm. My grandmother who died when I was fifteen was Neapolitan, with all the sadness, mad joy and intensity of that people. She would open beer bottles with her strong gold-tipped teeth. She drove real-estate agents crazy with her constant search for property, beautiful property that she could not afford. She spoke rich, rude Neapolitan dialect, she told risqué jokes — a favourite about men waking up in bed with cold porridge between their legs — and the word I hear her saying over the dark gulf of time is *Scialamm* — 'Let's enjoy ourselves, and to hell with it'. My maternal grandfather was a shadowy figure. I don't remember him saying anything at all. I have a strong visual image of him though: a short, balding old man in a white singlet and baggy trousers. He bottled tomato sauce; he made me willow baskets; he put cherries over a kitten's ears and made brown paper boots for the same poor cat. His silence was a Mediterranean type of silence and culturally at one with all his compatriots still in Pollara, on the western side of Salina: silent men sitting patiently on the wharf there, smoking as though it were their hobby, or sitting around a table in the bar, nursing their glasses, or their cups, their eyes vacant and calm.

When one is a child — perhaps always — identity comes from the very local and the very concrete. I neither lived in Italy, nor in Australia, but in an Italo-Australian enclave in Kensington, suburban Sydney. We ate Italian food, we listened to Italian music, we heard Italian dialects most days. I accepted all this without question. As a child I took Italy and Italianness for granted. My school-project 'on any country': Italy, *Paese del Sol*, with its packets of different types of spaghetti culled from my mother's larder, all, incidentally, crushed into sameness, was a completely spontaneous choice. The formal Italian lessons that we had on Saturday mornings were familiar to the point of contempt, and all I remember of them is giggling with my cousins and the word for butterfly, *farfalla.* I did not know, and still do not know to this day, whether some of our family customs were simply ours, or Isole-Eolian, or Italian. Pulling someone's ears affectionately on their birthday, for instance, or kicking them on the behind 'for luck'. Was the essence of aniseed that my nonna put in her strong morning coffee her own idea, or a Neapolitan one?

In childhood, the family was all: absorbing, maddening, all-encompassing, placental. My brothers, my sister, my parents, my cousins, my uncles and my aunts. They peopled a busy landscape for observation and amusement. Even when I knew very little about them, that little was itself fascinating and sufficient: my great-uncle Albert, a boxer, who one day intrigued me — I watched, eyes wide open, as he took a bunch of violets out of a vase, salted them and ate them with apparent relish; my great-aunt Vincenza (we called her Auntie Fishends, an approximation to the dialectical pronunciation of her name) who was racy, lived in King's Cross, and whose powdery pink flesh smelt of ladies' underwear and old Sydney. The generation between me and these mythical creatures was still tinged with a certain amount of mystery, but they seemed more Italian then than they do now; perhaps they as well as I have changed. When my generation, the cousins, got together as children, we had a type of hysterical fun the like of which I have not struck again as an adult. The implicit belief then was that this was 'family', *la famiglia*, and that therefore one was safe from betrayal. It was 'them' and 'us' — 'them' being that cold, cool Anglo-Saxon world out there.

All this time my addiction to reading was a tiny drumbeat of otherness, a secret counterpoint to the Italian womb. I learnt to speak Italian at university, knowing only dialectical phrases before then, and the odd word. I discovered for myself the articulate Italy of literature, not just the profound pleasures of Dante, Petrarch, Boccaccio, Ariosto, but — this with wonderment — the literature of an articulate South: Verga, Vittorini, Pirandello. My studies in English Literature taught me irony, and gave me imaginative access to the 'cold' Anglo-Saxon mind, and I found it actually to be deeply passionate and humorous, just my 'cup of tea' in fact. But it was still not until I was much older, and living for a time in England, that I realised that *famiglia* was not synonymous with trust, and that loving friendships could exist between unrelated people.

The immigrant experience changes over time, and with the lengthening of the generational link with the 'old' country. My father's experience could never be mine. There was much more anti-Italian feeling in Australia then, exacerbated by the Second World War. He was interned for a time during the War, but expediently allowed out to convert his lipstick-container manufacture into bullet manufacture. Australian society has, thank goodness, changed a great deal in its attitudes to 'foreign' food, music, culture. All of which makes 'being Australian' an evolving, broadening and therefore, to me, more sympathetic concept.

The common thread of migrant experience is a doubleness of reference. In my father's case, he could carry the twin epithets 'Italian' and 'Australian' with ease. The doubleness can be a source of elation and interest. The doubleness can destroy. I often think of another Italo-Australian girl — woman she would have been now had she lived. She was brilliantly clever, but split to her core by the rival personae she was meant to be: the intelligent, free, university spirit and the 'daughter in the house', bound by countless unwritten rules of tradition and protocol. She slowly starved herself and then took garden poison. At her funeral, representatives from the two sides of her life that she had been unable to unify in herself sat on either side of the Church: short men and women in black, faces sad and formal and students in motley gear whose expressions combined shock and seriousness. When I saw an official photographer photographing the coffin I realised the depth of the cultural abyss separating the two sides.

How am I Italian? The question is as difficult to answer as the matching question, 'How am I Australian?' I heard Manfred Jurgensen say he didn't know what being Australian meant, but he knew he was Australian. I feel I am Italo-Australian, but that very term puts the emphasis on 'Australian': a particular type of Australian, and that, I think, is the emphasis of my conscious mind. This essay is the work of an Australian sensibility — I find I have to check the Italian spellings even though I 'hear' them. There are however many other less conscious levels of being, parts of oneself that cannot be articulated, deep, but not vague cultural influences, motives. I now think that national identity is not an obscure, rather sentimental feeling of affinity with a particular culture or cultures, nor a mystical essence, but rather a composite of a host of little cues imbibed with one's mother's milk: a song, a scent, a language, a joke, an expletive, a gesture, a style of caressing. Myriad details build up layers in the onionskin of personality. There is no onion apart from its layers, so too there is no cultural identity separate from the too-numerous-to-count influences of a particular national or racial culture. Because identity is so local, I have to say that my Italianness was filtered through the migrant experience of living in suburban Sydney in an imperfectly sealed Italian cocoon. I was well outside the perceived mainstream of Australian life then, in the 1950s and 1960s. It was not until I left Australia that I recognised how Australian I was and that Australianness could be made up of such apparently little things as loving a particular quality of bright white light, or appreciating a particular sort of ironic humour.

But I am not Italian in the way that someone born and bred in Italy would be. For good or ill, one always has the perspective that distance lends. Italian face, Australian voice. The memory of a man, adventurer-type, in Naples trying to get me to board his Lambretta, telling me seductively that there are certain faces, like mine, that simply attract one like a magnet ... He didn't know, but I might have been related to him. I noticed that the word he used for 'face' was what one would use for a dog or a little animal. Another image comes, of a group of rich Milanesi at an airport in autumn. They were like exotic pheasants, their plumage subdued shades of brown and green, confident, self-conscious and self-possessed, but with that seeming lack of introspection that I had marvelled at before. They made me feel very much the itinerant student, which I was at that time, not belonging to any group at all. Then again, I am not a clubbable person. Like my father, an Islander. The Salinese are eerily familiar to me; they are my memory mirror. In the silvered, crackled glass I can recognise surliness, arrogance, pride, humour, self-sufficiency, seriousness.

My attitude to Italy is very ambivalent. I only experienced a rapture of empathy on my first trip there, and never again. I know it too well, and too deeply to be in love with it. On the other hand, it may be a real love affair, with those contrary elements of hate, knowledge, exasperation and reconciliation that lasting love has. The realisation that perfection and stasis exist nowhere this side of death liberates one to appreciate what does actually exist in this world, the differences, the many homes. There is no one way to be Italian, of course. That country's very different regions were unified late and barely. There is definitely no one way to be Australian. In humility, not arrogance, one comes back to the particularity of one's own being: Isole-Eolian and Neapolitan grandparents, Irish Catholic convent education, Australian life to age twenty. Oxford and England, a changed Australia again.

A double heritage gives you moments of precious recognition, 'race memories', as for instance, when I invented afresh the Salinese way of drying oregano by tying it in bunches with cotton thread; or when I was taught by a toothless old crone in Salina how to wash one's underpants spotlessly white by rubbing them with a stone in cold water from the well; or being shown how to bake the special Island Christmas biscuits *uastaduzz* and placing them in the enormous stone oven in the caverna of my paternal grandfather's house. My *paese*, where I come from ... in a way. This is the richness of reference that can be the best of sharing two cultures. Not the stereotypes, which by definition, are generalised and widely disseminated. The sobbing Italian male voice singing *Torna a Surriento* has always left me singularly unmoved. But the harsh close-harmonied singing of Salinese peasant women in the church at Santa Marina haunts me. That windy, salty island is not the paradise that my father continued to dream it was. But it has the same grip on my psyche that the Australian bush has. So my two homes become one. The story of cultural identity is a tale of winning the freedom to take or reject what one chooses from the parent culture, to enjoy, but not to be helplessly possessed. The nostalgia that grips the heart for wherever or whatever one has been, for youth, lost love, can, if unexamined and unchecked, turn into reflex and ultimately lose its meaning. Automatic tears, knee-jerk guilts, tourist-shop stereotypes.

So where does this leave us, with memories and feelings, choices that whisper to us across generations, with layers on layers of response and association: the frisson that I always feel on hearing *Vissi d'arte* and on making the Sicilian dish, *capponata*. The doubleness, indeed, multiplicity of personal, national and cultural reference, sometimes a burden, is much more often a gift.

1992

ROBERT HARRIS

The Carriers Off of the Dead

'The muzzy, brownish atmosphere of death' is a recurrent phrase in the notes I have kept from a short period in which I worked as a funeral driver/assistant, hearse driver, pall bearer, carrier off of the dead. Until that time I had never seen a corpse, now they became the ordinary material of my daily work. Master the few formalities and driving a hearse is easy: low speed, headlights, with coffin and remains aboard, and the tricks of thinking and moving in traffic for three or four cars. After that there's nothing left to learn. The main task is to get through the viewing (if there is one), the funeral service, the drive out to the crematorium or cemetery, the memorial service and burial without any embarrassing foul-ups. A foul-up would be anything from crashing the hearse to laughing at another driver's joke in the presence of mourners. Light, simple duties, but complicated of course by the proximity of other people's grief. Three middle-aged sisters in the company chapel, each with a bunch of flowers, 'What do we do with these? We want to take them to the cemetery and throw them in our father's grave.'

Doing funerals was like going to a fête compared to doing removes. On my third day I went out with John Crookes, a nineteen-year-old mortician's son, in the smoke to learn the industry before returning to Goulburn to enter the family business. I liked working with John. He had the level address and accents that go with wide, cold skies and flinty hills. A tour of hospital mortuaries, four removes before lunch: one van load. In the office at Prince Henry's mortuary are brains pickled in some sort of brine, brown cauliflower shapes in yellowish liquid. It reminded me of an American comic called *The Spirit* which was around when I was in high school. The turbid warehouselands, the huddling characters who spoke with multiple, sinister meanings, the plishing rain and trashcans of the world where the Spirit stalked his quarry. Back up the van, take the stretcher inside, find a trolley for it and wheel it down the corridor to the mortuary's swinging doors. Once inside, recognise the brains and look away, wait around for the attendant. At length he shows up, grinning as if he's won Tatts, and pushes our trolley into the freezer. Not many minutes later he brings it out to us, laden. It is not my first body by this time, but I am still surprised by its coldness and lifelessness. John and I open the head-to-foot white plastic wrappings at the feet and the middle, tearing the plastic away from the masking tape that holds it, to reach through to the fine, soft tissue of the shroud. Sometimes the shroud would get caught on the body's toes or fingers or more, inventively, in the crook of an arm, and a sharp little tug of war would result. We check the hospital's ID bracelets against those we are adding to the wrist and ankle, look around for jewellery (which must be catalogued) and anything out of the ordinary. The body is strapped into the green, rubberized stretcher, signed for, and wheeled out to the van. The vans are clean, but they all smell the same, faintly, in the rear. The lower two berths are saved till last, in case of an obese client. Then we climb into the cabin of our white, unmarked Hi-Ace and head for the next hospital mortuary. 'I will have that smoke now, John.'

Mortuary attendants are paid fifty cents per body collected by the undertakers. We got the money from the office before setting out on removes. Redolent as it is of rural underemployment in centuries past, the reference to Charon is nevertheless unmistakable. Crematorium operators are tipped twenty cents per body. The mortuary attendants, grey faced from working in the sickly, sweetish atmosphere of refrigerated human remains, have some of the muddiest eyes I have ever seen. We, at least, could drive around in sunlight and open air, chortle and bray in our canteens, and even at the Necropolis were birds of spectacular figure which made you decide to finally get a copy of *What Bird is That?*

First chore in the morning was washing down and polishing the hearses before changing into the bland drivers' uniform. It was the best time of day; we were not yet in death's harness. You smelt death as you clocked on (amongst the coffins), good morninged your way through to the drivers' tea room where the steaming urn and the recognitions excluded it; washing down the hearses, drying them with soft cloths prolonged this exclusion a little — what could be less disturbing than washing a car? It was a friendly company, first names were used throughout. If the pay was low, there were generous breaks. These strategies helped to keep staff who were on a rigorous roster system for night and weekend removes from private dwellings. There was little of the newly *chic* class-consciousness creeping through Australian life. This prelude of washing the vehicles was, for the drivers, the company's — perhaps the occupation's — happiness.

There was never any discussion of death among the drivers. You would never hear, among them, the faintly narcissistic drivellings about previous lives that might be heard over morning coffee in many a city office. The only discussion, and that was encoded in iconic Australian, was about how to cope. The workable view was that the dead people were strangers and the main thing was not to become involved by them. They were not disregarded or treated with any disrespect, but their status as stiffs was not to be enlarged, either. With the obvious exception of those in danger of breaking down, and with the exception of those disposed to be talkative, mourners were to be treated with relentless formality. The nearest thing to gallows humour was the offer of the use of a removal van to John Crookes so he could pick up his girlfriend, down on a visit from Goulburn.

Yet I thought that I detected a sense of shame in our work from time to time. An unspoken querying of himself which each man shared but which all bore alone, that he might not have somehow done better? If not this, then a social alienation: that one should be fit, if for nothing else, than to carry away the dead. The drivers, and no doubt the majority of staff, suffered socially. Their children were liable to be teased at school, their family life was disrupted by irregular hours, they and their wives could be shunned. This was one reason for the anxiety that I thought I sensed under the general affability. Every tea room I've ever sat down in has had someone with strong views about unionism, democracy, the noose and the lash, somebody cocked to pick a conversation about the most primitive morality. Here, however, the talk tended more than usually to material wealth. The prospect of buying a boat, pleasant as that is, would be aired with an additional tinge. It would begin to sound like there were really two boats, one the twelve-foot dinghy with the little outboard to use for fishing on the weekends, the other a raft of normality, worth striking out for at any cost.

For the main difficulty associated with this job had nothing to do with stress caused by noise or unrelenting pace or any other distortion of nature. Instead we dealt with a nullity alien to life itself, which instinct met with aversion and our culture met with platitudes or silence. Functionally, it was a trifle to tag a body, routine to walk in on the embalmer plying what are called his 'arts'. Often, driving the broad outer suburban roads, engaged in a conversation or by the traffic or the sky, you forgot that you had stiffs aboard. It would come back with a jolt. You were alive, with the window down and the breeze pouring in; they were not alive, their stretchers chocked into place, just behind you. On the hottest days I used to worry that they might bake back there, but they didn't. They were still chilled when we delivered them. I never saw a body, its features crossed with the expressionless expression, without a sense of shock, or wrote the names of the dead on the soles of their feet without being surprised that it didn't tickle. Once, fixing the safety-belt type straps over a corpse on a stretcher on the dank, cement floor of a mortuary, I had the sudden realisation that I was the paid agent this person had perhaps feared more than any other; it seemed to me at that moment that my jacket hung from my body like a crooked wing. This, I hope, will indicate the dislocation to be experienced in this work. Little wonder, then, that the tea room banter was coloured by futility, that scepticism was the predominant ethos.

Futility and scepticism are not confined to the unspoken realities of work in the funeral industry, of course. Rather, it's work in this industry which becomes illustrative of the internal dislocations required by a great deal of work in industralised society, for it is here that the divorce of will and action can be observed at its sharpest. The Telecom clerk who tabulates an oppressive phone bill does not wish it to invade her imagination. In order to evade the fact that it does, she need merely recall that I am a Telecom customer with an obligation to pay —

one of the 'dead'. The authorities who have introduced to Melbourne a new public transport system called Light Rail, a system of creeping discomforts and moderately spectacular inefficiencies, do not particularly mean the onus to fall on the lowest paid of their staff, the tram conductors, but if it does they make them 'dead', too. They are staff. It is part of their job. And on and on it goes, an ethics of disregard, assisted by mega-visual entertainments which rely on standardised roles and characters and one continuous, staple, subject: murder.

All drivers became students of the funeral oration. If it was a jockey's funeral, or a notable cricketer's, we listened closely in the chapel's ante-room to the address coming over the speakers. Civil celebrants and clergy were fawned upon in public where we wore our 'funeral faces', but the private attitude was contemptuous. They were in it for the money. (Somewhat unjust to the clergy whose fees were only half those of civil celebrants.) The stupidest line I heard in an oration was, 'His conversation was full of clichés, but they were good clichés … No-one ever really knew him', etc. The picture conveyed was of a fugitive but shrewd personality who tossed out a clutter of *bon-mots*, sayings, maxims, slang, argot and axioms to delay as long as possible the deathing of himself by the ascribed categories of his intimates. The most transcendant statement I heard was made by a priest on a rain-swept hill at a muddy graveside. He said that by dying Christ has made holy the graves of those who believe in him.

In the light of these experiences the recent death of a member of my family, an aunt, and the last of my parents' generation, was actually softened. Death, since it is irretrievable, is taken stoically by a majority of people, I have observed. My family is no exception. Grief is acknowledged rather than sealed over, yet the social aspects of the ceremonial are allowed to take over as soon as they may. It was appropriate that a woman whose researches into her family's genealogy were extensive should have gathered so many far-flung representatives of its various branches in one place at last. Great uncles, second cousins, friendly elderly identities familiar from early childhood, some of them not seen for over thirty years. An impossibly young-looking woman who played with you when you were a baby and she was ten, a long-dead grandfather's very lively 85-year-old sister. People with explanations of relation so complex that after the first paragraph or two you give up trying to follow and listen instead to the deep restfulness in kinship which their voices are telling you about. The fleeting sense of belonging to something large and tenacious, of lives related to your own reliably taking place in undreamed of parts of your city, and then of the city itself as a tough fabric largely made up of these invisible family networks. The Harrises, in all their formidable range, with their resilience and their sharp eyes. It was like being pummelled with flowers.

It is family, much more often than religion, that moves in to reassert continuity. The family's resources, variety, and shared human responsibility throughout its intimacy and society are the main support for the one or two present who are the most bereaved. I wonder what those ideologues hostile to the nuclear family imagine can replace this? There is no doubt that family can restrict, coerce and deform its members, but truisms are no substitute for kinship when kinship is needed.

I know that there are deaths which bring release. There are people who are able to counsel the dying, pacify might be a better word. There are people who accept death as a natural process, who expect or hope or intend to die peacefully and 'just sort of break up gently', à la Timothy Leary, as there are many people who consider that death is the final termination of individual identity. There are people who will believe any facile explanation of the most serious human predicaments as long as it is appealingly phrased, as there are persons who will accept the most brutal positions so long as they sound rigorous. Having handled the cold bodies, purging water onto my trousers from their lifeless mouths, I think of this arbitrary termination of a person's chiefest and only possession, life, as the greyest calamity. Neither the soporifics of pantheism nor the annihilation theory of death can afford to recognise pity for long. To one it is irrelevant, to the other unrealistic — or a metaphysical embarrassment. The popularity of these views indicates the low status given emotions, real, rare emotions, in our civilization. Both are, in my view, inadequate responses to death, this enigma, this insult, this source of grief and bewilderment, mud and trampled flowers.

Toward the end of my time as a carrier off of the dead I was forming the idea that life is visible. By looking at and handling the dead, whose features and bodies were intact, who had everything they needed to live except *life*, this peculiarly shimmering, light quality called animation began to become apparent. At first I thought of this quality as a component, which could be as it were abstracted, viewed and replaced. The disadvantage of this method was that it reinforced the inevitable sight of death on the features of living people. It was some months before the sight of life began to be involuntary again. It looked like something that curved, sang, flew, as we lagged along behind it, often following painfully.

1985?

KERRYN GOLDSWORTHY

Martyr to Her Sex

Ayers Rock, the place where Azaria Chamberlain disappeared more than five years ago, is in the region widely referred to by Australians as 'the Centre' — a word which in its everyday usage carries a vast weight of meaning: it means the heart, the middle, the core of things. It is what you measure and identify everything else against; it is the beginning place.

Australian history and literature have built up an ambiguous mythology about the Centre. It is a place of emptiness and disappointment, a place that failed to produce the hoped-for inland sea. It is a place where explorers failed and died. It is a metaphor for the allegedly vacant hearts and souls of the Australian population, a metaphor for spiritual emptiness frequently figured — interestingly enough — as infertility. But it is also a place of pilgrimage; most Australians regard a visit to Ayers Rock as a necessity if they want to know the country properly, to know its heart. It is a place of convergence; if you are travelling inland from any direction then it is the end of the journey.

Our histories and legends and stories of explorers, and especially Patrick White's *Voss*, have fixed Central Australia in the country's literary imagination as a place of redemptive suffering, a place where sacrifices must be made of individual lives for the sake of the population, as though the population must be made to pay somehow for the right to feel at home.

Ayers Rock, or, to call it by its rightful name, Uluru, is also a centre of convergence in Aboriginal mythology, a place where dreaming tracks meet. The Chamberlain episode was itself a convergence of mythologies; the spiritual significance of the Centre for both the indigenous and the imported Australian populations formed a kind of imaginative backdrop for two other sets of beliefs which figured specifically in the conviction of the Chamberlains: their Seventh Day Adventism, which brought out the latent hostility of Australians to minor or extremist religious sects in particular and to visible religious piety in general; and, more importantly, the mythology of motherhood.

The Chamberlain affair elicited a violent reaction from practically the entire population of Australia, as though it somehow involved everyone and therefore demanded a personal response. In a more spiritually sophisticated or religiously coherent country, much of this reaction might have been channelled into some version of formalised religious response. But, instead, the rhetoric of the court proceedings, of the media, and of public discussion turned on a more primitive form of worship: a semi-articulate, reverent and wilful mystification of the concept of motherhood.

Many of those who believed Lindy Chamberlain guilty maintained that the baby had been slaughtered in some kind of obscure sacrificial ritual; so it is deeply ironic that the trial itself turned out to be a sacrificial ritual on a national scale. Those who claimed that the name 'Azaria' meant 'sacrifice in the wilderness' spoke more truly than they knew; they simply mistook the identity of the victim.

The trial and conviction of Lindy Chamberlain was a public ritual involving the entire population in two essentially primitive religious phenomena: mother-worship, and — in this case growing out of that — the sacrificial and cathartic ritual of scapegoating. Lindy Chamberlain, like Camus's Meursault, in *The Outsider*, was condemned rightly or wrongly not for murder as such, but because of a public belief that like Meursault, whose worst proven crime was his failure to weep at his mother's funeral, she had violated the sanctity of motherhood.

In a way we are all responsible for Lindy Chamberlain's imprisonment. Motherhood is something which we are all so socially conditioned to revere — 'revere' as distinct from 'see clearly' and 'appreciate', which most of us do not do — that in our own tiny and daily failures with our own children, and our own mothers, we suffer a disproportionate guilt for which somebody, sooner or later, must be made to pay.

In almost all of the millions of words spoken or written about her in the past five years, the representation of Lindy Chamberlain — the construction of an image of her as public property — has been focused for good or ill on aspects of her femaleness: on her qualities as a mother, and on her sexuality. It seems to me that this is also true of John Bryson's recent book *Evil Angels*, which is an otherwise excellent account of the Chamberlain case and an extraordinary feat of writing and research. But in its implications and in the kinds of language that it uses, Bryson's book echoes and reinforces the public attitudes to motherhood and to female sexuality which informed and to a great degree shaped the course of Lindy Chamberlain's trial — a trial by jury, by media, and by the collective unconscious of an entire nation.

Bryson's book reflects the deepest paradox in Western society's attitudes to women, a paradox embodied in Christian iconography by the figure of the virgin mother. We combine a veneration of motherhood with a profoundly ambiguous attitude to female sexuality, a weird combination of fascination, condemnation and fear. Anne Summers's book, *Damned Whores and God's Police*, in its examination of women's place in Australian society since colonisation, holds as its central thesis the notion that there were, and are, ultimately only two roles available to women: the Damned Whore, whose sexuality is unconstrained and uncontained by the strictures of church and state, and who is therefore a disorderly, immoral and dangerous figure; and, alternatively, the role of God's

Policewoman, the virgin spinsters and respectable mothers who constitute the nation's moral guardians and in whom the restriction or repression of sexuality is seen as a direct factor in the maintenance of social order.

As archetypes go, these two roles are exhaustive and mutually exclusive, a binary opposition; if, as a woman, you do not meet the entrance requirements for God's Police, then you must perforce and by definition be a Damned Whore, since that is the only other position available to you. This paradoxical attitude is still around and is by no means confined to men, but is shared by those women who have not yet begun to question the values of the patriarchal society in which they live.

Apart from its strenuous and reasonably convincing attempts to prove that a dingo might easily have taken the baby from the tent, the evidence most heavily relied on by Lindy Chamberlain's defence counsel was that of numerous witnesses who attested that she was 'the perfect mother' — no attempt being made at any point, by either side, to analyse what this phrase might actually mean. John Bryson uses this kind of rhetoric himself with the same unquestioning attitude to it in *Evil Angels*. He makes constant, approving references to her 'motherliness', and he clearly shares the values implicit in such passages as this: 'It was then that Sally realised that Lindy had not planned to eat until the rest of the family was contentedly fed. Quite typical, she thought.'

It was certainly typical; Lindy Chamberlain's behaviour as reported by witnesses was consistently that of a model product of social conditioning in the role of wife and mother. She had spent that day riding around in a closed car with two little boys and a small baby, at least one of whom was carsick, while her husband took photographs. She had spent the time since their return to the campsite in attending to the comfort of her family; she must have been grubby, hungry and exhausted by the time that Michael Chamberlain asked, just as she was finally sitting down to eat, the now-famous question 'Isn't that bubby crying?' And it clearly did not occur to either of them that he could just as easily have gone and had a look himself.

John Bryson's book seems to imply that Lindy Chamberlain's obsessively self-sacrificing care and attention in the role of mother proves beyond doubt that she could not have murdered her baby. Not only does he fail to investigate the nature of 'motherliness' as a socially conditioned quality; he positively asserts, as though it were a virtue, his own and everyone else's failure — refusal? — to define, analyse or question it in any way. He writes at one point: 'The strength of the bond between mother and child is an intangible of a sort from which detectives like to keep well away', and later: 'All the messy complications of motherhood were beyond explanation.' This is, in effect, a declaration of male ignorance of female culture; of a desire to maintain that ignorance, as somehow admirable; and finally of a conviction that female culture cannot be accounted for in language — that it has no place in language.

Innumerable male journalists at the time of the trial became apparently quite obsessed with Lindy Chamberlain's body, an obsession resulting in a plethora of prurient prose. In an article on the Azaria case, in the *Australian Journal of Cultural Studies*, Dianne Johnson points this out and quotes from James Simmonds's 'Azaria, Wednesday's Child' to illustrate the point:

> The pert brunette had worn a different outfit to court each day so far ... and always managed to look striking. When she wore a filmy apricot dress with thin straps over the shoulders, male onlookers ogled her shamelessly, many tipping that she was bra-less beneath it. One middle-aged reporter felt the urge to comment on the 'soft roundness of her tanned shoulders', but he certainly was not the only man there to notice it ... One old-timer who spent hours sitting on the public bench watching the comings and goings at the court house was heard to tell his mate: 'It's easy to see why Michael is a pastor and not a priest.'

Sexy woman, or good mother? In our society it is difficult to play both roles convincingly at the same time; for what we call a 'good mother' is a figure who, in playing that role, affirms and reinforces the structure of society; she is defined, limited and kept under control by a patriarchal social order, and her reward is society's approval.

But female sexuality as such is something which, potentially or actually, threatens and disrupts that order, something for which, sooner or later, one will be punished. John Bryson fails in *Evil Angels* to negotiate or even recognise these confusions and contradictions. Early in the book, speculating on how nice it was for Michael Chamberlain that his wife's body betrayed almost no evidence of her recent pregnancy and delivery, Bryson writes, 'She had borne Azaria...less than ten weeks ago...yet the only detectable residuum was a certain slowness of the bosom when she moved.'

Apart from being puzzling — at what speed, and indeed in which direction, one wonders, will her 'bosom' move once it, too, has 'recovered'? — this observation has the same weird coyness detectable in a later passage, in which Bryson describes the same bit of female anatomy (not, this time, Lindy Chamberlain's; note, in fact, the absence of any personal pronoun) as 'the hummocky bust'. The general impression this sort of thing produces is that the word 'breasts' is one he fears might frighten his readers to death. Female sexual organs are dealt with even more strangely, and nastily, in his description of the Fertility Cave at Ayers Rock: 'Undulations in the walls and the ceiling were damp and anatomical, in contraction where she stood and dilating all the way out to the light. The insistent association was with the foetid passage of human birth.'

What we have here, in Bryson's dubious diction ('damp and anatomical' has at least the merit of being denotatively accurate, but the connotations of 'foetid' are potently suggestive), is the faithful reflection of his society's deeply ambivalent attitude to female sexuality, the shameful flip side of pure motherhood.

This ambivalence is also apparent in his description of what he calls the 'recovery' of Lindy Chamberlain's body — as though pregnancy were some kind of disease — after the birth of Azaria: 'It was a matter of pleasant and recurring wonder to [Michael] how quickly after childbirth her figure became girlish again.'

Here and throughout the book the words 'girl' and 'girlish', as well as the words 'little' and 'tiny', appear as terms of approval. What is a girl? A girl is an immature female, a person whose sexuality is latent and not yet a threat. Bryson approves, paradoxically, both of Lindy Chamberlain's girlishness and of her motherliness; it is only the necessary intermediate stage about which he is ambivalent, and with him a large proportion of Australian society. Hundreds of women, for example, were convinced of her guilt chiefly on the grounds of what they saw as her flaunting, during the trial, of her tanned shoulders and her large wardrobe; their 'logic' was that a woman interested in looking attractive at such a time must be a bad woman, and everyone knows that a bad woman cannot be a good mother.

Lindy Chamberlain, like Uluru itself, became a centre of convergence for Australians. She was a topic of national conversation, a topic on which everybody claimed their right to an opinion. The public image of her, that image to which Australians reacted so violently in one direction or the other, was an image constructed by the courts and by the media, both of which are overwhelmingly dominated by men; it was an image which was in turn dominated by aspects of her femaleness. Concentrated simultaneously on her sexuality and on her maternity, it challenged and violated the largely unconscious but deeply ingrained conviction that motherhood is good and female sexuality is not good and never the twain shall meet.

They did meet, in the person of Lindy Chamberlain, heavily pregnant and stylishly dressed and standing trial for the murder of her baby daughter. For pregnancy is that unique and unstable state which attests beyond doubt both to your sexuality and to your imminent maternity.

Male observers from the legal profession, including her own defence counsel, have said that Lindy Chamberlain talked her way into jail, and that if only she had kept her mouth shut she would have been acquitted. (Many men like their women silent, whether they be little and girlish, tanned and braless, or perfect mothers.) But I think it might well have been her pregnancy, more than her determined attempts to speak for herself — to construct her own image in her own words — which turned the scales against her, simply because she represented for Australian society a disturbing and unresolvable contradiction and therefore a threat to complacently held beliefs. There is a good chance that had she not been pregnant and prettily dressed when she stood trial she never would have been in jail.

1986

GREG MANNING

The Revolution That Never Was

For me, World Series Cricket came down to three watching days which, in retrospect, chart quite closely the peculiar parabola of its public history. Day one was the grand opening on 2 December 1977, when Kerry Packer's first Supertest on Channel 9 showcased the Chappells v. Roberts and Holding followed by Lillee pounding down ('like a machine') to Vivian Richards, while the official Test on the ABC began with Paul Hibbert and Gary Cosier playing and missing at Indian medium pacers, followed by a middle-order collapse. In the late 1960s Sir Neville Cardus used to insist that cricket matches were essentially contests between individuals, not between teams, that the mob were interested in who beat whom, but true connoisseurs of the game relished with disinterest the great conflicts of character. We soon saw how mistaken that notion was: nearly all the great clashes of character were on Channel 9, but all the self-styled 'true cricket lovers' were watching the ABC. Character, we were shown, cannot survive in a vacuum. In the public mind the Supertest was a sideshow, whereas the Test match inducted its players into a tradition that stretched back through Bradman and Trumpet to Demon Spofforth and Charles Bannerman, down to 13-year-old Mark Taylor at Wagga and fifth-grade no-hopers like me. If Packer's cricket was ever to gain credibility, he had to find some way to displace that immense and ancient structure of sympathy and support.

For a while it seemed unlikely that he would. The WSC Australians lost their first match before empty stands while the Test side won a riveting contest by just 16 runs. For the Test team Peter Toohey's gallant 82 on debut was a timely reminder that new flowers grow with every spring, while the second-innings 89 by 41-year-old Bob Simpson seemed like a gift from a simpler age, as if an ancestor had returned to shepherd the new generation. Simpson's tyros may have lacked the match skills of the battle-hardened pros at VFL Park, but they made up for it in pluck and romantic appeal. Day one belonged to the status quo.

Day two was January 14 1978, the opening day of the first Supertest against 'The World' at the Sydney Showground. Facing Roberts, Procter, Garner, Greig and Underwood, Australia was led to 304 by a limited little opening bat who was never in his life to make an official Test hundred. Bruce Laird's 106 was an innings of heroic resolution, claimed by sheer force of will over the limits of his own talent, off the most resourceful bowlers in the game. The next highest

Australian score was 44. Had it been played in a Test match, Laird's knock would now be preserved among the great ones, but as it was it lingered in the public mind scarcely as long as the bruises he collected in its compilation. His arena's proximity to Sideshow Alley made the indifference which met Laird's feat all the more desolate, and watching him I felt implicated, as if by paying for my ticket I had asked this man to risk his life for nothing more than my entertainment. The greatness of Laird's innings was profoundly moving, but it was moving precisely because it was denied meaning: transcending its forum, it exposed the truth that there was nowhere for it to belong.

Day three was 28 November 1978, the first major fixture of the second WSC season, at the SCG the night they turned on the lights. Forget the Supertests — everybody else has — this was the night we saw World Series Cricket for the first time. The ball was white, the umpires wore black (the players were still in white — the colours came in the new year) and the skies for a time were deep purple. For an hour at dusk the light seemed to come from nowhere. Everything glowed and nothing cast a shadow — and nobody knew the rules any more. The cricket scarcely mattered, as even the players seemed to realize (Viv Richards went third ball and Australia won in second gear) but in the otherworldly glow of the tips of 'Packer's cigars', which hovered over the 50,000 crowd like the underbelly of a Spielberg spacecraft, the artificial urgency of the one-day spectacle seemed like a close encounter with the future. That night, World Series Cricket did not so much win a positive verdict as usurp critical judgement. The Supertests had asked to be taken seriously, and had flopped. Here we did not know quite what to think — it probably wasn't cricket, but it sure as hell was theatre, and it was even better TV.

There was no stopping WSC after that. As the crowds and the TV audiences took to it increasingly, Graham Yallop's Test team (now known as 'the ACB eleven', as if they were playing more for the Board than for their country) was systematically dismantled by Mike Brearley's county pros. That season the Board's best card, an Ashes Tour, lost money; next season promised a haemorrhage. But many of Packer's stars were over 30 and would soon have to be replaced, so if he were to win the war too well, he risked destroying his own source of players. Truce was inevitable, and when at the end of the 1978–79 season the Cricket Board's broadcasting contract with the ABC came up for renewal, Packer won the prize that he had wanted all along, the exclusive right to televise and promote international cricket in Australia. In the compromise the Cricket Board were to continue to stage orthodox Tests at the traditional times in the traditional venues, and PBL took over on weeknights to turn the arenas into TV studios. The ACB staged the classic drama — *Richards the King*, as it were — and Channel 9 gave us *Hey Viv*.

For most of the two years that it lasted, the Packer 'revolution' seemed to threaten the very foundations of cricket in Australia, but in hindsight what is clearest is the amount of good it did. Not because WSC was necessarily preferable to the official alternative of the time, but because the official alternative was doomed anyway. One-day cricket was unavoidable; what mattered was how the one-day game would be incorporated into the Australian calendar. The obvious alternative to the present Australian season is the English one, where one-day cricket is played endlessly at county level, with only a handful of internationals. This has produced the present England team. The Australian system reserves heavy one-day schedules for players who have completed their educations, and sells those matches to the biggest possible crowds. That is precisely as it should be, and WSC worked it out.

There are of course many more traces of WSC in the modern game than white balls, coloured clothes, drinks carts and endless replays. Its preparedness to innovate has brought us helmets, fielding circles, triangular tournaments and thematically titled Test series. Its insistence on continuous international cricket has demeaned the Sheffield Shield, and the monopolization of top players' schedules that it inaugurated continues to deny young Shield cricketers the chance to play against the best opposition. The post-WSC schedule has made the Cricket Academy and the Australia A confection necessary; time will tell whether they prove sufficient to the task. Internationally, the World Series hothouse enabled Clive Lloyd to professionalize the West Indies fully by instilling a team commitment which overcame the regional loyalties that had divided their sides in previous years. Since then, their reign as the number one team in the world has been unbroken. Barry Richards believes that Richard Hadlee began to develop the self-belief that made him the greatest bowler of the 1980s during the WSC tour of New Zealand, when he kept knocking Australians over for nothing on dreadful pitches. Kepler Wessels' extraordinary international career began when he was made into an instant WSC Australian. And perhaps most intriguing of all, Imran Khan apparently first learnt to make a cricket ball jackknife by rubbing away the residual lacquer on the white ball. Subsequent Pakistani fast bowlers have learnt how to jackknife the red ball (which is not so heavily lacquered) and, by so doing, generated a degree of sensitivity about ball-tampering that has almost cost the head of the England captain.

Many of these changes are cosmetic, and the rest are evolutionary rather than revolutionary. Most of the innovations that WSC brought must have come in time, probably sooner rather than later. And not all the changes for the worse that are often sheeted home to it really belong there. It is often blamed for turning cricket into a blood sport and crowds into mobs, but while it is true that the Channel 9 ad-men seemed to think that low-scoring games on dubious wickets could best be sold by demonizing the fast bowlers, the fact remains that Thommo was talking about blood on the pitch and Rick McCosker's jaw was broken well before Packer came on the scene. In the late 1970s, cricket as blood sport was an idea whose time had come. And anyone who thinks that WSC invented hooliganism must never have been to the SCG in the early 1970s, in the palmy days of the 'KB Keg', or 'hand grenade', as it was known.

World Series Cricket emerged because Australian players in the mid 1970s were star attractions in an enterprise that was monopolizing their time, making millions of dollars, and paying peanuts. While there was no alternative employer, the official administration did not need to listen to the players' complaints. When Kerry Packer offered what seemed to them huge contracts (modest though they were in international terms), they had to sign, and when they did they were, if anything, even less free than they had been as Test cricketers. They were certainly made to work a great deal harder for their pay. Where, in the past, a player's season had mixed five or six Test matches with the lesser demands of Shield games and even club matches, the WSC Australians faced only the best and the fastest, day after day, often on ordinary pitches, usually in the one-day format. Lost form was almost irretrievable, particularly since the back-up competition, the 'Country Cup', offered more one-dayers against the next best on even worse wickets. Not surprisingly, some likely Test selections in official cricket who found themselves stranded on the Country Tour came to regret their decision to sign, but there was no escaping a Packer contract. When David Hookes tried to withdraw, he was laughed out of the room. The players, indeed, come through this story as in many ways tragic figures, who tried with every justification to change a system that needed changing, but were able to do so only by giving up what little independence they had, and handing power to someone whose feeling for cricket was always secondary. And now, fifteen years later, those once-impressive salaries have come back to the field, the intensified 'professional' schedules show no sign of letting up, and power is where it always was.

World Series Cricket threw forth any number of fascinating characters, but none more so than the two major players, Ian Chappell and Kerry Packer. Chappell's genius as a leader is well known, but no book I have read shows it as clearly as Gideon Haigh's *The Cricket War*. Whether he is encouraging a nervous opener, laying a talented young batsman's responsibilities before him, or goading his fast bowlers into fury, Chappell reads situations and people with unerring clarity. In the nets against an enraged Lennie Pascoe, Chappell produces what Phil Wilkins recalls as the 'the finest exhibition of net batting I've ever seen', twenty minutes of sustained self-exposure undertaken purely to spur his fast bowler, and perhaps to inspire his other batsmen. Even the better known exhibitions of vulgar bravado seem, in context, explicable parts of a broader strategy. Haigh writes at one point that 'Ian Chappell, rationally speaking, was too willing a self-abnegator to be a great captain', but Haigh's claim seems to me only to show how little reason has to do with great captaincy.

Countering Chappell's magnetism in *The Cricket War* is the inescapable presence of Kerry Packer. Perhaps his recent heart attack has changed him, but Haigh's Packer is a restless, haunted man. He reminded me of Saul Bellow's millionaire Henderson, who has a voice somewhere inside him saying 'I want, I want, I want', which will not be satisfied by the self-evident fact that he wants for nothing. What Packer seems to crave is real opposition, someone or something who can really test his resources, but every time he senses resistance he dissolves it on the spot with the perennial weapon, money. You sense that if he resents his father's memory, as he has been said to do, it is less for any boyhood neglect than for the start in life that Sir Frank bequeathed him, because it meant that he never had a chance to start from nothing, and so many of the really heroic achievements were denied him. The summer before World Series began Packer tried late to get the rights to televise Test cricket, opening his negotiations with ACB officials with the words 'Come on, now, we're all harlots. I know you haven't signed the contracts, what's your price?' They didn't have one, so he sank $12 million into finding the breaking point of the system. And yet, in his moment of triumph after the first night match in Sydney, as Tony Greig chokes back tears and Dennis Lillee gets a tingling feeling through his body, Packer seems inexplicably discontented. It is as if there is nothing so lonely as another fight won, another opponent gone.

Perhaps that is what makes him such an extraordinary overreacher. He seems to defer to no rules at all. Haigh tells the story of how during the fourth day-night final of 1978–79 it looked as if Chappell's Australians were not going to bowl their 50 overs by the shutdown time of 10.30 pm, so Packer ordered his manager to 'Fix it'. This was effectively a command to change the playing conditions during the course of the game, and the result was a fiasco. Ian Chappell received a message at 10.19 that the game would be played to a finish, which meant he needed to save Dennis Lillee's last overs and find a few from a part-timer, which in turn enabled the West Indies to slog their way past the Australian run rate. Then, at 10.30, with four overs still to go, the umpires ended the game. Neither they nor the West Indies had ever received the message. With Lillee not bowled out, Chappell looked a fool, he felt cheated, and the fact that the lost game cost his side the finals series and a shot at $33,000 only added salt. Soon afterwards Packer entered the Australian dressing room happy to confess his responsibility, full of apologies for what had happened, ready with the universal remedy: the Australians would receive parity of prize money. Whereat Ian Chappell looked him in the eye and said, 'You can take your money, and stick it right up your arse.' One can only wonder how much Haigh's Kerry Packer would give to have experienced, just once, a moment of such magnificence as that.

1994

ARCHIE WELLER

Portrayal of Aboriginal Men in Literature

Literature is a very important influence on a country's feelings since most thinking men and women will read and gain some sort of perspective from the Nation's authors. Therefore, writers have a responsibility to put as real an image as they can upon paper and, in this respect, Australian authors as a whole have failed dismally in the case of portraying the Aboriginal people. They only look at the one aspect of the image without attempting to explain it.

In the early days of the first settlement most writing consisted of journals or diaries kept by the pioneers. These books are to be found in the libraries around Australia today, such is the long life of the written word. This is another reason why writers should be authentic, since people die and take their feelings with them but the written word stays on forever.

The diaries on the whole portray Aboriginal people at best as 'Noble Savages' and at the worst as stone age idiots who never invented a thing and just wandered around Australia doing nothing, waiting for an accident to happen, until the white man arrived. There are very few books or stories that really try to understand the Aboriginal way of life that had withstood forty thousand years or more. The intricate totem system for instance, the complex food structures and the religious laws and closeness to the land that was the very essence of Aboriginality. Aborigines were considered childlike and clowns just as the Negroes of America were. They were written down as thieves of cattle, dirty, untrustworthy or, just as bad, nothing better than good faithful servants. Remember, the English upper classes thought of their own servants as mere belongings and not people and these new servants were black to top it off. Imperialism was alive and well in these days of the late 1700s to early 1800s so there was little thought as to the feelings of this nation of people, just as there was none about the Indians, Islanders, West Indians and other assorted 'Fuzzy-wuzzys or niggers' the world over. Indeed, there was even less than any thought for these people who were so gentle as to not organise themselves into warlike groups like the Zulu or Maori or betray their benefactors as in the Indian Mutiny. They welcomed these ghosts of the returned dead, hugging them in joy as they recognised a brother or sister.

There were, however, many heroes and warriors scattered throughout the land: Yagan, Midjigooroo and Calute from the West, Sandawarra as the Black

Napoleon, who led an army against the settlers in Tasmania, and the brave though sad Kalkadoon tribe who led a fierce charge, as did the Murray River tribes around Perth put up a fierce resistance that culminated in the so-called Battle (or massacre) of Pinjarra.

But one reads nothing of these exploits in the books and diaries of the settlers. These brave actions are put aside as isolated incidents of a few wild blacks, thus compounding the falsehood that there was no resistance to the taking over of Aboriginal lands that even today hinders the making of a treaty that would give Aboriginals back some of their land, dignity and purpose in life.

After the pioneers settled down and culture took its place in the new society (forget about the rich culture of legends and corroboree that was only so much wailing and fairytales to the whites) then the trend for Aboriginals in Australian Literature became fixed. The same people who wrote the diaries often wrote the books. In Rolf Boldrewood's *Robbery Under Arms* for example (published 1889) the halfcaste (a distasteful word but one used often in the early days) is a sly, sullen youth who dotes after his master in a doglike fashion. His name is Warrigal which itself means wild dog and gives some idea perhaps of how his creator saw him:

> As for Warrigal, Starlight used to knock him down like a log if he didn't please him, but he never offered to turn against him. He seemed to like it and looked regular put out once when Starlight hurt his knuckles against his hard skull.

We are told he is a fine shot and 'could catch fish and game in all sorts of ways that came in handy when we had to keep dark'. He is a good rider, tracker, and a plucky fighter but, as the narrator says, 'I was always expecting him to play us some dog tricks yet.' As, indeed, the author organises quite adequately that he does.

Another who seemed only to live for his master is Old Tim, a station hand at Wandoo in D. H. Lawrence's *The Boy From the Bush*. Aboriginal people in this novel are greatly conspicuous by their absence, although, in truth, around the period there would have been many families wandering the roads and being as much a part of the Australian landscape as the shearers, sandlewood cutters, swagmen and cockies described.

When Jack and Tom are setting off,

> the old black [actually he was a 'halfcaste'] was holding open the yard gate. He seemed to have almost forgotten Jack, but the emotion in his black, glittering eyes was strange, as he stared with strange adoration at the young master. He caught Tom's hand in his two wrinkled dark hands, as if clinging to life itself.

So we have another example of a faithful type of Uncle Tom figure that, as far as I could see, utters not one word throughout the whole book. He is the 'token Aboriginal'.

Another example from the same book as to total lack of interest in Aboriginal culture that was now becoming part of the art form. At least, in some of the diaries an interest had been shown in the living habits of the original inhabitants even though it was considered a bit of a joke:

'Wonder what Gingin means?'

'Better not ask. You never know what these natives'll be naming places after. Usually something vile. But gin means a woman whatever Gingin means.'

In fact Gingin comes from Tjennajen which means a footmark and here was an opportunity to wonder why a place would be named after a footmark. The foot must have belonged to someone important. But instead the remark about gins is made. Gin, like halfcaste, is a derogatory term, today unliked by many Aboriginal people. When coming from a white man's mouth it sounds dirty. This was written in 1924, the time of the dying pillow syndrome, when everyone was of the opinion that the poor old abos were due to fade away so let their last few years be kind, and integrate those with white parents into white society.

These attitudes are seen in the books of this period when Aboriginal people are mere shadows on the landscape. Mary Grant Bruce, who wrote the Billabong series, in all her books had only one Aboriginal, the Stockman Billy. It seemed that if Aboriginals were mentioned at all they were the good stockmen or excellent blacktrackers or bloodthirsty wild Aboriginals from the bush. The characters themselves were dehumanised. It was the era of the token Aboriginal, slotting one in to make it a truly authentic Australian story along with the gum tree or three and the kangaroo or two.

Yet all these writers — even Ion Idriess, Xavier Herbert or Douglas Stewart — could not really understand the land they were writing about. It is either hot and dusty, empty and inhospitable (Nigger country in other words, as Gavin Casey describes it) or it is full of the most descriptive adjectives. Yet these descriptions seem to miss something that Aboriginal writers don't miss, the soul of the country that is there for everyone to touch, but few have. It is hard for them to fully comprehend the beauty and especially the awesome power of their adopted country.

Perhaps here is an appropriate time to mention the artist Jolliffe, who also is an author in that he is a cartoonist. Some people today criticise Jolliffe by saying he is a racist and sexist but he did something no one else had done and that is portray with kindly humour and sympathy a society that many people thought of as just drunk and useless. Jolliffe had happy laughing people and amusing situations and his women were all beautiful when on the whole white society considered Aboriginal women as just someone to grab late at night when you were lonely; not beautiful humans, who often displayed intelligence. Speaking for myself it was Jolliffe's women I fell in love with as a boy and not the women in the pages of *Man* magazine which I sneaked from my father's drawer.

It was not only in novels but in short stories also that the Australian authors let us down. One of the greatest writers of Australian characters, Henry Lawson, when asked why he did not write stories about Aboriginal people replied that no one would read them. So an opportunity to use a powerful artform to describe the Aboriginals was never used. In *Coast to Coast 1943*, short stories compiled by Frank Dalby Davidson, himself an excellent writer from the bush, we find the first one is Xavier Herbert's 'Kaijek the Songman'. Here was one of the few writers who tried to understand the Aboriginal soul. But we can imagine the reader's amusement at silly old Kaijek, who would rather give up all the fame and fortune in the shape of gold nuggets to carry on into the desert with his newfound song. There is little attempt to explain that the song, to him, was as important as gold was to the white man. He is made to look silly and comical.

[...]

There were, in the mid seventies, a number of books written by whites who were disgusted and horrified at the plight of the Aboriginals. But books like *Children of Blindness* by Trish Sheppard and Richard Bielby's *The Brown Land Crying*, although well meaning, hold no hope at all. You see, Richard Bielby went around the camps for a few months with a tape recorder and Trish Sheppard spent a month in a country town. They did not, as no white person has really, grow up in an Aboriginal atmosphere and so glean all the little jokes and ways of life that still linger on from the past and help keep a depleted people together. The little settlements of Woongara West and ''Eartbreak 'ill' are filthy, full of empty bottles and dogs and dust or mud. The people there are ruined to a man, unless God has saved them. Prostitutes and thieves abound. There is absolutely no good at all here and no sign of the unique Aboriginal humour. It seems that the white people are so burdened with their guilt that the whole picture is colourless and too sad to be true really.

Of course there is dirt and drink and sickness, and racism is always rife in small country towns. But there are the football matches and the Aboriginal dances and the good times as well. There is the courtship of women and the stories of those who make it in work, sport or music. It is not all drunkenness and degradation. Not all parties turn into a drunken brawl.

Another thing that white people seem to harp on is that Aboriginal people can't handle the booze. This feeling persisted from the very first as with Warrigal in *Robbery Under Arms* who is a 'devil' when drunk, and it is by drinking that he is finally killed, when he blurts out his betrayal of the Marston boys to their father and also the betrayal of his 'master', Captain Starlight. Not mate: remember, Aboriginals were different and could never be a mate. So the drink ultimately destroys him — he, who is as good at riding, fighting, tracking and survival in the bush as any white — or indeed better — and who showed great cunning when helping Starlight to escape several times, but all this is forgotten at the thought of drink.

In Tim Winton's *Shallows*, the Miles Franklin Award winner, there is a rather interesting style of using Aboriginal people. They are seen as figures in the background only, and play no real role in the life of the town. One Abby Tanks, who is 'a promising new recruit', has had his knees shattered and his head and hand fractured by some who are obviously jealous of his fame. We follow his progress through the story in one-liners to his eventual death at the end in the shape of a headline. The forefathers of Abby are mentioned as well, sparingly in the journals of an old character. Yet, sparing or not, one can still imagine them. They are a part of the landscape.

One cannot write an essay on Aboriginal men in literature without mentioning Arthur Upfield's Inspector Napoleon Bonaparte, who really could have been a white man except for his amazing tracking skills and the odd little fear that trickled into his mind. Really this was a creation based on 80% fact as the author knew the man. I wonder if he ever paid this man any of the huge pile of royalties he gained as a result of exploiting an Aboriginal character. It is so obvious a gimmick, to have this amazing Aboriginal detective. I cannot lie and say I did not enjoy trying to work out in each story who the murderer was, just as I enjoy reading Agatha Christie, but it saddens me to think that a writer from a people who have ripped off another race's land can now dig freely into the soul of a member of that race and make up this wholly unbelievable chap with an equally ridiculous name. All the familiar clichés are there, with an emphasis on Boney's ability to think black and yet be accepted as a white person. But there are the wild blacks, the station blacks, the blacks with funny names and funny clothes. They somehow seem to lose their dignity.

Even in other stories by more modern writers we still find the filthy camps, the wastrel male figures and the young girls, doomed to be prostitutes and black velvet and pale Aboriginals ashamed of their colour. These are all ghosts; all true in a way but never explained as to why. They have no real body. They lack truth and thought-provoking feelings. We see them and read of them and think, Ah, well, that is what you expect from an Aboriginal.

Now, however, there are emerging Aboriginal authors who can dispel these myths and write about the real people. It was Jack Davis who said that only Aboriginal people can write about Aboriginal people and in the aspects of feelings and human dignity I believe he is right.

1988

ADRIAN MARTIN

TV Time Tunnel

In November 1991, the Museum of Contemporary Art in Sydney began an exhibition called *TV Times*, which subsequently toured the country. The theme of the exhibition was thirty-five years of watching television in Australia. Its focus was not really the history of TV, but its viewing: it was a show of memorabilia, fan magazines, colourful wheels from famous game shows, old TV sets, and huge, luridly glossy mug shots of the medium's stars (courtesy of *TV Week* magazine). I was one of several writers asked to contribute to the exhibition's catalogue. I had no particular brief or format to follow, only a broad topic: the effect of American TV on Australian culture.

When I received the finished catalogue, I was shocked to realise that virtually all contributors had, completely independently and probably unconsciously, whatever their specific subject, produced a piece of writing perfectly within the boundaries of a hitherto unknown genre, that of the TV memory. Writing about TV, it seems, naturally calls forth a stream of formative childhood memories, a telescoped life story, a chronology of key TV moments, and a passionate statement of one's personal critical position as formed in, through and against this stream of mass mediated experience. What follows is my TV memory.

When I was in Form 6 at a Catholic boys' school in 1976, all the smart kids loved *Monty Python's Flying Circus*. Eagerly banding together the morning after each broadcast, they would retell scenes, recite lines, imitate gestures. They were the true cultural elite of the school; as fiercely as they revelled in absurdist British culture (they were Goons fans as well), they already knew how to heap scorn on 'American trash': pop songs, TV shows, films. In the years to come, one member of this Python fan club became a prolific and respected poet; another flirted briefly with the Brotherhood before opting for a career in TV news.

I didn't mind Monty Python as a kid, but I was never invited into the inner sanctum of this schoolyard elite. My sense of the unnegotiable difference between myself and the group was summed up (then as now) by a particular joke its members once tried to share with me. A very serious and rather spiritually inclined boy in our class (who later became religious affairs reporter on a major daily newspaper) was also, as it happened, a player of the bagpipes. At the school he had previously attended (so the story went), the English teacher staged a passion-play. At the finale, as the Christ figure was taken down from the cross and carried off-stage, this student was prevailed upon to follow in procession, blaring 'Amazing Grace' from his pipes.

The Fellowship of Python roared laughing at the very thought of this absurd mismatch. I couldn't join in, because I sensed the cruelty and superiority in their mirth — and I knew I wasn't, ultimately, on their side of the cultural fence. This moment of alienation was one of the formative experiences of my life. A few years later, I discovered the terms that ever-so-feebly described that shock: I had encountered the difference between high and low culture. More exactly, I had suddenly found myself on one of the many points in between the poles of that great cultural divide, obviously and painfully out of place in the midst of a customarily binding social ritual.

Bagpipes in the middle of a passion-play would be clever stuff on *Monty Python's Flying Circus*, but when such a conjunction is produced naively or spontaneously, without the middle-class alibis of absurdism and irony, it figures as the very definition of bad art — shameless, opportunistic, spectacular, stupid, vulgar trash. And, of course, this bad art, this crazy mismatched quilting, is everywhere in what we loosely name popular culture: in B-movies, school eisteddfods, comics, TV shows like *Wrestlemania* or *Have a Go . . .*

Ultimately — as loving connoisseurs of popular art come to know — the so-called aesthetic badness of such works can be appreciated not as merely charming naïvety but rather as canniness, inventiveness, a sublimely mad and sometimes revelatory brilliance. Yet, in cultural realms that range from the aforementioned schoolyard elite to parts of the Academy via the weekend arts pages of classy newspapers, popular art is still routinely denied what, in the words of film critic William Routt, 'is conceded without saying to elite art: the ability to take one unawares, to question what one thought one knew, to confront one with one's self'.

Recently, I found myself watching a rerun of a typical and favourite show from my 1960s childhood, the American sci-fi series *The Time Tunnel*. To look back on it now, the show's operating level of unreality strikes me as absolutely astonishing. The time tunnel itself is a tackily painted spiral; objects are placed in it and miraculously appear right in the spot and at the second that the heroes need them; medieval battle scenes are unfussily conjured with stock footage or out-takes from more expensive productions.

Nowadays, I can marvel at the makeshift, involuntarily surreal art of *The Time Tunnel*. When I was a child, I think I took it not as a representation of reality — no kid could be that stupid — but certainly as my natural culture, my preferred and most comforting form of fiction, fantasy, spectacle. Recalling other favourite shows of my childhood — *I Dream of Jeannie, The Patty Duke Show, Twenty Thousand Leaques Under the Sea, Marvel Superheroes* — I realise that they all share *The Time Tunnel*'s unreal, patently artificial or fantastic aesthetic. I also realise they are all American.

It doubtless has something to do with my above-described formative experience, but I have a deeply ingrained tendency to equate high culture with British TV and low art with American TV. Rationally, of course, this proposition is nonsense: even as a young teenager I would have agreed that the proto American Playhouse TV special event *The Missiles of October* (with Martin Sheen as JFK) was high-class material, while *Dr Who* (another favourite) was hardly any more realistic than *The Time Tunnel.* But the kinds of prejudices I began to harbour, as my vague feeling of schoolyard alienation grew into a full-blown, passionately lived polemic, redefined absolutely my experience of the cultural field. Now, starkly spotlit in my vision forever more, certain signs of Britishness and Americanness rise like seductions or provocations from the TV screen.

To put it schematically, Britishness on TV — in the eyes of those who wish either to champion or abuse it — is tied up with basic operating notions of naturalism, realism, sophisticated wit, seamless production values, richness of detail, believable or in-depth characterisation, as well as more elaborate ideals of cultural worth, dramatic meaningfulness and artistic integrity. The spectrum of respectable Britishness runs from *Yes Minister* (at the light entertainment end) via *The Bill* to the never-ending Dennis Potter festival on the ABC.

Americanness, in an exact reversal of terms, is associated with hokeyness: one-dimensional or stereotypical characters, a paper-thin fictional illusion, drama or comedy in broadly melodramatic or burlesque strokes, spectacular sensationalism with no necessarily edifying goal. Think of *The A-Team, Wonder Woman, Charlie's Angels, Dallas* and *Dynasty.* It is perhaps in the daytime, no-frills American soaps that we encounter the full force of this surrealistically hokey aesthetic: dialogue that is abruptly cut off and returned to twenty minutes later as if not a moment has passed in the fictional world; the sudden appearance of visual effects or voice-over thought-tracks scarcely connected to the storyline; old pop tunes and stock bits of incidental music that cut in and out regardless of how they sit with the mood of a given scene. It's not exactly *EastEnders.*

It is perhaps another result of my formative experience that I have a hard time vibing along sympathetically with anyone who decries American cultural imperialism on our television screens. Materially, economically, in terms of ratings and package deals and prime-time slots, I guess the imperialist analysis is fairly correct. But whenever it is claimed that American popular culture, above all other cultural forms, contaminates and conditions our miserable colonised brains, I cannot help but hear the echo of those cruel Python lovers, so assured in their standards of good and bad. I cannot help but notice that, nearly every weekend in the *Australian,* TV reviewer Phillip Adams covers SBS and ABC fare (I especially remember his tribute to the documentary *Life of Python*), bullishly disregarding whichever typically American sit-com, cop drama or variety show has just started its run on a commercial channel.

Archetypally high culture, it is true, takes up very little time in the lives of most Australians — and the popular (mass-produced commodity) culture with which they more naturally sport is more often than not American in origin. Yet the feelings of shame and embarrassment among the unprivileged at being uncultured — feelings I know so well from my own upbringing, feelings that often surface in the most popular of pop texts (such as *Pretty Woman*) — surely these are causally connected to the regular, insistent, quietly powerful exercise of superior cultural taste that flows through our media and our education systems.

It is hardly a new table-turning ploy to suggest that Australian culture is more terrorised by British colonialism than American imperialism. There may not ultimately be that many Australians, country-wide, who submit to that terror, and eagerly seek out the appropriate blessing of Britishness upon the culture they choose to consume. But for some who have found themselves (as I did) in the wrong place at the right moment to be struck dumb by this British terror, disturbed by its fading, anachronistic but unmistakable force, the value of certain things American is that they provide a blessed path out of such a hell.

Those who argue that American popular culture has colonised our subconscious with its value system perhaps overestimate the efficacy of its messages. There is no doubt that American pop culture (from Capra and Spielberg to 'We Are the World' and the Miss America Pageant) is full of strident, proud, boastful messages. Yet there is something fortunately self-sufficient and myopic about the spirt of American cultural populism as it beams itself along the well-greased channels of the global media network. Where Clive James assumes the imperious role of mass-media guardian — monitoring and mocking the terrible spread of trash to unprotected peoples and cultures everywhere — Bill Cosby seeks only to speak his mind, to make money and to entertain. He probably doesn't worry much whether your or my Aussie family falls short of his ideal family on *The Cosby Show*; he probably couldn't care less.

It may well be the case that some media critics wildly overstate the role of ideological content — happy families, happy endings, Mom and Pop role models, the triumph of good over evil — when they target American culture for its brainwashing, socially determining effects on Australian life. Part of what we (sometimes ungenerously) construe as the innocence or simplicity of American popular culture resides in the obviousness, the blatantness of its ideology, and the familiar predictability of its ideological scenarios and icons. Everything — including the preach or the pitch — is on the surface, unlike more refined or sophisticated artistic forms whose message-mechanisms are usually more cleverly disguised, thereby excusing Dennis Potter's TV oeuvre from virtually any ideological examination in the quality press.

The ideological critique of American media continues apace in magazines like the *Independent Monthly*. But, alongside it in recent years, a strange cultural cargo cult has developed. Its acolytes, like the anti-imperialists, also fixate on the transparently plastic ideological markers of old American TV shows. Yet now, such content is to be celebrated and enjoyed rather than criticised. This is the kitsch-fun-trash cult, and its delight in reruns of *The Brady Bunch* or *Lost in Space* works on several levels. On the first level, these old programs have become camp, because they endorse values that now seem hopelessly naive to our cynical age — which is in fact how most cultural objects seem once they have lost their immediate link to the sensibilities reigning over a given time and place. This camp response is, in many ways, merely the reverse side of the lordly denunciation of bad art, but this time phrased defensively, and in bad faith: 'I know it's not great art, but it's fun'.

Complicating this assumption of cultural superiority, however, is an emotion that often blows its mantle of cool: nostalgia. Proposing a supposedly objective argument in favour of the golden years of television is one way of safely managing recurrent, embarrassing bouts of nostalgia. The naked face of this emotion, however, reveals itself often enough, as cultists unswervingly descend, in their fetishistic rituals, on one particular class of TV program: quite simply, the programs they happened to watch when they were children. When the elaborate defence mechanisms finally fail, cult members begin revelling in total psychobabble: I was so innocent then, TV was so innocent then, the families on TV were beautiful and happy, I wanted mine to be beautiful and happy too ...

When people time-tunnel back into their early experiences of TV, their accounts almost always invite an analysis of the complex yearnings that are in play: longings for a paradise lost, sometimes a paradise that never existed. The reminiscences I have offered are, at face value, little different. I too am drawn to reflect on a moment of innocence in the once-upon-a-time relationship between my youthful self and the TV set; some experience, some island of value and significance, that seems lost, crushed, whose memory must now be fiercely recounted and maintained. But I believe (unlike a lot of TV nostalgia freaks) that people's longings, their TV memories, are not just personal, patterned on some woeful cliché about happy families and perfect childhoods; they are also (and in no regular shape or formation) collective, cultural, social, political. Longings and memories can pinpoint lived contestations, strains, contradictions.

Personally, I can certainly pine for that lost era when I never felt obliged to jump to the defence of the bad art I naturally love. The innocence that calls to me like a siren's song is an impossibly precultural dream. I entertained the mad, egomaniacal wish that every grown-up could have the sensibility I had the moment before becoming aware of the brutal realities of taste and discernment, of the attribution of artistic value, of the division of culture into high and low spheres — the moment before the almighty, inescapable fall into sociality.

But the dream, impossible as it is, at least gives me in the here and now something to fight for, and to fight with. I don't believe the phantasm I have sketched here — the hurling of a vulgar, liberating America against a sedate, insidious Britain — is mine alone. As many have suggested, the British cultural presence in Australia is tied to ghostly notions of tradition and of empire, respectable notions of true and necessary art, and ultimately to a colonially subservient, nostalgic, bizarrely masochistic dream of 'our' national identity as bequeathed to us by the motherland of Britain. (This is the only possible explanation for *Woman's Day*'s perpetual fixation on the royal family.)

One does not have to love America to value, in a distant land, the gift of its popular culture. There are many recorded testimonies in the post-WWII period (by Wim Wenders in Germany, Umberto Eco in Italy, Raymond Bellour in France) of the personal and cultural liberations wrought by encounters with American jazz, movies and rock. American pop culture has the potential to trigger such liberation not because it is international or universal in character (as it pompously likes to believe) but rather because it is, in its decisive effect, stateless.

American pop culture conjures, from song to film to TV show, a self-enclosed, floating world of icons, images, sounds, fictions. It weaves not a heavenly utopia — the kind dreamed about on *The Love Boat* — but a strangely blank, abstract, unreal atopia, a no-place. This atopia offers its local subjects only the most chimerical and imaginary of identities — identities that are ultimately neither American nor Australian (and certainly not British).

If this idea of an atopia is true, then the papier mâché special effects of *The Time Tunnel*, the mysterious ellipses of *Another World*, the uniform alien landscapes of *Lost in Space* — all would become part of an airy, childish, ever-beckoning cultural revolution. This, at any rate, is what I choose to dream in public.

1994

MICHAEL McGIRR

At Home in Memory

Most of my friends have trouble spotting miracles. So do I. It's a pity because there are gentlemen in Rome only a miracle or two shy of declaring an Australian, Mary MacKillop, a saint. But to recognise a miracle, you have to cultivate a certain way of looking at things. It's a kind of art.

Mary MacKillop was born in 1842 at the top of Brunswick Street, Fitzroy, an inner Melbourne suburb with an ever-shifting personality. Some years ago, as regentrification was beginning to dictate the range of heritage colours allowed in the area, I was living in a community of alcoholics around the corner from where Mary MacKillop was born. One day, a woman came to the door and asked to be shown 'the birthplace'. There was no mistaking what she meant. Like most of our callers she was lost, but, unlike the majority, she knew what she was looking for. As we turned into Brunswick Street, however, we found a young couple lost in the wonder of each other over the very plaque which marks 'the birthplace'. In the circumstances, I was slightly embarrassed.

'Don't worry,' said the voice at my elbow, 'they're probably an infertile couple attempting a miracle.'

'Of course,' I replied, admiring the speed and determination with which she had reached the right conclusion.

. . .

Most of my friends, among whom I don't forget myself, are also losing the art of memory. There are too many cheap substitutes on the market. One substitute is nostalgia. Nostalgia is an industry. It thrives on bottling the past and selling it as a commercial proposition, whether that means a package tour, a model kit or a musical keyring. Some people are so keen on pickling the past as it happens that the proliferation of video and tape around any event of significance means that there is often very little more to these events than the taking of them down. It doesn't seem to matter. As long as we've got some decent photos, we can bring emotions on tap any time the craving hits us. We may never even have had these emotions at the time.

Another substitute for memory is data. We live in a new information culture. The number of recorded facts is bewildering. Whole industries have been adapted to the demands of storing them and allowing us access to them as randomly as historical answers pop up in an episode of 'Sale of the Century' or a game of Trivial Pursuit.

Memory, by way of contrast, is a human art. The ancients conceived of it along the lines of building a house. Cicero, Quintilian and others speak of walking from room to room within the memory and outfitting each chamber in such a way that every stick of furniture creates an association. The idea was that when we step behind one of the doors in our memory, the familiar arrangement of the space puts us immediately at ease within the body of material we have committed to memory. If we look within the drawers in the room, we find further detail and nuance carefully tucked away.

These techniques are so unfamiliar after two thousand years that it is difficult to imagine quite how they worked in practice. I find myself thinking it would take longer to create the house and furnish it than it would to learn things parrot fashion. Nevertheless, the assumptions underlying the technique fire my imagination. There appears a fine line, if any, between committing something to memory and being personally committed to that something. In the art of memory, there are no cheap souvenirs in plastic packets. Everything remembered has to be wanted and owned. Furthermore, there are no closets of tangled data which should really have been tossed out ages ago. Everything is deliberately placed. All this is possible, because, as the key image suggests, memory is the place where we live. It is home. Past, present and future, it is around us and beside us. It is under our feet.

. . .

A plaque in a pavement in Fitzroy noting the birth of Mary MacKillop, a woman only eight years younger than Melbourne itself, is a reminder that in some ways the whole world is furnished as memory. In Australia alone, there must be hundreds of plaques in pavements for all kinds of historical reasons, not to mention statues, cemeteries and obelisks. Lest we forget. Nevertheless, it was from this one plaque that, in early spring, I set out in fine fettle and good company to put something of the memory of Mary MacKillop under my own feet. As we walked to the train station, we caught a statue or two out of the corner of our eye, notably the one opposite the Windsor Hotel of the poet Adam Lindsay Gordon holding on hard to a pen as if it's about to throw him. But we were going to furnish a single room and did not delay.

Four hours later, having been first to the wrong cemetery, we stood in the Western District of Victoria at the grave of Mary MacKillop's father. Alexander MacKillop had initially studied to be a priest and disappointed those who'd put their hopes in him for this. In 1838, he arrived in Sydney from Scotland to make a fresh start and was one of the early settlers of the Port Phillip region. Suffering desperate financial embarrassment and separated from his wife, Flora MacDonald, he died in 1868. The kids jumping from headstone to headstone in the Hamilton cemetery seemed to mock him still. His grave remembers him principally, almost exclusively, as 'father of Mother Mary of the Cross, founder of the Sisters of St Joseph'. Some of Mary's biographers have suggested that her religious vocation came in no small measure from the one Alexander relinquished. I doubt it. Mary wasn't driven to make up for something her father lacked. On the contrary, her story is one of being drawn to love something her father became. He became poor. Not by choice either.

. . .

Mary MacKillop's story takes on a life of its own in Penola, South Australia, 126 kilometres from Hamilton. It was here in 1866, at the invitation of Father Julian Woods, that she began her first school for poor children. It was in a stable and became the progenitor of hundreds of schools for the disadvantaged which sprang up in her lifetime all over Australia and New Zealand. Throughout the twentieth century, these schools and the women who ran them have created an indelible impression on Australian culture and left their mark on our soul.

My companion and I had decided to walk from Hamilton to Penola. We are neither of us athletic and most of my friends said that if we made the distance, the event could be listed as a miracle in favour of Mary's canonisation. These are the same friends who wouldn't otherwise spot a miracle if a speeding truck stopped to offer them a ride. At least they were learning something. Cheered by this thought, we set off merrily and, after about ten kilometres, camped for the night in a field. Next day, however, we bit off more than we could chew. We thought we'd make it to Coleraine, a further twenty-nine kilometres.

There is something uncanny about walking the side of a highway. It's a far cry from bushwalking. Everything happens in slow motion as you are derided by the pace of life beside you. There's nothing in my experience as sarcastic as a sign which tells a walker to slow down and take a curve at seventy-five kilometres per hour. By mid-afternoon, our miracle looked severely in doubt. Traffic thundered past and meanwhile it was taking an hour to tramp from one marker triangle to the next. These markers, same as old milestones, are not the furnishings of memory. They simply create more data, dividing the world into a vast grid like a playing board. It wasn't until late in the day, just short of Coleraine, that we came across something a little different: 'Historical marker 500 metres'. We found a cairn piled up in honour of Adam Lindsay Gordon:

> the great Australian poet who rode in the great Western steeplechase, distance about 4km, and crossed the road at this point, first run in 1858. The great sportsman was a contestant in the famous event for 5 years, 1862–66.

'That's a lot of "greats" for one inscription,' said my companion, not feeling too great himself.

Apparently, the Great Western Steeplechase used to run a complete circuit of Coleraine. It says a lot for a culture that it devised entertainments so gruelling for both horse and rider. That hardness is still part of life. It is evidenced in

Coleraine by a man struggling alone in a wheelchair in the main street, going slower even than us. It is ingrained in a sense of humour.

'So you got here at last,' came a chorus from the bar of the hotel the minute we stepped in. 'We saw you on the road. We've been wondering when you'd get here and buy us a drink. It's your shout.'

After that first volley they ignored us for the rest of the night.

It's difficult to understand Mary MacKillop without pondering what it must have been like to have been a woman last century in a culture like this. There's a picture of Mary, aged nineteen, in the Catholic Church in Coleraine.

'That was given to us by the sisters when they pulled out after sixty years,' said the priest as a matter of hard fact. 'They didn't have the sisters to keep going.'

Even at nineteen, the face is strong. It needed to be. In a lifetime, Mary MacKillop was excommunicated by one bishop of Adelaide and harried mercilessly by another. She was besieged by the brothers Matthew and James Quinn, bishops of Bathurst and Brisbane respectively. She was estranged from Julian Woods who had guided the foundation of her work. Always and everywhere, the cause of tension was authority. The bishops wanted the sisters under their own control. Mary believed they should have a certain independence from the diocesan structure and be responsible to a single organisation of their own. In fact, she was pioneering a vision of one Australia well ahead of the federation movement. Ironically, when the Catholic bishops of Australasia met for the first time in 1885, a meeting which also anticipated federation, they voted fourteen to three in favour of keeping the sisters under the bishops' control. Mary stuck to her guns and was eventually vindicated on appeal to Rome.

In all this conflict, Mary lived with painful reminders that she was a woman. She suffered debilitating period pain. When brandy was prescribed as an analgesic for this, she was charged with drunkenness. Reading between the lines, it appears she went through a difficult menopause and was then doubled over in advanced years by attacks of rheumatism and finally by a stroke. These were the conditions under which she endlessly visited the burgeoning communities of her sisters. She virtually lived on the road.

My companion and I needed a lift to get over some of the hills between Coleraine and Casterton, the halfway point in our journey. This didn't stop us boasting of our exploits to the woman serving in the café.

'Don't worry,' she said, 'I walk further than that up and down behind this counter every day of my life.'

. . .

My companion said a friend of a friend had friends living on the road between Casterton and Penola. We phoned them and said we might be calling by in the next few days. Then, bracing ourselves, we walked out of Casterton into the teeth of a wind, the rain whipping us about the face. We camped that night in fear of being flooded, wondering what it was that kept Mary MacKillop going on one arduous journey after another.

Perhaps it was the joy of arrival. In the middle of the next day, a family sedan pulled over and a ten-year-old thrust a couple of pies at us. These were the friends of the friend of my companion's friend. We walked on to their property where they continued to bathe us in hospitality. Besides which, it was fun to be out of the weather and entertained by four bright youngsters. We told them our story of being on the trail of Mary MacKillop.

'Well, you should meet my father,' said Kevin, the father of the kids.

Kevin's father lived in an old house on the same property, further along the road. He said that his own grandfather had come over from Portland to start the farm. This meant that the youngsters were the fifth generation living on the same property, a rare continuity in Australia. Indeed, with the never-ending cycles of dislocation grinding on around us, it's probably rare anywhere in the world. But there was more. The man who had originally created the property married twice and soon found himself with nineteen mouths to feed. More to the point, he did some building work in Penola for Mary MacKillop. The story goes that Mary was unhappy with the job and called him back across to fix it up.

There is no shortage of biographies of Mary MacKillop but none of them contain this anecdote. Even if at some stage it had landed on paper, it would have to strike a historian as rather slight. But in the retelling of it, by an old man in an old house, it was anything but slight. It was a story that had been passed along the blood line. It came to us as part of the hospitality of a home which knew many other stories besides. It had the effect for me of creating a living presence within all the information I had piled up about Mary MacKillop. It threw into relief any nostalgia I may have felt about her world. In other words, it was the beginning of a personal memory of her. The tale was told in a dry manner, the words counted out like cash. But it was a living memory that had been tended and preserved with the timbers of the house.

The old man had more to say yet.

'Don't forget about Adam Lindsay Gordon,' he said. 'Gordon was a mounted constable for a while in Penola in the 1850s. He was friendly with the parish priest, Father Woods. They used to ride for miles together. But Gordon fell out with the sergeant because he had to have clean boots, left the force and went to break in horses on a property nearby.'

. . .

There are houses still standing in Penola which date from Gordon's time there in the 1850s, well before Mary MacKillop arrived. A number of them are owned by the National Trust and leased to storeholders. One of these is Sharam's Cottage. At the time of our visit, it sold toys and children's clothes. It's a charming place, almost a doll's house.

'People must have been much smaller in the 1850s,' said my companion, lifting a four-year-old's tracksuit off the rack.

The joke was spiked. It was difficult in such a dainty environment to appreciate the poverty for which this two-roomed bark-and-slab hut must once have stood. Seventeen people had lived in it at one time. Without the recent memory of the wind cutting through us on the road from Casterton, neither of us would have believed, between wafts of pot pourri, that people must have alternately frozen and baked in the place. They had nothing but hessian to line the walls. Thanks to the National Trust, something has been preserved. But it has been scrubbed up beyond recognition, sanitised and become a point of sale for consumer memorabilia.

After Mary MacKillop's first school had been going seven months, Julian Woods arranged for a more substantial schoolroom to be purpose-built. The 1867 schoolroom is still standing. For years, few people were allowed inside. Until 1984, the keys were jealously guarded by George Mapstead, an old-timer whose mother had been a student in the original stable school. It's said that you had to go down on bended knee to get them. Since then, the schoolroom has become a visitors' centre and place of pilgrimage, staffed by volunteers from the area. In September, they had just received their ten-thousandth visitor for the year. This places heavy demands on the human resources available for the work. According to the volunteer who met us, the National Trust is interested in taking it over and 'running it properly'. Thankfully, there is no real question of this. The Trust is unlikely to leave space for some of the material on display, such as children's drawings of Mary MacKillop, which are more objects of affection than good taste, the sort of thing you're more likely to see in a family home than a museum.

In the church next door, there were lists of people from Australia and overseas who were praying for God to work a miracle at the prompting of Mary MacKillop. Their medical conditions were moving. So was their faith. It made the church a welcome place to rest. In the choir loft, my companion and I were moved again to discover a painting that Austrian Jesuits had given Father Woods. It was leaning undisturbed against the back wall, quietly gathering dust.

Gradually, a dilemma was coming into focus. If some of the sick are favoured with a miracle (and who would hope otherwise?), Mary MacKillop will quickly become Saint Mary MacKillop. A tide, already building, will be unleashed. Penola will become a destination for such swarms of people that perhaps only a National Trust will be able to cope. But once the chance is lost to make a small discovery such as we did for ourselves of the painting, or of the old man's story about his grandfather, then memory becomes something different. It changes from a personal and painstaking art and becomes something mass-produced. It hardens. It accommodates less intimately. A character in Tim Winton's *Cloudstreet* discovers, when a pig starts speaking in tongues, that what you get in life is 'always the miracles you don't need'.

▪ ▪ ▪

In Penola we are introduced to a venerable nun. Sister Pat had been first stationed at Penola in 1936 and returned there in 1986. She tells us that when she was a young nun, the sisters didn't speak much of Mary MacKillop. And if they spoke at all of Father Woods it was entirely in the negative as the one who 'abandoned ship'. At that time, the elderly Sister Francis Xavier was still alive. As Blanche Amsinck she was one of the first to join Mary MacKillop's fledgling enterprise. She figures prominently in the biographies of Mary.

'She was known as *Ocle Omnium* because of the stentorian way she said grace,' said Sister Pat. 'We didn't know who she was. Not really. We went to such lengths to conceal our family names from each other in those days.'

In 1993, leg in a brace, laughing, Sister Pat sits at the kitchen table waiting for yet another busload of pilgrims who are already an hour late from Adelaide.

'You know Father Woods was the one who drew Adam Lindsay Gordon out of his melancholy and depression,' she says. 'They discussed Ovid and Shakespeare and Byron. It was Woods that got him writing poetry. Woods said their conversation broke the endless monotony of talking sheep, sheep and sheep.'

Sister Pat drums the table to emphasise the repetitiveness of what the menfolk discussed.

'And horses, horses, horses.'

I wonder aloud if telling pilgrims about Mary MacKillop has its own monotony.

'No. No,' she protests.

'Was there the same level of interest in Mary around here in 1936?'

Sister Pat tenants her own memories with pride.

'I can't remember that there was,' she says. 'But I can remember the face of every kid I taught back then.'

. . .

Writing about Port Arthur in *The Fatal Shore*, Robert Hughes remarks that Australia has many carparks but few ruins. Ruins certainly evoke something. They are haunted. They suggest untold violence and forgotten stories. Memory, on the other hand, is inhabited. It is where we live. Remembering means to embody. It means to take into your own person, your flesh, and your own faltering gait the unmiraculous meaning of someone else's simple stories.

The danger of becoming a saint is that of being kicked upstairs. Of being isolated as a wonder. Of being disdained as a curious datum by some and traded over with unctuous nostalgia by others. But neither of these responses does justice to anybody worth remembering. Not when home, the resting place, stretches out from under our feet.

1994

NOTES ON CONTRIBUTORS

BAKER, SIDNEY J. (Sidney John) (1912–76) b. New Zealand. Baker was a pioneer of the study of New Zealand and Australian English. He published several dictionaries and had a strong professional interest in all varieties of Australiana. His major work is *The Australian Language* (1945).

BANFIELD, E. J. (Edmund James) (1852–1923) b. Liverpool, England. Banfield came to Australia as a child. He spent many years working in Townsville as a journalist, but after an illness settled on Dunk Island, Queensland. He remained there for several decades until his death, and published numerous books about his experiences, including *Confessions of a Beachcomber* (1908).

BEAN, C. E. W. (Charles Edwin Woodrow) (1879–1968) b. Bathurst, New South Wales. Bean started out as a reporter with the *Sydney Morning Herald*, and many of his early articles on the outback, for example those collected in *On the Wool Track* (1910), are classics of documentary writing. He was an official war correspondent during World War I, and was wounded at Gallipoli. His collection, *The Anzac Book* (1916), is pivotal in the history and mythology of the digger. Bean's major project was the twelve-volume *Official History* (1924–42) of Australia at war.

BOOTE, H. E. (Henry Ernest) (1865–1949) b. Liverpool, England. Boote came to Australia in 1889, and spent the remainder of his life in the labour movement, principally as editor of the *Australian Worker*. As well as verse and fiction, he published many popular essays. His collections include *A Fool's Talk* (1915) and *Tea with the Devil* (1928).

BRENNAN, CHRISTOPHER (1870–1932) b. Sydney, New South Wales. After graduating at Sydney University Brennan travelled widely in Europe. He then devoted himself to poetry, in a heightened romantic style uncommon in Australia in the 1890s. Brennan taught for many years at Sydney University, but was dismissed in 1925 for his bohemian lifestyle and anti-British stance. Since his death his reputation as a poet has remained high; his essays are less well known. Brennan's major work was *Poems (1913)* (1914).

BUCKLEY, VINCENT (1925–88) b. Romsey, Victoria. Buckley taught English for nearly thirty years at the University of Melbourne, where he was a prominent Catholic intellectual and an influential poet and editor. Buckley's need to explore complex personal and spiritual questions places him, and those he influenced and encouraged, apart from the nativist tradition. As well as criticism and poetry, he published several books on Ireland and an important memoir of the 1950s, *Cutting Green Hay* (1983).

CLARK, MANNING (1915–91) b. Sydney, New South Wales. Clark was Professor of History at the Australian National University. He is the central figure in the understanding of Australian history, and one of Australia's handful of major public intellectuals. His most important work is the six-volume *History of Australia* (1962–87). Some of his essays and talks are collected in *Occasional Writings and Speeches* (1980). He is a figure of persistent controversy, partly as a result of his ambiguous flirtations with Soviet and Chinese communism.

CLARKE, MARCUS (1846–81), b. London, England. Perhaps the major essayist of nineteenth-century Australia, Clarke came out from England in 1863. After working in the bush, he settled into journalism in Melbourne. He was one of the founders of the bohemian Yorrick Club. (He is 'Perks' in Kendall's essay in this collection describing the club.) A prolific writer of fiction, journalism, and polemic, Clarke is most famous for his convict novel *His Natural Life* (1874). His final years were marked by severe financial difficulties that hastened his death.

CLIFT, CHARMIAN (1923–69), b. Kiama, New South Wales. After World War II, during which she served as an anti-aircraft gunner, Clift worked as a journalist. She and the novelist George Johnston, whom she married in 1947, lived away from Australia, mainly on Greek islands, between 1950 and 1964. They both wrote fiction. Returning to Sydney, Clift wrote newspaper columns, many of which were collected by Johnston as *Images in Aspic* (1965) and *The World of Charmian Clift* (1970).

COMAN, B. J. (Brian John) (1944–) b. Kyneton, Victoria. Coman grew up in 'rabbit country'. After studying agricultural science at the University of Melbourne, he began a professional career as a research scientist and consultant in the ecology and management of pest animals. As well as scientific papers Coman has published several essays in *Quadrant.*

CROSSWELL, BRENT (1950–) b. Tasmania. A leading VFL footballer of the 1960s and 1970s, Crosswell played in premiership sides at both Carlton (1968, 1970) and North Melbourne (1975, 1977). After retiring from football he worked as a schoolteacher and as a sportswriter for the *Age.* He lives in Tasmania.

DAVIES, ALAN (1924–87) b. Wangaratta, Victoria. Universally known as 'Foo', Davies was Professor of Politics at the University of Melbourne from 1968 until his death. He pioneered the study of political psychology in Australia. His books include *Private Politics* (1961) and a posthumous collection of longer essays, *The Human Element* (1988).

DENIEHY, D. H. (Daniel Henry) (1828–65) b. Sydney, New South Wales. The son of emancipated Irish convicts, Deniehy trained as a solicitor, but spent most of his life alternating between journalism, literature, and politics (including a period as a member of parliament). He founded and edited the *Southern Cross.* Admired in his prime by all who knew him, he died, disillusioned and alcoholic, following an accident in Bathurst.

DESSAIX, ROBERT (1944–) b. Sydney, New South Wales. Dessaix was an academic in Russian literature at the Australian National University before becoming an arts broadcaster with ABC radio. His books include a memoir, *A Mother's Disgrace* (1994), the novel *Night Letters* (1996), and, as editor, *Australian Gay and Lesbian Writing* (1993). He lives in Melbourne.

GARNER, HELEN (1942–) B. GEELONG, VICTORIA.
Garner's novels include *Monkey Grip* (1977) and *Cosmo Cosmolino* (1992). She has also written short stories and film scripts, but recently has turned increasingly to essays and non-fiction. *The First Stone* (1995), her account of the 'Ormond Affair', reflects her insistence on not allowing ideological verities to subsume personal relationships; it was hugely controversial. Some of her essays and articles are collected in *True Stories* (1996). Garner lives in Sydney.

GILMORE, DAME MARY (1864–1962) b. Goulburn, New South Wales. Raised in the bush, Gilmore qualified as a teacher, and began a lifelong association with the labour movement. In the 1890s, in Sydney, she became a friend of Henry Lawson and A. G. Stephens, but in 1896 she joined William Lane's New Australia venture in Paraguay. Returning to Australia in 1902, she began a long career as a poet, journalist, and activist.

GIUFFRÉ, GIULIA (1951–) b. Sydney, New South Wales. Guiffré studied literature at Oxford and Yale, and lectured at Sydney University before turning to full-time writing. Her publications include a book of interviews with female Australian writers, *A Writing Life* (1990). She lives in Camden, New South Wales.

GOLDSWORTHY, KERRYN (1953–) b. Curramulka, South Australia. A specialist in Australian literature, Goldsworthy teaches English at the University of Melbourne and is a former editor of *Australian Book Review.* She has compiled several anthologies, and has written a book of short stories and the critical study *Helen Garner* (1996).

GREER, GERMAINE (1939–) b. Melbourne, Victoria. Greer, who has lived in the UK since 1964, had completed a PhD on Shakespeare at Cambridge and was a university lecturer when her pathbreaking feminist work, *The Female Eunuch* (1971), made her an international celebrity. Since then she has alternated academic work with full-time writing, and has published many books of criticism, women's history, and memoir. Some of her essays and articles were collected as *The Madwoman's Underclothes* (1986).

HARRIS, ROBERT (1951–93) b. Melbourne, Victoria. Harris lived most of his adult life in Sydney. He was for a time poetry editor of *Overland,* and published five collections of poetry, of which the most successful was *JANE, Interlinear &*

Other Poems (1992). Harris's poems show an understanding of those who, like himself, have lived a hard life. The essay included here was found among Harris's papers after his death.

JAMES, CLIVE (1939–) b. Sydney, New South Wales. James has lived in the UK since 1962 but visits Australia regularly. A television reviewer for the *Observer* in the 1970s, he has been a television celebrity since the early 1980s. He has published many essays, notable for their wit and wide erudition, in the *London Review of Books*, the *New Yorker*, and elsewhere. As well as poetry, novels, and memoir, his collections of essays include *Snakecharmers in Texas* (1988) and *The Dreaming Swimmer* (1992).

JENNINGS, KATE (1948–), b. Temora, New South Wales. Jennings has lived in New York since 1979. She was active in the feminist movement in Sydney in the 1960s, and edited a well-known collection of women's verse, *Mother I'm Rooted* (1975). As well as poetry and short stories, she has published two collections of essays: *Save Me, Joe Louis* (1988) and *Bad Manners* (1993).

JONES, FREDERIC WOOD (1879–1954) b. London, England. Educated at London University, Jones held chairs in anatomy at London, Adelaide, Melbourne, Peking, and Manchester. In addition to his scientific papers he wrote many newspaper essays on natural history and other subjects. These were collected as *Unscientific Essays* (1924) and *Unscientific Excursions* (1934).

KENDALL, HENRY (1839–82) b. Milton, New South Wales. One of Australia's major colonial poets, author of the famous 'Bell Birds', Kendall was active in Sydney literary circles while still a very young man. His first volume was *Poems and Songs* (1852). Kendall's middle years were marked by poverty and alcoholism, but from the mid 1870s until his death he found settled employment outside Sydney, and both his health and his poetry experienced a renewal.

KERSHAW, ALISTER (1921–95) b. Melbourne, Victoria. Kershaw was active in Melbourne bohemian and artistic circles in the 1930s and '40s. He moved to France in the late 1940s and stayed there. He worked as a Paris correspondent for the ABC, and published books of poetry and memoir. He also wrote many essays — witty, conservative, sceptical — for *Quadrant* and other magazines.

KNÖPFELMACHER, FRANK (1923–95) b. Vienna, Austria. Knöpfelmacher served in the British Army in World War II, came to Australia in 1955, and commenced a long career teaching psychology and sociology at the University of Melbourne. A communist in his youth, he had witnessed Stalinism first hand in Czechoslovakia, and became an enemy of communists and fellow travellers in Australia. Some of his longer essays were collected as *Intellectuals and Politics* (1968).

LAWSON, HENRY (1867–1922) b. Grenfell, New South Wales. Lawson, Australia's major writer, grew up in poverty, first on the goldfields and later in Sydney. A radical and republican, he was closely associated with the *Bulletin* by the age of 20. He was by first instinct a poet, but his enormous talent emerged as a writer of stories and sketches: his best collections are *While the Billy Boils* (1896) and *Joe Wilson and His Mates* (1901). Lawson's last two decades were blighted by alcoholism, penury, and artistic failure.

LAWSON, LOUISA (1848–1920) b. Mudgee, New South Wales. The mother of Henry Lawson, Louisa Lawson spent the first half of her life in the bush and the second half in Sydney, where she was publisher of the *Republican* and founding editor of the *Dawn*, Australia's first feminist journal. She also published fiction and poetry, and was active in the movement for women's suffrage.

LINDSAY, NORMAN (1879–1969) b. Creswick, Victoria. Painter, sculptor, novelist, philosopher: Lindsay is one of Australia's seminal cultural figures. Through most of his life he wrote and illustrated for the *Bulletin*. Lindsay's vitalist philosophy contains a strongly sexual element that caused many of his works, both novels and paintings, to be banned. A number of his novels are still read, although he is probably best known for *The Magic Pudding* (1918).

LITTLE, GRAHAM (1939–) b. Belfast, Northern Ireland. Little, who came to Australia in 1954, teaches politics at the University of Melbourne. His books, which reflect his long association with Alan Davies in their emphasis on the formation of personality, include *Politics and Personal Style* (1973) and *Strong Leadership* (1988). Little has also presented interview programs on SBS television and on the ABC.

LOWER, LENNIE (1903–47) b. Dubbo, New South Wales. Lower served in the army and navy and knocked around in the bush before settling into journalism in Sydney in the early 1920s. For the next two decades he was a popular humorous columnist — noted for his love of puns and aversion to wowsers — in a variety of newspapers and magazines. He wrote the comic novel *Here's Luck* (1930). Cyril Pearl edited *The Best of Lennie Lower* (1963).

MCAULEY, JAMES (1917–76) b. Lakemba, New South Wales. A leading poet and critic of the 1950s and '60s, McAuley's biggest contribution to the essay in Australia is perhaps as founding editor of *Quadrant*. Some of his own essays are collected in *The Grammar of the Real* (1975); his *Collected Poems* appeared in 1971. McAuley, who was Professor of English at the University of Tasmania, stressed conservative moral and spiritual values in both his poems and his essays. Together with Harold Stewart he instigated the Ern Malley hoax.

MCGIRR, MICHAEL (1961–) b. Sydney, New South Wales. McGirr, who was ordained a Jesuit priest in 1993, is editor of the magazine *Australian Catholics* and a consulting editor of *Eureka Street*. He is the author of numerous essays, reviews, and short stories, as well as a travel book, *Travels with My Mother*, to be published in 1998. He lives in Melbourne.

MACLAURIN, CHARLES (1872–1925) b. Sydney, New South Wales. MacLaurin, whose father was Chancellor of Sydney University, completed his medical training at Edinburgh. During World War I he served on the French front as an army doctor. (His younger brother Henry, a colonel with the AIF, was killed on MacLaurin's Hill at Gallipoli.) After the war MacLaurin published two collections of essays, mainly clinical studies of historical figures: *Post Mortem* (1923) and *Mere Mortals* (1925).

MALOUF, DAVID (1934–) b. Brisbane, Queensland. Malouf, one of Australia's most admired writers, taught at the University of Sydney in the 1970s before turning to full-time writing. His novels combine close social observation with mythological undercurrents. They include *Johnno* (1975), *An Imaginary Life* (1978), and *Remembering Babylon* (1993). A collected edition of his poems was published in 1992. Malouf's essays are often autobiographical, and some of these make up *12 Edmonstone Street* (1985). He has homes in both Sydney and Tuscany.

MANNING, GREG (1954–) b. Newcastle, New South Wales. Manning teaches English at James Cook University of North Queensland. His essays and reviews have appeared in numerous magazines, including *Meanjin, Scripsi,* and *Australian Book Review.* He is co-editor of the journal *LiNQ.*

MARTIN, ADRIAN (1959–) b. Melbourne, Victoria. Martin is a freelance writer on the arts (especially film) who has taught media studies at several tertiary institutions. He has reviewed videos and films for the *Australian* and the *Age.* A collection of his essays was published as *Phantasms* (1994). Martin lives in Melbourne.

MARTIN, SIR JAMES (1820–86) b. County Cork, Ireland. Martin came to Sydney as an infant with his parents. After leaving school he worked as a journalist and solicitor, but in 1845 commenced a long career in politics that included three terms as Premier of New South Wales. Martin published an early book of essays, *The Australian Sketch Book* (1838).

MENNELL, PHILIP (1851–1905) b. Newcastle, England. Mennell came to Australia in the 1870s and worked as a journalist before returning to London a decade later as a correspondent for the *Age.* He continued to visit Australia regularly, and published *The Dictionary of Australasian Biography* (1892).

MURDOCH, SIR WALTER (1874–1970) b. Aberdeenshire, Scotland. Murdoch came to Australia in 1884. After studying at the University of Melbourne, he began an academic career that took him to the chancellorship of the University of Western Australia. Throughout the 1930s and '40s his short, witty essays in the *Argus* and, later, the Melbourne *Herald* made him a household name. His many collections include *The Best of Walter Murdoch* (1964).

MURNANE, GERALD (1939–) b. Melbourne, Victoria. Murnane worked as a schoolteacher and public servant before turning to full-time writing in 1973. Between 1980 and 1996 he was an influential teacher of writing at Victoria College. He has published seven extended works of fiction, including a much-discussed fable, *The Plains* (1982). Murnane has written a number of important essays that, like his works of fiction, explore patterns of memory and imagination in everyday life. He lives in Melbourne.

MURRAY, LES (1938–) b. Nabiac, New South Wales. Australia's major international poet, Murray grew up in the bush, where he now lives. His poetry identifies closely with the trials of the rural poor, particularly his own Gaelic forebears; some of it is spiritual and personal, while in another temper it belongs in the nativist tradition and debunks the multicultural social agenda of what Murray calls 'metropolitan élites'. As well as many books of verse and several anthologies, Murray's collections of essays include *Persistence in Folly* (1984) and *Blocks and Tackles* (1990).

OAKLEY, BARRY (1931–) b. Melbourne, Victoria. Educated at the University of Melbourne, Oakley was associated with the La Mama and Pram Factory theatres in Carlton in the 1960s. He has written numerous plays and comic novels, including the great Australian football novel, *A Salute to the Great McCarthy* (1970). Some of his essays and reviews were collected as *Scribbling in the Dark* (1985). Oakley lives at Wentworth Falls, in the Blue Mountains, and has for many years been literary editor of the *Australian.*

PALMER, NETTIE (1885–1964), b. Bendigo, Victoria. Palmer, together with her husband Vance, was an influential literary figure between the 1930s and the '60s. A pioneering critic of Australian literature, she edited several important anthologies as well as publishing poetry, diaries, reviews, leftist polemics, and many essays on diverse subjects in the popular press, some of which were collected as *Talking It Over* (1932).

PALMER, VANCE (1885–1959) b. Bundaberg, Queensland. Palmer grew up in rural Queensland, and devoted much of his work and thought to the outback. With Nettie Palmer he was at the forefront of the critical evaluation of major nineteenth-century figures like Lawson and Furphy. He wrote novels, biographies, poetry, and plays, but his major work is a cultural history, *The Legend of the Nineties* (1954). Palmer also wrote hundreds of reviews and essays, and gave a popular series of ABC radio talks on writers he had known (including Lawson, Paterson, and Dennis).

PATERSON, A. B. 'BANJO' (Andrew Barton) (1864–1941) b. Orange, New South Wales. Australia's most popular poet, author of 'Waltzing Matilda' and 'The Man from Snowy River', Paterson trained as a solicitor, but by his early thirties was established as a journalist and as a popular writer of prose and verse. He was a war correspondent during both the Boer War and World War I, and later edited the Sydney *Evening News.* As well as producing many books of his own verse, fiction, and journalism, he edited the anthology *Old Bush Songs* (1905).

PENTON, BRIAN (1904–51) b. Brisbane, Queensland. Penton worked as a political correspondent for the *Sydney Morning Herald* in the 1920s until complaints about his irreverent tone led to his resignation. He edited the Sydney

Daily Telegraph from 1941 until his death. A right-wing freethinker, Penton campaigned against government censorship during World War II. He published books of social criticism and several novels. The essay included here has not been published before.

PHILLIPS, ARTHUR (1900–85) b. Melbourne, Victoria. Educated at the University of Melbourne and at Oxford, Phillips was a schoolmaster at Wesley College, Melbourne, for nearly fifty years. Phillips was one of the most important and prolific Australian literary and cultural critics. His work emphasised the democratic theme in Australian literature. *The Australian Tradition* (1958) is an influential collection of his critical essays.

'POSSUM', 'PETER (Rowe, Richard) (1828–79) b. Doncaster, England. Rowe came to Australia in 1853 and contributed to various magazines and newspapers, bringing together some of his essays and verse as *Peter 'Possum's Portfolio* (1858). He returned to England in 1858 and published a number of books about his Australian experiences, including *The Boy in the Bush* (1869).

RINDER, SAMUEL (1823–1907) b. Liverpool, England. Rinder was a flour miller at Wedderburn, northern Victoria, who contributed several essays to the *Melbourne Review* in the early 1880s. He died at Mount Korong.

RYCKMANS, PIERRE (1935–) b. Uccle, Belgium. Ryckmans, a distinguished sinologist, came to Australia in 1971. He is Professor of Chinese at Sydney University and, as well as many scholarly works, has published a novel, *The Death of Napoleon* (1991), under the pen-name 'Simon Leys'. He delivered the Boyer Lectures in 1996.

SCOTT, SIR ERNEST (1867–1939) b. England. Scott came to Australia in 1892 and worked as a journalist and Hansard reporter. Following the publication of several works on French history, and despite holding no degree, he was appointed Professor of History at the University of Melbourne in 1912. His many books include *The Life of Captain Matthew Flinders* (1914).

SINNETT, FREDERICK (1830–66) b. Hamburg, Germany. Sinnett came to Australia in 1849 and, after working as a surveyor in South Australia, entered journalism in Melbourne and Geelong. He travelled widely around Australia and published several books based on his travels. His extended essay, *The Fiction Fields of Australia* (1856), is the first substantial critical work on Australian literature.

SORENSON, EDWARD S. (Edward Sylvester) (1869–1939) b. Casino, New South Wales. Sorenson spent his life working in the bush and was a prolific writer on the outback's natural setting and its social customs. As well as poetry and fiction he published journalism and essays, including the collection *Life in the Australian Backblocks* (1911). Many of his pieces appeared in the *Bulletin*.

STEPHENS, A. G. (Alfred George) (1865–1933) b. Toowoomba, Queensland. As inaugural editor of the literary section, or Red Page, of the *Bulletin*, Stephens was perhaps more responsible than anyone for the flowering of an Australian national, and nationalist, literature at the close of the nineteenth century. A selection of his contributions to the Red Page was published as *The Red Pagan* (1904). He also wrote poems, novels, and plays.

STOVE, DAVID (1927–94) b. Moree, New South Wales. Stove taught philosophy at Sydney University, where his heterodox views, voiced long before it became fashionable to denounce 'political correctness', involved him in numerous controversies with Marxists and feminists. A posthumous collection of his essays appeared as *Cricket Versus Republicanism* (1995).

STUKELEY', 'SIMON (Savery, Henry) (1791–1842) b. Somerset, England. Born into a prosperous family, Savery was transported to Van Diemen's Land for fraud in 1825. In Hobart he contributed a series of sketches to the *Colonial Times*, under the pseudonym 'Simon Stukeley', which, when reissued as *The Hermit in Van Diemen's Land* (1830), became the first book of Australian essays. Savery eventually secured a pardon but, after further financial misadventures, died in jail at Port Arthur.

VAGABOND', 'THE (James, John Stanley) (1843–96) b. Walsall, England. James, a journalist, came to Australia in 1875, via America. Under the pseudonym 'The Vagabond' he published hundreds of sketches of Australian life, mainly in the *Argus*. He also wrote numerous books describing his travels in Australia and the South Pacific.

WALLACE-CRABBE, CHRIS (1934–) b. Melbourne, Victoria. Since the 1960s Wallace-Crabbe has taught English at the University of Melbourne. His poetry combines philosophical speculation with a strong sense of Melbourne as a physical setting and, in this respect, can be compared with the work of his friend and colleague Vincent Buckley. As well as numerous volumes of poetry and several anthologies, he has published three collections of essays: *Melbourne or the Bush* (1974), *Toil & Spin* (1979), and *Falling into Language* (1990).

WELLER, ARCHIE (1957–) b. Perth, Western Australia. Weller grew up on an isolated farm, and has worked in a variety of occupations. His fiction includes *The Day of the Dog* (1984), which was filmed in 1991, and he co-edited an anthology of Aboriginal writing, *Us Fellas* (1988). Weller has also written plays and film-scripts.

WHITE, PATRICK (1912–90) b. London, England. Australia's major novelist, White received his secondary education in England. After serving with the RAF during World War II he returned to Sydney and began the series of intense, prophetic, deeply satirical novels that have become classics, including *The Tree of Man* (1955), *Voss* (1957), *The Vivisector* (1970), and *The Twyborn Affair* (1979). White was also a playwright. He won the Nobel Prize for Literature in 1973.

ACKNOWLEDGMENTS

The editor and publisher wish to thank copyright holders for granting permission to reproduce textual extracts. Sources are as follows:

Australian War Memorial for 'The Legacy' by **C.E.W. Bean**, from *In Your Hands Australians*, Cassell & Co., Melbourne, 1919; Penelope Buckley for 'Intellectuals' by **Vincent Buckley**; Mrs Dymphna Clark for 'Rewriting Australian History' by **Manning Clark**; **Brian J. Coman** for 'A Short History of the Rabbit in Australia'; **Brent Crosswell** for 'Vinny Catoggio'; Australian Literary Management for 'Nice Work If You Can Get It' by **Robert Dessaix**; Barbara Mobbs for 'The Fate of *The First Stone*' by **Helen Garner**; **Giulia Giuffré** for 'Who Do You Think You Are?' from *Who Do You Think You Are?*, Women's Redress Press, 1992; **Kerryn Goldsworthy** for 'Martyr to Her Sex'; Aitken & Stone Ltd for 'Sex and Society — Whose Rules?' by **Germaine Greer**, from *The Madwoman's Underclothes: Essays and Occasional Writings, 1968–85*, Picador, London; Peters Fraser & Dunlop for 'You Little Bobby-Dazzler' by **Clive James**, from *Snakecharmers in Texas*, Jonathan Cape, London, 1988; Margaret Connolly & Associates on behalf of **Kate Jennings** for 'Bad Manners: *Angry Women: An Anthology of Australian Women's Writings*' from *Bad Manners*, Reed Books, 1993; Barbara Mobbs for 'The Question of Ned Kelly's Perfume' by **Norman Lindsay**; **Graham Little** for 'The Flag My Father Wore'; Rogers, Coleridge & White Ltd for 'A First Place' by **David Malouf**, first published in *Southerly* 45, 3–10; Penguin Books Australia for 'TV Time Tunnel' by **Adrian Martin**, from *Phantasms*, McPhee Gribble, 1994; Curtis Brown (Australia) Pty Ltd for 'Poets Anonymous' by **James McAuley**; AMC (Aust) Pty Ltd for 'At Home in Memory' by **Michael McGirr**; **Gerald Murnane** for 'Some Books are to be Dropped into Wells, Others into Fishponds …' from *Verandah* 2, 1987; Margaret Connolly & Associates on behalf of **Les Murray** for 'The Trade in Images' from *Blocks and Tackles: Articles and Essays*, Angus & Robertson, 1990; University of Queensland Press for 'Meeting the Great' by **Barry Oakley**, from *Scribbling in the Dark*, University of Queensland Press, 1985, 1993; **Pierre Ryckmans** for 'An Amateur Artist'; **Chris Wallace-Crabbe** for 'Swaying in the Forties' from *Falling into Language*, Oxford University Press, 1990; **Archie Weller** for 'Portrayal of Aboriginal Men in Literature' previously printed in *Social Alternatives* 7:1, March 1988; Barbara Mobbs for 'The Prodigal Son' by **Patrick White**.

Every effort has been made to trace the original source of copyright material in this book. The publisher would be pleased to hear from copyright holders to rectify any errors or omissions.